Consuming Motherhood

Consuming Motherhood

EDITED BY
JANELLE S. TAYLOR
LINDA L. LAYNE
DANIELLE F. WOZNIAK

RUTGERS UNIVERSITY PRESS
NEW BRUNSWICK, NEW JERSEY, AND LONDON

LIBRARY OF CONGRESS CATALOGING-IN-PUBLICATION DATA

Consuming motherhood / edited by Janelle S. Taylor, Linda L. Layne, and Danielle F. Wozniak.

p. cm.

Includes bibliographical references and index.

ISBN 0-8135-3429-1 (hardcover : alk. paper) — ISBN 0-8135-3430-5 (pbk. : alk. paper)

1. Motherhood. 2. Consumption (Economics)—Social aspects. 3. Women consumers. I. Taylor, Janelle S., 1965– II. Layne, Linda L. III. Wozniak, Danielle F.

HQ759.C7253 2004

306.874′3—dc22

2003022260

A British Cataloging-in-Publication record for this book is available from the British Library.

This collection © 2004 by Rutgers, The State University of New Jersey
Individual chapters © 2004 in the names of their authors unless otherwise noted below.

"Motherhood under Capitalism" by Barbara Katz Rothman was originally published in *Recreating Motherhood,* 65–81. © 1989, 2000 by Barbara Katz Rothman. Reprinted by permission of the author and Rutgers University Press.

"How Infants Grow Mothers in North London" by Daniel Miller was originally published in *Theory, Culture, and Society* 14, no. 3 (1997): 67–88. © 1997 by Theory, Culture, and Society Ltd. Reprinted by permission of Sage Publications Ltd.

Portions of "Maternal Labor in a Transnational Circuit" by Ann Anagnost were originally published as "Scenes of Misrecognition" in *positions: east asia cultures critique* 8, no. 2 (2000): 389–421. © 2003 by Duke University Press. Reprinted by permission of the publisher.

"Going 'Home'" by Barbara Yngvesson was originally published in *Social Text* 21, no. 1 (2003): 7–27. © 2003 by Duke University Press. Reprinted by permission of the publisher.

All rights reserved

No part of this book may be reproduced or utilized in any form or by any means, electronic or mechanical, or by any information storage and retrieval system, without written permission from the publisher. Please contact Rutgers University Press, 100 Joyce Kilmer Avenue, Piscataway, NJ 08854–8099. The only exception to this prohibition is "fair use" as defined by U.S. copyright law.

Manufactured in the United States of America

For our mothers and our children

CONTENTS

Acknowledgments ix

Introduction 1
JANELLE S. TAYLOR

Con-Texts

Motherhood under Capitalism 19
BARBARA KATZ ROTHMAN

How Infants Grow Mothers in North London 31
DANIEL MILLER

Contributions

Maternity and Materiality: Becoming a
Mother in Consumer Culture 55
ALISON J. CLARKE

"What Will I Do with All the Toys Now?": Consumption and
the Signification of Kinship in U.S. Fostering Relationships 72
DANIELLE F. WOZNIAK

"Too Bad You Got a Lemon": Peter Singer,
Mothers of Children with Disabilities, and the
Critique of Consumer Culture 100
GAIL LANDSMAN

Making Memories: Trauma, Choice, and Consumer
Culture in the Case of Pregnancy Loss 122
LINDA L. LAYNE

Maternal Labor in a Transnational Circuit 139
ANN ANAGNOST

Going "Home": Adoption, Exclusive Belongings,
and the Mythology of Roots 168
BARBARA YNGVESSON

A Fetish Is Born: Sonographers and the
Making of the Public Fetus 187
JANELLE S. TAYLOR

Consuming Childbirth: The Qualified
Commodification of Midwifery Care 211
ROBBIE E. DAVIS-FLOYD

Mothers between God and Mammon:
Feminist Interpretations of Childbirth 249
PAMELA E. KLASSEN

Commentaries

Commoditizing Kinship in America 271
IGOR KOPYTOFF

Caught in the Current 279
BARBARA KATZ ROTHMAN

References Cited   289
Contributors   311
Index   315

ACKNOWLEDGMENTS

This volume has its origins in a panel on "Kinship and Consumption" that we co-organized at the 1998 annual meetings of the American Anthropological Association. We three coeditors have not met again in the same room since then, but we have worked together easily and well via telephone and e-mail over these several years, through births, relocations, and various other major and minor upheavals in our lives. We are very glad to have had such a team.

For their excellent and inspiring scholarship, their warm collegiality, and their patience through the time that it has taken to see this project through to publication, we are grateful to the panel participants whose work appears here: Robbie Davis-Floyd, Pamela Klassen, Igor Kopytoff, Gail Landsman, and Barbara Yngvesson. The original panel also featured contributions from several other scholars whom we would also like to thank: Daniel Thomas Cook, Valerie Hartouni, Susan Markens, and Judith Modell. We are grateful to Ann Anagnost and Alison Clarke, who joined this project later on in its development, for the graciousness with which they have responded to editorial suggestions aimed at integrating these chapters more closely into the volume as a whole. We would like to thank Daniel Miller and Barbara Katz Rothman for generously granting permission to reprint previously published pieces as "con-texts" for the original ethnographic essays presented here. Barbara Katz Rothman deserves special thanks as well for the openness and thoughtfulness with which she has engaged here with scholarly work that has pursued in some surprising—even unsettling—directions insights that she developed in her own earlier writings.

We have been very fortunate to work with Kristi Long, our energetic, creative, and unfailingly helpful editor at Rutgers University Press. We are grateful to Lynn M. Morgan and an anonymous reviewer for their close and careful reading of the volume and their incisive comments and helpful suggestions. Warm thanks to Joan Steiner for permission to feature her *Look-Alikes* artwork on our cover, and to the office of Susan Jeffords, dean of Social Sciences at the University of Washington, for providing funds sufficient to cover permissions costs. We would like to thank Joe Kemp for permission to reprint the artwork for his "Fetus Navidad" card, and we extend our warm appreciation to Ylva Hernlund, who prepared our index with the same care and skill that she brings to her own scholarly work.

Consuming Motherhood

Introduction

JANELLE S. TAYLOR

> We are facing the expansion of a way of thinking that treats people as objects, as commodities. It is a way of thinking that enables us to see not motherhood, not parenthood, but the creation of a commodity, a baby.
>
> —Barbara Katz Rothman, "Motherhood under Capitalism"

> Objects are the means for creating the relationships of love between subjects rather than some kind of materialistic dead end which takes devotion away from its proper subject—other persons.
>
> —Daniel Miller, "How Infants Grow Mothers in North London"

> The realm of human reproduction is one in which the difference between persons and things is particularly difficult to define, defying all attempts at drawing a simple line where there is a natural continuum.
>
> —Igor Kopytoff, "The Cultural Biography of Things"

Under a blue summer-afternoon sky in a well-tended city park, a woman perches on the edge of a sandbox, watching a little boy at play. Then, suddenly, the sandbox becomes a tambourine, and the toys resolve into a safety pin, an animal cracker, a starfish, a cork, and a spool.

This scene, featured on the cover of this book, comes from *Look-Alikes*, a 1998 children's book by Joan Steiner, which invites readers to engage in a game of searching out and identifying the familiar objects that she has used to construct meticulous dioramas of scenes of public life. The challenge of the game lies in the difficulty of disrupting the pattern of meaning that leads this image to cohere, at first glance, as a scene of motherhood. What we see is a mother watching over her child, one person caring for another, a relationship between two human beings. The pleasure and the interest of the *Look-Alikes* game, however, lies in the shock of recognition that comes when we first recognize, "hidden in plain sight" (di Leonardo 1998:10), the oddments of consumer culture of which this scene is composed. These humble objects, grown fantastically large, seem to take on unsettling new powers, thoroughly encompassing the human figures. And this moment of recognition invites, perhaps, a shock of self-recognition as well for mothers engaged with their children in the activity of puzzling together over an expensive hardback book, trying to pick out familiar consumer items.

Steiner leads her viewers, through a sort of poetics of the concrete, to perceive hitherto unsuspected affinities and potentialities within objects: a shoehorn can also be a slide, or a cork a child's bucket. In so doing, she also reveals to us the presence and the power of two different conceptual frameworks, mutually irreconcilable, that let us read this either as a scene of motherhood or as an image of consumption. As with Edgar Rubin's famous face/vase illusion, one perspective shows us people interacting, another shows us a thing of value. By analogy, one reading of Steiner's artwork points to motherhood as a relationship between people, while the other points to consumption as a relationship of people to material objects—and these two angles of vision, these two orders of meaning, seem as inextricable as they are irreconcilable.

We begin with Steiner's artwork because it raises, in a humorous and engaging way, the very serious questions that motivate this volume. How do motherhood and consumption—as ideologies, and as patterns of social action—mutually shape and constitute each other in contemporary North American and European social life? How can we, instead of oscillating between motherhood and consumption as ways of understanding what we see, hold them *both* in focus *together*? Or, to put it another way, how can we really hope to understand either motherhood or consumption *without* considering how they are in fact imbricated in social life? The project of *Consuming Motherhood* thus reprises a question that has been central to social theory since Marx: How are relations among people shaped and mediated by relations between people and objects?

To approach this broad question specifically through an interrogation of the relationship between motherhood and consumption might seem like an obvious move. On one level, it is obvious that mothering relationships are much *like* other social relationships and, like them, are bound to take shape from the broader political and economic order within which they are forged. In a consumer-capitalist society, mothers provide for their children by purchasing food, clothing, toys, and an ever-increasing range of other commodities (Seiter 1993; Miller 1998, this volume). Mothers also navigate the demands of paid employment and unpaid work in the home, from the very different class positions that they occupy, partly by purchasing and selling child care as well as other household tasks as paid services (Colen 1995; Nelson 1994; Romero 1992; Sampson 1998; Segura 1994). With the rise of new biomedical technologies of reproduction, even egg cells, embryos, and the gestation of the developing fetus—precisely those bodily realities widely thought to ground motherhood in biology, for better or for worse—are now readily commodified, purchased, and sold (Franklin 1997; Macklin 1996; Ragoné 1999, 1996, 1994; Roberts 1997; Rothman 2000 [1989]; Strathern 1992).

At the same time, motherhood also seems like an obvious locus at which to examine the workings of consumption precisely because of the ways that it is (considered to be) *unlike* other social relationships. Motherhood is supposed to be a special kind of human relationship, uniquely important because uniquely free of the kind of calculating instrumentality associated with the consumption of objects. It stands for "love," in sharp contrast to "money"—a simple but persistent opposition that structures American middle-class cultural values concerning family, parenthood, and child-rearing. Thus construed, motherhood offers a powerful model for human relationships that stands in opposition to the logic of the marketplace and has provided a vitally important grounding for social critiques, both conservative and feminist (Umansky 1994).

Practices that confuse and confound distinctions between love and money resist ready analysis for the same reason that they arouse cultural anxieties and provoke controversy: they reveal, by the very manner in which they transgress, the contours of deeply rooted ideological oppositions between that which is readily recognized as "real," good, or legitimate motherhood and the corrupting influence of consumption. It is precisely because they are so forcefully contrasted that ethnographic inquiry into the relationship between motherhood and consumption is so important. Like Viviana Zelizer's excellent historical studies of financial valuations of children's lives (1985) and of the social "marking" of currency (1994), the ethnographic essays collected here put the categorical distinction between love and money to the test empirically, through close and careful study of social life, and reveal how complexly they are intertwined.

Marilyn Strathern has argued that "what constitutes a natural or logical domain of ideas" is what gives an image or idea its distinctive cultural stamp, and that "this is equally true of what is thinkable in terms of combinations and syntheses—you can tell a culture by what it can and cannot bring together" (1992:3). One might understand the powerful opposition between love and money, in these terms, as a culturally unthinkable combination or synthesis. At the same time, however, such systems of thought must also be situated in relation to systems of social action—and at that level, the social practices of love and of money turn out to be quite inextricable. To modify Strathern's insight slightly, we might conclude, perhaps, that one can tell a culture by what it both keeps apart *and* brings together.

This tension between love and money is one that many women experience, in their own lives, as a problem. The vision of motherhood kept pure of the taint of consumption is one that many women value but few if any are able to realize in their own lives. Indeed, Daniel Miller (this volume) argues that for the North

London women he studied, the felt need to shield their children from consumption, coupled with their inevitable failure to succeed in doing so, form a central part of the social and cultural process through which women are produced as mothers.

If intrusions of "money" into the realm of maternal "love" are arguably inevitable for all women engaged in mothering in a consumer-capitalist society, they are perhaps especially troubling for those who most strongly value motherhood as that which stands for the promise and the possibility of human relationships not based on a narrow calculus of individual value, in contrast to the values that guide consumerism. The concern that encroaching commodification threatens to irrevocably evacuate from motherhood all that is best and most powerful about it, which Barbara Katz Rothman voiced so eloquently in "Motherhood under Capitalism" (reprinted in this volume), is one that many share. The home-birthing feminists of whom Pamela Klassen writes, for example, embrace home birth as part of a religiously informed feminist critique of the commodification of birth. They do so, however, from "the midst of their own location within a culture of consumption in which nothing, not even religion, is sacred. That is, religion itself is commoditized in complex ways" (Klassen, this volume, 251). As Klassen shows, ironies, ambivalences, and uneasy tensions arise as, in the course of their efforts to live out a vision of motherhood construed in opposition to consumption, these women inevitably "turn to the tools of their consumer culture, while also challenging its premises" (Klassen, this volume, 266). Similarly, Robbie Davis-Floyd (this volume) writes of home-birth midwives whose life work takes its meaning from an understanding of motherhood that, again, casts it in opposition to consumer culture. She documents their struggles to navigate the necessary process of commodifying their own services without compromising the values to which they remain committed.

Keeping "love" distinct from "money" may pose problems for all women, then, but it does so in ways mediated by class, racial, and other kinds of difference among women (Gordon 1994; Ladd-Taylor and Umansky 1998; Ragoné and Twine 2000; Roberts 1997). The ideological opposition between motherhood and consumption both casts individualizing blame upon and renders invisible the lived realities of many people whose life situations make it especially difficult to cherish the illusion that mothering can somehow remain free and pure of issues of consumption and commodification. These include, for example, women who find it necessary to purchase and sell childcare services (Colen 1995; Nelson 1994; Romero 1992; Sampson 1998; Segura 1994); those whose identity encompasses the historical memory of enslavement and the commodification of black women's reproductive capacities and children (Collins 1994; Roberts 1997); and those engaging with mothering relations in nonnormative ways, sometimes in the wake of encounters with infertility, through fostering, adoption, surrogacy, or assisted reproduction (Franklin 1997; Ragoné 1999, 1996, 1994; Layne 1999a; Sandelowski 1993; Wozniak 2002, 1999, 1997a, 1997b, this volume).

Keeping motherhood pure and free of the taint of consumption is especially challenging for women whose children are devalued and whose very mothering itself is often framed as an illegitimate form of consumption. As Gail Landsman's research has documented (1998, 1999, 2000, this volume), women mothering children with disabilities in the United States must contend with the devaluation of their children, in part because they are thought to be persons who are and will remain capable only of *receiving* and *consuming* resources:

> The personhood of those with disabilities is diminished in American culture in large part because such individuals have been viewed not only as incapable of giving but as needing the gifts of others . . . The consequences are serious in that physical and economic self-sufficiency serves as a prerequisite to being moral agents in North American culture. The devaluation of recipients of charity is consistent with a liberal political theory that assumes an opposition of autonomy and dependency; the act of giving to the "less fortunate" serves as a display of superiority ironically made possible by acquisition unfettered by the demands of others. (Landsman 1999:149)

The notion that mothering children with disabilities is a wasteful "consumption" of resources confronts most women today during pregnancy, if only obliquely, as they weigh the implications of prenatal diagnostic tests. All the other uses to which fetal ultrasound images are put notwithstanding, in the United States the only officially acceptable medical justification for ordering a scan is the reasonable expectation that it may reveal health problems with the fetus—and one of the primary justifications for offering ultrasound screening of pregnancies to all women on a routine basis is the expectation that fetuses exhibiting anomalies will be aborted (Taylor 1998, 2000b, this volume). On the basis of extensive interviews with women who have undergone just this sequence of events in connection with amniocentesis (another widely used prenatal diagnostic test), Rayna Rapp (1999) describes their experience as one of "chosen loss." Termination of a wanted pregnancy after a diagnosis of fetal anomaly is a course of action taken, often with great sadness, by women who, with careful reflection, judge it to be necessary. Part of what makes it *seem* necessary to individual women, of course, is a broader social context that provides precious little support of any kind for women and families endeavoring to raise and care for disabled children. In the medical literature, however, these "chosen losses" appear as simple "gains," insofar as they prevent the birth of disabled children who would "consume" the resources of their parents, the medical system, and the state. Thus, one article advocating routine screening of all pregnancies by ultrasound concludes that "long-term *gains* would include identification of a major anomaly and termination of pregnancy, thus avoiding the birth of a child with an anomaly who is likely to survive but with a poor quality of life" (Gabbe 1994:72; emphasis added). Women undergoing prenatal diagnosis find their "choices" seriously constrained, then, and mothers of children with disabilities find their mothering devalued, to the extent that the nurturing of disabled children is construed as unjustified "consumption" of resources.

Women whose mothering relationships are more closely enmeshed with social welfare institutions of the state face similar stigmatization as unproductive consumers of "other people's money." As the work of Danielle Wozniak (1999, 2002, this volume) shows, foster mothers find themselves burdened by others' perceptions that their children and their mothering relationships are of little value because they receive support from the state. As Wozniak documents, quite poignantly, these women use consumer goods to claim value for their children, and they also struggle to resist the state's commodification of their caregiving labor.

The stigmatization of forms of mothering, including foster mothering, that rely in any obvious way upon state support is, of course, a very short step away from the stigmatization of poor mothers, which in turn is deeply enmeshed with racism. At this end of the social hierarchy, the problems of "love" and "money" take quite different forms, and the taint of consumption takes on quite different flavors. Public discussions (and, too often, scholarly discussions as well) of policy measures to support the poor tend to proceed from the assumption that it is inappropriate forms of motherhood, especially among black Americans, that are the root cause of poverty: "According to the conservative vision, single motherhood is especially immoral and harmful, in part because conservatives believe out-of-wedlock childbearing causes poverty. . . . It is true that families headed by single females are disproportionately poorer than families with an adult male present. . . . But this correlation does not prove that single motherhood *causes* poverty" (Roberts 1997:223). When motherhood itself is falsely singled out as the cause of poverty, those few mechanisms that do exist to transfer public resources toward the support of poor women and their children tend to be decried and resented as an illegitimate use of "other people's money."

Not only is mothering blamed for causing poverty, but the specific terms in which this blame is cast frame motherhood itself when the mothers are poor, and especially when they are poor and black, as an illegitimate *consumption* of resources:

> Many legislators and their constituents will have a hard time seeing family caps and other laws discouraging procreation as penalizing women on welfare for exercising their reproductive rights. . . . Although these measures impose a deterrent to childbearing that wealthier people do not face, their proponents see them as replacing the constraints on poor

women's reproductive decisions that would exist but for the state's generosity. . . . The government already confiscates citizens' property in the form of taxes for a variety of social purposes. Tax money even goes to many redistributive programs, such as Social Security, farm subsidies, and corporate bailouts. But taxpayers reserve a special condemnation for welfare that redistributes income to the poor—and especially to support their children. (Roberts 1997:242–43).

If the racist and sexist implications of such views are quite clear, the extent to which they also draw upon ideologies of consumption has been less often remarked. The anger and moralizing directed against public support of poor women and their children may derive some of its force from negative views of *consumption* generally—and consumption by the poor in particular.

Consumption practices, like mothering practices, are often held to be the cause of poverty—and to similar ideological effect. As scholars such as Regina Austin (1994) and Elizabeth Chin (2001) have noted: "The not-so-subtle message often seems to be that if only those people would get themselves on track (by wanting the right things, dressing appropriately, buying the right foods), they too could be middle class. And there's the rub—getting on track is not simply an issue of willpower and stick-to-it-iveness" (Chin 2001:12). Arguments that locate the source of poverty in consumption, like those that locate it in motherhood, have the effect of individualizing poverty, depoliticizing it, and blaming it on those who suffer from it. Both come down together, and come down hard, on poor women who, like others in a consumer-capitalist society, seek through consumption not merely to secure the minimum necessary to maintain life but also to act meaningfully in the world and to create valued identities and social relations, for themselves and their children. Raymond T. Smith writes:

> It has been convenient to create statistical models that establish causal links between the supposed breakdown of the African-American family and the conditions of poverty and deprivation in which large numbers of people are obliged to live, without ever considering the constitutive relations between affluence and deprivation—between the extravagance of the rich and the desperation of the poor. That desperation is no longer as deeply rooted in starvation, disease, and physical deprivation as it was (though there is still a scandalously generous amount of those things), but it is no less deeply felt because it is produced by scorn, humiliation, and the lack of what Adam Smith referred to as "not only the commodities which are indispensably necessary for the support of life, but whatever the *custom of the country* renders it indecent for creditable people, even of the lowest order, to be without" . . . He cited linen shirts and leather shoes as necessary commodities for the maintenance of self-respect in the late eighteenth century, and we can easily compile an

updated list for our own time. However, there are few late-twentieth-century voices raised in support of according respect to the poor. (Smith 1996:2)

As this passage suggests, if consumption seems to taint motherhood, consumption also clearly enables it. In a consumer-capitalist society, consumption of commodities is an important avenue through which people seek to act meaningfully in the world, not merely to secure basic needs but also to achieve self-respect, social identity, and other important goals. Thus, for example, Alison Clarke's careful study of the provisioning of nurseries by women on a specific North London street shows how consumption plays a crucial role in the social production of infants and mothers alike, who are "'made' through a multitude of objects and social exchanges" (Clarke, this volume, 71).

Indeed, the role of consumption in the making of fetuses into social persons becomes quite clear to some women in the wake of pregnancy loss, as Linda Layne explains. Caught between "the emergence of the fetal subject and ongoing taboos regarding social acknowledgment of reproductive mishaps" (Layne, this volume, 122), women participating in pregnancy-loss support groups in the United States creatively use consumer goods to "make" memories of and social personhood for their lost children, in the face of strong cultural pressures to forget. In doing so, however, they also critique the hegemonic power of consumer culture, whose standards of value would deny to their children any meaningful identity or existence.

Documenting some of the historical processes through which "the fetus" has been made in and through North American consumer culture is the task of my own contribution to this volume. My account focuses on the role of sonographers, those mostly female technical specialists who perform obstetrical ultrasound examinations. As members of an emerging technical profession composed primarily of women, sonographers have worked hard to develop and promote ultrasound, and they have debated whether their professional identity ought to rest more on their technical "skill" or on their (feminine) capacity for "caring." Over time, the obstetrical exam has come to incorporate rituals of showing and telling and giving out pictures, which have allowed sonographers both to "sell" ultrasound and to respond to their pregnant patients in a "caring" manner. Ironically, however, these same elements have also set the stage for antiabortion advocates to use fetal sonograms to fetishize and commodify the fetus, and thus to "make" the public fetus that now inhabits mass-mediated consumer culture.

Women who adopt children transnationally experience the enabling powers of consumption in yet other ways. As Ann Anagnost documents, the effort to provide for transnationally adopted children a "cultural" identity reflecting their place of origins while also incorporating them into new families takes place to a considerable extent in and through the work of consumption, especially of "ethnically" marked dolls and toys. At the same time, the movement of these children, and the various exchanges of money and goods in and through which this movement is accomplished, can also bring to adoptive parents' awareness, in sometimes uncomfortable ways, the contours of the global circuits of power, privilege, poverty, and chaos that undergird transnational adoption as a special new form of migration. Anagnost argues that the "affective labor" of transnationally adoptive mothers—labor that takes place to a considerable extent in and through consumption—is profoundly enmeshed in these global processes, enabling and enabled by them even as it works to obscure them.

Yet, in mothering as in the rest of social life, ethnographic attention to "the margins" can reveal much about the workings of power and culture at the center. The imbrication of motherhood with consumption, intimate family relations with global power relations, is perhaps more visible in transnationally adoptive families, but it is hardly unique to them. As Anagnost notes:

> This labor of confronting consumption is not reserved only for adoptive parents but properly belongs to all of us who are, often unwittingly, articulated within a complex network of exchanges that propels the commodity to us across multiple disjunctures. Such reflection is critically important if we are ever to claim a political agency that exceeds the private confines of the family and works toward a wider call to responsibility. (Anagnost, this volume, 16).

The "roots trips" taken to their adopted children's countries of birth, by the Swedish families of whom Barbara Yngvesson writes, represent one way in which some have opened themselves to awareness of their own embeddedness in these global networks. To voluntarily retrace the paths of exchange that brought a child to oneself, and away from some other mother, "is to enter, imaginatively and in practice, the space of these exchanges," a space that Yngvesson calls "the eye of the storm." This space, she writes, "has revealed a kind of chaos, shaking up (and opening up) families, persons, and nations in the world that created international adoption and that international adoption helped to create" (Yngvesson, this volume, 185).

As this collection clearly demonstrates, interrogating the sociocultural and economic arrangements that position different groups of women very differently with regard to "consuming motherhood" is an important step toward documenting and analyzing what Faye Ginsburg and Rayna Rapp have named "stratified reproduction . . . the power relations by which some categories of people are empowered to nurture and reproduce, while others are disempowered" (1995:3). More broadly, attending to the dynamics of consumption and motherhood may offer us an angle of vision into the crucial questions of how emerging large-scale economic and political regimes take hold at the level of intimate relationships and how they are (re)produced in the bearing and raising of the next generation.

Motherhood and consumption, then, coexist in considerable tension as systems of ideas, even while they are inseparable at the level of social action. With a few important exceptions, however (Cook 1995; Layne 2003a, 2000b, 2000c; Miller 1998a; Seiter 1993; Taylor 2000a, 2000b, 1998, 1992; Zelizer 1985), the ideological opposition between motherhood and consumption has gone unquestioned, and their imbrication in social practice unexplored, as writings on motherhood have rarely centrally engaged questions of consumption and vice versa. Contributors to *Consuming Motherhood*, seeking to understand the complex and ironic ways that these intersect in the lives of the women about whom we write, have been compelled to draw upon—and to draw together—two streams of scholarly work that up to now have seldom flowed together: critical and feminist scholarly work on the topic of consumption, and on the topic of motherhood and reproduction.

One reason, perhaps, that these two streams have tended to run in parallel is that body metaphors of eating and digesting food remain implicit in theories of consumption, which mix rather badly with the metaphorical associations of procreation, making it difficult (or at least quite counterintuitive) to bring theories of consumption to bear specifically upon motherhood. The concept of consumption, now taken within social theory to refer to all kinds of uses of goods and services, still retains heavy traces of its older association with eating. Indeed, *Webster's* defines "consumer" as "one that consumes: as *a:* one that utilizes economic goods *b:* an organism requiring complex organic compounds for food which it obtains by preying on other organisms or by eating particles of organic matter." Indeed, hunger is inscribed as the paradigm for consumption already within Marx's definition of the "very queer thing" that is the commodity: "A commodity is, in the first place, an object outside us, a thing that by its properties satisfies human wants of some sort or another. The nature of such wants, whether, for instance, they spring from the stomach or from fancy, makes no difference" (Marx 1978:199). "Wants that spring from the stomach" stand here for real physical need (to the extent that any such unmediated needs might be said to exist), while other sorts of desires, "wants that spring from fancy," are refigured as a sort of mental or spiritual hunger.

This metaphor shapes—and, I would argue, hinders—our understanding in at least two ways. First, the consumer of social theory inhabits a body that, if not necessarily male (for, after all, women too eat and feel hunger), is at least not as easily imagined as a specifically pregnant body. The fetus is emphatically *not* "an object outside us," and although I would argue that it may nonetheless "satisfy human wants of some sort or another," it is difficult to imagine these wants as "springing from the stomach." This makes it rather difficult to conceptualize pregnancy, and by extension motherhood, in terms of consumption. How can the bearing of children be likened to the ingestion of food? The very suggestion seems to invoke that most frightening of all monsters, the mother who eats her own children.

A second, and related difficulty, stems from the assumption that consumption is—again, on the model of eating and digestion—primarily a destructive using up, the end point of a process whose beginning lies in production. Consumption appears to be simply "the end of the road for goods and services, a terminus for their social life" (Appadurai 1996:66). Motherhood, as an institution charged with producing new social persons, seems much more naturally to lend itself to analysis in light of questions concerning labor and production than to an analysis in terms of consumption—and, indeed, the analogy between reproduction and production has been enormously important and fruitful for feminist scholars and critics (Martin 1987; Rothman 1982; Taylor 2000a).

Of course, there is by now a considerable scholarly literature that *does* take consumption as a starting point, examining its social and cultural dynamics and consequences—and within this, a significant body of work addressing its specifically gendered dimensions (de Grazia and Furlough 1996; Lury 1996; Scanlon 2000). Scholars of consumption have quite thoroughly addressed questions of sexuality and consumption but have given the topic of motherhood comparatively little consideration. One reason for this, perhaps, is that consumption studies have tended to be cast as studies of "material culture," exploring the social and cultural role of material *objects*—while motherhood is understood to be a relationship between *persons*. The dividing line separating people from objects would seem, in this perspective, to be quite clearly bounded, fixed, and stable; the question is merely how they affect one another. The task of the analyst, then, becomes one of specifying relationships. Reproductive technologies and the controversies that swirl around them clearly suggest, however, that such distinctions—between persons and objects, bodies and commodities, mothers and consumers—are not so clear-cut.

If critical feminist studies of consumption and of motherhood are two streams that have largely run in separate courses, it is also worth noting that both are quite turbulent. Each of these literatures has been a site of heated debates over how to understand the object of study, in relation to the broader economic and sociocultural order of which it is part. Marxist scholars and critics of modernity have long recognized the centrality of economic production; by contrast, consumption has tended to be regarded as an unproductive using-up of that which is produced. When critical social theorists have turned their attention to consumption, they have generally regarded it as a mechanism through which social subjects who *might* conceivably be in a position to critique or resist the oppressive social relations of capitalism are instead enlisted in their perpetuation. Over the past two decades, however, scholars of consumption have argued persuasively that we must understand consumption itself as a site of cultural creativity and political agency, and also (at least potentially) of subversion and resistance. Consumers are not without agency, but rather appropriate mass-produced goods to their own projects and purposes, producing selves and making worlds in the process.

Feminist writings on motherhood have spanned a similar spectrum, from the pessimistic to the celebratory. Lauri Umansky writes:

> On the one hand, feminists have focused on motherhood as a social mandate, an oppressive institution, a compromise of a woman's independence, and a surrender to the half-human destiny that biology supposedly decrees to women. This "negative" discourse has occurred in conjunction with political agitation for birth control and abortion rights, and alongside a critique of the nuclear family. On the other hand, feminists have focused on motherhood as a positive force [which] holds the truly spectacular potential to bond women to each other and to nature, to foster a liberating knowledge of self, to release the very creativity and generativity that the institution of "motherhood" in our culture denies to women.
> (Umansky 1996:3)

There are, then, big theoretical issues at stake here: the limits of agency, the workings of power, the sources of resistance, and the possibility of transformation.

The relationship between motherhood and consumption is, however, far more than merely a theoretical question—it is a vital matter with which ordinary people struggle on a daily basis: What must I (and what *can* I) do and have and buy in order to properly love, value, educate, nurture, provide for, raise—in a word, *mother*—my child(ren)? *Consuming Motherhood* takes this up through ethnographic and historical explorations of how ordinary women, striving to build and maintain relations of kinship in the context of globalizing consumer capitalism, live out motherhood in and through, as well as against, ideologies and practices of consumption.

All of the essays collected here seek to document women's words and their actions with empathy, respect, and a keen sensitivity to the ironies and complexities of inhabiting social terrains cross-cut by motherhood and consumption. Beyond this shared commitment to ethnography, this collection reflects something of the wide range of positions staked out within the two streams of critical scholarship upon which the authors have drawn. Some essays, for example, primarily concern commodification—that is, questions of how, under what circumstances, and with what consequences something (such as a child, a reproductive organ, or a form of care-providing activity) comes to be regarded and treated as a commodity. Within this group, some authors understand "commodities" as being distinguished by the presence of a cash nexus, where money is exchanged for something or someone (Davis-Floyd, Klassen). Others understand "commodification" in more general terms, as the social process whereby something or someone comes to be made exchangeable—for example, by being stripped of social identity (Anagnost, Yngvesson, Wozniak, Taylor). Another set of essays, meanwhile, primarily address consumption, especially the subjectivity of the consumer, and focus on people who exhibit (or resist, or critique, or are attributed) stances toward mothering and kinship that echo the stance of consumers toward the objects of consumption (Landsman, Layne, Clarke).

Crosscutting these broad theoretical differences among the chapters are a number of common themes and topics. For example, some address the role of consumption practices in the making of fetal subjects (Layne, Clarke, Taylor). Others document dilemmas of midwives, specialists in home-birth rituals, and sonographers, showing how they have carved out professional niches through the commodification of their services, while struggling to adhere to their various visions of what it means to care with integrity for pregnant and birthing women (Davis-Floyd, Klassen, Taylor). Several essays deal centrally with motherhood lost, and the ways that material things come to concretize or stand in for loss, showing how motherhood and consumption are linked in the work of memory (Layne, Yngvesson, Anagnost, Landsman, Wozniak).

Our aim, then, is not to somehow reconcile or stabilize the debates about either consumption or motherhood, nor do we seek to produce a one-size-fits-all theorization of their relation. Rather, we seek to document a range of different kinds of motherhoods, and different kinds of consumption, and thus a variety of interrelations between the two. In so doing, of course, we also seek to do two things that ethnography at its best always does. First, we seek through our scholarly work to bear witness to the lives and views and struggles of ordinary people and to honor them with close attention and thoughtful, careful, well-informed reflection. At the same time, we also seek to allow social life—in all its richness, its complexity, and its capacity to surprise—to "speak back" to the scholarly literatures upon which we have drawn, which we have found both indispensable and imperfect, but always eminently worthy of serious critical engagement.

Clearly, there remain many topics not explored in this collection that invite consideration as other instances of consuming motherhood. We hope that the scholarly directions charted out here will be pursued further by others who will ask and seek to answer similar critical questions concerning the relationship of motherhood and consumption in a far broader range of specific circumstances than are considered in the chapters collected here. Much remains to be learned about, and from, the situation of single mothers, "welfare mothers," lesbian mothers, immigrant mothers, and others who, from specific positions within global social and economic systems, struggle to build and maintain meaningful family relations both against and through consumption. It is perhaps worth emphasizing, however, that this is not simply a call for a bookshelf full of studies to document a supermarket-shelf array of identities and family forms.

Consuming Motherhood does not, in other words, endorse or embrace the argument one often encounters to the effect that proliferating varieties of family and motherhood are to be understood primarily as new consumerist options. Rather, we hold that the questions addressed here touch on quite basic matters concerning the relationship between social life and economic life, the ordering of persons and the ordering of objects. As such, the questions engaged here carry implications far beyond merely the specific groups of mothers discussed and the small communities of scholars who study them.

As a way of helping readers to situate the ethnographic essays presented here relative to the literatures on consumption and on motherhood, we have included here in a section titled "Con-Texts" two classic pieces that approach the problematic of consuming motherhood from very different perspectives. Barbara Katz Rothman's "Motherhood under Capitalism," which first appeared in 1989 as a chapter in her book *Recreating Motherhood: Ideology and Technology in a Patriarchal Society*, we present here as a strongly stated and influential view from within feminist discussions of motherhood and reproduction. Alongside it, as one example of how similar questions have been approached from within the scholarly literature on consumption, we present Daniel Miller's "How Infants Grow Mothers in North London." This piece, which originally appeared in 1997 in the journal *Theory, Culture, and Society*, draws upon fieldwork conducted for (and partially replicates arguments presented in) Miller's influential 1998 book *A Theory of Shopping*, which analyzes women's activities of shopping for their families as a form of ritual practice. Taken together, these pieces will, we hope, give readers some sense both of the considerable differences between these two streams of scholarly literature and of the intriguing ways in which they might speak to each other.

The next section, "Contributions," presents nine essays that explore questions of consuming motherhood through ethnographic research. These we have touched upon already. Each chapter stands on its own, though all are in quite close dialogue, and they may be read in any order. Rather than seeking to flatten out theoretical differences that remain, we sought instead to highlight them. For this reason, we have presented the chapters in an order intended to chart out the wide spectrum of approaches that the authors take to the central term *consumption*. First come those that hew closest to a material culture studies understanding of "consumption" as having to do primarily with tangible goods; next come those that focus on situations of consumption and fetishism, where the line between material objects and persons is both troubled and troubling; and, finally, at the other end of the spectrum, come those that address as instances of "consumption" such intangibles as caring services and even spiritual practices.

The book concludes with a third section, "Commentaries," which presents reflections on the volume from two quite different scholarly perspectives. Igor

Kopytoff, an anthropologist and scholar of Africa, has made a large and lasting impact on scholarly discussions of consumption through his influential article "The Cultural Biography of Things: Commoditization as a Process," which appeared in 1986 in *The Social Life of Things: Commodities in Cultural Perspective,* edited by Arjun Appadurai. In that piece, Kopytoff considers the case of slavery, patently a case of the commodification of a person, as illustrative of problems inherent in trying definitively to separate "persons" from "commodities." In Kopytoff's view, commodities are best understood not as members of a separate class of things, but as objects occupying a specific moment within a social *process* of being rendered available or unavailable for exchange—a process to which human beings, like other objects, may be subjected. In his commentary on *Consuming Motherhood,* Kopytoff contextualizes the cases considered here within a broad comparative and historical view of the variable and changing relationship between economistic relations and kinship relations. He concludes that a sort of cultural balance that had previously existed in Western societies between economism and opposition to it has been undermined with the advent of industrial capitalism—with the result that more and more spheres of life have been invaded by economistic behavior, while at the same time conscious resistance to economism (so far, relatively unsuccessful) has also grown stronger.

Certainly, a sense that economistic behavior has invaded the sphere of kinship, as well as a conscious effort to resist this process, have long been central to the writings of Barbara Katz Rothman on motherhood and consumption. We close with a commentary by Rothman, who situates the ethnographic essays presented here within a reflection on the historical trajectory of feminist approaches to questions of motherhood (a trajectory that her own work has, of course, significantly shaped). She ends with a question: What, she asks, are we to do? Where do we go from here? In the wake of the insights made available by attending to the problematic of *Consuming Motherhood,* how does one continue to work for that which one values about motherhood and contest that which is troubling about consumerism?

These are, of course, what I often describe to my students as *real* questions: questions about the world that were not designed solely as a teaching exercise, that have no single obvious answer, on which thoughtful people may deeply disagree—and, above all, questions that matter. They also resonate with other questions of concern today; it is not only in the context of troubling and troubled relations between motherhood and consumption that we encounter problems of love and money. How do we usefully situate not only motherhood but also any of the other social relationships that people hold to be meaningful in their lives, within the broader economic orders that undergird and encompass them? Approaching such questions as scholars, how can we best grasp the relationship between systems of thought (about kinship, economy, or other manifestations of love and money) and systems of social action? And, approaching such questions as people committed to feminist and other visions of social justice, how can we seek through our scholarship not only to document but to help transform social life? With such real questions is exactly the right way to close this volume, and the right place from which to move on to the work that lies ahead—the vital work of building and maintaining and transforming the world that we all inhabit, of which scholarly work is one small but important part. Ultimately, it is not in this or any other book, but in that ongoing collective work that answers to such real questions—answers that must necessarily remain always partial and provisional—will have to be worked out.

Con-Texts

Motherhood under Capitalism

BARBARA KATZ ROTHMAN

> The ideology of technology dehumanizes people by encouraging a mechanical self image–people viewing themselves as machines. Capitalism adds that not only is the body a collection of parts, its parts become commodities. In the United States the essential fluids of life–blood, milk, and semen–are all for sale.
>
> –Barbara Katz Rothman, *In Labor: Women and Power in the Birthplace*

That is my basic starting point in understanding the meaning of capitalism as it exists in the United States: there is a price tag on everything. This chapter will explore what the experience of motherhood comes to mean when prices are affixed.

From the standpoint of the ideology of technology, we have seen that motherhood is perceived as work, and children, as a product produced by the labor of mothering. Mothers' work and mothers' bodies are resources out of which babies are made. From the standpoint of the ideology of patriarchy, it is men's babies that are being made. From the standpoint of the market, not all work is equally valuable, and not all products are equally valued. There is not a direct relationship between the value of the worker and the value of the product. What is essential to capitalism is the accumulation and investment of capital, of wealth, by people who are in a position to control others. Under capitalism, workers do not own or control the products of their own labor.

Babies, at least healthy white babies, are very precious products these days. Mothers, rather like South African diamond miners, are the cheap, expendable, not-too-trustworthy labor necessary to produce the precious product.[1]

This is where it is all heading: the commodification of children and the proletarianization of motherhood.

This is the end result of the evolution of these three ideological perspectives. This is what ties together the new technology and the old technology, the legal, the medical, the political, and the psychological re-creation of motherhood.

We are no longer talking about mothers and babies at all—we are talking about laborers and their products.

Capitalism alone is not responsible for the deep trouble motherhood is in, but it is a very important part of it. Societies that have resisted the commodification of life tend to look at the situation in the United States as a kind of warning. Responding to work of mine on new procreative technology, Margaret Stacey called it a warning that should be well heeded, lest the United Kingdom go the way of the United States: "Although the UK, like the US, is predominantly a capitalist society, we have hitherto consistently sought to prevent the intrusion of capitalist values into our health and welfare services. In the UK, issues associated with health and reproduction are less blatantly exploited for profit than in the US" (Stacey 1985:193).

Exploitation, profit, and motherhood: an unseemly combination. How do capitalism and market values fit into the re-creation of motherhood?

While there is much disagreement about the relation between patriarchy and technology, on the one hand, and patriarchy and capitalism, on the other hand, clearly capitalism and technology are intertwined ideologies. One can envision a technological society without capitalism—though many would claim that the technological societies which claim to be socialist really practice state capitalism. But it is possible to envision people as cogs in a wheel, without the wheel turned to profit. It is harder to picture full-blown capitalism without the technological ideology.

But my goal here is not to answer chicken-and-egg questions about the relationship between these three ideologies. Rather, I am going to take this ideology as a given right now—in America we do live in a society in which capitalism is an economic system and a guiding principle, shaping the way we see life. Ideas such as supply and demand, cost-benefit analysis, and profit permeate our lives. We think of the profit motive as if it were a basic human desire, greed as if it were part of "human nature." It is the nature of capitalism to raise the motive for making money and owning goods above all else: that is not an inevitable part of the human spirit, but very much a part of American life.

This chapter will focus on one essential aspect of the capitalist ideology, the extension of ownership or property relations in ways that are at best inappropriate and too often morally wrong. There is a great deal of modern social criticism that makes exactly that claim, including, for example, the ecologists. They argue that it is inappropriate to think we can own the land, the waters: the earth, they claim—significantly—is our *mother*, not our property.

But what happens when we start thinking of motherhood itself in terms of property? As wrong as it is to think of the human relation to the earth this way, it is worse when we start thinking about our relations with each other in the language of property.

The actual word *property* gets used relatively infrequently in discussions of human relations. More often the key term is *rights*. "A right can be interpreted as an entitlement to do or have something, to exclude others from doing or having something or as an enforceable claim" (Smith 1984:202). There are two directions in which property rights have extended that are directly relevant to motherhood: rights of ownership of one's own body and rights to one's own child.

The way an ideology works is to force our attention in certain ways, to give us a point of view, a perspective—often expressed in language as metaphor. People do not necessarily talk of or even actively think of their bodies or their children as *property* in the sense of real estate. But what Janet Farrell Smith says of parenthood can be said equally of bodily ownership: "In applying a property model to parenting, it is important to remember that a parent may not literally assert that a child is a piece of property, but may work on assumptions analogous to those which one makes in connection with property" (Smith 1984:201).

Women are not just passive victims of capitalist ideology: we use it in our interests as well. Women, like men, lay claim to their own bodies and to their own children and call on the basic values of capitalism to support those claims. As I shall discuss in the next section, feminists have been able, in some sense, to capitalize on the value of ownership to gain certain rights for women, particularly what are called "reproductive rights." But there have been attendant costs, with regard both to the owned body and to the owned child.

The Owned Body

Within a capitalist system we cannot legally force or forcibly prevent people from doing something with their own property without very compelling reasons. The right to own, and therefore to control, property is among the most valued of rights.

In technological society, I have argued, the body is treated as a thing and as a resource. In capitalist society, where the emphasis is on private ownership, the body is viewed not as a resource for the community or the society, but as private property, a personal resource. Rights of privacy are in a sense just a variation on other rights of ownership, of private control.

Given the view of the body as owned property, the extension of ownership to all of our body parts allows women some measure of control over the use of our bodies in procreation. If women are full persons, then we are moved out of the category of owned property and into the category of owners of our own bodies. Men can no longer entirely legally barter in women's bodies.

Feminists have made use of this concept of bodily ownership to make American society recognize that, just as we cannot force a woman to have some particular surgery, we cannot force her to have an abortion—even if either one, the abortion or the surgery, would save her life, or save the state much money, or save other people much difficulty. And we have as a society also concluded that we cannot stop her from having an abortion, just as we cannot stop her from having, say, her gallbladder removed, even if we think it is unnecessary surgery, bad for her, or risks a loss to the society or to her family and friends. It is, after all, her body.

But while ownership is a useful legal analogy for one's relationship with one's "own" body, it is certainly far from the essential experience of being embodied people.

Often we do not feel as if we own our bodies. If we view them in ownership terms at all, it may be as rented space. John Quincy Adams said, shortly before his death: "I inhabit a weak, frail, decayed tenement; battered by the winds and broken in upon by the storms, and, from all I can learn, the landlord does not intend to repair" (Fadiman 1985:6).

Sometimes we feel as if we *are* our bodies: intense physical sensation or effort can have that effect. In pain, sex, and athletics one can sometimes achieve—and some people strive for—a true unity of mind and body. But such intensity of physical experience can also make a person feel as if there is a distinct inner self, the owner of the outer body, "distanced" from physical sensation. And people can strive for that experience, too, to step outside the body, to "rise above" the body. The experience of bodily change over the life course can also distance us from our bodies—is this middle-aged woman really me? Or am I in here somewhere, looking at a weathered hand working a pen across a page? It is a hand I control, I own, a hand that is *mine* but surely not *me*—not the *me* that played with clay, that learned to hold a crayon. And sometimes—with terror or with humor or both—we experience the body as inhabited *without* any of the control of ownership. The loss of strength or agility with age or illness can make a person feel trapped inside the body.

That last, Adams's view, is close to an essentially religious view that our bodies are ours to use for a while, but that our bodies, and our souls, come from a god-force and do not belong to us. That perspective does not give the individual infinite control over his or her body, since the body is not the person's but God's property, and God sets the rules of tenancy. We speak of tenancy, but we know we have no coin with which to pay our rent but our own subservience.

There is another way of seeing the body as not "ours" to own but as not coming from God. That is to see the body—and perhaps the mind and soul as well—as part of something much larger: the stream of life, the gene pool, the evolutionary chain, the fatherland or motherland, the family.

In American society we may be able to talk about and think about the body in all of these ways, but legal recognition goes only to the view of the body as individually owned. That is an idea deeply rooted in our liberal political system and our capitalist economic system. And it is not a bad way of *legally* viewing the body. Every time a society removes individual ownership of the body, it opens the way to state control. So viewing the body as property, privately and individually owned, protects each of us from all of us, protects us as individuals from the power of the state.

Given the present economic and political system, it would be dangerous to argue against this view of the body as privately, individually owned, legally expressed as a right to privacy. "Privacy, as it is connected with a model of property relations, is not only an ability to deny others access to certain aspects of one's life, but also a right of entitlement to exclude others" (Smith 1984:202). Other views of the body, even if more satisfying ethically or spiritually, are dangerous politically. As Janet Farrell Smith points out: "Since some of these rights (to form a family, to decide whether or not to have children and to raise those children) are now established in U.S. constitutional law on a basis of the right to privacy, it would be a strategic mistake to extract that basis from procreative choice" (Smith 1984:201).

Within the American system, intelligent feminist use of the individualist ethos has been invaluable in assuring women's rights in procreation. Once women themselves are recognized as full citizens, then individual women must be accorded the same rights of bodily autonomy and integrity that men have. For women, that means sexual and procreative autonomy. Because it is her body, she cannot be raped. Because it is her body, she cannot be forced to bear pregnancies she does not want. Because it is her body, she cannot be forced to abort pregnancies she does want.

This does not mean that women are not forced by circumstance into these very situations and eventualities. It only means that the society will not use the official power of the state to force her. Women are in fact prevented from having abortions they might want by family pressure, by economic circumstances, and by religious and social pressures. And women are forced into having abortions they might not want to have because of poverty, because of lack of services for children and mothers, because of lack of services for disabled children and adults. By offering amniocentesis to identify fetuses who would have disabilities, and by cutting back on services for disabled children and their families, we effectively force women to have selective abortions.

Because of our current battles over the right to abortion, Americans tend to think of the state as "permitting" women to have abortions, as if the drive for continuing pregnancies came from the state, and the drive for abortions from women. In fact, the legal protection works also to permit women not to have abortions. When women's ownership rights over their bodies are lost, the rights to have and the rights *not* to have abortions are likewise lost. Such was the case in Nazi Germany, where some abortions were indeed forced, but it is equally true that women lost the right to have the abortions they themselves chose, the abortions they as individual women felt they needed.

In American society, when we bring it back to the simple legal question—who can force an abortion or forcibly prevent one—we wisely retreat to safety, calling forth our most sacred value. It's *her* body. We invoke a higher power, the power of ownership.

This then is the way that women have been able to combine dominant American liberal philosophy with capitalist ideology to our benefit. We've made use of the mind-body dualism to allow a view of the body as owned, like a shelter which houses the more important mind. If one claims rationality for women—the essential liberal claim for all people—then simple fairness gives women the same rights of bodily ownership that men have, and the very high value of ownership, of property rights, is then turned to the advantage of women who can claim exclusive rights to our own bodies. In the name of ownership, women have demanded access to contraception, sterilization, and abortion. And given the prevailing liberal philosophy, we've gotten those rights to control our fertility—although given the capitalist class system, we have fared less well with access to the necessary means.

While the "owned-body" principle has worked for women in avoiding motherhood, it is less clear how it can be made to work to empower women as mothers. Our bodies may be ours, but given the ideology of patriarchy, the bodies of mothers are not highly valued. The bodies are just the space in which genetic material matures into babies. In a patriarchal system, even if women own their bodies it may not give them any real control in pregnancy. Women may simply be seen to own the space in which the fetuses are housed. This is the argument on which attempts to control women's behavior during pregnancy are based: owning her own body is not enough to assure her civil liberties if her body is believed to contain the property of someone else, somebody else's baby.

Of course, if women's bodies are understood to be the space in which sperm and egg grow to be a baby, and women are understood to be the owners of that space, then the acceptance of "surrogacy" follows logically, almost inevitably. The woman can rent out space in her body just as she can rent out the spare back bedroom. And she will have no more ownership rights over the inhabitants of that space in her body than over the boarder in her home.

The combination of patriarchy and capitalism explains the powerful reluctance to engage in the open sale of babies by their mothers while permitting surrogacy. The baby is considered precious, even beyond sale, but it is not owned by the mother. The mother's capital is her body; it is her property, but it is cheap. In surrogacy contracts only about a third of the total cost paid by the potential adoptive parents goes to the "surrogate" for her "service." The legal and medical fees take the rest. Those services are of course highly valued, and a few hours of work by an attorney cost more than months of gestation.

Is it possible to make the legal concept of the owned body work in the interests of mothers? We could take advantage of mechanistic thinking and claim "sweat equity" for women in their babies: they are ours because we have done the work to make them. We would then have made the connection between the owned body and the owned child. But the "sweat equity" idea will work only if women's labor, the "sweat," is valued. And because pregnancy is bodily work, and because it is women's work, it is not likely to be highly valued in American society.

What is valued is the child. In patriarchal ideology, the child is the extension of the man. In capitalist ideology, the child is the repository of wealth.

Mothers may not be much valued in America, but children are.

A Child of One's Own

When people talk about becoming parents, about wanting a child, they often use the word *own*. They want a child of their own. They want, it sometimes sounds, to "own" a child. The word *have* gets used in its blurred meanings: they want to "have" a child. They want to have it to *own* it, and they want to have it to, well, to *have* it.

What exactly is it that people want when they want to "have" a baby? I will now explore what it has come to mean to want to have children in a market-oriented society and how that wanting is experienced and met.

Having a child *is* a lot like owning something. It's more complicated than the sense of possession of a pretty little object, a vase or a painting. Rather, it's like the complicated owning that goes with a house—you own it, but it takes an awful lot of energy, or work. The demands make one sometimes feel more owned than owner.

When a woman gets pregnant easily, readily, she doesn't have to think about what it means to "have" a baby. But when a woman, or a couple, cannot readily have a baby of their own, on their own, they take the complex whole of "having" a child and start sorting it out into the parts they can and the parts they cannot have for themselves.

Some people want the opportunity to be part of a child's life, to help a child or children. They want the good times—the trip to the circus, the help with the science fair project—and they want the bad times, to be there psychologically, physically, financially for a kid who needs them. Some of these people realize that they don't have to "have" a child to be there for a child. Many of us have had the experience of the childless aunt or uncle or family friend, the one who was not all tangled up with his or her own kids, who saw us as real people, who went to bat with our parents for us, who came up with the extra time or energy or money when our parents' supply gave out. Mostly it is people who are not tied up with kids of their "own" who can do that. Sometimes it is people who never had kids, and sometimes it is grandparents and older people whose parenting is, basically, behind them.

Some people, when they say they want to have a baby, are talking about the having of it, the actual act of bearing the baby. That is a life experience a woman may very well want, and more than once, for herself. When we offer such a woman adoption as an alternative, it does not meet all of her needs. An adoptive mother may feel exactly in every way the same about her child as does a mother who gave birth to her daughter or son. But she may feel differently about herself, about her body. "Having" a baby is something a woman may want for herself, for her own experience, independent of her relationship with her child or children. When I think about that personally, I know that the depth, the intensity, the quality of my feelings toward my child by adoption are no different than my feelings toward my children by birth, but I am sure that I relate differently to my own bodily experience than I would have had I never been pregnant and never given birth. And while it is not my own experience, I can imagine that a man may well want that experience of pregnancy as well—he may want the experience for himself of a pregnant wife, a pregnant lover, of feeling the baby move against him through her.

For some people that physical experience of bearing a baby matters, and for some it doesn't much matter, and for some it matters, but negatively—that's the part of "having" a baby they'd prefer to avoid. I've talked to men who are just starry-eyed over their wives' pregnancies, who want home births and the most intimate physical connection with the entire pregnancy and birth experience. And I've talked to men who have resented every moment of the demands of the pregnancy and the birth on their wives. And it is just as true of women—I've talked to women who fantasize about going through pregnancies and births and suckling again and again, just for the sheer joy of it—and to women who feel revulsion at the thought of it all.

The genetic tie is another part of having a baby, a baby of one's "own." Part of having a baby is reproducing part of oneself. Whatever it is that is genetic in who or what we are, part of that part gets passed on to our children. For myself, I feel that it's just the physical body that gets passed on—the shape of a nose, body build, tendency toward diabetes, a bad back, strong legs. Other people feel that it is also intelligence, wit, sometimes even "character." But whatever it is, some of us want very much to reproduce parts of ourselves in this world.

Being involved in a child's life, physically experiencing pregnancy, having a genetic tie, a feeling of "owning" a baby—all of these are aspects of the experience, but they are not all of the aspects of what people mean when they say they want to "have" children.

In a capitalist system, when people want to have something, they become a "market" for it. When people want something simple, the path of success is to find a cheaper way of producing more of that thing. If people want, say, coffee, one could just grow more coffee cheaper. But one can also start thinking about what it is about coffee that people like and don't like, want and don't want, and start marketing different products to meet the coffee need: decaf, instant, coffee substitutes like chicory, herb teas, and instant broth, caffeine tablets.

And so it is with babies. Since there are a lot of things people want when they want to "have" a child, there are a lot of ways of marketing parenthood. Just looking at these few meanings of "having" a child, we can see the potential and the actuality of a range of marketing strategies.

When people want a child to help, to take care of, to be involved with rather than to "have," it doesn't lend itself to commercial exploitation, but it certainly does open up nonprofit "marketing." Donations to many good causes rely on pictures of children. Physically disabled and mentally retarded adults are probably more needy as individuals than are children with the same problems—after all, the children most often have parents tending to them, advocating for them, buying for them. But it is poster children, retarded children, children on crutches that we are shown when asked to help people with disabilities. Grown-ups starve in families, too; but, oh, those children's eyes and swollen bellies just tear us up. We give. Arthritis is not just an old people's disease, the arthritis foundations tell us, so we give. Villages in underdeveloped nations need fresh water supplies, so we "adopt" a child and mail off our sixteen dollars a month to save the children. These are all good things to do, but it is easier to get people to do them when the pitch is helping children. And so it is a kind of marketing that goes on. Some say it is an exploitation of children to use their sad faces, their large eyes, their skinny braced limbs to make us give.

When people want a more direct relationship with children, more than just sending money, another kind of nonprofit marketing steps in. "Big Brother" and "Big Sister" and "Foster Grandparent" programs all address the needs of people who want to relate to a child in a real and direct way. Foster parenting does the same, with more of the demands of the full parenting experience.

All of these ways of giving—of money and of ourselves—address part of what it is people want when they want to have children in their lives. When people want children to "have" children of their "own," then the potential for more directly commercial marketing takes over. The current push in reproductive technology can be seen as ways of segmenting this market into different parts of "having" a child and addressing these various needs.

When it is the pregnancy experience that people want, and then all the parenting that follows, the focus is on creating a pregnancy and allowing parenting to follow from that. Most of infertility research has been directed at exactly this: how to get the woman pregnant. If the problem was her blocked tubes, unblock them or, with in vitro fertilization, bypass them. If the problem was his sperm, fix whatever caused the problem, replace the sperm with artificial insemination, or use fertilization techniques—in vitro fertilization (IVF) again—that require fewer viable sperm. The treatment is a success if the woman is pregnant and going to "have" a baby.

Treatments for infertility that promise to do this have been very successfully marketed. Sadly, the marketing success far exceeds the pregnancy successes. By the late 1980s we had seen an incredible expansion of in vitro clinics, most of which had never produced a baby, and a top success rate hovering around 10 to 15 percent. More than a decade later, the success rate is still only 22.9 percent according to the American Society for Reproductive Medicine, which represents the doctors and clinics who provide IVF. The felt desperation of infertile couples has been used to sell a high-risk, high-cost, low-success treatment.

Achieving a pregnancy is not always the answer for people who want to "have" a baby—even for those who very much want the pregnancy experience, the technological fix may not work. And for others, the pregnancy is not the issue. When the need is to "have" a child to parent, then the focus is on getting a baby. I sometimes hear infertile people say that quite clearly: "I just want a baby to hold, to love; I just want a baby in my arms." Getting the woman pregnant with all sorts of high-tech, invasive procedures is not the only way for infertile people to "have" a baby. There are nontechnological ways of obtaining babies; they are being produced all over the place. One possibility is to tap into that overproduction and effect some redistribution. Nonmarket adoption aims to redistribute the babies some people "have" but don't want to "have" to other people who want to "have" babies but cannot "have" them. A little juggling around between the haves and the have-nots and everybody's happier.

Most of the people in the private adoption sector are not "brokering" babies but just trying to match up babies with families. When that works, it works well. Nonmarket adoption started to break down into its current chaos when the demand for healthy white babies—the standard "replacement" baby for the white majority of couples with infertility—far exceeded the supply. When there were more potential adopters than there were babies, we had a "market" with unmet needs. It was inevitable in this society at this time that more traditional marketing strategies would take over. Profiteers sell babies. Some of the profiteers are the mothers themselves, women who have extra babies that they don't want to have but would like to sell. Some women have gotten pregnant deliberately, just to sell a baby and make a profit.

More commonly, the profits are made by the brokers. Often these are lawyers who make the profit out of their charges for adoption services. Money is changing hands, but no one is technically selling a baby. When the whole project slips right out of the legal sphere and black marketing takes over, babies are simply sold for whatever the market will bear.

In this situation, so-called surrogacy adoption began. While the commodification of babies, treating them as products, has gone a long way in our society, it probably still feels—and almost certainly felt in the mid-1970s when the first surrogacy contracts were drawn up—inappropriate to simply say that the time has come to put babies up for sale. Such sales would also raise the difficult question of ownership, of who owns a baby in the first place. What the brokers did instead was to say that if a wife cannot carry a pregnancy and have a baby of her own, a man can hire a surrogate to carry a pregnancy. He hires someone to substitute for his wife in bearing the husband's "own" baby.

This strategy sidesteps the laws against selling a baby because, as Noel Keane, the "founder" of surrogacy-for-hire in the United States and the man who brokered the contract between William Stern and Mary Beth Whitehead, says, "You have to look at who the baby is sold to." The contracts are between the man, the sperm donor, and the woman, the mother. How, Keane asks, can a man buy his *own* child? Keane says the woman gives the baby "*back* to the father," as if it came from him in the first place. And so here we have the marketing of patriarchy: the mother just incubates the man's child, for a fee. For Keane, the child is at least as much the father's (the sperm donor) as the mother's because not only is his genetic contribution equal to hers, but it is his by intention, by contract.

When one starts dealing with parenthood in terms of sales and contracts, and most especially broken contracts, questions of ownership loom large. When the "surrogate" changes her mind and wants to keep the child, the question we ask is "Whose child is it?" We talk as if the child were indeed property, as if it belonged to someone.

Most often we get trapped into a discussion of mother's versus father's ownership rights over their children. We talk as if the child were the property of just two people, as if the genetic tie to the parents were the only definitive relationship for the child. The child is seen as the product of the sperm and, perhaps reluctantly conceded, the egg, and that defines *who* and *whose* child it is.

But is that how any of us define ourselves—as the product of an egg and sperm, as the property of the egg and the sperm donors? The children we produce are people, who like us see themselves as individuals in a social context, in relationships, including the very important but not *defining* parental relationship.

The idea of owning children as property is more closely tied to the traditional *rights* of fathers in patriarchy than it is to the ongoing *responsibilities* of raising a child. The need is far more pressing to extend the responsibility ethic than the rights ethic to the care of children in America.[2]

It is not that the view of children as property is totally unrealistic, inevitably evil, and manipulative. Given our great respect for property, there are ways in which, in this society at this time, it works in the interests of children to treat them as property. But the combined forces of capitalism, technology, and patriarchy encourage us to commodify children in some of the least desirable ways.

NOTES

1. I want to express my appreciation to the Texas midwife who found it so hard to understand how babies could be valued and mothers not—reminding me yet again

why I so deeply value midwives—and to the other Texas midwife in the audience who explained it by giving us the example of the South African diamond miners.

2. This is a point made clear in the work of Carol Gilligan's *In a Different Voice: Psychological Theory and Women's Development* (Cambridge, Mass.: Harvard University Press, 1982) and brought home repeatedly to me by Caroline Whitbeck.

How Infants Grow Mothers in North London

DANIEL MILLER

A Joke

As a middle-class Jewish academic living in Northwest London, it is not surprising to note that I have several friends who are involved in psychoanalysis, either professionally or as clients, or simply through a deep interest. I have reacted largely with a skepticism based on an attraction to certain traits in anthropology that are antithetical to psychoanalysis. I regard psychoanalytical theory, on the one hand, as too universalizing with a strong essentializing tendency in the more vulgar forms and, on the other hand, as too focused upon individuals when compared to anthropological approaches to social relations.

Based on the little reading I have done in the area, mainly papers by Melanie Klein, I have come up with a joke which I have aimed at my various friends working in this field (in most cases at least twice!). I suggested to them that psychoanalysis is really a huge act of projection. The stages of development described by Klein are not really about infants at all. Instead, they describe the various stages which a parent goes through in order to develop as a mature parent. This is the result of collective repression in which the psychoanalysts all had such problems coming to terms with parenting that they shunted all the key problems onto the infant.

So, for example, I would suggest that what is called the paranoid-schizoid position (Klein 1975: 1–24) occurs when relatively new parents cannot resolve their sense of the infant as both utterly wonderful and completely appalling, while the depressive position marks a stage wherein the parents start to understand how these can both be aspects of the same object-relation. Since many of my friends are also parents, this "joke" usually gets some sort of laugh. I would not pretend to be knowledgeable about psychoanalysis. I have read little and understood less, though when I started reading the biographies of Klein (Grosskurth

1985) and other key analysts, this seemed to reinforce the joke, or at least make it more poignant.

In this article I want to take my joke a little more seriously and consider the stages by which the development of the mother is revealed through her child care and shopping.[1] Indeed, it does seem to me that one fault in much of the literature I have gone through is that there is surprisingly little serious attention given in psychoanalysis to the stages of "mother" development as opposed to infant development. My inspiration is derived from Strathern's (1988) marvelous use of Melanesian ethnography to question Western assumptions about gender. According to her account, in Mount Hagen (Highland New Guinea) it is understood that in some sense the child grows the mother (250, 252). My aim is not then a serious review of psychoanalysis, for which I am not qualified. It is rather to use this joke to explore through ethnography possible stages in the development of mothers, within a particular class and region.[2]

The article presents a generalized trajectory in order to make theoretical points. These points do not apply to all of my informants and, indeed, are least appropriate to two of my main informants. Almost all the discussions and observations were held with women, which accounts for the relative absence of male voices here. The analytical structure used is clearly imposed by myself, but the ideas of what should or should not be done by mothers and the concepts of maturity, gender, and guilt which constitute the evidence for my argument derive from conversations with and observations of mothers during the fieldwork.

The recent literature on mothering seems to be heading in the direction of a concern with difference. Woollett and Phoenix (1991) note that there is increasing emphasis in psychology on differing styles of mothering and differing degrees of child-centeredness (see also Glenn, Chang, Forcey, 1994; van Mens-Verhulst, Schreurs, and Woertman 1993). I find Chodorow the most congenial of the accounts that I have read, since her use of object-relations theory is more sensitive to social and contextual environments than most psychoanalysis, and in her recent work she has argued for an anthropological sensitivity to local differences in mother-infant relations (1995). Some recent work has taken a more ethnographic turn and included a concern with middle-class mothers that seems similar to that expressed in this article (Everingham 1994; Ribbens 1994). Everingham includes in her study a group she calls the "alternative" mothers, who appear similar to the National Childbirth Trust (NCT) group presented here, and she focuses upon the ways in which mothers interpret their sense of the needs and desires of infants.

My own ethnography forms part of a larger research project on the topic of shopping and identity.[3] It is based largely on a single street in North London, and within that the material for this chapter comes from the more clearly middle-class informants. Almost the only group within this street that in any way approximates to the idea of a community is formed by mothers who belong to the NCT. In particular, there is a group of ten mothers who have children of around two years old and have been with the NCT for those two years. They meet together every week, and a number of them also meet a second time in an associated toddler group. My information on the topic of mother-infant relations comes both from members of this group and from other parents in the area who have belonged to other NCT groups. The chapter also reflects on my own parenting and that of my friends, since many of my informants come from a similar social milieu as myself.

The NCT

Although the letters NCT stand for National Childbirth Trust, it could more appropriately have been called the Natural Childbirth Trust since its most active members and literature often express an almost obsessive concern with the concept of nature where applied to childbirth and childcare. At the most extreme its members are attracted to semicultic practices such as rebirthing, where the mother is expected to relive the experience of her own birth (though such practices are formally outside of the NCT). More generally its members tend to favor various other manifestations of a concern with nature such as recycling household rubbish or homeopathic medicine. With respect to the birth itself, NCT members are encouraged in their local magazine to avoid any kinds of assistance in the birth process such as painkillers or doctors. These are described as "interventions" and are considered to intrude into the natural course of the birth, which is axiomatically preferable for both child and mother. It is clear, however, that this advice is not intended to be taken where it might constitute any risk to either mother or infant. Not all NCT groups and certainly not all members share such views, but I have certainly encountered mothers who have for various reasons found it necessary to have a cesarean section and who clearly feel half guilty and half deprived by the sense that they thereby missed out on a natural birth.[4] There is evidence, however, for some decline in this degree of enthusiasm and zeal for natural births in the last few years.

Becoming an NCT mother commonly involves months of preparation, including attendance at classes, reading relevant magazines or books, and listening to many comparative stories about other people's experience of giving birth. It would be quite surprising if such a weight of emphasis during this period did not have consequences for the subsequent relationship between the mother and the newly born infant. One effect is to highlight the specific experience of childbirth and to dwell upon it both before and after the event. Since such mothers are less likely to use painkillers, they are more directly exposed to the extreme pain and intense focusing upon one's own body that is associated with traditional childbirth. This may assist in the creation of childbirth as a kind of rite, whose subject is not merely the birth of a new infant, but in equal measure the birth of a new form of adult—the mother. She has performed a most literal "rite of passage," which is often associated with pain (Van Gennep 1960). As will be argued later, most of those involved had hitherto devoted themselves in large measure to escaping from the constraints of biology and family. It may well be that this sudden negation of their previous values requires a kind of ritual purifying through pain. In effect, these women are engaged in an act of recycling themselves to return to the world as natural.

If this appears to describe a process more akin to a religious rite, then this may well be appropriate. The intensity of devotion which follows the birth of the infant also appears to create a new figure of the mother as "born-again," analogous with reentry into religious devotion. Indeed it may well be that the virtual cult of the infant that will be described here has for some people replaced religion as the main experience in life within which the sense of transcendence of one's individuality is felt and avowed.

The Paranoid-Schizoid Position

According to Klein (1975:1-24) the paranoid-schizoid position is one in which the infant is profoundly incapable of reconciling its experience of the "good" and "bad" breast. These represent two entirely opposed senses of the mother as the source of all positive and all negative feelings. I would argue that is an entirely apt description of these newly born mothers. The experience of being a member of the NCT contributes directly to the construction of the infant as a "good" breast. The period of idealization is shared among other women. Some of these mothers only join the NCT after the birth as a means of finding a community of women who are also having to be at home looking after infants. This adds to familial and other pressures which ensure the idealization of the infant. The goodness of the infant is intimately associated with its complete dependency upon the mother. It is regarded as helpless and without anything more than rudimentary agency. It is the pure product of a natural birth.

One of the key gestures of such births is that the newborn baby is placed immediately at the breast, preferably still covered in blood and other natural surrounds, substances that at all other times are considered dirty or to be avoided. Thus, as little distance as possible is put between the mother as natural feeder of the embryo prior to birth and the infant after the birth. The stress is on the infant as the biological extension of the mother. Furthermore, the NCT probably places almost as much emphasis on natural breastfeeding as on natural birth. All assistance is given to the mother who is prepared to breastfeed and who avoids substitutes for as long as possible. For example, the NCT will supply pumps that allow babies to be fed on the milk expressed by their absent mothers.

At this stage, then, the mother has given birth to an infant that is perceived as largely an extension of her own biology, the main difference being its absolute purity and innocence. It represents a version of the mother that has all that she feels is bad about herself filtered out. New mothers will typically spend considerable amounts of time gazing both privately and publicly with an adoring expression at a being that objectifies the very quintessence of goodness.[5] This is moreover a goodness that at the same time presents a narcissistic image of herself as refined and purified.

This identification has a specific social and historical context, and I do not wish to imply that it is the case for all mothering. To describe these people as middle class represents less their current income levels than the level of their parents' income and their educational expectations. While some are too young to be called the 1960s generation, they were all affected by the impact of feminism in the 1970s. In general they were brought up with a strong sense of their personal potential and of the importance of their autonomous development as individual women. Key moments in this development include their time as university students but also a period of employment. In most cases their present sense of style or "taste" developed in one or other of these stages. Those more influenced by their student days tend to a more "ethnic" and Eastern look, using shops such as Monsoon for their clothes, while those whose sense of style matured while in early employment are more likely to express themselves in the kind of interior decoration found in journals such as *Marie Claire* and *Elle Decoration*. As students their individuality was mainly expressed in the formation of left-of-center political opinions, but as their incomes rose with employment, emphasis turned to developing themselves as consumers and into people with taste.

In Britain, women with university education tend to have children relatively late and some years may elapse between the formation of relationships with partners and having children. The nature of their relationships to partners varies considerably, but unlike expectations in earlier times and in other class fractions, living with a man may not be viewed as particularly limiting to developing a skill for self-objectification through commodities. Both the males and females tend to have a high regard for feminist thinking and are quite self-conscious about the importance of continued autonomy for female self-development. What partners may often represent is a marked increase in household income. Buying clothes is joined by house decoration and eating out as important areas of consumption. As noted by the local hairdresser reflecting on the dominant conversations that take place in the salon: for these professional women the main concern up to this point is that the men they meet do not seem either mature enough or competent enough to assume the equal partnership roles these women desire. They feel that their abilities and success frighten off eligible males, who prefer the deference associated with younger and less-qualified women.

This is the context into which the infant is born, and it is not surprising that the skills of consumption form part of the process of positive identification.

Several mothers noted that almost instantly the sense of pleasure that they had developed in buying clothes and items for themselves is transferred directly onto the infant, at least for a period.[6] There is considerable concern that the material culture associated with the infant should represent the stylistic aspirations of the parent. While in other communities mothers are concerned to get back their figures and clothing style lost in pregnancy, these mothers tend to channel all their knowledge and ability as consumers into the task of shopping for the baby. For example, one mother noted that:

MOTHER: When I was working I was buying myself clothes a lot more often and I think clothes were probably my greatest indulgence. . . . Since I stopped working, I have transferred it to her so that if anybody gets indulged it's her.

DM: Does it matter that she can't appreciate them?

MOTHER: I suppose buying clothes for her is as much my indulgence as hers.

In Klein's work, however, some of the most commonly ascribed attributes to the new infant are rage, jealousy, and, above all, a kind of primitive guilt. I believe (see also Parker 1995) these are equally applicable to these same mothers' attitudes to these infants. The construction of the infant as bad breast takes on a particular form which reflects the social background and typical social trajectory of these mothers.

The important distinction between this group and most British mothers is their comparatively high degree of individual autonomy. For most women in Britain a struggle for autonomy in late teenage life is developed in relation to their own parents, but this is then negated in the early formation of their own families. Within this group, by contrast, the quest for freedom represented by being a teenager is able to mature into a more sustained and fully fledged self-construction. Rather than being ended by settling down with a home and partner, the impact of feminism has allowed them to build on this earlier struggle for autonomy. These mothers often see their generation as the first which is able to compete with males. They may feel they have a moral duty to strive to fulfil the new potential that history has given them, and their ambitions for their own careers are usually clear and explicit.

Although I have noted the importance of consumption in the lives of these women prior to becoming mothers, my studies and theories of consumption (see Miller 1987, 1995, 1997) suggest that consumption is more often an expression of relationships than of some mindless materialism. I do not want to suggest or imply that these women are particularly individualistic or selfish or superficial. Quite the opposite; they are characterized by a high degree of empathy with others and a strong sense of responsibility. But they also have a powerful experience of the modernist concept of freedom, where responsibility is felt to be an outcome of their own agency rather than merely an obligation. Arising out of teenage and student rebellion against assumed and prescribed obligations, they have tended to insist that if they act as dutiful children to their parents, or if they give their time to a worthwhile cause, it is their personal decision rather than merely a duty or unreflective compliance. Similarly, they give their love to their partners, making clear that this cannot be taken for granted, rather than "falling in love" as though inevitably succumbing to fate and destiny.

What is astonishing is the degree to which these same mothers allow the infant to represent the complete negation of their previous life project. The infant's constant demands are accepted as essential priorities and at no point should the mother's own desires prevent them being attended to. Particularly in the case of the first child, this goes far beyond the practice of most mothers in Britain. If the infant was understood as a separate entity or opposed agency to herself, this would represent an act of complete self-repudiation. All her skills of self-construction through agency become negated. This negation is acceptable because the baby is not viewed as an other, but part of this newly recycled dual persona of mother-infant. This may be related to Freud's observation that "parental love, which is so moving and at bottom so childish, is nothing but the parents' narcissism born again, which, transformed into object-love, unmistakably reveals its former nature" (Freud 1984:85).

At the very first stage, then, the mother (projected as the infant in psychoanalytical theory) has little conception of any separation between herself and this new environment in which she is reborn. Rather she has merely extruded a perfect objectification of her own ideal and pure nature in an act of narcissism. The infant as an object becomes the sign of her immanent goodness. But this infant as good breast is soon accompanied by the infant as bad breast. The degree of constraint upon the mother's freedom becomes quickly apparent. These mothers were all aware that changes would occur and often made provision in their career or educational trajectory to make space for the birth. But in most cases the reality of this constraint was far more severe than they foresaw.

This negation is exacerbated by the focus upon the infant's natural development. The understanding is that the infant should be allowed to pass through natural stages with minimal parental "intervention." The ideology follows from regarding medical authorities as interventions in the birth process. Infants often start life by waking up their parents several times a night, but for many of these parents it is important that they grow out of this naturally and are not disciplined by some contrivance (for example, allowing them to cry themselves back to sleep). There are many versions of this devotion to the natural. Some may see daily routine as unnatural and are concerned that feeding, sleeping, and other activities are entirely dictated by the apparent mood of the infant. Others who believe that a routine is in some sense natural may become obsessed that this is never varied, since the welfare of the infant is seen to depend upon the maintenance of the order they have become used to. Either of these strategies may be used to constrain the action of the mother, who is also likely to continue breastfeeding for as long as possible, which becomes a primary mechanism for transforming the desires of the infant into constraints upon her freedom.

In many religions the most effective way of establishing a relationship that is ontologically privileged (that is, which transcends the separation of the two entities) is through acts of sacrifice. Here, too, mothers will construct acts of self-sacrifice. For example, women who frequently went out at night for entertainment may refuse to go out even once for more than a year after the infant's birth. Even though they may have male partners who are more willing than most British males to participate in child rearing, the emphasis upon the biological and natural relationship between mother and infant in some ways reconstructs them as gendered in a sense that they have so far struggled to oppose. These are just some instances of the way becoming a mother is based upon the systematic negation of the mother's previous self.

Everingham (1994) noted that for the "alternative" play group she studied, a dominant belief is that the mother should never intervene in the natural development of the child. All infant demands express their purity as nature, which should be immediately met. This is evident in the idea of the breast, which is never refused, and in the response to crying, which is regarded as never occurring without good reason. Later on, however, the parent is confronted by areas in which the need for intervention seems undeniable, such as when her infant bashes another infant in the playground. At this stage the negativity that has been channeled into the experience of self-sacrifice develops into a powerful sense of guilt. Every time the parents act directly to discipline the child they experience this as their own loss of self-control. They will publicly berate themselves and tell other parents of their own viciousness. Instead of trying to understand the infant and the contradictions of their relationship, the tendency is to refer the infant's agency back to themselves and their own inadequacies. This guilt can be reinforced by any subsequent infant misdemeanor, since the failure of the infant to be perfect can be related back to the imperfection of the mother in having disciplined the child. All of this may be reinforced by reference to a popular literature on child rearing (books by Penelope Leach, Hugh Jolly and others; see also Urwin 1985) with their vulgarized "Winnicottian" emphasis upon the mother and a general tendency to assume there is always a good reason for the actions of infants (such as crying). These have reinforced the dependency of the mother on the omnipotent infant. Several of the mothers criticized these books for having fostered their guilt through promoting a particular ideology of child care.

The combination of immediate constraint, such as being woken up several times a night, and the long-term constraint upon her ambitions, together provide the foundation for projecting the infant as the bad breast—that is, an entirely negative force that should be the subject of rage and jealousy. Given the prior objectification of the infant as good breast, the mother may be said to be passing through the paranoid-schizoid position. At such a time it is extremely difficult for her to consider that this source of such benign and such negative emotions can really be the same object. First sacrifice and then guilt are important as mechanisms for preventing this contradiction in coming to the fore, since they allow her to project all the negativity represented by the child back onto herself. Alternatively, she may deflect her anger by projecting it onto her partner or her own parents. The birth of a grandchild/grandmother is often seen as grounds for reentry into the nuclear family by the older generation and may remind the mother of her own struggles for separation. As such her mother or mother-in-law are often first in the firing line as the source of badness.

This may also help explain the extreme reluctance to discipline the child. Not only does discipline represent an "intervention" in the natural development of the child, but it may well expose the adult to some sense of their own rage and jealousy of the child. It is not surprising therefore that the mother is extremely fearful of allowing such emotions to surface, since this might lead to an acknowledgment of the child as "bad breast." If the child must be punished, it should always be done as a highly controlled rational and premeditated action. The worst punishment is viewed as one done in the spirit of anger at the child's actions, such as would lead to an admission of the presence of this anger in the mother (Parker 1995:83–99).

The Depressive Position

According to Klein, the movement from the paranoid-schizoid position develops into the depressive position when the infant learns to confront the realization that what previously had been clearly separated into the good and the bad are actually both attributes of the same object—that is, the mother. If we regard this as a stage of mother development, then it clearly represents the start of a process of separation in that, as Winnicott notes, this represents for the child (and for us the mother) a new clarity with regard to what is part of and what lies outside of the infant (mother) and a new capacity for object relations (Winnicott 1980:153). Although Klein used the observation of child's play as a technique, Winnicott argues that she does not explore the full potential of playing itself as a subject of study (46). Winnicott's interest in the activity of play with toys helps provide a bridge to the topic I employ here to study the depressive position in mother development, which is that of shopping.

Shopping, the main topic of my research, plays a relatively small role in this initial phase of mother development, apart from transferring some of the mother's passion for self-construction through clothing to her infant. Most of these children have a variety of cuddly animals, of which one may be singled out by the parent. At this stage, however, the infant may exhibit relatively little concern for this animal, and it is the mother who appears frantic at the idea that it may be lost. It is possible that this particular toy becomes her "transitional object" (Winnicott 1980:1–30) representing a vicarious vision of the infant and playing an important part in allowing her to emerge with a stronger sense of the infant as other.[7]

Once shopping returns as a major activity, the development of mother-infant separation takes on a very particular form. There begins an unceasing struggle between what is regarded as nature and what is seen as the artificial world of commodity materialism. During this struggle the mother-infant relationship passes through a series of battles which the mother must always lose. This culminates in a final battle in which she attempts to don the armor of her opponent, through "buying back her children" (see later). It is essential to the mature development of what would be regarded as normal relations that she should once again lose this battle. I will restrict my argument to observations about fighting over commodities, but an alternative source of evidence would have been my observations of the embattled relationship between mothers and infants while they are together in the shops.

The first battle relates to the substances the infant is allowed to ingest. There is no problem at first, since the infants are entirely breast-fed and initial foods are usually homemade pulp from vegetables. Soon, however, a villain appears in the form of sugar, against which the mother strives to protect her child. The problem of sugar seems to be taken from images of decay, as in the constantly quoted case of the tooth which decays in a glass of Coca-Cola. Since infants have no teeth, this must be generalized into the sense that sugar is one of a class of additives which will result in some less defined pollution to the child as a whole.

I have seen mothers react to their toddlers reaching for a cookie as one might respond if the infant were about to stick its fingers into the socket of a plug. Jewish parents (of which there were several either in this group or observed elsewhere) were sometimes the most fastidious. Drawing on a tradition of searching out non-Kosher ingredients, they are here able to secularize this training through comparable scrutiny of ingredients for artificial additives. Of course I am not suggesting that the avoidance of sugar represents an unreasonable concern. Indeed, I doubt if this whole edifice could have developed if each aspect of it could not be legitimated by the parent as reasonable. However, inevitably the battle ends in defeat, as sooner or later the infant acquires considerable access to a wide range of biscuits, sweets, chocolates, and similar substances. The problem is generalized where the baby is viewed as losing its "organic" status through the ingestion of artificial substances. So the defeat over sugar is compounded later on as the child resists the taste of homemade and "healthy" foods pushed by the mother and resorts to a diet of fishfingers and baked beans or, if sufficiently victorious, burgers and pizzas.

Parents do not give up without a struggle, within which their concept of biology plays a major role. It is very common for such parents to insist that their infants have an allergy to anything artificial. It is as though the infants' bodies have antennae attuned to the mothers' ideology of nature. Infants are said to come out in spots as soon as they ingest any kind of additive or the wrong E-number (a number specifying food ingredients that is included on product labels in the UK). If the children do not oblige (with spots) then the parents may claim that these additives cause behavioral problems, which is a harder claim to contest. This cosmology of nature has already been formulated in regard to the parents' understanding of their own health. A generation ago we regarded death and disease as natural phenomena to be combated by artificial drugs and medication. Today such mothers are attracted to a variety of alternative health schemes, where the symbolism is reversed. Sticking needles into parts of their body or emphasizing particular colors and smells are seen as more "natural" than formal medicine, which is regarded as often dangerous. As Coward (1989) has argued, good health has become regarded as our natural state to be retained through a proper balance of elements. Disease and death are no longer regarded as forces of nature but as unnatural affronts to our proper state of being.

Some of the mothers recognize that the restrictions they impose are specifically middle class. For example, a childminder may be blamed as the source of early corruption, since they are held to be unable to resist giving the children sweets despite being requested not to do so. The parent may also resort to subterfuge in this struggle. One mother, referring to an NCT meeting, noted: "There was definitely a time when mothers would say 'Here's your biscuits I brought them with you' and produce a rice cake or something like that."[8] The defeat when it comes may be poignant, as recorded by a mother in a different NCT group:

> There was that kind of incident a couple of weeks ago. We went to the first third-birthday party of the little group of children, and it was done by one of the mothers who probably has the same attitude as me—they love Smarties; it's a party, give them Smarties. I was sitting next to my friend whose child has not had sweets, and she said, "This is the end of my beautiful pure upbred, pure things for my daughter," and I said, "Yes it is, it is. You have to accept she's going to come to these birthdays. You can't, you know, you can't not," and so we were laughing at the whole thing, and she agreed that that was the end really, and I said "Look you've given her a good start. She'll just have to learn that there are limitations that go."

The next defeat of the parent comes with the eruption of gender as an attribute of the child. Gender, in particular masculinity, comes as a defeat to the feminist mother. She believes in natural equality and that gendered behavior is a cultural construction rather than a biological given. This is complicated by a contradiction in her own position, which makes daughters a slightly more "natural" extension of themselves than sons. As Burman (1995) notes, the quintessential infant in Britain is a girl, while the stereotypical youth is a boy, and the transition between the two is perhaps one of the means by which we objectify the problem of separation. Some mothers claim a kind of semiconscious empathy and understanding between themselves and their daughters that takes on a mystical aura.

This is not evident at first, since the baby is largely degendered, which helps in incorporating the male child within a generic naturally feminine baby. These parents resent, rather than welcome, cards and gifts in pale pink and blue. If anything, as members of the NCT their children are green: the embodiments of natural childbirth and rearing. As the infant develops its own agency, parents may expend considerable effort in trying to prevent any association with gendered toys. This includes trying to prevent girls from becoming particularly interested in dolls, but the greater effort is usually expended on avoiding guns, swords, and other weapons. In conversation, parents may tell with pride of their young sons' enjoyment of dolls.

The first major defeat in this area is almost always phrased in the same way. The mother tells how there was finally no point in preventing her son having access to toy guns, since he was found to be using every household object from pens to coat hangers as gun substitutes, happily shooting adults and siblings. A typical comment was, "Yes, we've not had guns, but they've got swords and bows and arrows, which I'm not terribly happy about, but I sort of gave in, because they were making guns out of pieces of wooden things. It's very difficult." In generalizing from such statements, one does not need to suppose that sons are somehow naturally given to violence or daughters to dressing up dolls. What infants may well pick up on from quite an early stage is that there are key normative possibilities open to them through which they can most effectively assert their autonomy. The seizure of gender within a feminist household may be just as effective a symbol of autonomy as the refusal of gender has been for children brought up in families with a strong gender ideology. At this point the parent (since it is often the father) may intervene and buy less harmful examples of the genre. Parents will usually also attempt to reason with the child. For example, one mother noted with respect to the influence of Power Rangers: "Yes, he loves it and I do give him lectures about you mustn't, because he does start doing the kicks and things immediately afterwards and I have talked to him about how dangerous it is and that children have ended up in hospital and he does listen."

The situation is usually less straightforward with a second child, and there seems to be considerable diversity of practice with respect to subsequent children. Some parents are at least as adamant in their battles with the second child as they were with the first, seeming to see this as a second chance to gain victory for their values. More common are parents who see the corrupting influence of the first child as so powerful that such battles have become pointless. Their struggles are clearly more halfhearted the second time around.

The term *depressive position* may be applied to mothers who have come to terms with the simultaneously good and bad qualities of their infants. While there is more acknowledgment of the infant as a separate entity, the mother retains a desire to remain the primary source of all potential gratification for the infant. She in turn develops an ambivalence which may have a number of effects. For example, in seeking to retain the sense of the infant as a projection of her own qualities, she begins to play with several possible versions of this relationship. This may be illustrated by reference to the kinds of clothes bought for daughters by mothers. Depending upon the mother, there may or may not be status competition involved in such dressing. I have encountered groups that clearly do value designer OshKosh and other labels as part of status competition between sets of parents, but there are also many mothers who are genuinely neither interested in nor involved in such competition. The child may, however, still be understood as the narcissistic projection of the better (or idealized) aspect of the mother. As one mother noted: "The difference is she has got a fantastic little figure and I have put on weight since having kids, and the honest thing is that I don't get so much pleasure, as I need to lose about 2 stone, that's the reason. Everything I look at I don't like myself in any more, but everything on her looks fantastic, so it is such a pleasure. I enjoy having a little girl for that reason."

More revealing are the dominant styles used to dress daughters. These represent the first moves toward the construction of style as infant girl rather than female baby. One mother delineated the two major possibilities for dressing the infant for NCT meetings: "It's very popular to have them in the smock type dresses on the one sort of school, but its also quite trendy for them to be in leggings and tops." These styles are of considerable interest when taken in relation to clothes worn by the mothers. There is no adult equivalent to the cotton dresses with lace collars and smocked chests, often ornamented with flowers or folk designs. The emphasis is on hand-smocked, or at least machine made to look like hand-smocked. They represent a generic "folk" look, which in turn evokes a sense of natural persons based on the land and on tradition.

These dresses are in direct contrast to outfits based on leggings, which are more likely to include artificial fibers, such as various plastics, and to be stretchy, with Day-Glo colors and lustrous textures. This style has more direct bearing on an adult equivalent, which was mostly associated with a generation somewhat younger than these particular mothers, who by national standards had come to mothering relatively late. The two styles then project two images of the mother through the infant. The smocked dresses show more continuity with the narcissistic projection of the infant as the purified and authentic goodness of the mother. The other style expresses the mother's desire to be a younger, fitter, and more streetwise version of herself. This opens up a new potential for the infant which gradually increases in importance as the infant comes to be seen as a substitute younger sister that might, as she grows up, become a means of rejuvenation for the mother through a sharing of youth.

The child may start to represent an independent presence here, taking on one or the other style in opposition to her mother. A common situation is represented by the following quote: "I would prefer her in shorts and leggings and things like that. She will wear dresses any day of the week. If I let her loose on choosing her own dresses she would come up with, I would think the most awful things, full of ribbons and bows and flounces, which isn't me at all." It is this conflict which leads to the next stage in the development of the mother.

The Vengeance of Barbie

Having come to terms with the opposed good and bad ideals represented by the infant, the next stage toward maturity is represented by the mother's acceptance of key external influences upon her child. This involves a further series of defeats. In the case of daughters, one of the most common trophies of battle is the Barbie doll. I have been struck by the observation that mothers, who previously had maintained strict control over the images available for the child's self-representation (dominated by anthropomorphic animals), find themselves, much against their will, buying not merely one Barbie doll but sometimes a dozen or fifteen Barbie-type dolls.

The particular significance of Barbie (or Sindy) is evident given what has already been said about feminism and the passionate commitment to nature and the natural. The mothers do not object in principle to their infant dressing an anthropomorphic toy. This is seen as a learning and nurturing practice. But their preference would be for a figure that was both reasonably naturalistic and in many cases androgynous, such as to be suitable for both sons and daughters. Barbie, by contrast, is aggressively feminine and seems deliberately invented to anger such mothers. Not only does she represent the prefeminist image of woman as sexualized bimbo—she can't even stand up. This is a crushing defeat for parents who swore that their children would never succumb to such sexual stereotyping. A typical negative comment, in this case from a father, was the following:

FATHER: My partner feels quite strongly about Barbie dolls, we're quite firm about dolls really. She doesn't have dolls very much.

DM: What's the objection to dolls?

FATHER: Stereotyping I think, yeah, and with Barbie the absolutely unrealistic figure that she's got. I think she's very keen that she shouldn't be stereotyped into being a traditional little girl and of course that's all she wants to be.

As a mother noted, "Judy always wants Barbie dolls and any old trash she sees on the telly really—my little ponies, my little rhinoceroses. If she sees it, she'll want it. Barbie dolls is one. She would love a Barbie doll."

There are likely to have been precedents. An earlier battle may have been fought over the equally aggressively artificial My Little Pony, but at least in that case parents feel there is an innocence attached to the love of brushing hair and ponies. This is sinful but forgivable. Barbie, by contrast, comes across as unmitigated negation to the narcissistic projection of the infant as purified mother. The capacity of children to establish radically opposed countercultures objectified in toys as vengeful insistence upon their autonomy is already well documented. Alison James's (1979) analysis of children's sweets showed how these represent a systematic objectification of the adult's category of the inedible. In the time elapsed since James wrote her paper, this process has evolved still further. Any visit to the local sweetshop will reveal new versions of pocket-money sweets as snot, poo, corpses, and similar transgressive forms. Psychoanalysts most likely have their own ideas about the implications of the symbolism involved in these sweets and toys. For the anthropologist, who eschews universalistic symbolism, the concern is with the specific oppositional social relations that are being enacted.

In the case of sweets we can understand the victory of the child as reflecting the early use of pocket money as an independent resource. While such candy is very cheap, Barbie dolls and their outfits are expensive and become relevant at an earlier age than these sweets. It is the mother who is purchasing the objects she detests. Why should she acquiesce so fully in this tragic defeat for her own desires?

In conversations with many mothers it becomes clear that they regard materialism as the major pollutant for the older infant. The fear of commerce is evident even prior to the birth. Hirsch (1993:67–95) in his analysis of adults' discussions of new reproductive technologies found that these echoed more general attempts to forge a morality of value. In reading press coverage of the issues involved, one of the things potential parents abhorred were practices such as renting out the womb or anything that might be regarded as "shopping" for babies. Intimate social relations are themselves defined by their opposition to the world of commerce. In crossing over this boundary to invade the infant world, commerce becomes viewed not so much as evil but as an inappropriate presence which is thereby, in Douglas's (1966) terms, polluting.

Many mothers claim it is television advertising and similar external influences which turn the natural infant into a machine desiring quantities of artificial commodities. As a result, the infant becomes entranced by a world whose values are diametrically opposed to those intended by the parent. This is a world where foods are bright colors and full of artificial ingredients and additives, and where toys are equally garish, noneducational, and nonfunctional. The toy shop as "Early Learning Center" is soon replaced by the toy shop as TOY shop. The single most loathed outlet is without doubt Toys "R" Us (see Seiter 1993:205–13). There seems to be no other shop that evokes so much revulsion among so many shoppers. This might at first appear to be a rejection of the modern warehouse-sized anonymous shop, but similar size stores selling other products do not create the same reaction. In some cases the scale and anonymity are welcomed. The problem with Toys "R" Us is that it represents a move both to TOY shop and to toy SHOP, where there is no escape from the sense of toys as mass commodities reeking of materialism. It is this that fills so many shoppers with almost physical nausea.

These battles over foods and gender are often viewed by mothers as evidence of the natural infant-mother bond becoming overwhelmed by capitalism. While most of these women reject the idea that they would be much influenced by television advertisements, they see their children's desires as almost entirely emanating from this source. Typically they will state, "She is very influenced by the TV. She gave me a lecture on washing powder straight from the adverts." The child's expression of agency in the form of desire for different objects from those preferred by the mother can thereby be understood as the corruption of the child by an external force acting against its own welfare.

By this stage the sense of defeat is palpable. Its poignancy derives from the fact that the corruption of the child by materialism directly invokes what the mothers see as their own major defeat in life. They recall their student life brimming with ideals and a certain purity forged out of their rejection of their own parents' values. This was followed by their decline into more materialistic concerns of homemaking and self-styling prior to their rebirthing as mothers. Mothering may have been intended to replace consumption as a superior form of self-construction through a new social relationship.

That it is the mother herself who buys the fifteen Barbies and the multitude of other toys that she had previously forsworn may be evidence that she has not changed her goal so much as developed a new strategy. Up to this time the mother has been seen as the major and the natural source of all that goes into the making of the infant. It may be that, when faced with an opponent that threatens to overwhelm her, her response is to attempt to introject this enemy and make herself once again the primary source of pleasure for her child. Since she has had plenty of experience at constructing herself through commodities, it is not difficult for her to reinstate her role as the means through which the desires of the child may be gratified, this time through the supply of commodities.

This development in mother-child relations is likely to be redolent with contradictions. This was suggested when observing one mother shopping at the local Woolworths. She had just complained to me that her daughter wanted a Barbie for her birthday but that her daughter already had about fifty Barbies (a large exaggeration). After looking around for some time, she chose a Barbie using a Dustbuster. Two minutes later she remarked that she did not have a Dustbuster herself but wanted one. Just after paying she noted that she regretted buying the doll, since it would have been better if the child's grandmother (her own mother) had bought it.

These Barbies represent the moment of reversal when the child is almost overwhelmed by finding that its constant demands for objects, which where originally formulated in opposition to its mother, are now satisfied liberally by its mother. In effect, then, the mother is attempting to collude with her erstwhile enemy and buy back her child. As they develop, the children may themselves express some ambivalence about the parents' attempt to seize control over commodities as a source of gratification. This becomes clearer when the evidence is extended to later developments. Interviewing ten- and eleven-year-old children in a local primary school revealed a number who see their parents as ready to purchase whatever they demand. For example:

CHILD: People just let you do what you want to do. If you say that one. Say wants to buy for me this jumper, and I don't want. I want this, she says this one more warmer. I say but I don't want that, I want this one. She goes ok then. She just goes and pays for it.

DM: Why is that bad and not just a nice thing?

CHILD: Because I am just spoilt too much, like they just buy me everything I want.

Ribbens (1994:168) has recently shown that similar mothers are highly concerned with the kind of balancing act between budgeting, spending, and caring, within which the concept of "spoiling" tends to fall.

The sequence that has been described here forms part of a much larger and slower transformation in values and moral attitudes that go well beyond the particular issues of this article. In my larger project on shopping I have described a polarity between thrift and expenditure that has more to do with the construction of value systems and cosmology than with purely economic considerations. Using an analogy with traditional sacrificial ritual, I argue that this forms part of an attempt by most shoppers to create others as desiring subjects. This would be the case of parent-child relations but also for a much wider variety of household and other relationships. As such contemporary shopping is better understood as a means for maintaining but also restructuring social relations than as either hedonistic or materialistic activity (for details see Miller 1998).

Toward Maturity

I have suggested a normative pattern within this community where the practice of parenting is experienced as a series of inevitable defeats. Parenting becomes a form of tragic practice, in which—as when infants vainly attempt to stem the tide with sandcastles—parents obsessively attempt to build dams and repair breaches through which pour the growing agency and autonomy of their infants. This sequence often continues into a much more explicit series of conflicts as the child grows into teenage life. The battleground moves to areas such as computer games and videos. Later still there may be fraught conflicts over sexuality, drugs, parties, and other genres of teenage life. In many of these cases there will be a similar tension in parental strategy between direct opposition or the attempt to buy back children through becoming the primary source of commodity purchase.

Just as the Kleinian tradition is prepared to regard the stages Klein outlined as necessary steps toward the development of the mature infant, I would wish to view these stages of parenting as the foundation for the construction of a mature parenthood that has learned to deal with problems of separation that are intrinsic to a relationship that starts with such a powerful bond of identity and is supposed to end in autonomy.[9]

This conclusion may be illustrated by observation of these same mothers' relationship to their own parents. There may be some initial hostility to grandparents' involvement with the newborn baby where this is seen as rivalry for the parents' exclusive control over their infants. But once the relative position of the generations is established there may develop a period in which the new parents, to some extent self-consciously, reconstruct their views in line with their own upbringing. For example, they may return to some of their childhood religious practices "for the sake of the children." By this means they reposition themselves within a larger line of descent through the generations, as indicated by a new interest in family history and origins. This also gives them an authority over their children derived from what can be represented as the continuity of an inherited tradition.[10]

Quite often shopping remains one of the most important mediums through which this parent-child relationship may be expressed and negotiated. It is possible that this strategy of buying back one's children will be sustained for a considerable period. This is suggested if we turn from the parent-child relationship to that of the parent-grandparent relationship.

The new parents often speak about their shopping experiences with their own mothers, who are relatively common as shopping companions. In professional households grandparents may enjoy still higher incomes than their children. Even where this is not the case, grandparents prefer to retain a sense of themselves as the buyers of gifts rather than accept gifts from their own children. But the older generation no longer flaunt their generosity, but are subtle in a manner that shows their respect for their daughters. When shopping, the grandparents will give advice but only when this is asked for, and they are otherwise quiet but supportive. A typical comment from a new mother is that: "See my mum, and dad as well, don't tend to buy me things unless they know specifically what I want. Because they know their taste is different from mine."

This ideal is described in terms of the sensitivity of the older generation. They have now come to recognize that they cannot enforce their own taste and that they should be content merely to provide resources and allow their children freedom to choose their own style and image. This is regarded as a mature period of mutual respect. Any attempt to exert greater authority may now be rebuffed, for example, by restricting access to the grandchild. The grandmother may be viewed as having come to terms with the issue of separation, which, given its narcissistic roots, is partly a relinquishing of control over her own fate. The new parent, who has in many senses become her own mother, now dwells upon the degree to which the person who previously held that position is subservient to her in relation to the infant.

This ideal may be contrasted by parents with the image of the pathological grandparents who have failed to develop to this stage precisely because they were unable properly to separate from their own infants. Such a grandparent continues to project upon her child. She has failed to accept her series of "defeats" and has reacted with bitterness and resentment, projecting her sacrifice and guilt to all around her. She is condemned as the mother who continues to use her finances to attempt to retain control, and impose her taste, and for whom nothing the daughter ever does quite matches her expectations.

Conclusion

I hope it is evident that I am not trying to oppose or denigrate these stages, which are based, at least in part, on my own experiences as a parent. As far as I can tell similar trajectories may result in mature relationships as long as the constant defeats are accepted. The process is a dialectic in which a form of what might be called a "healthy" narcissism is gradually negated and separation therefore recognized. The sequence is also epigenetic (in the Piagetian sense), leading to growing profundity as each stage is exposed as contradiction and negated in order to create the foundation for the next.

The methodology of anthropological research, based on participant observation, is likely to lead to a focus upon the external environment, here shopping and social groups. Psychoanalysis, by contrast, tends to focus upon the patient's introspection and the internal dilemmas of individuals. I believe that the main factor which lies behind what I have observed is the cultural development of a normative category—"the mother" among a particular class fraction. This in turn derives from emerging cosmological models of nature and materialism. Although these parents' own childhoods are clearly relevant, I suspect individuals with a wide variety of childhood experience may nevertheless undergo this rebirthing process that reflects more general contemporary ideology. Beck and Beck-Gernsheim (1995:37, 76, 102–39) have recently attempted, using evidence from within Germany, to situate this development of obsessive child-centeredness within more general social trends. Movements such as feminism have helped transform this into the last relationship and opportunity for love that is not subject to radical doubt. Their observations may in turn be situated within the larger history of changing objects of love and devotion (see Miller 1998).

This suggests that although such a movement from identification to autonomy may well be commonplace, the particular structure and features noted here are specific. I do not intend to present these developments as intrinsic to mothering per se. The mothers described here are very different from the working-class mothers living on the other side of the street I am studying. The latter do not have the same concept of nature and do not so radically negate a feminist project of autonomy in mothering. This concern with nature can be mapped against ideological and consumption shifts within particular fractions of an evolving British middle class in the 1980s and 1990s (Savage et al. 1992: 99–131).

Similarly, these practices may change with time. Indeed, they almost invert the typical middle-class parenting of the first half of this century. The concept of spoiling and the spoiled child, which was used to legitimate constant punishment, held that the natural child embodies many evil inclinations and that it is the responsibility of the parent to protect the child from the main source of badness which lies within the child itself. As such, parenting was a civilizing process. The NCT mother, by contrast, has constructed a sense of the child that is naturally good and repressed her hatred of her own infant. The goodness of the child is a biological projection of her own original nature and goodness and is only corrupted when outside materialistic forces come and wrest the child away from its biological roots. I do not know how far it is psychoanalysis itself which has helped to develop this cosmology, but it does seem as though Rousseau has finally become the standard-bearer of middle-class socialization.

NOTES

I should like to acknowledge the help of my coworkers on the shopping project, especially Alison Clarke. Stephen Frosh has been my friendly guide to psychoanalysis for many years, though he should take no blame for what is expressed in this paper. Thanks also to Erica Burman for ideas on mother-child relations, and to all those who contributed comments when the paper was presented at seminars in Lund, Sweden (Department of European Ethnology) and at Manchester, Great Britain (Department of Anthropology). I am also very grateful to one of the anonymous reviewers of this chapter who provided detailed criticisms of both the content and the style in which it was originally submitted.

1. From here on I will refer mainly to mothers. Much (though perhaps not all) of what I report could apply to males, but, although I have come across cases of near equal parenting, the material upon which this chapter is based derives mainly from observations of cases where it is females who occupy this social role.
2. Since writing this paper Stephen Frosh introduced me to the excellent book *Torn in Two* by Rozika Parker (1995). Parker parallels my argument that the maturity of mothering may develop through coming to terms with ambivalence toward the infant. In her case, however, the argument is both more serious and is constructed within a sympathetic stance to psychoanalysis in general and Klein in particular. I would suggest that for some readers her book may provide a powerful antidote to my own article.
3. This is an ESRC-funded project (Ref. No. R000234443). It includes two geographers, Nigel Thrift (Bristol) and Peter Jackson (Sheffield), and two anthropologists, myself and Michael Rowlands (University College, London), and a research fellow, Beverly Holbrook (UCL), who specializes in research methodology. The ethnography is being conducted jointly with Alison Clarke, a professor of design history and material culture at the University of Applied Arts, Vienna, Austria.
4. I should make it clear at this point that I write as a member of the group described in this chapter. I attended an NCT like class with my partner. Both our children were born without "interventions" such as painkillers, and if we were to have another child, and my partner was so inclined, I would follow this route and subscribe to these values.
5. The term *objectify* is used throughout this paper in the sense given in Miller (1987:19–82).
6. I have not attempted to address here a major complication. Because of their staunch antimaterialism, many of these women would not, in an interview context, admit to such pleasures which are viewed as illicit. It does not take long, however, within the ethnographic study of what people actually do, to discern this contradiction.
7. I discovered during my research that I had not been the only parent to have purchased and stored "reserve" copies of my favorite cuddly toy, out of fear that the original might be lost, before realizing that the passion was mine rather than that of my infant.
8. Rice cakes are made without sugar and are usually purchased at health food shops. They do not taste remotely like biscuits.
9. The phrase "I would wish" refers partly to my desire to construct this argument in order to account for my observations. It also represents my personal desire for this argument to be the case in as much as I regard myself as an example of the type of parent that I have been discussing.
10. This use of the child to reenact their own history may be related to Steedman's recent suggestion that childhood as a category has been used to help construct both the concept of history and of the self as objectified through interiority (1995).

Contributions

Maternity and Materiality

Becoming a Mother in Consumer Culture

ALISON J. CLARKE

As an analysis of kinship, anthropology commonly recognizes the mutual constitution of mother and infant (Strathern 1992; Miller 1997). Since the publication of Barbara Rothman's *Recreating Motherhood* (1989) a growing literature around motherhood, capitalism, and consumer culture has similarly highlighted the dyadic relation of commodities/markets and infants (Layne 1999; Miller 1998b; Taylor 2000a; Zelizer 1994). Most significantly, these literatures emphasize the relational process of "having" a child, a social process far more complex than the mere bearing or biological creation of an infant.

Through analysis of the provisioning of infants and infant-related spaces on a specific street in North London, England, this chapter explores the mutually constitutive process by which "mother" and "the child" are made through the collation of objects, processes of acquisition, and their ensuing relations. Previous studies have shown how the minutiae of social exchanges around "things" generate ideologies and normative practices surrounding the practice of mothering (Clarke 2000; Layne 2003a). The case studies presented here reveal how object/subject relations not only make women and infants as social beings but how such relations then go on to form part of broader social trajectories. The projections associated with "having" a child are not just biological or innate but rather are formed through social desires (Rothman 1989). In her study of infant loss, Layne describes how women do not just experience the emotional loss of the baby but also the loss of belonging to "the motherhood club" (Layne 2003a:245). Material culture, the materiality of the mother/infant relations, is integral to this social transformation.

From the onset of pregnancy, the conceptualization of motherhood is bound up with facets of provisioning and consumption choices that mark imagined trajectories for both women and infants. Increasingly, the "act" of birth itself is presented by advice literature, public health bodies, and popular media as a significant choice a mother makes for herself and her baby (Davis-Floyd 1992; Longhurst 1999; Sharpe 1999). The type of birth desired (if not actually experienced) and the choice of godparents, mentors, or similar are part of a mapping out of resources and of aesthetic and practical selections made in the course of constructing mothering.

The birth of a baby most often signals a significant change in the makeup of the home in terms of its social relations and physicality. This most frequently manifests itself in the rearrangement or redecoration of the home as an explicit expression of a pending shift in the composition of the household. Rooms that may previously have acted as kitchen extensions become play areas; home offices are transformed into nurseries as the prospect of a new child takes on a spatial and aesthetic dimension prior to its actual physical presence. A baby seat might be added to a household's car or a new vehicle purchased (as advertisers are well aware) on the premise of its increased safety or enhanced space (Taylor 1992). The relation between a new birth, household life-cycle and consumption is made apparent in the proliferation of advertising, specifically aimed at this event (Larson 1992; Seiter 1993; Taylor 2000b). As a whole arena of new activities, roles, and behaviors presents itself to the mother-to-be, products (their exchange and acquisition) become the key means through which types of mothering are constructed and negotiated. Male partners, kin, and friends may be involved in this process, but, as shown in the ethnographic detail that follows, it is the actual practices themselves and their ensuing knowledge and exchanges that gender the act of "mothering" (Clarke 2000). This transitory process varies widely according to the resources available to the parent/s and caretakers, but it forms the beginning of a sustained relationship between activities of provisioning, their objects and values, and the construction of "mothering" and "the child." Although there are superstitions attached to the acquisition of goods (borrowed, given, or purchased) too early on in pregnancy (Layne 2003a), the process of "becoming a mother" involves simultaneity of materiality and social conceptualization.

The Realization of Mothers and Things

In her research concerning fetal loss, Linda Layne (2003a) maintains that it is through the accumulation of goods and gifts pertaining to a new child, most often initiated prior to birth, that a baby and mother are socially constructed. The rituals of baby showers (parties for a mother-to-be in which she is gifted by female friends or colleagues), the receipt of presents from relatives and family shopping trips organized around the baby-to-be, are processes that lend the fetus personhood at an early stage of development. Similarly, Janelle Taylor (2000b) argues that, contrary to the "production" analogy commonly identified by feminist scholars of reproduction, consumption has now become a more fitting way of understanding reproduction, from the cultural consumption of sonograms to the commodification of the fetus.

Feminist scholarship has tended to avoid analysis of cultural dimensions of the fetus in Western society as a counterresponse to the contentious pro-life (antiabortion) stance of locating personhood at the point of conception. However, the increasing visual presence of the fetus in medical procedures and popular culture has caused, it has been argued, a widespread shift in attitudes toward a baby's social presence (Kaplan 1994; Taylor 1998, 2000a, 2000b). In terms of materiality, this increased social presence is manifest in the intricacies of consumer goods. In Layne's research around pregnancy loss support groups in North America, for example, "things" emerge as the principle means by which women "make" (often far in advance of the anticipated birth) their babies and themselves as mothers: "Through the buying, giving, and preserving of things, women and their social networks actively construct their babies-to-be and would-have-been babies, real babies and themselves as 'real mothers,' worthy of the social recognition this role entails" (Layne 2000a:321).

Using homologies of children's goods (fluffy animals, miniature forms, brightly colored rainbow-decorated items, pastel clothes) women bring the fetus to life as a social being, and these specific and sensual forms of material culture become the treasured objects of many women who lose their babies. Booties or cot blankets become mementos stored carefully in cupboards; footprints of a still-born baby might be made into a special framed picture commemorating the "realness" of the child. In the process of grieving their loss, mothers consistently draw on the sadness of unfulfilled provisioning as expressed by one mother: "If you were here I'd buy you a red velvet dress . . . I'd give you dolls and dishes and all the play-house toys I loved as a child" (Layne 1999c:260). In the life of a "real baby" these objects would be part of an ongoing consumption process, but, with the loss of the child, they are transformed into objects of memory and devotion. Layne's argument, by focusing on the specificity of material culture in the context of mothering, opens up what she describes as an alternative feminist perspective, "one that focuses on the iterative process by which individuals and their social networks materially and socially produce (or opt not to produce) a new member of the community" (Layne 1999c:252).

Layne considers the *discourse* of material culture (her evidence is drawn from verbalized accounts and the writings of pregnancy loss support group newsletters) rather than ethnographic context of the persons and objects. It is a point of rupture, the loss of a child, that highlights the significance of "baby things" and their provisioning. Material culture in this context, while socially constructing motherhood, also defines the end of a lived relationship and the beginning of a transcendent relationship.

Through their archaeological interpretation of an abandoned apartment in a British state-provided housing complex, Victor Buchli and Gavin Lucas (2000) also consider the relation of material culture in the construction of the "intertwined dyad of mother and child" as embodied, in this particular case, in the politics of the state. Analyzing the contents of a council (state-provided) flat, abandoned by a twenty-five-year-old mother after the breakdown of the relation with her drug-addicted partner, Buchli and Lucas consider the ways in which the home has been appropriated by the mother (despite the conflicts with her partner) and used almost solely in terms of the "child" and "childhood." The authors surmise, through examination of documents and analysis of the number of material items, such as baby books and cherished toys, abandoned in the apartment that the mother left hurriedly with her young children. Child-associated artifacts and clothing predominate throughout the flat and the mother has decorated the bedroom with Flintstones cartoon character wallpaper (depicting the archetypal nuclear family). The mother had created a "distinct realm or transcendent futurity through the constitution of her children, their objects and spaces" made evident through the jarring abruptness with which the scheme was abandoned (Buchli and Lucas 2000:137). As the mother vacated her home through her own volition, she has lost her entitlement to social housing, forfeiting (as it is seen by the state) a "fit home" for her children. Despite her attempts at creating a "good" home (as made evident in the materiality of her abandoned life), in institutional terms this mother has cast herself as an "unfit mother," a definition that will have real implications for the trajectory of herself and her children.

Buchli and Lucas illustrate, then, in their archaeological "excavation" of a living space, that within the "mutually constitutive circumstances of the 'child' and 'mother'" there exists a "highly conflicted and ambivalent role" in which "women's identities and futures [are] mediated through children" (Buchli and Lucas 2000:132). It is in the child-related material culture (from abandoned baby books to Flintstones character wallpaper), set within the context of state-provided housing, that these conflicted and ambivalent roles become so visible. The examples offered by Buchli and Lucas, and Layne, reveal the significance of material culture as a key means through which mother and child are constituted and how ideologies surrounding mothering are bound to, and enacted through, specific images and conglomerations of goods. Both examples use rupture as the point for analytical intervention, as it is at such moments that otherwise embedded practices become visible and that the role of material culture becomes most poignant. How, though, does a study of mothering and material culture in process, rather than rupture, differ in its potential findings?

The studies offered above, while effectively showing the intertwining of materiality and maternity, also represent consumption largely as a practice dislocated from the actual immediacy of the social relations in which it is enacted. Yet objects and images consumed with the infant or infant-to-be in mind are most commonly consumed in relation to other subjects such as mothers (real or imagined), friends, and relatives, and it is in pregnancy that this process most commonly begins.

Rothman suggests that gestation, along with nurturing, has been systematically undervalued in accordance with a patriarchal ideology that places the onus on genetic ties, and "the seed," as the basis of kinship. Similarly, Layne observes how feminist scholarship tends to deal with "the beginnings and ends of pregnancy" (Layne 2003:244), thus neglecting "gestation" and pregnancy as a process whose theorization might lend weight to the social understanding of motherhood and renderings of infant personhood.

By considering how the infant-to-be is provisioned, through gifts, shopping trips, decorative schemes, and the construction of domestic space, it is possible to see how objects take on an active role in the social process of making mothers and babies (Latour 1993). Brands, gadgets, and styles take on extraordinary significance in this process, and, while marketing companies and retailers are fully aware of this fact (Cook 2003; McNeal 1999; Seiter 1993), it does not render the materiality of motherhood "inauthentic." Rather, it has become the key means, in contemporary society, of negotiating the increasingly complex processes of "making" a baby.

Making Babies and Mothers: From Nurseries to Baby Showers

Young families living on a single street in North London referred to here as Jay Road engage in a range of infant-related consumptive activities, from the decoration of nurseries to the exchanging of secondhand babies' clothes.[1] The examples presented here are representative of a range of practices associated with the provisioning of infants and, in particular, the ways in which these activities related to a localized meaning of mothering and class. The broader fieldwork, carried out between 1994 and 1997, concerned the nonformal retail means by which households were provisioned, including homemade goods, gifting, nearly new sales, catalog purchases, and related practices (Clarke 1998, 2002; Clarke and Miller 2003). These informal modes of provisioning were considered alongside complementary research, carried out on the shared field site by Daniel Miller, who investigated supermarket and formal retail shopping (Miller 1998a, 1998b, 2000).

The informants featured in this study are not necessarily defined as middle class in terms of formal definitions of education and income (Marshall et al. 1988). Jay Road has no discernible "community" or class-specific demographic as such. Rather, social class arises as a definition through the actual practices of provisioning, which, in terms of the construction of mothering, lends the neighborhood a particularly significant cultural geographic meaning.

Many residents with small children, or those planning a family, identified the greenness, easy access to parks, and associated amenities as an attractive feature of the area. For Jay Road is equidistant from a overtly white, middle-class, cosmopolitan area (Ibis Pond) and a more urban, ethnically mixed and predominantly working-class area (Wood Green). The polarization of these areas becomes a pronounced means by which, in the process of conceiving of motherhood, women construct a class disposition toward place and practice. The safety and intimacy of Ibis Pond, with its green, village-like atmosphere, is often contrasted with the harsh urbanism of Wood Green. In the following excerpt, taken from a conversation with Sally, who moved to Jay Road several months prior to the birth of her son, the harsh urbanism of Wood Green was encapsulated by a seemingly portentous shopping trip for the baby-to-be: "The first time we went to Wood Green [High Street] was the week before he was born, and I went with my mother-in-law to look for a cot. We were walking under the car park area and got hit by a flying bottle. We got cut, so I've not had good associations with Wood Green, not my sort of place." Middle-class dispositions in and around Jay Road are not a priori reflections of economic and cultural privilege. Rather, many inhabitants on the street are less stable in their class positions. This may transpire in the use of oppositional geographical locations such as Ibis Pond and Wood Green. In this sense Miller (1998b), discussing this locality of North London, describes a process of "shopping for class" as people "try on" different class positions; "The problem of job insecurity combined with better possibilities of class switching is not somehow less 'authentic' or more superficial than a consistent identification with a particular cluster of values. Many people inhabit not one or other site, but encompass the relationship itself and the field of difference" (Miller 1998b, 157–58). Class here, then, is understood as a social practice rather than as a static identity.

In Sally's description of her ill-fated shopping trip, the idyllic innocence of a baby's cot, and the social process of provisioning the nursery is contrasted with the anarchic alienation of the working-class urban area. Sally uses the symbolism invoked by the incident to mark the end of any potential relationship with Wood Green and, by association, any of the urban "messiness" it denotes. But this is not merely a straight enactment of a class disposition (Sally herself was brought up in a working-class area of a major city); rather, it is the intersection with a new and burgeoning social identity as a mother that makes this encounter specifically poignant. It also marks the beginning of imagined and enacted trajectories around provisioning and its values, which are inextricably linked to the social making of infants.

The nursery, a room given over to the nurturing of infants and the housing of their related material culture, has evolved as a key site of desire and fantasy in the context of mothering in contemporary consumer culture. While women, such as Sally, might have the space and resources to go shopping for their nursery, even mothers on Jay Road precluded from physically making a nursery often fantasized about their "ideal" baby room. Popular childcare consumer magazines, recommending nursery styles ranging from the Scandinavian "natural look" to the cheery primary-colored "modern look," promote the idea that a major project of pregnancy is the construction of this child-centered space. While fantasizing around this space offered some women pleasure, for others, making sense of the multitude of styles and objects associated with its construction was an onerous task. Provisioning an unborn infant requires choices and expertise in an unfamiliar arena where the stakes could not be higher—for every object and every style has attached to it some notion of a "type" of mothering or an expression of a desired mother/infant relationship.

Historically, the nursery itself has evolved as a morally pertinent domestic space. In Britain, from the mid-nineteenth century onward, it emerged as a discrete domestic space within middle-class housing, coinciding with the proliferation of child-rearing advice literature aimed at mothering as an increasingly ideologized arena (Hardyment 1983). The nursery was seen as an essential space for the correct instruction of infants, and its hygienic, thoughtful decoration was viewed as an instrumental part of this endeavor. Although nannies and other child-related servants may have used the space, the middle-class mother was expected to oversee its decoration and provisioning.

By the turn of the century the nursery was seen as such an integral part of "proper" child rearing that popular advice literature pleaded with mothers to turn their drawing rooms over to their children if they had no other rooms available. Books such as *Nursery Management* (1914) stressed the importance of modern decoration and recommended nonmorbid decorative subjects, creamy yellow walls, a sunny disposition, short neat curtains, and simple stained floors with removable rugs (Hardyment 1983:141–42).

With a new emphasis on development rather than nurturance, by the mid-twentieth century the nursery became more commonly referred to as the "playroom." With its new nomenclature came new understandings of the nursery's role in the development of the independent child. However small the space, pleaded one contemporary advice source, its existence was essential in maintaining a healthy separation of infant and mother, for "if in hearing distance of mummy [the infant] will constantly call out to her" (Page 1953:101).

In the context of North London homes, nurseries and playrooms have taken on a meaning more indicative of an idealized, child-centric culture described by contemporary scholars of childhood (James and Prout 1990; James, Jencks, and Prout 1998). In practical terms, a *nursery* generally refers to an infant's bedroom and the *playroom* denotes an area of daytime use and toy storage. But ideologically, these areas have become a key means of valorizing the otherwise ostensibly mundane and utilitarian aspects of caring. Although such areas are not formally designed into any of the informants' homes, the conjuring up of the nursery, if only metaphorically, is a key means of imagining the physical presence of an infant-to-be and its objects.

Gemma lives with her husband, Anthony, in a two-bedroom Victorian terrace house (on one of the less expensive streets adjacent to Jay Road), and she decided to convert a guest bedroom into a nursery. In the latter stages of her pregnancy, Gemma gave up work as a part-time salesperson in a natural health food store to spend more time at home preparing for the birth of her son. The couple depend on the single income generated by the husband's position as a visiting lecturer in a London art school and so are fully aware that a new child will drastically change their relaxed attitude toward household budgeting. In this case, Gemma's extensive redecoration and refurbishment of a customized nursery relies solely on homemade and customized goods rather than brand new, shop-bought models of furniture and equipment. Gemma and her husband did not originally own their home together. Once Anthony's bachelor home, the house has been gradually transformed into a family home through the joint purchase of secondhand furniture and collected artifacts. For Gemma, however, the creation of a themed nursery, a project initiated prior to the birth of her son and extended several months after, is not shared with her husband. Rather, it is the major focus of her time spent at home alone with her unborn and now her new infant son: "I've got all the furniture in his room, Charlie's room at the moment I'm going to paint, I'm going to stencil on little cowboy motifs and stuff to make it look all 'Westerny,' so I've got a constant running list of what I'm going to do; it's just having the time. I've . . . taken a very long time to do it. And it's not like nursery rhyme [themed], it's like cowboys and stuff, it's a bit more grown up than a typical nursery, which drives me mad." Although Gemma insists the nursery is incomplete (she intends, for example, to make three-dimensional cacti from vivid green felted fabric), upon entering six-month-old Charlie's room, one is stunned by the minute attention paid to detail in the decor, from the embroidered cowboy hats on the bed linen to the tasseled "poncho" lampshade. Provisioning for Charlie's room is an integral part of Gemma's present mind-set as, like the majority of nonworking mothers on the street, she spends a large proportion of her time alone with her child in the home. But in Gemma's case, her enthusiasm for home crafts and design generates a type of motivation and sociality that carries beyond the domestic sphere. She visits local furniture auctions and charity shops, for example, with her baby, looking for cheap items to renovate and paint. Because Gemma left her country of origin (the United States) twelve years prior to her marriage in England, she does not have direct contact with any extended family, and her new role of mother is largely self-taught. Although she has had contact with middle-class mothering organizations in the area, such as the National Childbirth Trust (NCT), she remains peripheral to this social network and disassociates herself from what she views as typically British middle-class mothers' concerns. She is less purist, for example, in her critique of consumerism, gleefully telling of how she combined her trip home to America with a massive shopping spree in which she managed to fit out Charlie with a wardrobe of branded clothing half the price of that available in Britain. Similarly, she happily receives gifts of branded toys unavailable in the United Kingdom from relatives and friends in the United States.

Unlike the core of middle-class mothers on Jay Road, previously sociable women who self-sacrificially deny themselves a social life with the birth of their new child (Miller, this volume), Gemma makes concerted efforts, within weeks of her child's birth, to visit pubs with friends and generally regain her social self. In this sense, Gemma's nursery project melds the knowledge and skills of a previous identity with those of a new mother to create a revalorized role expressed in her concerted effort to use an atypical nursery motif indicative of her and her son's perceived individuality.

Unlike Gemma, Brendan and Katrina approached the redesign of their home in preparation for the birth of their child as a joint project. Although couples often have prerehearsed tastes in furnishings that form an integral part of the process of becoming "a couple" (Clarke 2002) in the construction of the nursery, the application of such tastes often becomes problematic. The couple are no longer solely constructing themselves in relation to each other; rather, they are constructing themselves in relation to the unborn and imagined infant. And, as becomes apparent in the following description, gestation is not merely a biologically delineated period but also a socially delineated process.

Brendan and Katrina, both in their early thirties, have been married for several years and own a three-bedroom, 1930s semidetached house on Jay Road. Brendan works in the information technology industry, and Katrina has a part-time position as a personnel administrator. Since the conception and birth (eighteen months ago) of their first child, Serena, they have transformed the largest of their bedrooms into a fully equipped nursery. Wallpapered in bright striped colors and carpeted in deep pink, the nursery contains a large cot with *broderie-anglaise* drapes, a range of toys, a diaper-changing table, and a cheerfully colored pink chest of drawers. While many of the stencils along the nursery wall were applied by hand, the contents of the room were purchased at Lilliput, a large retail outlet that specializes in nursery furnishings, prior to the baby's birth. The decor incorporates stylized pictures of animals and teddy bears, and around the bay window a cloud-effect paint technique is used to depict fluffy clouds on a sky blue background. The couple are extremely proud of this room as their favorite space in the house and describe at it as being their "ideal" baby room. The couple did not meet the extensive costs of this refurbishment alone, for the room is scattered with gifts from grandparents and other relatives, as described by Brendan: "Even before Serena was born we had wardrobes full of baby stuff. I'm not saying we didn't go out and get things ourselves that we liked, but most of it, like the cot, has come as gifts, even if we might not be too sure about some of it! Katrina's tried to make things fit in but some of it just isn't what we would choose, but it's Serena's [the child]." Unlike the majority of informants on the street, Brendan and Katrina have several relatives living within a twenty-five-mile radius with whom they maintain strong social ties. Most weekends are spent paying visits to them with baby Serena. Although Katrina is not actively Christian (she describes herself as a Humanist), she bowed to family pressure more than a year after Serena's birth and held an elaborate christening, with the celebration taking place in the couple's newly decorated home.

Katrina and Brendan are exceptional in comparison to other informants on the street. Firstly, their home is comparatively spacious. Secondly, they have acquired a large proportion of their furniture and appliances (brand-new) as gifts from their extended family or from specifically organized shopping trips, instead of acquiring them over several months or years. Since becoming married they have self-consciously set out to transform their home, and they consider the relandscaping of their garden as the only outstanding objective before the house is complete and they contemplate their second child.

Brendan and Katrina are perhaps exceptional as regards the extent of their explicitly planned approach to the physical transformation of their household in relation to the bearing of children and as regards their almost exclusive use of brand-new full-price goods. Also, they are one of the few couples that actively approach the furnishing of their baby's room as a joint project (although Katrina acts as supervisor, having full control of decisions related to decor, etc.). The couple's relatives were extremely active in the direct provisioning of their household, acknowledging the presence of the unborn child with their chosen gifts of clothing and equipment. Despite some misgivings regarding the extent of their relatives' involvement, the parents-to-be happily reciprocated on behalf of their unborn child by signing their Christmas greetings cards with a "?" as a gesture from the as yet unrealized and unnamed child.

For Brenda and Katrina, their choice of baby-related goods is largely circumscribed by relations with extended kin. But Katrina's role as taste supervisor is crucial to her construction of self as mother and her infant as social being. After reading an article in a baby magazine about the hazards of mobility toys, she sensitively integrated an unwanted gift of "an all singing, all dancing baby walker" from her mother-in-law into the supervised play repertoire of her daughter (at least in the grandparents' presence!). However, when other mothers from the neighborhood visit, she is quick to condemn the item as "a waste of space."

Lynn Morgan (1996:53) describes the reluctance of feminist scholars "to allow relationality to 'leak out' into a pregnant woman's social world," as the acknowledgment of vested interests (for example, parents, friends, fathers, government agencies) might undermine the "sovereign control" a woman has over the fate of her pregnancy. Yet, it is clear from the descriptions above that materiality is a key means through which the relational nature of pregnancy and early motherhood are negotiated and that mothers "become" mothers through this ongoing process. The next ethnographic example describes a woman for whom the "relationality" of her early motherhood is proving problematic despite the fact that she has self-consciously sought to generate a social context for her mothering throughout the course of her pregnancy.

Katherine is a first-time mother in her early forties who describes feeling isolated from the conventional younger mothers on Jay Road. With little disposable income and an anticonsumerist stance, Katherine relies almost exclusively on secondhand and homemade goods to furnish her new son's nursery. As a single parent living on income support, supplemented sporadically by her estranged boyfriend's maintenance payments and a small amount of savings, Katherine rarely buys household items from formal retail outlets. The birth of a much-wanted baby has drastically changed Katherine's life and has become the exclusive focus of her decision making and planning. Despite living on welfare support, Katherine is the owner-occupier of a three-bedroom Victorian house (purchased several years ago when she had a full-time teaching job) on one of the leafy streets adjacent to Jay Road. The house is furnished with items from previous households, therefore much of the furniture is of late 1970s and early 1980s styling, and she describes these items as belonging to her "previous life."

Although Katherine regularly asserts her indifference toward homemaking and issues of fashion and style, two rooms in the house have been completely transformed since the pregnancy and birth of her son, Rory. The double bedroom adjacent to her own has been made into a pastel-colored nursery designed, painted, and stenciled solely by Katherine. The woodwork has been stripped to its natural state, and an old fitted wardrobe painted in deep purple and gold has been designated as Rory's special toy cupboard. In the center of the room stands a contemporary cot, above which a handmade mobile of colorful shapes dangles. A 1920s wardrobe (acquired from a neighbor by exchanging a pile of unused plywood in her loft) is filled with secondhand and hand-me-down clothes awaiting Rory to grow into them. On a pine chest of drawers a collection of toys from Katherine's own childhood is mixed with furry animals from local nearly new children's shops. In the hallway a wooden peg plaque with "Rory" carved in wooden letters is attached in a prominent position to the wall.

Downstairs the main reception area has been extended, with the addition of an outdoor wooden deck accessed through large French windows, into an all-season playroom. It is decorated with bright alphabet pictures and is filled with toys ranging from a full-size toddler slide to a miniature cooker. The room is reminiscent of a fully equipped, upmarket kindergarten. The entire contents of the playroom (with the exception of a reduced-price Ikea shelving unit) have been obtained through the free advertising section of the local mothers' organization newsletter or from local nearly new sales specializing in children's ware. Plastic toys, other than secondhand (or recycled), are banned from the house in favor of wooden versions more oriented toward education than stimulation.

Although Katherine would describe her values as being broadly middle class (particularly in terms of attitudes toward education), she is proud of her northern, working-class origins and, even after living for more than twenty years in London, disassociates herself from what she views as the competitive, materialist values of the south. As Rory has grown up, Katherine has deliberately acquired toys she considers to be nonsexist and educational. She openly tries to counter gender stereotypes by encouraging Rory to play with baby dolls and prams. In this respect, she does not consider her overtly child-centric home, with its nursery, playroom, and extensive toy collection, as materialistic but rather as educational. Katherine views the alternative ways in which she acquires goods as subverting the market and constructing an added value around the specific forms.

Separated from her extended family in the far north of England, estranged from her child's father, and alienated within her specific peer group, Katherine is the sole decision maker in the upbringing of her baby. Consequently, the projection of the ideal through her child is relatively unmediated. Katherine's moralities around consumption, as with the majority of middle-class mothers in this study, are legitimated around understandings of education. In Katherine's case, however, "middle class" is being constructed as the "other," to be opposed through the correct appropriation of certain goods and cultural forms in the form of her values and strategizing. It is in the material manifestation of the home, and its child-related contents, that the contradictions and conflicts in this endeavor become evident.

Katherine's frustrations and contradictions in positioning herself as a mother on Jay Road, as played out in the materiality of her home, are couched in class terms as understood in relation to the specificity of a local culture of mothering. Ultimately, Katherine, disillusioned with the materialism of London and its lack of community, decides to "sell up" her house and move to a village on the Scottish borders, where she believes she and her infant son will make "proper friends."

Jay Road is neither working nor middle class, but as a street it has taken on a particular significance within the lifecycle of aspiring young families because it offers comparatively cheap property, allowing owner-occupiers to get a foot on the property ladder. As Werbner observes in her study of British Pakistani communities, the meaning of property is not fixed in the materiality of bricks and mortar; rather, it is forged through fluid historical and cultural processes. "Values, markets and meaning inter-relate to create both immigrant ghettos and exclusive suburbs. What a house or neighbourhood *is* is, first and foremost, what it *means*. Even with a single city, the 'natural' concept of housing varies both synchronically, over time, and diachronically for different local populations" (Werbner 1990:15).

It is not the housing stock, then, that dictates a particular demographic and therefore a particular form of mothering in the area. Rather it is the process of setting up homes and the provisioning of infants and children that a version of middle-class mothering emerges; though not wholly embraced by any individual mother, this mode of mothering has begun to develop a normative context in the area.

In and around Jay Road there are a limited number of formal organizations and activities, such as toddler and mothers groups, the NCT, playgroups, and local mothers' groups. But it is through the everyday work of consumption, and a variety of loose social networks and tentative encounters, that women's sociality as mothers is most visible. Meetings at the school gates, passing comments, or the exchange of pleasantries make a basic form of sociality for part-time employed or nonworking mothers, and it is here that children are directly identified with specific women and their households. But in particular, the brands, goods, and gadgets associated with infants offer a type of public currency that allow otherwise unthinkable forms of unsolicited social interaction.

A typical example illustrating this phenomenon is that of Jessie, the mother of a five-year-old daughter who makes a new friend by asking where she purchased her "fantastic ultra-modern" Maclaren buggy. The brief conversation over technical details and comparisons with other brands and models expands into a discussion of coping with the work of looking after twins and an older daughter. In this short encounter, Jessie, through a consensual process around the buggy, establishes the parameters of her own and the other woman's mothering.

The chain of potential contact between mothers often begins with pregnancy, through attendance of the antenatal clinic, or even through a random comment regarding a piece of baby equipment whilst taking a shopping trip, and then might go on to the attendance of birthday parties or the sharing of school runs. These social trajectories, as recalled by one mother, may begin with a passing comment over baby equipment: "I remember when I was pregnant, I was looking for a buggy and I saw a girl pushing one that I liked, and I went up to her and I said, 'Where did you get your buggy?' That's right. We exchanged telephone numbers in the bakery. And we do see each other occasionally [now]. We saw each other quite a lot when Lilly was smaller. The girls went to the same birthday parties and then got into the same schools, so it was quite good really."

Just as decisions over birth plans and nursery colors are perceived as part of women's reproductive work, so too is the task of locating an appropriate school and then assuring a child's place (David, West, and Ribbens 1994). Similarly, it is mothers' social activities, as attendees and organizers of children's birthday parties, as chatting neighbors waiting for their children at the school gates, and as avid buyers and donors at nearly new children's ware sales, for example, that provide the crucial underpinnings of such trajectories (Clarke 2000; Hill 1989; McCannell 1988). This it not to suggest, however, that these seemingly peripheral activities of women as mothers are merely an extension of gendered work (Bell and Ribbens 1994; Finch and Groves 1983; Gullestad 1986), but rather that they are inseparable from broader consumptive activities through which women "make" their babies as social beings and themselves as mothers.

Numerous approaches to mothering highlight the dominance of ideology (for example, patriarchy, conservatism) in the construction of mothering (Dally 1982; Everingham 1994; Glenn, Chang, and Forcey 1995; Ruddick 1982; Stacey 1986; Thurer 1994; Tivers 1985). However, the ways in which larger external ideologies, such as class and ethnicity, intersect with and create modes of mothering is seen in the experiential detail of the everyday material worlds of mothers provisioning their infants.

On Jay Road, on the Sparrow Court council estate, Lola Santos anticipates, at the age of forty-one, her third child. She and her husband had originally intended to confine their family to the two girls they have brought up in London since leaving Colombia more than twenty years ago. Lola knew how happy a baby boy would make her husband, and when she became pregnant, the family, including the two girls, became very excited (despite remaining uncertain as to the sex of the infant). They have been making tentative plans for the new arrival.

Taking the bus alone to the Brent Cross shopping mall, Lola recently bought herself a pattern for a maternity dress and fabric for curtains in the new baby's room from the John Lewis department store. This store is renowned as a high-quality outlet and is embraced by the middle-class mothers of the area as something of an institution. Even as a one-time purchase, this marks, for Lola, entry into a new realm of provisioning.[2] The choosing and buying of nursery curtains from John Lewis marks a transition from allegiance strictly to the local ethnic area from which Lola came to a new allegiance in an area dominated by normative middle-class motherhood as engendered in the values of John Lewis (renowned as a rational, sensible retail outlet offering value for money and high-quality merchandise). While Lola uses the bargain fabric shop to supply the material for her own maternity dress, the specialness of the new baby's curtains is marked by the significance of purchasing in a completely new arena requiring different competencies and class associations.

Unlike the descriptions of prebirth announcements, conspicuous consumption, and baby showers in North America (Layne 1999b, 1999c, 2000a; Taylor 2000b), there is much superstition attached to the premature acquisition of baby-related items in South American culture. Indeed, the personal and cultural reluctance to disclose the pregnancy too soon has made it quite difficult for Lola to arrange some of the provisioning associated with the birth, as she plans to borrow most of the necessary and expensive baby items. Although the pregnancy was not explicitly planned, Lola had deliberately kept aside the cot used for her daughters but anticipates borrowing a pram from one friend and a baby bath from another. Another friend, whom she describes as spending "lots and lots" of money on her own children, will, Lola anticipates, be handing down large amounts of expensive clothes in very good condition for the new baby. A bench upstairs will be converted into a changing area, and the only items really necessary to buy brand new, Lola surmises, will be Baby-Gros, as she long ago passed on her previous baby clothes to friends and relatives.

Although other informants preparing for birth receive one-time baby-related gifts individually from friends and relatives, in the course of the ethnography Lola's baby shower party constituted the most public and ritualized prebirth gifting event in the vicinity of the street. Lola's own party belonged to a series of other parties, and to have turned down the offer of a celebration would have meant explicitly extracting the family from the Colombian community as a whole. During the course of the ethnography Lola attended over half a dozen such events. Although the items chosen for the expectant mother differ according to her particular needs or request, the format of the celebration is well rehearsed and considered as an inevitable part of the pregnancy, as described by Lola: "The baby shower is usually around seven months because at the beginning you are not sure if something is going to be wrong and at the end it's too close to the birth. So seven months is just the age you need to buy things if you are pregnant—so it's the best time to do it."

As well as dancing, chatting, and eating, the main focus of the event is the point at which the pregnant woman is seated on a chair in the center of the room surrounded by gifts. After games, many of which refer to the impending motherhood, the mother-to-be publicly unwraps the baby shower gifts. Lola makes flattering comments to the donors regarding suitability of gifts as she discards the wrapping paper. There is a repertoire of gifts that every mother-to-be in this community receives (the layette, the fluffy toy, the traditional Colombian baby dresses, etc.). None of the gifts is expected to be expressive of an individual relationship within the group but rather representative of the whole. Although there are many smaller gifts offered by individual families, the shared gift, negotiated through word of mouth, is considered as the opening gift of the party. This gift is consensual within the immediate social group and is considered as a thoughtful, practical gesture to show an understanding of the mother-to-be's needs. As illustrated by Lola's description of the most recent baby shower: "We took a baby alarm, you know, a baby listener. And we all gave her a carry-cot and some clothes—we asked her what she needed because, you know, there's no point in giving her something and somebody else already has—and she said, at first, she said she wanted one of those things to carry baby things in but someone gave it to her so she said [she wanted instead a] 'baby listener.'"

Becoming a mother for the third time, with an entirely new set of resources at her disposal, Lola is able to combine the normative middle-class culture of her area in Jay Road with the formal and ritualized traditional culture of her old ethnic ties. Her infant-to-be is materialized in the nursery curtains purchased from the white, middle-class department store, as well as in the well-chosen, prescriptive gifts from her ethnic community. Unlike her previous two children, who struggled to fit in as first-generation British Colombian children, her infant-to-be is socially constituted in both arenas of the family's newly established life.

Conclusions

In her study of personhood, Morgan (1996:57) critiques a feminist scholarship that arbitrarily views the birth of the infant as the dawning of its personhood, as if it were a blank asocial canvas upon which personhood is ascribed. She urges instead that, with the advent of new reproductive technologies, the fetus is consumed in entirely different ways that might allow us to embrace a notion of personhood that acknowledges corporeality, as well as social cognition, as being socially constituted. An alternative perspective, she argues, might "view the fetus/infant as a motley amalgam of many social influences which enable its constitution. These might include social events (such as the failing contraception or acquisition of better-paying job), personality traits inherited from important persons (such as the whistling grandmother or gardening dad), and substances (such as prenatal vitamins, or peanut butter or seven-grain bread)." Taking on board Morgan's plea for the acknowledgment of the social constitution of the corporeal, and its integral role in the making of personhood, we might similarly consider how her thesis extends to the role of material culture. The putting together of nurseries, the receiving and deciphering of infant-related gifts, and the competencies and social relations implemented in the everyday consumption of baby-related goods simultaneously makes babies and mothers. The agency of the subjects and objects involved in this process also lend themselves to broader trajectories. In a literal way, the choice of baby buggy may in turn lead to the attendance of a specific round of children's birthday parties (Sirota 1998; Zelizer 2002), which themselves revolve around a nuanced repertoire of gifts and decorative schemes), and finally a particular school and peer group affiliation.

Renderings of personhood may be tied to specific normative trajectories, such as those negotiated by the mothers in this particular area of North London, but ultimately the making of babies is a social process that involves both objects and subjects. This process is not dissimilar to that described by Conklin and Morgan in their study of the Wari' Indians of Rondônia, Brazil, who constitute their infants' personhood gradually through bodily composition and social exchange: "Sociality, body, and person are intimately interwoven and conceptually inextricable from one another" (Conklin and Morgan 1996:687). The Wari' do not consider there to be a "natural" social body upon which personhood is ascribed; rather, the bodily self and the personhood are the result of an ongoing process of social exchange.

Consumer culture, the accumulation of things, the investment of time in style and homes, may not be as individualist as it first appears. For commodities and infants are inextricably bound through the social processes and networks of consumption; they are the "made" through a multitude of objects and social exchanges. This analysis of maternity and materiality is not, as Taylor has suggested in her critique of anthropological and material culture studies, merely another rendition of the "hungry subject inhabiting a world of needed-and-desired objects external to himself" (Taylor 2000b:414). Rather, it has shown how the materiality of things (made and mass-produced) is inseparable from the politics of mothering and the construction of mothers and babies as social beings beyond the domain of the expressive individual or the "hungry subject." The process of consensus through which certain items, such as the "right" baby monitor, an "ethical" toy, or a "pretty" dress, are identified is an entirely social process through which mothers are made in relation to each other, as much as individuals in relation to their infants. The objects implicated in this process are neither arbitrary nor passive, for their biographies (Kopytoff 1986) and social worlds are intimately tied to those of the infants whose personhoods they come to make.

NOTES

1. The names of informants, areas, and streets involved in the study have been changed to protect anonymity. The very nature of ethnographic inquiry means that one is not studying specifically class or taste as discrete categories, but rather the intricacies, social relations, and activities of mostly unconnected households. The intended study was not, then, of mothering (which evolved as a major theme) but the nature of provisioning.

   The main street in the study, Jay Road, was selected because it lacked any outstanding features and defied any one definition, in terms of class or ethnic makeup, of a neighbourhood. One side of Jay Road is occupied by a 1960s council estate (still predominantly tenant occupied); the other side, by owner-occupied and rented maisonettes and houses. Adjacent streets are comprised of larger Edwardian and Victorian family homes, many of which are more recently occupied by middle-class inhabitants keen to take advantage of the lower than average price, in comparison to immediate surrounding areas, of such properties. In terms of ethnicity, the study includes inhabitants of Greek Cypriot, West Indian, Southern Irish, Asian, Korean, Jewish, and South American descent. In short the street is typical of North London in being cosmopolitan but manifestly ordinary. Although preliminary interviews were conducted with more than 150 households, 76 households formed the core of the ethnography cited here.

2. See Miller (1998b) for a comprehensive discussion of the significance of the John Lewis store in relation to middle-class identity in North London.

"What Will I Do with All the Toys Now?"

Consumption and the Signification of Kinship in U.S. Fostering Relationships

DANIELLE F. WOZNIAK

Introduction

Cindy sits at the kitchen table looking at her hands, the three-year-old boy in her lap alternately resting quietly and then fidgeting with her blouse and hair. He is holding a red plastic suitcase. I ask her how it will be when the two brothers she has raised from infancy leave for their adoptive home. She looks away and begins to cry. She strokes the boy's hair. She takes a long time to answer. "I have gotten very attached," she says slowly. "We have all bonded with each other. They are a part of our family."

Cindy Harris is a thirty-seven-year-old housewife. Her husband is an electrician. They have two teenage daughters. They have fostered Michael and Nathan for three years. A year after being placed in foster care their biological mother's parental rights were terminated. Two years later the state asked Cindy and her husband to adopt the children. Prior to this request the Harrises had little contact with the state. The boys have severe emotional and developmental delays. Cindy's grown brothers and sisters, their spouses, and her parents all provide some kind of care and support for the two boys and for the Harrises. Michael and Nathan also attend a special school and require myriad state-provided home-based services. Once the boys are adopted, many of these services will have to be provided by the adoptive parents, and the board and care payments the Harrises receive from the state will end.

Quietly, the youngest boy, Michael, slides off Cindy's lap as though no longer able to endure only half of her attention and opens and closes his toy suitcase with a snap. He looks up at his foster mother and initiates a game I think they must have played before. With a smile he says, "Bye-bye mommy."

"Where are you going?" she asks.

"I'm going," he laughs and backs away from her waving his suitcase.

She reaches for his stomach and tickles him. "You're not going anywhere, bug," she says.

"Yes, I am. I'm going," he repeats laughing as though this is further enticement for her to play with him. "Bye-bye mommy," he taunts.

She reaches for him and takes him into her arms. He buries his face under her neck and smiles. "You're not going anywhere, bug," she says. "You're going to stay with me forever." He smiles and reaches his arms around her neck to hug her and asks for lunch. I realize that in this moment I have become invisible to them. He is delighting in her touch, her hug, her smell, their game. She is engrossed in and with him. She does not seem to be aware of what she has just said to him and the apparent contradiction. But as I continue to watch them I begin to suspect what is confirmed for me later through continued research with dozens of other women. She will keep this child with her forever; this and a thousand other memories will become a permanent part of who she is and how she relates to the world. And thus in the face of a relationship that is physically transient, she will maintain a permanent kinship bond. He is and will remain *her* child.

As I get ready to leave, Cindy walks me to the door. Michael sits in the kitchen pulling a diaper out of his suitcase. Again she begins to cry. "I have been getting the boys ready for their new home for a long time now. But now that the time is here, it is really hard. I'm scared of letting them go. I know them so well. I just wish I could put the whole thing on hold and wait for a while and let them stay with me longer." As she talks, she stares through the kitchen window into the backyard. It is littered with children's toys, tricycles, trucks, dolls, puppets, bats, and balls. "The adoptive mother," Cindy says, "doesn't want any of these toys to go with them. She wants to buy all new toys." She is silent for a moment, staring, and then asks, "What will I do with all the toys *now?*"

I heard this question asked by all of the foster mothers I spoke with either directly or symbolically as each woman struggled with, and ultimately resolved, the meaning of her experiences as a mother of children who left her—children who were at once indelibly and indisputably her children and who simultaneously and legally belonged to someone else. Thus it is a question about the meaning of identity and kinship within a context that disputes women's claims to motherhood, and it is a story about the ways in which items associated with childhood and family life act to mediate social and cultural disjuncture. Within a consumer culture foster mothering is both naturalized in a Saussurean sense as it is an affective relationship between a woman and a child, occurring in a home, in a nuclear family, thus in a specific context, and is "denaturalized" as an artifact of industrial capitalism in which the context is no longer part of the natural experience, and can be changed, perhaps purchased at will (Haraway 1989). Foster motherhood is constructed as a time-limited if not transitory identity conditioned and defined solely by the presence of foster children. Since foster mothers can exist only vis-à-vis foster children, they have no presence, no identity *sui generis*. Thus rather than being regarded as thinking, feeling human beings who engage in relational work, foster mothers are regarded as disembodied means to an end.

As wards of the state, foster children are excluded from the nuclear family ideal articulated in popular discourses of American kinship. They are stripped of one of the essential elements that make "children" in American society—that is, belonging to parents and family in which care and dependency needs are met. As "nonchildren" or "temporary children" in a temporary relationship, foster children lose the singularization generally reserved in Western culture for human beings (Kopytoff 1986) and assume the quality of a commodity, a "case" that can be shifted from one location, one owner, to another.

In this chapter I draw on ethnographic research to examine how American foster mothers, working within state-imposed commodity relations, both contest and use these relations to create constructs of motherhood and belonging that ultimately critique historically discriminatory labor practices that devalue women's labor and subordinate mothers as devalued workers.[1] I also examine the ways in which foster mothers transform children, who through foster care are treated as alienable commodities, into inalienable possessions of their foster family. In so doing, they critique aspects of consumer culture as they commute the commodity relations of fostering imposed on them by the state into kin relations and transform themselves from workers for the state into mothers capable of bringing about social transformations.

As foster children become a part of their foster mothers' lives and memories and a part of the foster family, some left-behind objects, especially those used and favored by children and thus imbued with the contagion of "real" or "true" children in "real" families, become signs of children's inalienability.[2] This is important since foster mothering relationships are often delimited in ways biological mothering is not. Procuring and often preserving tangible commodities after a child leaves not only signifies the emotionally enduring, ongoing, and singular nature of the foster mother/foster child relationship but also symbolizes the child him- or herself. Left behind toys, clothing, and especially photographs objectify shared familial memories, the relationship, and the child and make it possible for family members as well as those outside the family to recognize the child as a loved and valued member even long after the child has physically departed.[3]

Another practice associated with the resolution of tension between commodity versus kin relations was the storage or curation of children's belongings over several years in the hope and belief that the foster child would someday return for these treasured items, reclaiming both their belongings and their family membership. While this practice for foster parents appeared to be connected with bereavement, it was not uncommon to hear of foster children who found their way back to their foster homes after they reached majority. Similar to Hendon's (2000) analysis of Mayan and Trobriand storage pits, items such as bronzed baby shoes, a favorite dress, or stuffed animals, kept in a box in the attic for a period of years, carried for foster parents a moral imperative. On one hand they suggested that foster parents maintained their vision of the foster child as a family member despite social constructs that contradicted that vision. On the other, preserved memories demonstrated that foster parents were "good parents" who did not and would not forget children they have loved and for whom they have cared (as distinguished from "bad parents" who either let their children enter foster care or who simply regarded foster children as commodities and did not become emotionally attached to them).[4] As Weiner (1992) suggests, "human beings live in memory and by memory . . . the basis of social life [is] the effort of our memory to persist . . . to transform itself into our future."

But the process of family-making and the desire of memory to persist is itself problematic since, culturally, children are viewed as the exclusive possessions/property of their biological parents, and kinship through child welfare policy and practice is defined solely through blood or legal relationships. When fostering relationships end and children move on, items of consumption accrued through the foster mother/foster child relationship symbolizing the child's inalienability are often rejected by adoptive or biological parents because they signify that the child "belonged" to someone else and so may not completely belong to them. Thus the question Cindy Harris asks is also one about the artifacts of isolation. On one hand, commodities associated with a foster child's presence in the foster family symbolize an intransigent belief that no matter where the child is, the relationship continues, even though in some respects it has ended, and thus are a way for women to maintain their claims to a maternal identity. And on the other hand, they suggest that foster mothers' claims to motherhood exist in a fixed liminality in which they contest prevailing cultural ideals of kinship by enacting alternative forms but consistently fail to have their vision officially recognized or integrated into practice or policy.

Part of the Family: From "Foster" Children to "My" Children

With few exceptions fostering was defined by women as mothering work.[5] This related primarily to a sense of belonging to a child and to a sense of responsibility and obligation to care for a child. It was also transformative work, since, through claims of belonging, children were incorporated into women's lives and families and their inalienability restored. Foster mothering was consistently couched in terms of women's abilities to give to children. This required women to engage in the other-centered process of knowing and seeing children in order to meet their needs. It was an outward manifestation of the intimate knowledge of another and overtly indicated a familial relationship. "This isn't a stable, this is a home and these kids . . . when they come to our home . . . are a part of the family. [Y]ou're not an outsider. Everything that I can give you that I think you need or every normal little child needs or wants, we try to give the kids. We never ostracized or separated any of the children from our little circle. Everybody is part of the whole" (Celestine Gordon, a Euro-American married woman in her late forties).

Transformations were also accompanied by a discourse of possessiveness and commitment that wove themes of permanence and stability through a context of physical and temporal impermanence. Through kinship rhetoric premised on affective claims of belonging, women reconstituted relationships commodified by the state into kin relations. As Delia Johnson explained to me:

> I got her when she was thirteen, and we had just moved into an all white neighborhood. And you know how it is when you move into an all white neighborhood. You've got to be cool. Don't make a lot of waves, 'cause people are watching you all the time, seeing how you are, what you like. And I got my last one when she was thirteen, and we had just moved in, and she had seven foster homes before coming to me; they saying she was all out of control and all. And don't you know the first week we was there, she stole $500 from a neighbor. And she says to me, "So, I guess now you gonna have me moved, huh?" And I said, "No, baby. You mine now. You one of my children. You gonna stay here. You gonna turn that money back, you gonna go to court. You gonna suffer. But I'm gonna suffer with you. And you never gonna do that again." (Delia Johnson, a single African American woman in her early thirties)

While women looked at children as belonging to them, as evidenced in possessive rhetoric, its meaning must be qualified since it varies significantly from discourses of ownership conveyed in consumer culture premised on exclusivity. On the contrary, possession and belonging for foster mothers was consistently seen as inclusive and shared. While women claimed a stake in children, they simultaneously recognized that they shared this stake with others and through it increased their own kin network. For example, foster mothers often counted children's biological grandparents or parents as family members and often co-parented foster children through carefully negotiated kin relations. The basic unit of kinship in fostering was not a mother-child relationship but numerous mothers and numerous families, all of whom or some of whom shared a kinship relationship and child-rearing responsibilities. This was possible because foster mothering was based on the assumption that children were not the sole possessions of either the state or of their biological parents. Those who worked to jointly meet a child's needs were kin. Thus while women appropriated the rhetoric of children as private property (for example, "my children"), they simultaneously critiqued this practice through their construction of kinship as inclusive and shared. Unfortunately, their appropriation of the language and the content of contemporary families, but not the form, often contributed to their sense of isolation from other nonfostering families and ultimately exacerbated their conflict with the state.

When talking about themselves in relation to their children, many women expressed discomfort with the term *foster*, believing that it connoted a temporary, fake, or pseudo mother and, reflexively, referred to a nonfamilial relationship with children. Foster mothers were also aware that through these designations foster children were signs of failed nuclear family ideals. Children were "state" children because their "real" parents, echoing the words of a nineteenth-century social worker, "didn't love them in the right way" (Zelizer 1985) and failed to meet state-specified parenting standards. As products of failed families, foster children themselves were tainted and seen as damaged, failed, or non-children and could legitimately be excluded from resources.

> We had a problem with one girl in glasses, she became a teenager and needed glasses. She wouldn't wear them because the state said only "X" amount of dollars paid for this type of glasses and the children laughed at her, made fun of her. So she didn't wear them. So we went out and put out money and bought her some glasses so she would wear them. I asked them, "What do you have?" to the eye doctor. He said, "These are all we have for state children." I said, "What do you have for normal children? We don't have state children. We have children." (Norma Peel, a married African American woman in her early seventies)

Their tasks as mothers were to convey to children, themselves, and those around them that foster children had worth and value, that they mattered enough to be well cared for and provided for, and that caring and provisioning emanated from within a familial context. These discussions often assumed a compensatory nature as foster mothers tried to "make up for" the state's failure to value children and its failure to recognize children as inherently singular beings.[6] In part, women's struggle against the commoditization of children and their own labor related to cultural ideals that human beings were by definition singular and thus could not be objects of exchange (Kopytoff 1986). By constructing foster care as "home" and "family" in which children became singular and inalienable members entitled to all the resources the family could provide, women were able to commute the exchange from money for care-taking services (controlled by the state) to transformation and singularization in exchange for kinship (a process controlled by foster mothers). In this way, women kept children, their memory, and a sense of their active presence in the family by retaining their kinship claims to the children even after they left and by retaining images of themselves as independent service providers rather than as "foster" mothers. Another way foster mothers resisted fostering as an imposed commodity rather than a kin relationship was through the act of sacrifice. Through women's sacrifice, children assumed a singular, perhaps even a sacred, nature. Deleah Smith, a married African American woman in her late forties, relates the following:

> I . . . can't help myself 'cause I like kids. I tell all these little crumb snatchers around here, "Why do you come to my house?" They won't leave. They keep coming back. This one over here [a mother in the neighborhood] says to me last night, "Could you buy [her daughter] a pair of shoes?" I don't have *enough* kids that I got to buy shoes for? Now you want me to buy your kid a pair of shoes? Today, I'm gonna go to the store and buy the kid a pair of shoes. I can't let the kid go around barefooted. I watched her for two weeks barefooted. I can't do that no more. So it's like, you know, you do what you gotta do. . . . I'm not a foster mother. I'm just a mother because I've got children and I'm their mother. They're mine.

Since foster mothers have been largely constructed as women raising "other people's children" or temporary child-care *workers,* their ability and desire to sacrifice for children, and the meaning of sacrifice as a signifier of kinship, has either been overlooked or actively contested. Linda Vanderbrink, a married Euro-American woman in her late forties, relates how painful this ultimately is:

> Once I was at the hospital with a sick baby. He was going to be in the hospital for three weeks. It was really hard on me to get there every day. I had a four-year-old at home and everything. But that little baby didn't know anyone at the hospital. He didn't know anybody. When I came early in the morning, he would brighten up . . . I got him to eat. I was talking to a nurse, and she said, "If its so hard for you to get here, you don't have to come. You're *only* the foster mother." I left the room crying, and my pediatrician who knew me asked me what's wrong. I told him that she had said I was *only* the foster mother. . . . Only foster mother? Can you believe that? These kids are part of my *family.* I make arrangements to be there [for them].

Giving items or services that signified singularized children was also a part of direct resistance to the state. For example, Mr. Simmons, a married African American man in his mid-thirties, talks about how the state encourages a market relationship between foster parents and children in their training sessions. His response is to hold on to a sense of family by providing his foster children with the same experiences as his biological children, even though to do this ultimately means to make a sacrifice. In this situation it is a financial sacrifice since the Simmons are a working-class couple who, in order to save for vacation, have to make significant sacrifices in their daily living.

> If you go by the training, right, you would take being a foster parent as a type of business thing, you know. I mean, this training would make you an artificial parent, you know. I personally think that these kids need to be incorporated into your family as a family member. The last training session, I had a serious problem with it, you know. Everybody was just taking things as a business.... I mean like for the money, not for the love and affection. [When asked if DCF was encouraging this attitude, Mr. Simmons said:] In fact, almost mandating it, you know.... To me, my kids to me, are our family. To me, we are a family here, right. We took these kids, we took them on vacation with us. Last year we took them to Jamaica. That cost me over eleven grand. [But] to me, these kids are part of my family. They will be for as long as they're here. (Thomas Simmons)

Providing for children's material needs, no matter how difficult, as Miller (1998a) suggests, "transcends any immediate utility and is best understood as cosmological in that it takes the form of neither subject nor object but of the values to which people wish to dedicate themselves." For foster mothers this entailed the process of taking "any" child and transforming it into "my" child, but it also included images of a larger social transformation by caring for potentially any and all children in need. Much of this discourse was couched in terms of financial sacrifice, since most foster parents, like the Simmonses, had very little disposable income and providing for children's needs meant that they themselves went without.

> I don't care who pays the bills. It doesn't matter to me. They send [the bills] to me and I put them in the garbage, because the [children] will be taken care of as long as they're here. I'm not going to allow them to be here and something is going wrong and then ten years down the line we have a murderer or a rapist or something and it could have been prevented... I just have a love for children and I look at these children as my kids. (Althea Hansen, a married African American woman in her late fifties)

> All the clothes that they came here with to this day are in boxes in my basement. [And] that's where I want them to stay. They weren't fit to be worn. It took us three months for DCYS to give us a voucher for kids clothes, and then they give you $150. They give you $150 a piece. How much can you buy if you're starting from scratch? We're talking about starting from underclothes. That's what you get. It was crazy, but we stuck it out. (Deleah Smith)

Sacrifice that implied love and devotion to children was also consistently paired with obligation and duty and thus may suggest a sacrifice in the more literal sense. As Miller (1998a) points out, "The crux of the ritual . . . is the separation of the sacrificed into two elements, one of which is given up to the transcendent and the other returns back to the mundane." Through their sacrifice, women consistently spoke of healing society, contributing to making the world a better place, healing injustice in their own lives, and/or correcting society's inequitable distribution of resources. Thus mothering was intimately connected to a larger social fabric. What they did with and for children mattered, it "made a difference." The act of purchasing or acquiring commodities for children was at once something transcendent, it was a sacrifice that repaired a portion of a fractured society, and something ordinary, since it provided for children's daily material needs. Rather than simply being consumers of children's goods or services, through sacrifice, women became producers of social healing and guardians of society's future.

This was very important since all foster mothers were aware of the stigma associated with fostering and accepting "state" money. Most (especially poor and working-class) women had experienced having their motives for fostering questioned and felt that they were often regarded with the same suspicion and hostility as "welfare mothers"—women who are unwilling to earn an "honest" dollar and who exploit taxpayers by sponging off of the state (Jewell 1993) and making a living off of children. As one woman reported when she took her three foster children (all of whom came from different families and were of different ethnic origins) and three biological children in to the grocery to use her WIC coupons, the clerk at the checkout register was so rude to her and the children that, incensed, the foster mother proclaimed, "Look, these are my *foster children*. I work hard taking care of children. I'm *doing* something for our community."

Through sacrifice, and the obligation to sacrifice, children became the objects of women's devotion and in so doing assumed "the image of the transcendent that one would willingly give one's life for" (Miller 1998a). This also acted to distance women in their own minds from the images imposed on them through popular culture and often through social relations with the state in which they were constructed as mercenary women who would profit from their nature and being, motherhood. As one foster mother says, "When I look at these children, I am absolutely in awe of them. [She is holding her three-year-old foster daughter. She spreads her foster daughter's fingers out on the table and looks at them.] I think, What an incredible thing God made. I am absolutely in awe. . . . The problem is that society doesn't really care about these children. People in our society don't really care about each other. All they care about is themselves" (Judy Harrington, a Euro-American housewife in her early fifties). As images of the transcendent, the sacred, children became powerful referents for an ideal maternal identity. "In their devotion to these objects people objectify their ideal of stable identity, in the sense that the objects come to constitute the materiality of social identity" (Miller 1998a). Alicia Miller, a divorced African American woman in her early sixties, says about her foster son, "You end up, the way that I do for my kids, I end up using my personal money. How much personal money do you have when you're on pension and Social Security, because that's what I get . . . [But] I'm not going to allow my kid to have on shoes that's two sizes too small. I'm not going to go out in the street with my kid looking like a little rag doll. I am not going to do that. I would do without myself. What do I need? I just don't buy a lot. I go out and I see some little kid and he looks like a little rag doll, I just shake my head and I say, what are they doing?"

The Meaning of Things: Kinship and Consumption

The way in which foster mothers talked about their purchases and acquisitions on behalf of children suggested the hoped-for transformation of children from alienable possessions to inalienable family members and were thus also about women's own transformation from workers to mothers. Most of their stories were about the importance of children's "before" and "after" picture. Children came to care with little or nothing—that is, they came to care as commodities, as interchangeable items of trade, or as "cases," and left with things that signified both their status as cared-for family members and their status as consumers, or full social beings. Thus the toys, clothes, books, school supplies, or behavioral reward treats women provided foster children signified both a kinship relationship between the giver and the receiver and the social transformation of "foster" to "true" children, and it simultaneously signified their own transformation from worker to mother.

Women's ability to provide for children themselves allowed foster mothers to marginalize and resist the significance of the state's presence and thus became as Gell (1986) suggests a type of identity badge through which women enacted family obligations. "I know there are some people who rely very much on their social worker. I sort of consider these kids my family and I don't treat them any different than my biological children, so I don't really have the need for a social worker. I take care of my own business as far as their needs and everything else. And I think my kids that have been in other foster homes appreciate that more. That's what makes them feel more like a family, you know" (Belinda Evans, a Euro-American married woman in her late fifties).

While foster mothers talked with pride about being able to provide for their children, they simultaneously greeted the need to provide basic clothes or school or medical supplies with a degree of resentment. For most women, providing for foster children, especially initially, was financially difficult.[7] It was also difficult when in the course of an afternoon, with little or no warning other than a heralding phone call, a woman's family went from two to six children and stayed that way indefinitely. While completely outfitting a child presented a practical problem for many foster parents, more important, their resentment stemmed from their interpretation of children's status upon arrival as negligence by the state. In their opinion, little care or attention was given to the transfer of children's possessions and thus to their needs. As wards of the state, children were simply commodities, a symptom of which was that they became dispossessed of their right or privilege to own, possess, or retain objects and instead became themselves owned objects who were moved from home to home as though all foster homes were interchangeable and as though affective fostering relationships were impossible. Mr. Hobbs, a Euro-American foster father in his late fifties, suggests that one way the state could improve the transfer of children was to actually see the personhood of the children imbued with needs for ownership. "When the child is taken, no matter what the circumstances, get a hold of his blanket or get a hold of his pillow or get a hold of mother's sweater—Something to put in the crib with the baby. And that way he hasn't lost everything and it's something to cuddle. Because he (referring to his foster son) didn't have anything. He didn't have anything when he came."

Karen Smith, a married Euro-American foster mother in her late thirties, makes a similar observation. "I always try . . . to get some of the kid's belongings brought here—like a stuffed animal. Because usually when they take them they just sweep through and you're gone. Most of the time when they get here they don't have hardly anything clothes-wise. Cory got dropped off in a pair of pajamas and that's it. I still have the pajamas, I saved them. I don't know. It's like I try to put myself in their place, how I would feel if somebody took me away. And they have to be terrified."

Deleah Smith suggests that it is the overall lack of care with which children are given new homes that signifies their commodity status and their ultimate emotional demise and reflexively signifies foster parents' interchangeability and their lack of value. "It was like they were 'placed.' Thank you, we placed them, fuck you! That's what it was like. Excuse my French. But that's what it was like. It was like, okay, we got three kids placed. Fuck it, let's move on to the next. There has to be a lot more. They're gonna lose a lot of children that have great potential. . . . Once they're placed, nobody really gives a damn."

All foster parents expressed concern about children's care as wards of the state and ultimately saw the state's treatment of children as abusive or neglectful, and thus as harmful as the treatment children received in their families of origin. In fact, while social workers expressed the desire to "rescue" children from abusive homes, most foster parents expressed the desire to "rescue" children from the state's management and care. In response, most women acted quickly to accept children into their homes and began the transformation process immediately as a way of undoing the harm they saw the state inflicting. As one woman stated when asked when children became family members, "the moment they walk through the door." This perspective often led women to accept more children than they ultimately wanted and to assume greater financial hardship than they were able. For example, another woman relayed a story about how she was called by a young male social worker to see if she could accept twin babies. The mother initially said no since she had three children under two, but when she found out that the babies were in car seats on the social worker's desk and he was guessing at what formula to put in their bottles, she immediately agreed to come and get them, saying, "That is no way to treat babies."

While no woman felt she could change the way the state treated children or the assumptions upon which their treatment was based, all women felt that through their care they could undo some of the harm done. So while women talked both about the difficulty of providing for an instant family, they simultaneously spoke about the resourcefulness and creativity with which they managed it. Women related with pride their frugality, thrift, and the importance of being well connected to other mothers who recycled their outgrown children's clothes. Sharing relations with other foster mothers was also important since women had a mirror that confirmed the important and familial nature of individual foster parent/foster child relationships. This was something they could not count on from nonfoster parents nor from state social workers.

Sharing goods with other mothers contributed to women's ability to transform "foster" children into "real" children and to overcome economic hardship. By providing for their children, and by passing on and acquiring secondhand goods that had already been singularized (Hermann 1987), foster mothers were able to symbolically become a part of a larger network of mothers, memories, and family-making through the transfer of possessions laden with meaning and life history. That is, secondhand goods were imbued with "the sympathetic magical law of contagion" (Rozin et al. 1989) and contained the familial relations women constructed and enacted through fostering. Through the transfer of these items, foster mothers were able to share that legacy with other mothers. These items were also imbued with the contagion of "real" or "true" children—that is, children who had been transformed from objects of trade into singularized well-cared for family members. As Hermann (1997:920) suggests about items purchased in garage sales, "The transfer of possessions . . . is therefore far more laden with meaning than merely deriving use value from secondhand goods. Since buyers act as though they take home some essence of the sellers."

Through the transfer of goods, women furnished items "imbued with the identity of their owners"—that is, the identity of children who were inalienable possessions—and the commodities themselves assumed the characteristics of inalienability through the conveyance of sentiments, memories, and the conveyance of the context within which items were used. For example, in one household I visited, while the mother talked to me, a mother's helper ironed dresses she had received for her three-year-old foster daughter from another mother. The dresses were regarded as an important gift, not only because they would allow the three-year-old to be "properly" dressed for church and therefore fit in with the rest of the family, but also because the context from which they came was one in which another foster mother used the dresses to transform her own foster child from a "state" child into a "real" one.

Through these trade networks women were engaged in work that situated them socially as *mothers* and supported the construct of foster mother as mother through the transfer of meaning-laden and history-laden items to other women who recognized the meanings inherent in each item. That is to say, the life histories these items accrued were about mothering, the arrival and departure of children, loss and change, the sacralization of children, and the need to provide quickly for children. They were thus items associated with the essence of foster mothering and transmitted the essence of foster mother/foster child relationships to women who were capable through their own experiences of empathetically understanding these meanings. In a social and familial context marked by change (both in terms of children joining and leaving the family and children's changing needs) foster mothers created a sense of continuity by primarily trading with other foster mothers who recognized and added to the singular nature of items and shared in the rituals and demands of singularizing children. They also expanded kin relationships from within the foster family to a much wider community.

Interestingly, juxtaposed to foster mothers' pride in frugality and reliance on secondhand goods were social workers' scorn and mistrust of women who purchased or acquired them. Social workers tended to regard foster mothers' preferences for secondhand clothes as nefarious. Most social workers felt that if a woman was not purchasing new clothes for children, then she was pocketing the money and making a profit from her foster children. Social workers failed to see the value added to secondhand clothes and regarded new clothes as superior. They also tended to believe that the money women got from the state should be spent directly on foster children. Money from the state was rightfully money *for* the foster child and so was seen as the child's money. Social workers often questioned foster mothers' motives for fostering and interpreted secondhand clothes as a sign of the foster children's secondhand status. That is, they saw this as an expression of foster mothers' beliefs that these children did not *deserve* new clothes and were not being treated like other family members. Thus, while foster mothers used their exchange networks to erase perceived differences between foster and "real" children, social workers interpreted this strategy as one that imposed or maintained difference.

Foster mothers' friends and relatives also consistently provided for children and provided children with possessions associated with family life. They thus participated with foster mothers in the creation and recognition of kin-based social relations, shared the financial burden, incorporated children into a larger kin network, and gleaned recognition, support, and affirmation for their motherhood status. In addition to gifts at Christmas, birthdays, and the beginning of the school year (times of increased expense), often extended family members provided care, nurture, and support to children and respite to foster mothers throughout the child's physical residence in the foster mother's home. Through their gift-giving foster mothers' families and often neighbors or friends recognized a woman's instrumental and sentimental obligations to these children and claimed a similar relationship for themselves. An example of this is found with Bertha White, a divorced African American woman in her early sixties.

> Well, they would come over and would hold the baby and play with the baby, help me do different things. And when Christmas time came and that's how I really supported my first kid, because when Christmas came he had everything. Everything. I didn't have to worry about that. Any clothes. I called the people that I knew and they had smaller kids, smaller grandkids. They brought stuff over, even for the baby that I had for twenty days. I had more stuff. See, because my niece sent me . . . she called up friends of hers that had babies, they brought all kind of clothes and stuff, oh yeah . . . Even my neighbor down here, when Christmas came, he'd come over with a big shopping bag full of stuff. It's been great.

Secondhand trade networks were important to foster mothers, but so was shopping for new items. Through shopping, these mothers gained a sense of proficiency and competence as providers. In part, this may be related to the way shopping erased or made irrelevant the boundaries between public and private, production and consumption, and in this respect mirrored the work of fostering (also see Wozniak 2002). But it also has several other referents, such as sacrifice, social transformation, and ultimately the ability to take a situation in which women had little or no control over children's fate and through provisioning create a situation in which they had control. That is to say, through their consumption practices women commuted the meanings of foster children's status and legitimated for themselves and their extended families a kinship relationship in which foster children became their children. Interestingly, while women on one hand critiqued a consumer culture by contesting the commodification of mothering, they simultaneously purchased mass-produced consumer goods to contest the commodification of children. As Martha Hollingsworth suggests, "To me, I'm very thrifty. So I go to like Filene's or Macy's when they're having a sale and I could buy, find Healthtex shirts, if I shop [that is, hunt for bargains], for $3.00 apiece, and I'll buy five for each boy, different colors. You know? And do certain things. Because I'm a shopper that looks for bargains. Okay? And I buy good name-brand clothes and everything. And I just shop and I buy them. And I never felt that money is an issue for me as far as—[whose money is being spent]. These boys need a tremendous amount of clothes."

Fostering and the State

As we have seen, fostering was based largely on a gift exchange in which what was given (knowledge, expertise, love, clothing, or shelter) both signified and established a mother-child relationship between the giver and receiver (Mauss 1990; Hermann 1997). But this gift exchange was effected within a context that overtly defined fostering as a commodity exchange. Rather than simply contesting these relations, foster mothers used them, selectively choosing aspects of commodity exchange as a part of fostering and reinventing the meaning of others in service of a foster mother identity. For example, Lillian Rosebud, a Native American married woman in her early forties, uses the idea of mothering as a "service," something usually used in the context of a market economy, but reframes it as a gift women give to children and thus as something recognizably familial.

> If you look at yourself as a temporary mother, although you know its a temporary situation, I don't think you can provide the proper kind of service to the kids, because children deal with emotions and they are very susceptible to picking up on things that maybe you don't think about. But if you hold back from them in any way, they can sense that. If you really want . . . to be good to the kids and provide them with all the love and attention they need, you have to put all the other feelings aside and just let yourself completely fall in love with a kid basically. . . . That's what you have to be willing to deal with. You have to be willing to take [the pain that comes from an ending].

This same woman also explains her attitude toward the money received from the state for fostering. When asked, "Does the money help?" Lillian Rosebud responded with sentiments characteristic of many women.

> Oh yeah. Yeah, now it does. I mean years ago, it really didn't help a heck of a lot, but now, with the increase in rates and everything else, I can afford to go to a [foster care] conference in California, take a vacation, and I can afford to fix up my house and do all the things that years ago, when the rates were so low and the kids were beating up on your furniture and you have to buy a new fridge because they ripped the door off the old one, and the washer and the dryer are breaking down because of the amount of laundry you're doing [you couldn't]. I just had another brand new floor put down, the other floor was only six years old and it was trashed because of all the kids in and out of the home. You're talking about a $1,500 kitchen floor. And if you have to replace that every five or six years . . . The carpeting in here is only six years old, my couch is only six years old, and it's trashed. Having only one biological child who's now moved out of the home, my husband and I could have had a real nice

home and we would have had all these nice things and being a foster parent should not keep you from having the things that you want. If I was to go out to work and I was bringing home my paycheck, my husband and I could afford to do all kinds of things. Being home and being a foster parent should not stop you from doing those things. You should have enough money coming in and we do, now. Now that foster care rates have come up to a half-decent level, we do have the money coming in that we can afford to take the vacations that we deserve and still be able to afford to take those kids along with us. We can afford to replace the appliances as they wear out and to keep the home in decent condition instead of it being trashed. You need that increased rate in boarded care to keep up with expenses.

No woman saw this money as *earned*—that is, as a quid pro quo for labor provided—and most were against the idea of a salary for foster mothers as well as against the idea that fostering was or should be a paid a "job," since this would ultimately allow the state to own women's labor to an even greater extent. Instead, women tended to see themselves as independent service providers who gave a gift to the community or to society at large and within this context commuted state money into support for providing this service. That is, the state was in some sense an ally acting to facilitate or enhance women's ability and desire to care for children in need.

While women themselves had little problem accepting money from the state, they resented and resisted the way the state cast fostering exclusively as commodity-relations in which fostering more closely resembled production line work, where workers interacted with a product for a short time, then moved on to the next product, rather than parenting. Similar to Goffman's (1961) findings about the deliberate lessening of selfhood through institutions such as mental hospitals or prisons, most foster mothers experienced the state as intentionally diminishing their sense of motherhood and thus their sense of self. When asked, "How do you think the state sees you?" these mothers responded:

> The whole agency sees you as a temporary caretaker. You're being paid to take care of that kid and feed 'em and clothe 'em and that's as far as it goes. You're not supposed to love 'em, not supposed to get attached to 'em. If you get attached to the child and try to advocate on the child's behalf, the department will step in and take that child out of there because they're afraid of going up against you. (Lillian Rosebud)

> I don't think they [saw me]. I think they just looked at me as another person to take on their kids. I think they don't look at foster parents as being people. They look at them as being places to put bodies . . . Even from things you see on TV with the news, it's like it's just a business to place

kids. And there's no personality in it. There's no nothing. I mean like when I got these kids they never came to see if these kids had a bed to sleep in. (Deleah Smith)

DCF thinks they're steering you some money. They think you're not in it for anything except to get the money. I really don't think that they understand that our hearts are right there. And I don't think that they understand that when they're shifting a child out of your home it's not only the child suffering. It's us suffering. It's the biological parents [suffering] because their contacts have now been broken. Everybody suffers. It's a no-win situation. But the agency's attitude is, "You have to learn to deal with it. It shouldn't bother the child. It shouldn't bother you." [But] you can't just be standoffish. You just can't ignore that child.... We were told that they were "foster children." That means emotionally we should be cut off from them because they can come and go.... So be standoffish. Don't get attached. Don't fall in love. [But] it just doesn't work that way. (Eleanor Gordon, a married Euro-American woman in her late thirties.)

While women talked about the way in which state money helped their households, they also talked about the inadequacy of state money and the need for women to use their "own" money to adequately provide for children. Privileging the importance of providing for children's needs regardless of whether or not the state provided assistance was one way of intentionally holding on to a particular sense of self in the face of relations with the state that consistently dehumanized mothers and commodified their labor. Using or distinguishing one's personal money relative to state money was a way of asserting an identity discourse in which consumption, as Miller (1998a) suggests, "is more often about expression of relationships than of some mindless materialism," in this case signifying maternal sacrifice, responsibility, and empathy. When talking about the way she provided for two boys upon their initial arrival, Martha Hollingsworth, a married Euro-American woman in her early thirties, talks about the importance of shopping for them and providing for them like family. Martha uses her "own" money to provide for these children since state reimbursements do not arrive for up to four weeks after children are placed in care. Later she stated that she is lucky enough to be able to provide for her children regardless of state reimbursements since her husband has a well-paying job and she works part-time as an accountant at home.

> The boys ... that came to us ... had nothing when they came. Just a plastic bag with some stuff in it and that was it. We took them out and bought them all new things and everything, clothes and everything. To tell you the truth, when the children came, they didn't have much clothes or anything like that.... So we went out and bought them whatever they

needed. You know? So we had to go out and spend a few hundred dollars. We had to buy them sneakers, clothes. But we had no problem with that because, you know, money is not a big issue with us. And, you know, there was no problem. [I]t's like they need, you know, shoes or clothes, whatever they need, if they want to go to the movies, we take them to the movies; whatever they want.

Real Mothers, Real Loss

Knowledge of the potentially temporary nature of the foster mother-foster child relationship seldom if ever conditioned whether or not foster children became full members of their foster families. Women explained that they became emotionally attached to children in the face of imminent loss because not to do so would be a contradiction of mothering, would be to know need in another and not respond. Thus, just as stories about mothering were about providing for children and including them in the family, they were also about the pain of loss and the hope of one day again being reunited with children who had left their care. As Alicia Miller says about her foster son, "[When he leaves,] oh, I'm just gonna lay down and die. It's gonna be hard. And I know the day may come." Or, as these mothers suggest, bereavement and a sense of absence or severing from the object of their devotion itself became a permanent marker of motherhood.

> Giving up babies was the hardest part. Every time a baby left, it left quite a hole in our lives and in our family . . . It was always like handing over a part of your body, like your arm or your leg. Sometimes I couldn't do it. You would have to go down to the state and hand over the baby. Sometimes my husband had to do it. I don't know how he ever did it. It was like losing a part of you. (Sara Rill, a married Euro-American woman in her late fifties)

> It messes up your whole life. I mean it's hard. It's hard for you to deal with your own emotions. It's hard for your spouse, it's hard for your family because they've grown attached to each other, especially when you've got adopted children, because it reminds them that they're vulnerable . . . You end up lashing out at everybody, if you're like me. I'm a very emotional person. Little things get to you because your emotions are just flying all over the place. . . . Well, *every single time* a child leaves, that is what you go through. You go through the grieving process. . . . you get frustrated, you lash out, you'll be busy washing dishes and you'll just stand there and cry. . . . Your husband may come through the door and you lash out at him, your kids come home from school and its like, ahhhhh. And that's what you go through every time a child leaves if you're attached to them. And even if you're not attached to the child and even if it's a situ-

ation where you want the child to go home, you still go through a grieving, because you know that when that child walks out that door, you're probably never, ever going to see them again. (Lillian Rosebud)

While regarding children as inalienable and permanent family members in the face of imminent separation or loss appears somewhat contradictory, it is in fact this seeming contradiction that enabled most women to foster. As *identifiable* family members, foster children were given aspects of their foster parent and foster family identity, and this could not easily be removed.[8] Not only did foster mothers seek to retain something of the child, but when children were given to other families, they were given in such a way as to retain some indelible mark of their foster mothers and foster families. In most foster mothers' minds, children were loaned, given, or shared with other families, but foster mothers' claims to kinship and claims to one's extended sense of self represented in the children's care were retained.

Many women talked with great pride of the things they were able to send with foster children, like bags of clothing and toys, possessions that bore the individual mark of the sending family indicating that this child was a cared-for family member. Similar to the findings of Finch and Mason (2000), women and children implicitly understood that these keepsakes carried the memory of those who gave them and thus acted as an embodied reminder of the child's family. As one mother states:

> He came with nothing and he went back with a great big bag full of clothes and—So he has something when he goes into that other home now. He has something to associate with us . . . you know. I did get a voucher for, you know, a hundred dollars to buy him some clothing. I go up to the Goodwill up here in Monroe. And the lady that runs it used to be a foster mom. She was a foster mom fifteen, twenty years. And she knows I'm a foster mom. So, you know, I get clothes and things practically for nothing. So I didn't even use the hundred dollar voucher I had because I had gotten him shorts and T-shirts and shirts and long pants and three pairs of shoes. So I just gave the vouchers to the worker who picked him up. And if they want to—you know, I says, "He doesn't have a jacket." So if they want to use the vouchers to get him a jacket or whatever, they can. (Betty Hobbs, a Euro-American married foster mother in her late fifties)

Other mothers talked about the importance of giving foster children something (of theirs) to take to their next home. In most cases these were "special" gifts separate from those commodities that signified the child's well-cared-for status. Not only did these items indelibly mark the foster child as part of the foster mother, but they also insinuated the presence of the foster mother into the child's next family. As this mother comments, "I always buy them something, something they are going to be able to keep, so they will know that we were there. And it is usually in the form of jewelry most of the time. So something, you know, that they can [keep]. Some of them I buy crosses, necklaces, some I buy a ring for, some I have given my mother's rings to—the ones I am real, real close to. You know, something, you know, it is a part of me, for them. And almost always they want pictures of us, so we have pictures and we just give it to them" (Linda Snell, a Euro-American married foster mother in her early fifties).

When foster mothers had regular contact with the biological mother or grandparents and child care tasks and responsibilities were collaborative, foster mothers attempted to retain an ongoing relationship with both the parents and the child and thus retain their kinship claim when the child left their care. In most instances, however, the state discouraged this contact or simply made it impossible by telling foster mothers little about where a child came from and even less about where a child was going. Since foster mothers had no legal claims to foster children and the state considered this information "confidential," women had no access to this information.

Most women told stories of their attempts to stay in touch with foster children in spite of the state and to convey to the next family both their kinship claims to the child and the child's singularization through foster family life. Women sent their telephone numbers with children, most sent pictures of the foster family that included the child, others sent their address with the child, still others talked about pinning a note to the inside of children's clothes asking the next mother to call them. When it was possible to know the address of the next home, especially once a relationship had been established in which both (foster and biological or adoptive) parents' claims to children were recognized, many women sent packages to the child of small gifts or sent gifts at holidays or birthdays as a way of maintaining an active relationship. These gifts were clearly equated with kinship and reproduced on a smaller scale foster mothers' obligations to provide for their children. For example, one woman whose foster daughter left after two years to join her grandparents stated, "I just called her. I was at the mall and got her a pair of earrings."

When women were allowed no contact with children after their departure, when they were not able to ascertain the child's destination, or when the biological or adoptive mother was threatened by the foster mother's claims of belonging and prohibited contact, most foster mothers still retained their claims to kinship and still included the child as an active member in the family household, but they held their ability to act on their claim in abeyance. In these cases, which occurred perhaps more frequently than their ability to maintain contact, women held the hope that in some way at some time children would remember their life in foster care and would find their way back to the family. Since this was enacted at all stages of the life cycle, where children after several years of absence called or wrote to their foster mothers or simply came back, this hope was not unreasonable. As this mother suggests, the idea that children are permanent family members is often a mutual understanding. "One little girl lived with us for four months the first time and then a year and a half the second time. She was like ten or eleven when she was with us the second time. She's twenty-six now. I heard from her for a while after she left, then I hadn't heard from her for a while. And then this past Christmas, we got a card from her with a picture of her and her two children, and you know . . . its just kind of neat. Here she is an adult and we got a card, saying, "Dear Mom and Dad" . . . you know she still considers us mom and dad" (Jacqueline Rosehill, a Euro-American woman in her early forties).

When an embodied relationship was not possible, the preservation and curation of commodities associated with individual children, along with shared reminiscing consistently conducted in the present tense, was one way foster mothers retained their claims to children who had left their homes. Many foster parents developed rituals of remembrance that legitimized their bereavement for the member they had lost. Through commodities associated with particular children, foster parents were able to tangibly mark the child's existence, to affirm the kinship relationship, and to retain their identities as mothers to particular children. For example, the Samuelses, a Euro-American couple in their middle thirties who have adopted four children and have three biological children, maintain the active presence of foster children who are no longer physically present by creating a Christmas tree ornament for each child. The tradition was started when the Samuelses were grieving over the loss of their first foster child, Amy, who lived with them for more than four years and then suddenly died. Each ornament was fashioned in the likeness of something that reminded the family of that child. Christmas became a time for reminiscing and for sharing with new children the presence of former children and thus in some respects holding their ever-changing family constant. Since the Christmas tree was public, this was also a way in which nonfamily members were educated about these kinship relations. As Claudette Samuels says:

> We have, for every child we had, we have a gold ornament [for our Christmas tree] with their name on it and the year that they were here with us. When we're doing the Christmas tree, I'll say, "Oh, remember him," and then we'll tell little stories and remember. My Christmas tree is a memory tree. You know, there's ornaments on the tree that my twenty-one-year-old son made when he was in kindergarten. And each year we bring them out . . . And we clean them off, and they'll [the children] say, "Well, tell us about this one," you know. And "Why is this one [ornament] a football player?" And we would tell stories about how he liked football, or "Why is this one a fire truck?" Or you know, "Tell us about the angel,

Mommy. Tell us again about the angel," which is Amy. Amy was our angel and you know [her voice trails off and she pauses]. We would sit for days and talk. . . . And people come over and say, what a beautiful tree, you know. And we'll say, this is our memory tree.

Many foster mothers also spoke about the importance of photographs. All parents had their walls or tabletops adorned with photos of their foster children. When asked who was in their families, women consistently relied on photographs to chronologically relate members' coming and goings, to indicate their age at arrival and their current age, and to talk about where children were (or were when the women last knew) and what they were doing. Most of the photographs depicted typical scenes of family life and most featured several members interacting. Portrait style photos were consistently displayed next to other portraits of family members. Thus, through the dialectics of present and absent images, women preserved children's membership while also creating an interstice for bereavement—both of which preserved their *right* to kinship claims with foster children. As Marcia Granholm, a married Euro-American foster mother in her forties suggests, the hope that children will return or that an embodied relationship will continue does not preclude mourning nor the creation of a permanent place in the family for the absent child.

Well, we keep memories of the person that's left by pictures in a photo album and by contact. We talk about it. It's not a hidden thing. Elisha is six, she's my daughter, and Dawn is thirteen. Elisha was nine weeks old when she came here, Dawn was five, and they've seen it, they've seen the children come in crying, they've seen children who leave crying, and they've made best friends, you know, with a lot of the children that were here, especially the ones that were close to their age when they came or that were here the longest. And that's what you do, you keep their memory there. We always [also] give them our phone number, we always give them a notebook with our names and addresses in it. And we always keep their photos in our photo album.

Foster parents also often retained a child's toy, an outgrown article of clothing such as a favorite dress or baby shoes, or items children made as tangible, sentient symbols of particular children's presence and concomitantly of foster parents' parenthood. These items were often curated in a designated place within the home, such as an attic room, a cupboard, or a shelf. This is similar to Layne's (1998) findings about objects preserved after late-term miscarriages in which items associated with "real" babies and "real" babyhood were preserved and used to normalize the lost child as well as communicate the child's value. By keeping these items, foster parents also asserted themselves as "good" parents by invoking a connection between what is moral (loving children, holding on to them) and storing their active memory. Consistent with the argument Hendon (2000) asserts about Trobrianders and Tzotzil-speaking Maya of Mexico, "storage acquires a moral dimension because it is part of the process connecting resources with people's needs and desires, and because the social evaluation of people or groups may take into account their connection to the practice of storage." By curating objects left behind by children, by, if you will, storing them, foster parents connected themselves with "real" parents and thus intentionally distanced themselves from parents who love and then lose their children or from the state-commodity-relations model of fostering.

Clearly, the need to ritualize inclusion and preserve symbols of kinship was incurred through social relations with the state. Since foster mothers' claims to kinship were seldom recognized, their grief when a child left was not acknowledged by state social workers or their nonfostering friends or acquaintances. As one mother states:

> You have the agency on one hand saying, you've got this child coming to your home and you're supposed to love it for however long you have it in your home. Then all of a sudden, a year later, you've got this agency saying, now you've got to stop loving this child because it has to go someplace else, but we've got this other child and now we want you to love it. How do you just say, OK, this one's gone now, so I don't have to love her anymore. Its like—a part of you just *dies.* And there were certain kids that left, there were this certain few, that when they left . . . they say that when your heart breaks, there's no such thing, but you actually feel like there's this part of you that is just dying. And you can't explain this kind of thing. I always said that its worse than losing someone to death. Because when someone dies, they're gone. And you know that it's permanent and that wherever they are they're OK, and you don't have to worry about them any more. But when you lose a foster child, and they go off, either back to their biological parents, which is sometimes worse, or off to adoption you're always wondering—I wonder where they are, I wonder if they're OK, I wonder how they're doing, I wonder if their life is OK, and if the parents—if their marriage lasted . . . You know what I mean? Constantly. You worry about them. But when somebody dies, you don't worry about them anymore. (Jacqueline Rosehill)

Most women attributed the state's inability to see their kinship relations with children to the commodity model of the foster mother/foster child relationship. Women's grief was exacerbated through these transactions since children often disappeared from their lives without a trace.

> [When] this little girl left, I have never heard from her. And I was devastated by that. I thought that, you know, I know that everything was for this

little girl's family and getting her through this as best we could. And [the social worker and I] both worked towards that. But she left a household that missed her. And I just thought that it was not very—it wasn't a very nice thing to do. I think that we deserve the consideration of the phone call, not that it's going to change anything, but . . . I would like to be able to follow how this child was doing. I know that there are some things that they can't report to me. But certainly I would feel better just having contact with the worker at that point so she could reassure me that all was going well. (Sarah Perkins, a Euro-American married woman in her forties)

[When she left, I was told] that I was doing a job and my job was terminated. It was ended and it was over and so that's the end of it. I don't need to deal with her anymore, as though it was no more than that, you know? (Sandy Wallace, a Euro-American woman in her late forties)

While the state consistently abrogated women's kinship claims to foster children and thus their rights to simultaneously maintain a relationship *and* to grieve children who had left their care, biological or adoptive mothers *did* recognize foster mothers' claims and were often threatened by them. Toys, gifts, and photographs given to the child within the context of foster family life often became problematic for adoptive and biological mothers who, according to foster mothers, asked that these items not accompany children or refused to allow children to have those that were sent and returned them.

Betty Hobbs relates her thoughts about a child she and her husband, Al, fostered from birth to age two. Their attempts to retain their claims to kinship have been rebuffed by the adopting mother. The child's presence, however, is maintained in the household through numerous pictures scattered throughout the house and on both Betty's and Al's key rings, and through shared reminiscing. The items rejected by the adoptive mother, though reminders of the problematic nature of their kinship relations, are carefully curated until that time when they might see her again.

Well, the lady [adoptive mother] promised she would keep in touch. [Y]ou know, she says we were such a valuable part of [Betsy's] life that she was going to make sure we kept in touch and all this and that and she was going to have Betsy christened such-and-such a time and we were invited up for the christening and all this. And then nothing. And then I sent her a package. [The adoptive mother] didn't even let her have a picture, have the package. And I thought, well, maybe—you know, maybe working so much, she probably couldn't get to the post office or whatever. You know? So I re-sent it out. And it was sent back. It says "Not Wanted" or something like that. So I said, "Okay. I guess she doesn't want to—[stay in touch]." I've asked [the social worker] how [Betsy] is doing. And all I get is, "Yes, everything is going fine." But I figure, well, we'll probably see her someday, hopefully.... So I put the box in the attic. Its got pictures and a pair of her bronzed baby shoes and some real cute little dresses. You know, maybe she will want them for her own child, you know?... [H]opefully some day we'll see her.

When a child went from foster care to adoption or returned to the biological mother, signs that the child had been part of another family or had another mother were problematic since they signified a familial membership outside of the context of a legal relationship. The very fact that some mothers were threatened by foster mothers' claims indicated that they recognized these claims to kinship and recognized the child's inalienability within the fostering context but were compelled to reject them since they contradicted kinship vis-à-vis the conferring agency, the state, and signified that if the children belonged to someone else, they might not belong exclusively to them. These parents were thus anxious to "redeem" children, make them *their* exclusive property, and erase all signs of contagion from their last family.

Adoptive parents' rejection of commodities symbolic of a child's inalienability points to another cultural disjuncture inherent in fostering relations. Legally children are considered to be the exclusive property and possessions of their biological parents. Culturally, children are ideally considered inalienable possessions. But the very fact that children are being passed from mother to mother, that their inalienability is being intentionally suspended through foster care, violates this ideal. From this perspective, foster and adoptive mothers' attempts to transform the child into an inalienable possession, one bearing the marks of family membership, are attempts to resolve this contradiction. The difference for foster mothers is they have accepted as a condition of their motherhood the recognition of multiple kinship categories and communal or shared ownership and in so doing have maintained fostering as gift rather than commodity relations. Adoptive and biological mothers, however, because their rights are defined and conferred by law, do not see possession as communal and therefore must reject these claims if they are to retain the ideological ideal of children as inalienable possessions since the very notion that they have come from another mother indicates that they are in fact alienable. From this perspective biological and adoptive mothers can only recognize foster mothers in terms of a commodity exchange in which there existed no claims to kinship and thus, rather than allying with foster parents, they acted to support the state.

Conclusion

Most foster mothers felt there was little they could do to change policies, practices, or sentiments in which they and foster children were constructed through commodity relations. Many foster mothers pointed to "the system"—that is, the social relations based on policies and practices that established this paradigm—and felt helpless and often hopeless as they confronted impossible choices. The social relations foster mothers experience through their interactions with the state, and with adoptive or biological mothers, were tremendously isolating. When commodities threatened adoptive or biological parents, they became signs that foster mothering existed within a set of cultural contradictions.

Left-behind and preserved commodities were a reminder of the physically fragmented relationship women must endure in order to maintain their vision of the child as a family member. They were at once signs of women's success at reconstituting a commodified foster mother/foster child relationship into one of kinship *and* a sign of women's failure to have that vision recognized or legitimated within a larger sociocultural context. Commodities signified both the continuity of the relationship *and* its fragmented and broken nature. Children's possessions and reference to them in regular family discourse were part of rituals of inclusion and remembrance that legitimated foster parents as *parents,* and thus their sense of loss and bereavement, and were a constant reminder that they had no social or legal claim to children, thus socially, no right to grieve them.

By transforming transient children into inalienable family members through claims of belonging, foster mothers not only affirmed their motherhood by approximating the American ideal of mother-child relations in which children belong to their parents, but also acted to "secure permanence in a serial world that [was] always subject to loss and decay" (Weiner 1992:7). Foster children inevitably left their foster mothers' homes. But foster mothers retained their claims to motherhood and retained their kinship relationship with particular children, even when these were ignored. They thus contested the commoditization of foster children and the commodification of their care-giving labor by insisting that fostering was not about an exchange in which foster mothers received money for care giving, but about the heroic efforts to keep children even when they had to give them away. That is, to be "real" parents to "real" children and thus, paradoxically, about continuity in the face of change and humanity in the face of otherwise alienating and impersonal social relations.

NOTES

1. My data comes from participant observation and intensive informal and semistructured interviews conducted over the course of three years from 1993 to 1996 in Connecticut with more than fifty women. I also conducted structured ranking interviews with sixty-nine women and conducted four focus-group sessions. In all, I talked with more than two hundred foster mothers. Among the women from whom I collected a significant amount of data, the sample was divided between African American (43.5 percent) and Euro-American women (47.8 percent); a very small portion were Hispanic or "other" (1.45 percent). The majority of women were married (about 75

percent), and the rest were either divorced or had never been married. Women's ages ranged from twenty-eight to seventy-eight years old. The number of children women fostered over their careers ranged from those who fostered no children (there were some who had not yet received any) to those who cared for 250 children. Of the children women currently had in their homes, a small proportion were biological relatives. Study participants also included women who had adopted up to eight children and those who had adopted none. The length of time children stayed with foster mothers varied from as short as an overnight stay to as long as eight years. Foster mothers also cared for children from a wide range of ages, from birth to late adolescence. While my unit of analysis was foster mothers, I also included a small sample of foster fathers since no woman fostered in isolation. All of these men acted in concert and support with their wives relative to their views of fostering and, like their wives, articulated a strong fostering identity. I thus include some men's comments while focusing primarily on women's experiences.

Women's comments included in this paper are excerpts from transcribed interviews. While I do not wish to portray foster mothers as a unidimensional group, an analysis of the codes through Ethnographic and an Ethnographic-like system revealed strong patterns in women's conceptualization of foster mothering, parenting norms, mothering, and parent-child relationships. Foster mothers expressed a high degree of consensus on the core features of foster mothering (how kinship is established through fostering, the permanence of fostering relationships, and the criteria for motherhood [see Handwerker and Wozniak 1997]).

2. I use the terms "real children" and "real families" in this context because I often encountered foster children and foster parents talking about themselves and their experiences in these terms. For example, my own foster daughter, when asked how many children her former foster mother had, answered, "four foster children and two real children." On another occasion, as we were going to her school open house, she asked me not to tell anyone that she was a foster child because she wanted children to think that she was a "real" child. She used similar words to describe why she wanted to be adopted. This rhetoric was not isolated to her and was often articulated by other foster children I spoke with formally and informally. Similarly, foster parents talked about how their foster children were often discounted as not really belonging to their family, thus not being "real" family members, or of the parents not "really" having a family that could include so many children and often so many transient children. Again, thus not being a "real" family. Foster parents also encountered people who separated foster parents' "real" children (that is, biological children) from their foster children in conversations. Consequently, the idea that foster children were "real"—that is, were loved, cared for, and belonged with the same degree that biological children did—was a very important point for most families and is a very important part of understanding the meaning of foster parenting.

3. I often describe fostering relationships as "physically transitory" relationships since children often leave their foster homes and since women create permanent kinship relationships in the face of children's imminent departure. I also talk about fostering relationships that are physically enduring—that is, those in which the foster child does not leave but physically remains with the family, generally through adoption. It is important to note that to foster mothers there was little if any difference in the *quality* or *meaning* or *intensity* of either of these relationships. Whether a child stayed with the family in an embodied relationship or whether a child physically left to join another family, women were clear, the relationship they created with children

endured and neither was more or less permanent.

4. During my research I heard many foster parents refer to bad foster parents—people they had heard of who fostered "for the money." I relentlessly pursued the "bad foster parent" without much luck. I have concluded that while there were homes in which I was more comfortable than others, and there were families I liked better than others, the "bad" or mercenary foster parent is a cultural archetype against which many parents measured themselves and one that has been well represented in the popular media. However, it is not one that necessarily existed or existed to the degree foster parents suspected or the media portrayed (see Wozniak 1999). The significance of foster parents invoking this archetype is in their suggestion of memory's importance. By holding on to both memory and membership they define themselves as opposite those who forget or who do not curate possessions and memories and who thus accept commodity relations imposed by the state. Commodity relations are thus equated with children's impermanence—they assume the properties of a low-value and interchangeable commodity.

5. The exceptions were the few older women I interviewed who described themselves as grandmothers and saw their mothering work as short term and delimited.

6. Foster mothers' discussions of the state's inability to value children were based on their daily dealings with state social workers and with the agency as a whole. Women referred to the state losing children—that is, placing them and then forgetting where they were placed—to social workers' lack of contact with children, to their abbreviated visits and limited knowledge of children's needs, goals, or even partial history, and to the meager resources the state actually provided for children (this was especially evident during times of increased need, such as birthdays, high school proms, or when children needed sports equipment to successfully play after-school sports, or to purchase class rings).

7. This was especially true for poor foster mothers and somewhat less so for middle-class or wealthy foster mothers. However, since the majority of women fostering for the state of Connecticut were poor or working class, it was the dominant discourse. See Wozniak (1997) for additional socioeconomic data.

8. Data analysis reveals that the theme of transformation is prominent in women's discourses about their foster children (see Wozniak 1997a). This is part of the discourse of inalienability. Through the foster mother/foster child relationship the child is transformed from a state or condition to something else. This something else, in terms of health, behavior, appearance, demeanor, all become a part of what is *recognizable* as familial and was an important part of adding the child to the family. This was especially so since many of the foster child's outward behaviors or actions and even appearance initially appeared foreign or unacceptable within the foster family.

"Too Bad You Got a Lemon"

Peter Singer, Mothers of Children with Disabilities, and the Critique of Consumer Culture

GAIL LANDSMAN

The hiring of utilitarian philosopher Peter Singer as professor of bioethics at Princeton University's Center for Human Values was met with loud protest, and his speaking engagements, including an address at a government sponsored conference on genetics, continue to arouse angry voices of dissent among disability rights activists.[1] Among the most controversial points surrounding Singer are his statements that disabled infants do not necessarily qualify as persons, and that under certain circumstances it is morally acceptable to kill infants up until the twenty-eighth day after birth. In his book *Rethinking Life and Death,* Singer notes that his earlier commentary on the Baby Doe rules, published in the journal *Pediatrics* in 1983, had included the statement, "If we compare a severely defective human infant with a nonhuman animal, a dog or a pig, for example, we will often find the nonhuman to have superior capacities, both actual and potential, for rationality, self-consciousness, communication, and anything else that can plausibly be considered morally significant." This sentence generated numerous letters at the time protesting the comparison of the intellectual abilities of human beings with those of dogs or pigs. "Yet the sentence that so disturbed them," Singer claims, "is not only true, but obviously true" (Singer 1995:201).

Singer's is a stance against what he calls speciesism and lends itself well to the animal liberation movement of which he is a founding member.[2] Erasing the moral line between animals and humans, Singer argues instead on the basis of personhood, suggesting that some animals have a greater claim to personhood than do infants or severely disabled adults. By the same token, he argues, some humans fall into the same moral category as nonhuman animals. "There are many beings who are sentient and capable of experiencing pleasure and pain, but are not rational and self-conscious and so not persons. I shall refer to these beings as conscious beings. Many non-human animals almost certainly fall into this category; so must newborn infants and some intellectually disabled humans" (1993:101).

As Nora Ellen Groce and Jonathan Marks point out in a recent essay in *American Anthropologist* (2000:819), making comparisons between humans with disabilities and other species is not scientifically new; it was, they remind us, "a hallmark of the eugenics movement in American biology." More important, Groce and Marks warn, in the current context such comparisons can have devastating implications worldwide, as they potentially justify the prioritizing of scarce health care resources and rationalize doing harm to the most vulnerable segments of a society (821). As specialists in the study of human beings and of cross-cultural concepts of personhood, it would seem that anthropologists might usefully contribute to a discussion that has heretofore been carried out primarily at the crossroads of the academic domain of bioethics and the politics of disability rights. The inclusion and analysis of ethnographic data, in this case focusing not on disabled humans themselves but on the experience of those who have recently given birth to and nurtured them, can offer insight into American meanings of disability, reproduction, and lives worth living, as well as into the processes whereby those meanings may change.

While the issue of ending life is "not without complications," Singer admits, nevertheless for him "the main point is clear: killing a disabled infant is not morally equivalent to killing a person. Very often it is not wrong at all" (Singer 1993:191). Thus removed from the domain of persons in Singer's model, do infants fall into the domain of the exchangeable commodity? I propose to use the debate over Singer's position as an entry point for analyzing the relationship among concepts of personhood, the transformative experience of mothering infants with disabilities, and the commodification of babies in North American culture.

According to Singer's total utilitarian position, infants not only can but *should* be understood to be replaceable, in that the birth and continued life of a disabled infant may stand in the way of what he believes to be the more happy occasion of the birth of a normal child. In a society with readily available birth control and in which a woman may have predetermined the size of her family, one child, in essence, takes the place of another. Because raising a child with a disability often places additional financial and time demands on a family, Singer argues that allowing a disabled child to live may prevent the birth of a future child whose own life might be happier and whose family's life, less burdened by the care of a disabled child, would also presumably be happier. Thus, in addition to questions of who qualifies for personhood, predictions of the total amount of happiness are critical for determining moral action in such cases. "When the death of a disabled infant will lead to the birth of another infant with better prospects of a happy life, the total amount of happiness will be greater if the disabled infant is killed. The loss of happy life for the first infant is outweighed by the gain of a happier life for the second" (Singer 1993:186).

Harriet McBryde Johnson, a disabled lawyer, writes about her conversations with Peter Singer at Princeton, "He insists he doesn't want to kill me. He simply thinks it would have been better, all things considered, to have given my parents the option of killing the baby I once was, and to let other parents kill similar babies as they come along and thereby avoid the suffering that comes with lives like mine and satisfy the reasonable preferences of parents for a different kind of child. It has nothing to do with me. I should not feel threatened" (Johnson 2003).

Parents, Singer states, should have the right to decide to kill a newborn infant up until the age of one month; this is morally acceptable, he argues, because (1) at that age *no* infant is a person, and (2) infanticide has the advantage over abortion of allowing parents to have more information about a child's condition than might be available during pregnancy. Singer points out that most mothers, given notification through prenatal testing of a fetal abnormality, do choose abortion; they may do so because they believe the quality of life for the child, were it to be born, would be unacceptably low and/or because the burden for the family raising a disabled child would be too high. Conditions caused by birth complications, however, could not have been predicted from prenatal screening, and infanticide would therefore enable parents of children with brain damage caused at birth or with defects undetectable by current prenatal screening technologies to also have the option of discontinuing the child's life.

For this and other arguments, Singer has been targeted by, among others, the disability rights group Not Dead Yet (which also protests the right-to-die position of Jack Kevorkian), the Consortium for Citizens with Disabilities, and an Internet-based group of parents of children with disabilities calling themselves United Parents Protesting Singer (UPPS). Nevertheless, as anthropologist and disability rights advocate Adrienne Asch remarks, Singer's views are not very far out of the bioethics, public, and medical mainstream.

> I can give you a long list of names in bioethics and practices in medicine that would speak to the sentiments that Peter Singer is talking about and voicing. Furthermore, I would suspect that there is not a single person who is the parent of a child with a disability of whatever age, or the friend of someone with a disability who hasn't been looked at and clucked at with great pity and told, "You're a saint. It would be better if your child had never been born. It is so sad. You deserve so much credit. You are such a hero." There probably are a few disabled people with visible enough disabilities that the public can ceremoniously come up to them and ask, . . . "Have you considered killing yourself? . . . Are you sorry you were ever born? Wouldn't you like to be some other way?" (Asch 1999)

Asch goes on to point out that Singer is correct in stating that many women do avail themselves of technologies to diagnose fetal abnormalities, and "if they don't like the information they get, go on to have abortions of otherwise wanted children." The issue, Asch argued in her public discussion with Singer at Princeton, is therefore not Singer himself but the extent to which the public shares pieces of his views. The widespread acceptance of Singer's underlying assumptions about the lives of disabled persons is similarly acknowledged by Johnson, as she poignantly justifies why she, even as a disabled person and disability rights activist, cannot bring herself to hate Peter Singer.

> If I define Singer's kind of disability prejudice as an ultimate evil, and him as a monster, then I must so define all who believe disabled lives are inherently worse off or that a life without a certain kind of consciousness lacks value. That definition would make monsters of many of the people with whom I move on the sidewalks, do business, break bread, swap stories and share the grunt work of local politics. It would reach some of my family and most of my nondisabled friends, people who show me personal kindness and who sometimes manage to love me through their ignorance. I can't live with a definition of ultimate evil that encompasses all of them. I can't refuse the monster-majority basic respect and human sympathy. It's not in my heart to deny every single one of them, categorically, my affection and my love. The peculiar drama of my life has placed me in a world that by and large thinks it would be better if people like me did not exist. (Johnson 2003)

It is precisely this—not the extreme consequences Singer proposes, but rather the broad availability and public sharing of many of the ideas upon which they are based—that interests us as anthropologists. Not in Singer's view alone is it culturally acceptable for the worth of a disabled child to be compared to the worth of another type of child and to be found wanting.

In what sense do Singer's arguments have resonance with mainstream views of personhood, reproduction, and lives worth living? And under what conditions do these views come to appear as problematic? Analysis of narratives of mothers of infants and toddlers diagnosed with, or at risk for, disabilities suggests that the experience of mothering a disabled child foregrounds the widespread presence of a North American discourse in which infants are categorized as commodities.[3] This experience in many instances leads to the development by mothers of a critique of the commodification of the reproductive process and of children themselves. Mothers' critique of commodification, often defined by professionals as denial but understood by mothers as acquired knowledge, in turn both converges and conflicts with the discourse of disability rights.

Infants as Commodities

Out of the total range of things available in any society, Igor Kopytoff reminds us, only some of them are available for marking as commodities (1986:64).

Commodities have use value and can be exchanged in discrete transactions; the transaction itself indicates that a counterpart has an equivalent value. Salability and exchangeability for other things thus suggests that an item has something in common with other exchangeable items that, "taken together, partake of a single universe of comparable values." In other words, Kopytoff points out, to be saleable or exchangeable is to be common, as opposed to singular, unique, and therefore not exchangeable for anything else (69).

In contemporary Western thought, Kopytoff points out, there exists a commonsense divide between commodities and noncommodities: that between things and people. That is, the universe of commodities is understood to comprise things (physical objects and rights in them), while at the opposite pole we place people, who "represent the natural universe of individuation and singularization" (64). In the West, then, the establishment of personhood is critical for defining a human being as outside the realm of commoditization. Human beings to whom personhood has been attributed are neither salable nor exchangeable; each is unique and irreplaceable. Human beings who fall outside the category of full person are, in contrast, potentially replaceable.

As reproductive body parts and processes (including eggs and gestation) are increasingly subject to sale in the marketplace, the relationship of reproductive technologies to baby selling has become a topic of heated public debate. The distinction, for instance, between public attitudes toward commercial versus altruistic surrogacy (Baker 1996; Cannell 1990; Ragoné 1994, 1999) can be attributed to the existing cultural exclusion of full persons from the commodity domain and to the cultural opposition of the public world of paid employment and the presumed "natural" world of motherhood and family. The motives of surrogate mothers who are paid to carry a baby for a commissioning couple are therefore more suspect than those who do it as a "gift of love" for an infertile relative (Narayan 1995), just as foster mothering in the United States is culturally "tainted" by the fact that foster mothers accept financial reimbursement from the state (Wozniak 2002).

The blatant commercialism of the "Ron's Angels" Web site, in which the ova of physically attractive women were to be auctioned to the highest bidder, provoked public disdain. Public acceptance of new reproductive technologies in contemporary Euro-American culture, on the other hand, may be aided by the use of naturalizing language—that is, language that presents reproductive technology as simply lending nature a helping hand (see Franklin 1997), enabling natural instincts for parenthood to be realized (Cannell 1990; Ragoné 1994), or, as in the case of gestational surrogacy, ensuring what is seen as the more natural, genetic relatedness of parents and child (Ragoné 1999). Such language diverts attention from the financial transactions involved in procreation under these conditions. As Ann Anagnost (this volume) reveals, a "resignification of the meaning of monetary exchanges" characterizes not only the use of new conceptive technologies, but that of international adoptions as well. Anagnost documents "rhetorics of disavowal" through which adoptive mothers of Chinese girls attempt to keep at bay the "anxiety that a child might be a commodity" as a consequence of "baby flights," tour packages, and financial transactions with adoption agencies. The recent possibilities of using technologies for purposes of selecting specific traits of children such as sex or compatibility for bone marrow donation have opened up even more arenas for public controversy over the commodification of reproduction. The question emerges: Are we shopping for babies? A large literature, much of it feminist, has focused our attention on just these issues (Corea 1987; Hershey 1994; Rothman 1989, 1992; Rowland 1992; Schmidt and Moore 1998).

But regardless of what commercial arrangements might have been made in order to bring a specific baby into a family, once there, the normal baby in contemporary North American culture is considered a person and is decommodified; rather than being salable, the child itself is now "priceless." When a baby or young child is diagnosed with a disability, however, the cultural attribution of full personhood is far from assured. Giving birth to and nurturing an anomalous child reveals to a woman the presence of competing cultural categorizations, which in some instances do relegate children to the domain of commodity exchange.

Consumption Practices in Pregnancy and the Futility of Choice

In the contemporary United States, mothers of infants with disabilities are not seen as morally equivalent to mothers of normal children (Landsman 1999:135). Compared to mothers of normal children, mothers of children with disabilities are seen either as better—"special" mothers chosen by God to have special children or, worse, as "bad" mothers who through their drug use and irresponsible behavior during pregnancy cause imperfect children. The much publicized teenage mothers of "crack" babies epitomize the latter.

According to Daniel Miller's theory of shopping, there exists a normative expectation that most shoppers will subordinate their desires to a concern for others. Shopping for commodities is, in this scheme, an act of love, in which love is a practice compatible with feelings of responsibility and obligation (Miller 1998a:18–19). Housewives, researching their families' preferences as well as trying to influence their eating habits for the better, assume they are acting on their basic responsibilities as wives and mothers; shopping in supermarkets, Miller claims, is a major form in which love is manifested (18).

Similarly, in pursuing normal, healthy babies, pregnant women are publicly expected to subordinate their own desires—such as for caffeine or alcohol—for the health of the baby and to consume instead according to a particular pattern. By sacrificing one's personal desires during pregnancy on the one hand, and by consuming specific goods and services—food deemed nutritious for the fetus, prenatal vitamins, expert prenatal health care, prenatal screening tests, pregnancy guidebooks—on the other, pregnant American women, like Miller's North London housewives whose grocery shopping becomes a "means by which relationships of love and care are constituted by practice" (Miller 1998a:18), also turn their expenditures into a devotional ritual that affirms the transcendent force of the baby-to-be.

Miller himself refers to the rise of the infant as the object of contemporary devotion; he calls on his observations of the emphasis among middle-class London mothers upon "the infant as a recipient of their shopping," which he considers part of "an obsessional concern with what foods, clothing and other materials infants should be allowed to consume or be prevented from consuming" (Miller 1998a:124). Among American women this devotion to the infant may be present well before birth and may be manifested in women's consumption practices during pregnancy. My research suggests that during pregnancy a woman acknowledges that there is within her body a subject-in-the-making for whose health she is ultimately responsible and in whose interests she makes many of her choices in the marketplace. Living in a society in which signs in restaurants and bars publicly proclaim that pregnant women should refrain from alcohol consumption, cereal boxes remind her to eat folic acid, and pregnant drug users may be subject to arrest (Biskupic 2000; Roberts 1991), a woman's very consumption practices mark her as pregnant and help to create and verify for her and others the existence of this transcendent baby-to-be. At the time, she is not seeking to "buy" the perfect baby; rather, through her consumer choices, she is manifesting love for and responsibility toward the child she carries.[4]

Thus, inherent in the image of the "bad mother" is the assumption that the pregnant woman, who was supposed to have been involved in self-sacrifice, instead consumed on her own behalf, not showing proper devotion to the baby. Indeed, as I have documented elsewhere (Landsman 1998), few women, *upon first hearing about their child's disability,* failed to reflect upon their behavior during pregnancy.[5] Questions of whether eating particular foods, working too much or too late in the pregnancy, having an alcoholic beverage before knowing one was pregnant, or using a painkiller such as ibuprofen or acetaminophen might have caused the child to have a defect were the norm for women in the study. But as time went on, these same mothers themselves came to claim that compliance with recommended consumption practices, be it dietary regulation or undergoing prenatal testing, simply did not and could not bring about the results promised. Jenna Mosher, a teacher at a private girls' high school, talked about finding out a year earlier that her infant son had a chromosomal anomaly that would cause him to have multiple disabilities, including profound mental retardation, vision impairment, speech delay, and severe motor impairments.

"All I could think of was, God, this is my first child. I did everything right during my pregnancy. I didn't have one cup of coffee. I ate all organic food, exercised. How come someone who doesn't take care of themselves and doesn't even want the kid, has a completely normal child? Yeah, I went through that. Why am I being punished, what did I do, I must have been really bad in a past life. Now do I ask myself why? I don't really. That was more of a response to the shock of discovering it all, I think."

The vast majority of mothers in the study reported modifying consumption practices in their daily routines in order to ensure the birth of a healthy, normal child. They attempted to comply with advice they received from medical staff or through public media and/or friends and relatives regarding diet, often reducing or eliminating intake of otherwise desired foods and beverages such as those containing caffeine, excessive sugar, or alcohol. Most reported taking special vitamins; getting exercise; obtaining prenatal care early in the pregnancy; and abstaining from the use of tobacco, illegal drugs, and even prescription and over-the-counter medications. Most utilized whatever prenatal screening and diagnostic tests were offered to them. In this sense, as I have pointed out elsewhere (Landsman 1999:148), mothers in this study can be understood as analogous to what James Carrier has called "Wise Shoppers." "Wise Shoppers" actively exercise choice. They invest effort prior to and during the act of shopping itself, thereby stamping their commodities with personal identity (Carrier 1990: 586–88). But neither "wise shopping" nor the practice of what Miller calls "devotional duty" could in this case bring the desired or expected result. As a consequence, many mothers reflect upon what they *now* define as their prior assumption that babies could be shopped for, for there is no real control over what you get, no real choice. In the words of Denise Rivers, a married medical transcriber whose young daughter has cognitive and physical impairments due to hydrocephaly, "This is not my choice. This is not your choice.[6] These are not our choices. These are not choices that we were given. You never grow up in school saying, I'm going to grow up and have a handicapped child. . . . This is a whole new 'here it is, take care of it, handle it' situation, you know."

On Calculating Happiness and the Exchangeability of Children

Singer suggests that it is possible to develop a calculus of human happiness. If the death of a disabled child would lead to a greater total amount of happiness—that is, more happiness for more people—the child could justifiably be killed as long as it is within the time period before which a child could be expected to have self-awareness. The disabled infant would then be replaced by a healthy child to be born later. Singer discusses this in terms of the birth of a baby diagnosed as a hemophiliac, noting that, in fact, most hemophiliacs themselves do find life definitely worth living. In the scenario Singer presents, however, "the parents, daunted by the prospect of bringing up a child with this condition, are not anxious for him to live." Under such conditions, Singer asks, can we defend euthanasia? Singer answers in the affirmative.

> The total view makes it necessary to ask whether the death of the haemophiliac infant would lead to the creation of another being who would not otherwise have existed. In other words, if the haemophiliac child is killed, will his parents have another child whom they would not have if the haemophiliac child lives? If they would, is the second child likely to have a better life than the one killed?
>
> Often it will be possible to answer both these questions affirmatively. A woman may plan to have two children. If one dies while she is of child-bearing age, she may conceive another in its place. Suppose a woman planning to have two children has one normal child, and then gives birth to a hemophiliac child. The burden of caring for that child may make it impossible for her to cope with a third child; but if the disabled child were to die, she would have another. It is also plausible to suppose that the prospects of a happy life are better for a normal child than for a haemophiliac.
>
> When the death of a disabled infant will lead to the birth of another infant with better prospects of a happy life, the total amount of happiness will be greater if the disabled infant is killed. (Singer 1993:186)

When considering "normal children," the idea of trading one live child for another in American culture appears abhorrent. Exchangeability, a basic feature of the commodity, is out of place in the domain of full persons. But as I and other scholars have described elsewhere, in many cultures, including the United States, disability denies, delays, or diminishes personhood (Hrdy 1999; Landsman 1998, 2000; Scheper-Hughes 1990; Weiss 1994; Whyte and Ingstad 1985). Thus, once disability enters the picture, the door is opened for the language of commodification. Upon diagnosis of disability, a fetus or a young child may publicly move from "baby" (person) into the commodity state—that is, it may come to occupy what Appadurai refers to as the "commodity-situation . . . the situation in which its exchangeability (past, present, future) for some other thing is its socially relevant feature" (1986:13).[7]

This transition is not without moral ambiguity for pregnant American women. In her study of women and prenatal diagnosis, Rayna Rapp (1999:138) found that white middle-class women in particular expressed a preoccupation with selfishness and self-actualization; they melded the right to abort a disabled fetus with the right to plan an adult life. Reserving the right to choose what type of baby to bring into the world, these women were at the same time self-critical about their motives. Rapp's finding suggests that in utilizing prenatal testing and selective abortion for disability, some pregnant women do see the themselves as "shopping" for babies but describe themselves doing so in Miller's sense of shopping, making choices *based on love* for family members, existing or potential. A pregnant woman receiving a positive test result for a chromosomal anomaly, for instance, may conclude that regardless of the mother's own desires to bear a child, the quality of life would be unbearably low for the disabled infant, or the burden for other family members, particularly siblings, would be too great if the baby were to be born. She may conclude, perhaps, that she herself is not strong or "selfless" enough to give a disabled child a good life; or she may believe that only "special" women are capable of mothering a child with special needs and qualities (Landsman 1999). Rapp finds that recent immigrant women, especially those from Central America, South America, and the Caribbean, also act on concerns that a sick baby will be an obstacle to their project of geographic and social mobility (Ginsburg and Rapp 1999:294). In all these situations, exchanging a potential disabled child for a potential "normal" child can be represented either as selfishness *or* as an act based on motherly love and commitment to family.

For the mother nurturing an *existing* child with a disability, however, the language of commodification is brought to the fore for a specific, living child in her care. Full personhood, the very quality that disqualifies a being from commodity exchange, is now in question for her child. Many mothers' narratives describe a sense that a woman must justify her continued investment in what is publicly perceived as a defective commodity. Tina Graham, whose child is mentally retarded, explains:

> I did have a few people say things to me like, "Oh, I'm sorry," and trying to console you in some fashion or another and make comments like, "Well, you can always have more." You're like, well, I happen to love the one I've got now.... "Too bad you got a lemon." It sounds like that coming from some people almost, and we even had one woman say to us, she said, "Well, now you need to decide if you're going to sink your whole life into Jonathan or if you're going to have more kids and create a normal family environment." And I thought to myself, what is she saying by that, you know?

The metaphor of "getting a lemon" in common parlance refers to the purchase of a defective automobile and implies that one was cheated or did not get what one paid for. "Lemon laws" enacted in all fifty states are designed to protect consumers from continued investment in the maintenance and repair of hopelessly and permanently defective products. For instance, New York's "lemon law" (General Business Law, section 198-a. Warranties) states that if within a specified period a manufacturer or its agents "are unable to repair or correct any defect or condition which substantially impairs the value of the motor vehicle to the consumer after a reasonable number of attempts, the manufacturer ... shall replace the motor vehicle ... or accept return of the vehicle from the consumer and refund to the consumer the full purchase price." Similarly, California's lemon law (California Civil Code Section 1793.22) requires that if a manufacturer cannot fix a vehicle to conform to the warranty within a reasonable number of repair attempts, the manufacturer may be required to replace the vehicle or reimburse the buyer for its purchase price. No level of commitment to maintenance and repair will bring a "lemon" up to normal acceptable standards, and thus such a product should be considered replaceable. The metaphor of child as lemon thus implies that the child is a permanently substandard commodity in which a parent's ongoing investment of resources and energy is futile. No amount of medical treatment, rehabilitative therapy, special education, or mother's love will result in the child reaching standards of normality; only the birth of a normal child in its place (physically and/or emotionally) can bring about "a normal family environment."

Patricia Marks, who adopted twin very low birth weight premature girls at high risk for cerebral palsy and numerous other disabilities, found herself noticing a similar attitude in the public response to her children. She tells of taking the babies to visit in her older son's classroom. "One of the teachers in his grade came right up to me and said, 'When are you going to know if they're okay?' And I said, 'Not for years.' 'Well, what are you going to do then?' I knew what she was asking, and I said, 'Whatever it takes.' I had to bite my tongue and not say, 'No, we are not sending them back.' This was not a 'we come with an exchange policy.'"

Mothers recognize that it is society's lower valuation of their child that makes it necessary for them to justify their parental investment (that is, "sinking their whole life into the child") and possible for others (as well as themselves, perhaps) to imagine replacing one child with another. Jenna Mosher stated, for instance, that "right after Victor was born, I wanted to have another child immediately. Because I just felt so gypped on my whole experience." Taylor (2000:415) has pointed out that while in a consumer-capitalist society pregnancy and the fetus have increasingly been experienced as commodities available for consumption, at the same time the fetus is, with the help of technology, increasingly construed as a person from its earliest moments; I would argue, however, that in the case of a fetus or child found to have permanent disability, this very personhood is often rescinded. The following poem written by a birthmother who chose to give her disabled baby up for adoption speaks to the issue of not getting what one bargained for; in this poem we see the subject shift from a state of personhood as a wanted fetus into the commodity situation as a disabled baby:

I feel so cheated.
You were so perfect, my little one
the small life inside of me
my tummy still flat, I knew you were growing
the first flutter
then a kick
A boy or a girl? We wondered
But never would you be right
the whole time you grew
from pinpoint tiny to person-sized
you were never right
never perfect
We rejoiced and planned
we raised glasses to toast and
cried tears of joy
through autumn, then winter
You kicked and stretched
my tummy swelled
But even then
you were different
even then
you didn't look like us
or think like us
Precious as you were, a life we created
you weren't the baby we'd waited for (J.W.S. in Finnegan 1993:9)

Mothers in my study, all of whom voluntarily kept and are raising their disabled children, responded to the notion that children are exchangeable commodities in at least two ways. It is important to recognize that although the two responses may appear contradictory, they may nevertheless be expressed by the same woman at different times. One response, often presented in mothers' narratives in the context of interactions with physicians, is to highlight that the child has value and is worthy of commitment because he or she has the potential to overcome disability—that is, the child will not necessarily be disabled in the future. Another response, to be discussed later, is the conviction that the child is valuable and worthy of love and commitment regardless of his or her permanent disabilities.

A common character in mothers' stories utilizing the first response are doctors who are interpreted by mothers as having "written off" their kids. An example, taken from an interview with Becky Romano, mother of a child with a chromosomal anomaly, follows. "So the thing I was upset with Dr. Jones about is he had formed his opinion before he even walked into the room. He told us that.

He said, "When I read the report, I knew this child was going to be severely retarded." And I says, "Well, as you can see now, he's not." And he told me he would never be self-sufficient. He would never go to college. And you don't say 'never' in my vocabulary!"

Similar stories are told about doctors who reported a child might never live through the night, might never speak, never walk, etc. While common among the mothers of infants *newly* diagnosed with disability whom I interviewed, the theme of overcoming disability made only a small appearance in the public debate over Peter Singer's appointment to Princeton. During the fall of 1999, parents on a Down syndrome listserv engaged in discussion that led to a protest action over Singer, called United Parents Protesting Singer (UPPS). In September of that year, a woman named Catherine reminded listserv readers to "always keep in our minds the stories of people in comas whose families have stood by with hope and faith for months against all medical advice and have seen them emerge well and whole."

Doctors and nurses commonly refer to parents who reject diagnoses of disability as being in denial. Physicians often give what are perceived as more pessimistic prognoses out of concern for parents' needs to "face reality." Reality is often uncertain, however. Numerous studies have indicated the difficulties involved in predicting cerebral palsy within the first year of life, for instance (Dubowitz et al. 1984; Harris 1987; Nelson and Ellenberg 1982), and note high rates of false positives for various assessment tools (Bierman-van Eedenburg et al. 1981; Morgan and Aldag 1996). And, according to the American Academy of Pediatrics (2001), research shows that when pediatricians use only clinical impressions rather than formal screening tools, estimates of children's developmental status are even less accurate. Mothers are rarely aware of this research. However, they do incorporate examples of their own child having overcome past dismal predictions within a larger story that represents the child as currently experiencing a developmental delay that will eventually, with a child's perseverance and a mother's hard work, be overcome in the future. This concept of developmental delay thus leaves the future open, with parents able to retain hope that their child will not, in the future, fit into the category of the seriously disabled. Personhood is here attributed and justified in terms of the projected impermanence of the label "disabled" (see Landsman 2003). Disability itself remains a threat to personhood.

It is in part this focus of some parents—their concern to find a "cure" and/or their linkage of their child's value to the child's valiant efforts to overcome disability—that place parents and the disability rights movement at cross-purposes. That is, the latter opposes the viewpoint that they refer to as the "cure 'em or kill 'em" mentality. Many disability rights activists argue for a social or civil rights model of disability that locates the impediments to a high quality of life not within the body of the disabled person (such that the person should be cured, put out of his/her misery, or prevented from being born in the first place), but rather within the society that discriminates against persons with disabilities. Indeed, they argue, a life with an impairment is well worth living; oppressive social conditions and inaccessible built environments are what disable individuals born with or acquiring impairments. The "Statement of the Disability Rights Education and Defense Fund (DREDF) Against the Philosophy of Peter Singer" complains that "in his work on the ethics of killing disabled infants he (Singer) makes little distinction between the barriers imposed on people with disabilities by society and the inherent limitations of a physical or mental disability." By ignoring the body of work of international scholars from a social model perspective, the DREDF statement claims "Singer tacitly permits socially sustained barriers to justify infanticide rather than addressing the injustice of these barriers" (DREDF 2002). As for the suffering of the family raising the child with disabilities or the burden to society, those are less the inherent consequence of an individual's disability, the disability rights position holds, than of "a society that fails to provide adequate resources, and sees disabled people as a financial burden and a drain on scarce resources" (Triano 1999).

Singer's miscalculation, many disability rights activists therefore argue, lies in his assumption, shared by many, that there can be a calculus of happiness for an individual determined by the presence or absence of impairments. "I question his replacement-baby theory, with its assumption of 'other things equal,'" Harriett McBryde states. "I draw out a comparison of myself and my nondisabled brother Mac (the next-born after me), each of us with a combination of gifts and flaws so peculiar that we can't be measured on the same scale" (Johnson 2003). Anne Finger, under the penname "Peter Stinker," writes a satiric piece, "with apologies to Jonathan Swift," entitled "A Modest Proposal for Preventing Disabled Children from Being a Burden to Their Parents and Society, and for Making Them Beneficial to the Public." Mocking the assumption that one can measure the value of one life versus another, the "proposal," published in the disability rights online journal *Ragged Edge*, notes that while malnutrition is rampant in the nonindustrialized world, "the lives of disabled infants are sustained at enormous social cost in the neonatal intensive care units of modern hospitals. . . . These infants will, of course, survive only to live lives which are nothing but pitiable and miserable." As a solution, the proposal's supposed author satirically suggests firstly diverting the money "heretofore wasted" on preservation of the lives of grossly deformed infants to the nurturance of the nonhandicapped of the Third World; and, secondly, that these disabled infants be slaughtered and their carcasses sold on the open market as luxury food, with proceeds donated to charities (Finger 2002). In the perspective of disabled adults actively opposing Singer's position, people are not defined, nor their futures determined, by their disabilities. Asch argues with Singer:

> I think it is simply wrong to say that you can put all desires, pleasures, goals, on one calculator and one measure and decide that life without disability is always better than life with it. One could say that life without disability means that you don't have to expect a certain number of problems, but that's all you can say. It doesn't mean anything else about what that life will consist of . . . I want to argue that the reasons that people wish to terminate the lives of disabled newborns, the reasons that physicians have given for withholding treatment, the reasons that many people choose abortion of their diagnosed fetuses, flow from many of the same views that Singer holds and they are misguided views: assuming that there is only one standard of what makes a life valuable. (Asch 1999)

Many mothers' narratives in this study indicated self-reflection on just this point: that they themselves had once held views that put forth a single standard of value and that they have since come to reject such views. The recognition that one's child is a valuable life as it is, regardless of whether or not the child "progresses," thus is another stance that mothers of children with disabilities may take. But it is important to note that the research suggests this stance is *acquired,* the outgrowth of the act of mothering. It is through the process of nurturing children who fail to meet cultural standards that the commodification of infants in American culture is highlighted. Many mothers reinterpret their own behavior during pregnancy in these terms. What during *pregnancy* women had understood as their efforts to do what was best for the baby and family, mothers *now* represent negatively as "shopping" for the "perfect" baby. As Suzanne Dalton explains, "I mean, of course, I always think, you know, when we had had those discussions earlier on in the pregnancy, what if the child had Down Syndrome. . . . I mean, I wouldn't say punishment, but this is the answer that you wanted the perfect child. How selfish of you for wanting perfect children, you know. Children come in all different ways and I would have to say, if anyone asked, that I would say I have the perfect children."

Rejecting their public image as irresponsible producers of defective merchandise or duped consumers ending up with flawed commodities in which they tragically, perhaps even nobly, continue to invest, these mothers now provide a critique of consumer culture. It is not only that there is no real choice or control over what you get that makes it impossible to "shop" for babies, they suggest, but that each child is singular and unique; unlike cars, children cannot be compared to each other according to a set standard of functional or aesthetic qualities. In telling their stories, mothers position themselves against the public discourse which would have, as Singer proposes, a normal child replace a flawed one; in essence, against a cultural "lemon law" for defective children. "Before I knew Billy was handicapped, I still had that regret that it wasn't a girl," Becky Romano commented. "Well, people ask me now and I say, 'I don't care if somebody handed me twin baby girls, infants, right now, to swap for Billy, I wouldn't,'" she continued. Pam Karcher's son has Asperger's syndrome, a disorder on the autistic spectrum. Talking to a friend who was pregnant and worried about her ability to cope if the baby was born with a defect, Pam reassured her, "Chances are you're going to have a healthy baby . . . But if you don't, I'm like 'look at him. . . . I wouldn't take it back,' and so, no, I don't wish I didn't have him or you know, I'm like that's not even thinkable." So, too, Tara Vernon, mother of a young girl diagnosed with autism, reflects upon the irreplaceability of specific children. Apologizing for crying during the interview, she explains, "I think that's one reason I don't bring it up with people. It's because lots of times I do end up getting weepy, and I don't want them to think it's because I don't love Nicole, because . . . if somebody said I could have a normal child, I would definitely say 'no.'" What is significant here is not only that these mothers claim they would not exchange their children, but that they are, or imagine being, asked whether they would do so. Their stories suggest that Asch and Johnson are correct in claiming that Singer's views are widely shared.

Indeed, mothers sometimes describe their own earlier failures to attribute personhood to their disabled infant. Jane Sawyer's baby was born prematurely with a very low birth weight and later was diagnosed with cerebral palsy. She describes the experience of first seeing her child in the neonatal intensive care unit and of only later coming to accept that this was indeed a person. "I definitely looked at it as a tragedy. I mean, I didn't see one—I didn't see her as her, I didn't have the attachment to her. As a matter of fact, I think the first time I held her, I probably felt that, where I looked at her more than—I guess I saw her as a *baby*, and not as something that—a terrible thing that just happened."

On Determining Lives Worth Living

Research suggests that parents of disabled children rate the predicted quality of life for hypothetical conditions of infants higher than do health professionals, and that parents are particularly more accepting of the more severely impaired health states than are health professionals (Saigal et al. 1999). Representing UPPS, "Emily's mom" writes on the Internet that her group "would like to send a personal message to Princeton University and the world: our children are enjoying their lives and we are enjoying our children."

The inappropriateness of measuring or comparing the value of children based on the single criterion of disability, which emerged over time in the narratives told by mothers I interviewed, became the theme of parents' organized political action. Mary Wilt, a Virginia Beach nurse and mother of a child with Down syndrome, had been doing a search on the Internet when she happened upon information on Peter Singer. She became "appalled that everybody wasn't appalled," shocked that this was "going down smoothly" among medical professionals and among "people who had no life experience." Spreading the word about Singer's appointment on a Down syndrome listserv on the Internet and communicating by e-mail with disability studies scholars and activists, Wilt and others began to develop a strategy to get their voices heard. Consisting primarily of what Wilt calls a "bunch of mad moms" and organized through the Internet, UPPS eventually set up a Web site and collected what she estimates to be about a thousand e-mails and several hundred letters that were hand delivered by protesters to the president of Princeton University (Wilt 2003).

Writing to the listserv, Wilt explains that "the danger of Singer is NOT that he asks hard questions, NOT that he rubs our noses in some of our own hypocrisy, and NOT that he talks about quality of life issues. It's the conclusions he comes to that disability AND NO OTHER CRITERIA is a reason in and of itself to declare someone's life of less 'quality' and therefore less worth." Quality of life was portrayed by UPPS members during the protest as less dependent on impairment than on whether a child was valued and given a place within some human community. "How about including letters from our grandparents, aunts, uncles, cousins, teachers and neighbors who love our kids and think them worthwhile, too," suggests another mother on the listserv. Calculation of a person's value, yet another contributor suggests, cannot be done "without putting into the equation the identity of who is doing the valuing ... Absolute objectivity is neither desirable nor possible."

Through nurturance, women not only redefine criteria for personhood but also appear to be recalculating what counts in determining quality of life, both for their child and for themselves. In these arguments we see maternal, affective labor (Anagnost, this volume) celebrated not only, as in earlier examples, for its potential to move a child from the disabled to nondisabled category (and thus to full personhood as defined by mainstream culture); but for its role in both recognizing and validating the personhood of a *permanently* disabled child. It is here that the discourse of mothers of disabled children converges with that of adult disability rights activists using the social model. And indeed, UPPS coordinated its protest both with the disability activist group Not Dead Yet and with disability studies scholars (Wilt 2003).

In claiming to have come to reassess what really matters in life, American mothers of disabled children may critique consumer culture but do not necessarily remove themselves from active consumerism in regards to their children. What are we to make of this apparent contradiction? Scholars have addressed the way that material objects validate identity and personhood for fetuses (Layne 1999c; Taylor 2000b). On the surface of it, the same process might seem to be taking place here; buying consumer goods for a disabled child involves recognizing that the child is a person and valued enough to justify expenditure of a family's funds. Yet many mothers of disabled children claim to purchase consumer goods for their children not as a public or private expression of their own belief that real persons have, need, or are entitled to consumer goods, but rather as a conscious and active strategy to protect their children from the burden of added discrimination in a commodity-driven culture that sadly fails to recognize their child's true identity and value. Thus the mother of a deaf child in the study is concerned to make sure her child is well supplied with Disney and Sesame Street characters to help ensure the girl's ability to socialize with future nondisabled peers. Kim Boland, mother to a boy with Down syndrome and autism, is willing to purchase items beyond what her son's Medicaid covers because "you know your kid gets picked on if he wears cheap sneakers. You know they're going to get picked on if they look different, if they act different . . . When we first got him glasses we had Medicaid, and all Medicaid wanted to cover was those big plastic, cat eye, ugly . . . I'm like, 'Why do they do that?' This kid has enough problems without having to be picked on about his glasses . . . we'll always make sure that he has at least the things that make him look the same as the other kids." And Patricia Marks makes sure to dress well and carefully her twin daughters, who have cerebral palsy. "I make a point when we go out that they look spectacular . . . without it being, you know, overkill . . . because I always want the first thing that they hear somebody say is 'How pretty you look' or 'How pretty you are' . . . before you get the 'How come you've got those on your legs?' or 'Why do you wear glasses?' or whatever." These women are concerned to purchase culturally approved material items for their disabled children, but do so within a critique of the commodification of babies and of consumer culture more generally; they describe themselves consuming as a conscious strategy to shield their children from emotional pain and to foster acceptance of their children within a public less knowledgeable than they of the true worth of children with disabilities. Not able to change a society that commodifies children, they purchase so as to help their children fit into that society.

Peter Singer and the Complications of Love

Mothers in the study generally credit love for their reinterpretations of pregnancy and of disability: to the love they have for their child, and for the "gift" of knowledge of unconditional love given to them by their child (see Landsman 1999). Mothers of infants and toddlers with disabilities recognize and critique the discourse of commodity exchange of children in large part because it reduces the personhood of those they love; at the same time, they describe their acknowledgment of their disabled infant's personhood as a *consequence* of love. But immediate and unconditional mother love, as scholars have shown (Hrdy 1999; Scheper-Hughes 1990; Weiss 1994) and as these mothers attest, is not necessarily a universal script. Mothers throughout the world abandon disabled (and other unwanted) children, give them up for adoption, or let them die from neglect. "Scrutinizing newborn group members is a primate universal," Sarah

Hrdy (1999:463) tells us. "But consciously deciding whether or not to keep a baby is uniquely human."

How then do the narratives of mothers of infants with disabilities speak to the issues raised by Singer? Let us take one small excerpt. Here a mother describes the first days after learning that her newborn son was born with agenesis of the corpus callosum, that is, without the part of the brain that connects the right and left hemispheres. "I remember when he was born wishing that I didn't love him, wishing I could just give him away and that we didn't have to bring him home," Lorraine Hamilton tells me. "But it was too late; I was already, we were in the hospital for 5 days and had to stay a little longer because he was having feeding problems . . . It was too late, I was already in love with him."

On the one hand, this statement might lend support to Singer's argument favoring infanticide. Singer recognizes that once a life is well established, parents become committed to that life, possibly forgoing the birth of a normal child and resulting in a reduced total amount of happiness. Better, Singer suggests, to end the life of that child early and replace it with a normal child with a projected higher quality of life and fewer burdens to bear for the family.

What Singer fails to account for in his calculus of parental happiness, however, are the changes and redefinitions mothers claim are generated by love and nurturing. This study suggests that while most American women would indeed choose for their children to live without disabilities, and do often hope for and work toward cures (placing them at odds with the discourse of the disability rights movement), through the act of mothering a child with disabilities they also come to redefine the criteria for happiness and for lives worth living. The variables involved in determining the relation between personhood and disability in the United States are thus not only class, race, ethnicity, religion, or resources, important as these are, but also personal experience. "As far as maximizing happiness is concerned, he needn't worry about me. David (disabled son) has shown me the real meaning of that word," writes one mother to the Down syndrome listserv regarding Singer. "We are the experts here. You people making judgments about our children's worth and quality of life simply do NOT know what you are talking about!! Let us show you!!" Mary Wilt describes as the parent group UPPS's most important message to Singer's supporters. Singer is wrong, the parents organized against him argued, not because of flaws in his logic but because he lacks concrete knowledge they have acquired through acts of nurturance of unique, particular, disabled children. Access to this information, they suggest, would alter Singer's conclusions.

Disability rights activist Harriet McBryde Johnson (2003) points out that as a "disability pariah," she struggles

> for a place, for kinship, for community, for connection. Because I am still seeking acceptance of my humanity, Singer's call to get past species

seems a luxury way beyond my reach. My goal isn't to shed the perspective that comes from a particular experience, but to give voice to it. . . . As a shield from the terrible purity of Singer's vision, I'll look to the corruption that comes from interconnectedness. To justify my hopes that Singer's theoretical world—and its entirely logical extensions—won't become real, I'll invoke the muck and mess and undeniable reality of disabled lives well lived.

It is here, in the "corruption that comes from interconnectedness," that the position of mothers I interviewed as well as those who organized against Singer's appointment, converges with that of disability rights activists. Unlike academic theorists pursuing logical arguments, or medical experts who so often appear to pit their knowledge against that of parents and of disabled people themselves, mothers raising disabled children also live and love in the "muck and mess and undeniable reality" of disabled lives. With this experience comes new knowledge. Finding herself having to justify her investment in what is culturally represented as a product of permanently reduced value, many an American mother of a child with disabilities returns that child to the domain of "individuation and singularization" that characterizes persons and offers a critique of the consumer culture that devalues her child in particular and commodifies babies in general. Peter Singer, seeking to increase happiness, would save us from the heavy burdens that love brings upon us. Others would say they have learned that a life that would deny love's burdens is itself not worth living.

NOTES

This article is based on research funded by the National Endowment for the Humanities, Program in Humanities Studies of Science and Technology, from 1995 to 1998. The work would have been impossible without the goodwill, trust, and time generously extended by the women who participated in the study; I will forever be indebted to them for all that they shared with me. I am also grateful to Dr. Anthony Malone, section head of Developmental Pediatrics at the Children's Hospital at Albany Medical Center, for providing a supportive environment in which to conduct participant observation and to recruit interviewees for the study; and for engaging in an ongoing and productive discussion of my research findings. Mary Wilt and Susan Thomas were most kind and generous in providing valuable information about the efforts of parents to organize a protest against Peter Singer. Thanks also go to Linda Layne, Janelle Taylor, Margaret Lock, and Ichiro Numazaki for their useful comments on earlier versions of this chapter.

1. Peter Singer was invited as a keynote speaker at a conference sponsored by the New Hampshire Governor's Commission on Disability, scheduled for October 2001. The conference was entitled "Genetics: Ethical Concerns of the Disability Community"; in August 2001 Diane Coleman, president of the disability rights organization Not Dead Yet wrote a letter to the executive director of the Governor's Commission objecting to Singer's participation. Not Dead Yet's position was that Singer is not just controversial but dangerous in that "he advocates changes in public policy that would deprive millions of people with cognitive disabilities equal protection of the law and allow those

who do not meet his fuzzy criteria for 'personhood' to be killed by medical professionals with the 'consent' of their parents" (Coleman 2001). Speaking for the Governor's Commission on Disability, Executive Director Michael Jenkins replied that Singer had been invited precisely because he represents a "philosophy which shows that we, as a society, may well be on our way to an ethical and moral abyss as we ascribe less and less value to those who are 'less than perfect'" (Jenkins 2001). The New Hampshire Executive Council voted to allow the commission to have Singer at the conference but blocked the use of state funds to pay his fee, a fee that Singer later waived. Singer's appearance divided the disability rights movement, with some arguing in favor of having members of the disability community openly "take Singer on" in debates with prominent disability rights figures, and others claiming that the invitation provides a form of legitimacy for Singer's views (Johnson 2001).

2. Singer authored the book *Animal Liberation*, published in 1975, which "is widely regarded as the touchstone of the animal-rights movement" (Specter 1999:46). He is also the cofounder and member of the steering committee of the Great Ape Legal Project, the goal of which is to establish legal rights for great apes.

3. Narratives were collected by the researcher in interviews with sixty women whose children, ranging from newborn to five years old, were recently diagnosed with, or at risk for, disability. Participants were recruited from those bringing their children for evaluations to the Newborn Followup Program, Department of Developmental Pediatrics, at the Children's Hospital of Albany Medical Center in Albany, New York. All mothers in the study were raising the child or children in their home; the study does not include women who chose to give their disabled children up for adoption. One-third of the women were interviewed approximately a year following the first interview. All interviews were audiotaped and transcribed verbatim. The researcher also carried out participant observation at the Newborn Followup Program, observing 130 developmental evaluations, most of which were taped. All names of interviewees in the study have been changed. While there was minimal variation in race among the women interviewed (the majority being white), there was wide diversity in mothers' ages, level of education, religion, and socioeconomic class. The latter was in part made possible because the law requires that developmental evaluations and any services for which a child might be found eligible must be available at no charge to parents. For discussion of the methodology of the study, see Landsman (1998, 1999, 2000). While names of interviewees in the study have been changed, real names of public figures such as the bioethicist Peter Singer and the organizer of the group Parents United Against Peter Singer, Mary Wilt, are used in this chapter.

4. Rapp's research suggests that contrary to the arguments made by many scholars that genetic testing raises expectations that one can choose to have a perfect baby, most pregnant women are actually seeking basic health and normalcy (Ginsburg and Rapp 1999:287); Press et. al (1998:56) similarly claim that the majority of pregnant women are not seeking perfect children, but rather "perfectly normal" children. I agree; but I will argue that after nurturing a child with disabilities, many mothers reinterpret prenatal testing and other aspects of expected behavior during pregnancy as efforts to purchase perfect babies.

5. Layne suggests that women in the United States who experience pregnancy loss are similarly prone to such reflection and self-blame, as messages received by women from their doctors, popular culture, and the women's health movement all stress the importance of "women's agency in 'producing' a healthy baby by maintaining self-discipline and submitting to the authority of experts" (Layne 1999:172).

6. Here the narrator is referring to the fact that the researcher also has a child with a disability (cerebral palsy).
7. Disability is not the only quality that moves a child into commodity status. Wozniak notes that foster children are "stripped of one of the essential elements that make 'children' in American society, i.e. belonging to parents and family in which care and dependency needs are met. As 'non-children' or as 'temporary children' in a temporary relationship," Wozniak argues, foster children assume the "quality of a commodity-possession, a 'case' that could be shifted from one location, one owner, to another" (2002:69).

Making Memories

Trauma, Choice, and Consumer Culture in the Case of Pregnancy Loss

LINDA L. LAYNE

In my book *Motherhood Lost* (2003a), I describe how in the last quarter of the twentieth century women in the United States who experienced pregnancy loss (miscarriage, stillbirth, and early infant death) found themselves at the confluence of two contradictory forces: the emergence of the fetal subject and ongoing taboos regarding social acknowledgment of reproductive mishaps. I describe how these circumstances exacerbated the experience of loss and led to the establishment of more than nine hundred pregnancy loss support groups during this period. In this chapter I explore pregnancy loss as a traumatic event and draw on contemporary interdisciplinary scholarship on trauma and memory in analyzing problems of memory that befall individuals who experience such losses. I also draw on consumption theory to explore the ways that members of pregnancy loss support groups marshal resources from consumer culture to deal with these problems, and at the same time offer a critique of many of the core assumptions of consumer culture.

Research focused on three pregnancy loss support groups: UNITE (not an acronym), a regional group with about ten support groups serving Pennsylvania and New Jersey; SHARE (Source of Help in Airing and Resolving Experiences), the nation's largest pregnancy loss support organization, with more than ninety groups throughout the United States; and the New York Section of the National Council of Jewish Women's (NCJW) support group in New York City. Research involved attending support group meetings, participating first as a "parent" and later as a "professional" at pregnancy loss conferences and other special seminars and events sponsored by these groups, interviews with founding members of these and other groups, and a textual analysis of the quarterly newsletters of UNITE (from their first issue in 1981 to 2003) and the six annual issues of the SHARE newsletter (from 1984 to 2003), which include contributions from members throughout the country. I also draw on the personal experience of seven miscarriages.

Most support group meetings are attended by white, middle-class, heterosexual couples. Women, mostly bereaved mothers but also sometimes other female relatives, friends, and nurses, write the vast majority of the newsletter items, with men contributing about 12 percent of the pieces in SHARE's newsletter and about 4 percent of UNITE's. Miscarriages are by far the most frequent type of pregnancy loss, with most losses occurring during the first trimester (Bongaarts and Potter 1983:39), but second, and to an even greater extent, third trimester or postpartum losses are much more frequently discussed by newsletter contributors. More than half of the 447 losses reported in the newsletters from 1981 to 1994 refer to a loss after twenty-four weeks' gestation—that is, after the point in the pregnancy at which the fetus has some chance of surviving ex utero.

Problems of Memory

Many members of pregnancy loss support groups experience their loss as traumatic. Brison (1997) begins her piece "Outliving Oneself" with the observation that "survivors of trauma frequently remark that they are not the same people they were before being traumatized." Though originally used to refer to "a physical wound (a . . . break in the body produced by an outside force or agent)," trauma has come to be used to describe "invisible injuries inflicted on the mind, self, or soul" (Young 1996:89). Along the same lines, Hacking (1996:75) describes traumatic experience as "painful experiences that corrupt . . . one's sense of oneself."

Pregnancy loss clearly poses challenges for would-be parents' sense of themselves. Memory is "an intrinsic part of selfhood," and the "identity-building act" (Lambek 1996:243, 249) of remembering is especially critical for those whose sense of self has been jeopardized by trauma. Yet pregnancy loss poses a number of challenges in terms of memory. Some of these problems are general problems of memory, at least as understood in our culture; others appear to be widely shared by those who suffer trauma; and still others appear to be, if not unique, at least a distinctive consequence of this particular type of trauma.

Members of pregnancy loss support groups, like the general population, are troubled by the effects of time on memory. Memories are commonly understood to be like photographs (Lambek 1996; Kirmayer 1996; Forty 1999). This analogy highlights the perceived objectivity and accessibility of memories. It is also used to exemplify the deleterious effects of time on memory. "Like photographs, memories may fade" (Kirmayer 1996:176). Members of pregnancy loss support groups fear the corroding effects of time on memory. Iris Rubinstein (2001), a

UNITE support counselor, tells of meeting a woman at a basket-weaving class who had lost her third child at full term twenty-five years earlier and who shared her story, including the fact that although people had told her that "time heals all wounds and she would forget this pain, . . . she had not. In fact, the pain seemed to be getting worse as the years went on." Iris asked her to come share her story at a UNITE meeting, explaining that "many of us fear that we'll forget our lost babies as we move through the years . . . [You] would provide great reassurance that these precious souls are never forgotten." This fear explains why bereaved parents are so determined to "fix" their memories securely. Heil (1989) recalls how during the first week after her daughter's stillbirth she felt she "had to record every detail of her life and death for fear that I might ever forget her."

Scholars have noted the importance of others in the construction and maintenance of memories and selves. "In order to construct self-narratives . . . we need not only the words with which to tell our stories but also an audience able and willing to hear us" (Brison 1997:21). But as survivors of trauma often learn the hard way, many people do not wish to hear their sad, disturbing stories. Brison describes the "intense psychological pressures" that make it so difficult "for others to listen to trauma narratives," noting that this reluctance stems from "an active fear of empathizing with those whose terrifying fate forces us to acknowledge that we are not in control of our own [fates]" (26). The difficulty of finding empathetic interlocutors is one of the most common themes in narratives of pregnancy loss. For example, Karen Craig, whose sister's infant son died for unexplained reasons after one week in an intensive care unit, describes how hard people's unwillingness to hear was for her sister. According to Karen, what hurt her sister most was not the insensitive things people said, such as, "At least you didn't have a chance to get to know him," or "At least you have your daughter," but "those people who didn't know what to say so just avoided the issue, or my sister, or both, altogether."

A related, though different problem that affects those whose memories are of traumatic events is social pressure to forget. Like other trauma victims, members of pregnancy loss support groups keenly feel such pressure. One grandmother describes how she keeps finding the silver-framed photograph of her daughter holding her stillborn grandson face down on the credenza in her office. She wonders, "Who is doing this? What is their problem? Do they wonder what kind of person would love a picture like this?" and ends by asserting, "We should be allowed to remember him" (Zorn 2001:8).[1] Frank Pavlak, who along with his wife formed the Association of Recognizing the Life of Stillborns, writes of his stillborn daughter, "Sadly, our society does not recognize the fact that she was ever alive. I will remember Sarah for eternity even though some others think we should forget her" (Pavlak 1984:3).

One way to understand this pressure is in terms of culturally specific schedules for forgetting. Barb Knopf acknowledges the good support she received from her family and "everyone around her" at the time of her loss "and even a long time afterward" but then observes that "four whole years" later others think she "shouldn't be crying about Danny anymore . . . everyone assumes that four years should surely be enough time to 'get over it'" (Knopf 1999). These pressures often lead bereaved parents to silence. Iris Rubinstein (2001) concludes her piece "Storytelling with Our Hearts" by noting that "frequently we censor ourselves before we speak and as a result, the story often doesn't get told. But the tales of our babies—loved and lost—need to be told."

While difficulty in finding empathetic listeners and social pressure to forget are problems that appear to be widely shared regardless of the type of trauma, other problems of memory seem to be particularly associated with certain types of trauma. For instance, for those who suffer childhood sexual abuse, the problem tends to be retrieving buried memories so that painful experience can be consciously dealt with (cathected) and integrated into one's life (Antze 1996; Hacking 1996; and Young 1997). For rape or Holocaust survivors or those who undergo "combat trauma," however, the problem is more likely to be one of disruptive, overwhelming memories that come unbidden (Kirmayer 1996; Brison 1997). For pregnancy loss, the challenge is neither to uncover buried memories nor to keep them at bay, but rather to create adequate memories and then to retain them.

"Babies" that die during a pregnancy or shortly after birth pose special problems because of how little there is to remember. Take for example, Lisa Jeffries (1998:5), the UNITE group facilitator who wrote of the "baby" she miscarried at eleven weeks, "I will remember you in so few ways it hurts"; or Mary Zeches (1989:2), who writes of a boy who died at birth due to prematurity, "I hunger for images—there was so little time and so little to remember"; or David Nagele (1986a:3), who observes, "The reminders will always be with us, but not in the things we remember; his life was too short." Instead, he anticipates that they will remember their son through reminders of "the things that will never be—No first steps, no words, no baseball gloves or scraped knees." Similarly, Stacy Bricker (2000:1) describes sitting each Mother's Day in the garden she has planted in honor of her stillborn son Geoffery and "dream[s] of our missing memories."

The problem is not only that the "life was too short" but also that this "life" was experienced by so few, and oftentimes indirectly at that. Frank Pavlak describes his daughter "Sarah's Secret Life" in a piece by that name. He begins by noting the fact that she was "made in secret" and describes how "very few people knew Sarah. My wife knew her very well. I knew Sarah indirectly through my wife but only saw her for part of one day." He also mentions his son, two friends, and his parents, each of whom saw her for a short time at her baptism. "No one else really knew Sarah" (Pavlak 1984:3). Sue Palmer of Winterville, Ohio, also addresses this issue in her poem "Knowing You"—"You are so real to me. But this is understandable because I am the only one who ever knew you."[2]

The risks of forgetting are greatly increased by the fact that there are so few social reinforcements for these memories. Time and time again, contributors comment on the fact that others have forgotten. For example, Colene Rose (1984:4) of Grand Marais, Minnesota, in a piece written one year after the stillbirth of her daughter, writes of this anniversary, "it's nothing special to others, even those who were there. They won't remember that one year ago today, our beautiful little girl was born. But, my darling Erin, I will never forget." Sue Chaidez writes, "Everyone's forgotten you, Lacy. Everyone but me" (1985:16). In her piece "Remembering," Lisa Jeffries (1998:5) writes, "They would have forgotten had I let them." Leaders of the pregnancy loss support movement are acutely aware of these problems, and an explicit part of their agenda is "helping parents know what rituals, procedures and mementos will be helpful in remembering their babies" (Laux 1988:12). Consumer goods are routinely employed as technologies of memory by pregnancy loss support group leaders and members as they make, maintain, and share memories.[3]

Preserving Memory

In an era in which children have great sentimental value (Zelizer 1985; Spigel 2001), childhood, and especially babyhood, is felt to be a precious time that is over all too soon. Part of the ideology of contemporary middle-class motherhood is that one should raise healthy, happy, competent, self-confident children and also be sure not to get so caught up in all that is required to accomplish this that one forgets, or is too tired, to enjoy them. Mothers must constantly self-monitor to be sure that their children not only have all they need but also are enjoying each moment of their childhood. That is not all. One must also record these "precious moments" so that they can continue to be enjoyed as "priceless memories" for years to come. This two-part enterprise—providing children with "memorable" experiences and then assisting them to remember them—is an exercise in the contemporary management of childhood and hence an enactment of love.

Bereaved parents engage in these prescribed, value-laden practices as much as they are able. For early losses, there may be sonogram photos, the home pregnancy test dipstick, or nothing at all; for late losses, there are often baby blankets, caps, hospital ID bracelets, locks of hair, photos, foot and hand prints, and perhaps a toy (Layne 2000a, 2000b). But even for late losses, compared with the attic full of such trappings that one can accumulate over the course of one's child's childhood, there are so few mementos that special care is often taken to preserve them.

Support group newsletters give advice on how to care for "precious photos" (Friedeck 1995b) and periodically provide contact information for a company that "produces a line of archival quality photo albums and storage boxes which preserve photos" (SHARE 1988:11[5]:8). As SHARE coeditor, Michael Niehoff explains, such photos "deserve special care. Many commercial photo albums and mounting devices damage rather than preserve these precious pictures utilizing harmful adhesives which can tear, stain or fade photos and actually erode the images over time." He had photographs taken of the five ultrasound images of his stillborn son because "ultrasound pictures given parents are not a permanent record and will fade over time" (Niehoff 1994:4). Others have photos transferred onto commercial products like plastic plates or mugs, or commission paintings or drawings based on them. One contributor explains that she and her husband "thought of a safe deposit box because there is only one [picture of their daughter]. What if the house burns down?" (Dirks 1988).

And like other parents, some members of pregnancy loss support groups have their infant's shoes bronzed. Cheryl L. Miller of Perry, New York, explains that even though her baby never got to wear the shoes she had purchased for her, she had them "forever bronzed" to "withstand the test of time. A frozen memory of your quiet departure. The shoes you left behind" (Miller 1988).

As these examples suggest, rather than thinking of memory as a cognitive phenomenon, pregnancy loss support members oftentimes treat memory as things.[4] This model of memory has a number of consequences. Once memories are understood as things, they then share with things a number of important characteristics. They can decay and decompose, be lost, or ruined; they can be also be kept, stored, lovingly cared for, and preserved for posterity.

Another instantiation of memories as things can be found in the use of "memory boxes." Many hospital bereavement teams present memory boxes to bereaved parents, and UNITE presented attendees at their twenty-fifth anniversary celebration with a small, white, heart-shaped "memory box." SHARE markets "padded, fabric covered" boxes produced by Memories Unlimited and advertised as "the perfect place to hold the cherished mementos that connect with the tiny child. With the ribbons tied, the box is closed and the memories are kept safely inside. When the bow is untied, the open box reveals the things that touched the tiny life and left footprints on the heart" (SHARE 1994:3[5]:13). A number of contributors to the newsletters mention using "memory boxes." For instance Mary Zeches (1989:2) laments "that all our dreams should come to this—a box of memories and my mother's sketch" (see also Doherty 1991). Pieces like these reveal the common elision between mementos and the memories they evoke.

Memories are not just any sort of thing, however, but special, precious things, and, like the babies, are sometimes likened in size and value to jewels. For example, in a piece by Joann Meredith (1988:2) of Beebe, Alaska, written in the form of a question/answer session with God, God explains "your little jewel was mine to have." Another woman describes the tiny casket her daughter was buried in as a "treasure box."[5]

Prompting and Sharing Memories

Consumer goods are also employed to address the problem of inadequate social prompts for these memories and outright social pressure to forget. These may be the same items used to preserve memory (things purchased for the baby in anticipation of its birth, or traces of the baby's body) or they may be goods acquired after a loss specifically for the purpose of acting as *aides-memoire*. For instance, memorial jewelry (pendants, angel pins, and mother rings that can be "personalized" with a birthstone), figurines, Christmas ornaments, and items for the garden are often used to stimulate or prompt memories (Layne 2000a, 2000b).

The choice of aides-memoires and where they are stationed signal different goals in terms of whose memory is meant to be aided. For example, they may be aimed at prompting memory from one or more of the following—oneself, members of one's family, guests to one's home, coworkers, or strangers who might perhaps comment on an unusual piece of jewelry.

There are clear differences in understanding, both between bereaved parents and between parents and members of their social networks, about the appropriate place for such mementos and of such memories in one's life. Memorial objects are sometimes placed in a box in a closet, in a curio cabinet, or on the mantel in one's living room, on a window seal in the kitchen, on one's desk at work, in one's pocket, or on one's person. In other words, they are sometimes kept in private spaces or segregated to the more formal, ritual spaces of one's home. In other cases, people attempt to integrate memorial goods and the memories they prompt into the ebb and flow of daily life. Some explicitly use goods to assure that the dead baby is included in the annual ritual cycle and is a part of everyday family life. For example, Michael Niehoff (1994:4) explains that "a week before Christopher was stillborn, we bought him a soft, cuddly raccoon puppet named Ragamuffin," which is "now one of Zachary's [the surviving older brother's] favorite buddies to sleep with, and is one of our most constant reminders of Christopher." Cathy Hintz, a UNITE member, explains how the crystal snowflakes she bought as memorial Christmas ornaments one year and has since hung in her sunny kitchen window produce rainbows that "reaffirm symbolically how the children were and still are a good part of our lives" (Hintz 1988:3).

Thus, for some the goal is to continue to remember an important event in their lives, an event that may be experienced and understood in various ways—for example, as a miscarriage, as the death of a would-have-been baby, or baby. For others, the goal seems to be more. By keeping "the memory alive," they may feel that, in a sense, they are keeping their baby alive. For example, as Martin explains in a piece addressed to her baby, "Only in our memory do you live." This sentiment is also expressed in a prayer from the Reform Judaism prayer book reproduced from time to time in the newsletters entitled "We Remember Them." The prayer consists of a long list describing the moments in which "we" remember [the dead] and ends with the verses "For as long as we live, they too shall live, For they are now a part of us, As we remember them" (for example, SHARE 1985:8[6]:1).

Making Memories

We have addressed the problems of the effects of time on memory and the lack of social support for remembrance. Now let us turn to the problem of quantity. Bereaved parents handle this problem in two rather contradictory ways. One strategy is to purposively "make memories." For at least twenty years anthropologists and historians have embraced a model of memory (and history) as constructed, as an account of the past that is made and remade in the present. The concept of memory-making prevalent in narratives of pregnancy loss likewise shares an understanding of memory as something that can be constructed. But whereas the anthropological/historical understanding of constructed memory focuses on present reconstructions of the past, in the case of pregnancy loss, memory-making is proactive. This model of memory is no doubt influenced by the rhetoric used in advertising for vacations, particularly family vacations, encouraging us through our consumer choices to make "priceless," enduring, and, in the language of Disney, "magical" memories.

Disney is one of the most prominent purveyors of this concept. In October 2003, a search of the Disney Web site (www.Disney.com) produced 1,110 references to "memories," and the prompt to "create" or "make" memories featured prominently in the advertisements for Walt Disney World, Disneyland Resort, and Disney Cruise Line. The rhetoric of memory making is frequently used by other vacation businesses as well. For instance, in the 2001 AAA tour book for Colorado and Utah, a riverboat company has a color photo of a family in a white-water raft, and the header reads, "Share an adventure. *Make a memory*" (AAA 2001a:91, emphasis added), and the Lake Powell Resort and Marina advertisement reads, "This year, enjoy the best of Utah and *make the memories of a lifetime*" (2001a:155; emphasis added).[6] Advertisements for cameras and film also frequently advocate memory making. A summer 2001 advertising flier for disposable cameras explains, "ball games, picnic, boating, weddings, fishing, the beach—these are the places where summertime memories happen," and uses a header "Memories in the Making."

The rhetoric of memory-making is not confined to activities, however, but also applies to some consumer goods. This seems to be especially true for certain categories of gift—either precious, enduring, romantically freighted ones like diamonds or handmade gifts, especially perhaps those made by children and/or grandparents. An example of the latter can be found in the Vermont Country Store's mail order catalog for Christmas (2000:2), which begins with a letter from the proprietor explaining why he has filled the pages of his catalog "with items that will create lasting memories for your family to cherish." The header on this and the facing page reads "Making Memories," and together they advertise five kits for handmade gifts.

Children, especially girls, are socialized into such memory-making practices at a young age. For example, the popular children's "Dear America" series of historical novels structured around the diaries of children (mostly girls), marketed in elementary schools by Scholastic, has a "my memories club." In addition to books, members receive a "memory-making kit" and instructions to guide them on how to "create your own memories through hand-made keepsakes."[7]

Some members of pregnancy loss support organizations agree that memories are something that not only can but should be created. For instance, in a piece entitled "Healing Memories," Michael Niehoff describes how during the two and one-half days after learning that their son had died in utero and would be stillborn, the SHARE director "worked with us to create and collect as many memories of our little boy as possible." He explains, "this was especially important to us because we wanted 'material memories' that our then four-year-old son, Zachary, could cherish with us for years to come." He goes on to instruct his readers, presumably the care-giving segment of the membership, that "someone must help [parents] create memories. They may not want to save anything at the time, or think taking pictures is repugnant" (Niehoff 1994:4). Bernadette Foley, a certified social worker and contributor to the UNITE newsletter also encourages bereaved parents to "make memories." She writes, "making memories of a child who never lived outside the womb, or whose lifetime after birth was brief, seems very difficult. But we do have memories of our pregnancies, no matter how short. It takes some effort and a little creativity to make these memories concrete, but it can be done. I encourage you to make memories of your child, for yourself, your family, and your future" (1985:2).

Niehoff and Foley both use the concept of "making memories" to describe ways of documenting the baby's life. This involves both "saving" and "collecting" things that relate to the child and also purposively creating documentation of the baby's life—for example, by taking photos.

Some parents go further and continue to "make memories" after the loss. Sue Friedeck (1995c), one of the coeditors of the SHARE newsletter, whose son had survived fetal surgery for congenital diaphragmatic hernia but then was born prematurely and died thirteen days later, explains, "I have been able to make some memories where none may have been. Some are symbolic, like the water globe that I bought that has a Snowbaby," which has bright blue eyes similar to those of her son. Another woman tells of how she brings home a gift from each of her trips. "Every new place I go, I bring something home in Matthew's memory."

More Is Not Necessarily Better: A Critique of Consumer Culture

The other, not necessarily mutually exclusive, strategy for dealing with the scant quantity of memories available in cases of pregnancy loss is to challenge quantity as a measure of importance. In doing so members of pregnancy loss support groups articulate a critique of a number of related core assumptions of capitalist consumer culture. For example, a foundational premise of contemporary North American consumer culture is that "more is better." One version of this is found in the words of Morrie Schwartz, as conveyed in the best-seller *Tuesdays with Morrie:* "We've got a form of brainwashing going on in our country" that works by repeating "something over and over"—for example, "Owning things is good. More money is good. More property is good. More commercialism is good. More is good. More is good. We repeat it—and have it repeated to us—over and over until nobody bothers to even think otherwise" (Albom 1997:124).

Members of pregnancy loss support groups frequently challenge these standards of value. They argue that size and amount, whether it be of the body, length of a lifetime, or number of memories, are irrelevant as markers of value. They turn this on its head and stress the merits of the small instead. This ironic reversal—that a little is not what is seems, but is actually quite grand, grander in fact than things that are of more apparent size and worth—is a common theme in narratives of pregnancy loss. Rhetorically, this move is in the style of the late-eighteenth, early-nineteenth-century natural theologians William Paley, Charles Bucke, and Thomas Carlyle, who refocused "the sublime from the vast and infinite to the small and immediate." "This perception of the miraculous in the ordinary, the infinite in the small becomes the basis of sort of finite sublime (what Bucke termed "the infinite little") (Cooksey 1992:6, 7). This sensibility is well captured in the familiar lines of William Blake's poem "Auguries of Innocence": "To see a world in a grain of Sand / And Heaven in a Wild Flower / Hold Infinity in the palm of your hand / And Eternity in an hour."

Images of nature are often used in narratives of loss to similar ends. For example, in a piece reprinted in the SHARE newsletter from an anthology on pregnancy loss, Kim Steffgan elaborates an analogy between miscarried babies who never get a chance to develop and "brown dwarfs" or "prestars," which "have all the same elements to become a star, [but] for some reason do not." The author describes the "full lives" that most "stars" go through, hot bright white dwarf stage to their aged cooler and dimmer red giant stage. But "'brown stars' only go so far. Instead of being born to live a normal star's life, they remain cool and dim. . . . But like our babies, their roles in the universe are very important. In fact scientists believe they serve as a link between the small things and the big things, holding the universe together, a mid point between the beginning and ending of our universal story. As we grieve our babies who died before reaching the stardom of their earthly lives," perhaps we can find comfort in the possibility they were "designated for this very special, universal role" (Steffgan 1999:7).

In another piece, memories rather than the babies act as a link or bridge between this world and the next. As Connie Harmon puts it, "memories are the bridge between heaven and earth, cherish your memories, even if they are few, They are like a rainbow, from you to heaven, from heaven to you" (Harmon 1988:11).

Flowers are probably the most commonly employed analogy from nature for dead babies. In an interesting variation on the "little equals a lot / more is not better" theme, Susan Schwaegler of Moline, Illinois, uses the symbol of a "full-blown flower" to represent her stillborn daughter. She explains why she chose "full-blown" pink roses instead of unopened buds to remember her daughter on her birthday. "A life full-lived. For a thimble of water is as full as a pail . . . her life as complete in all its brevity" (Schwaegler 1989:1).

With or without analogies to nature, bereaved parents routinely contrast worldly time and value, which we obsessively measure with transcendental time and things whose value is beyond measure. For example, David Nagele deploys this trope, both in terms of describing the enormity of that which was lost, "We lost something . . . that cannot be measured—a lifetime," and in describing his memories of his son. "Jonathan's memories are in hours and not in years as we had hoped. Just an instant, an instant, an eternity of emotions grasped in a handful of time" (Nagele 1986a:3).[8] In another piece, Nagele (1986b:4) asserts, "Time should be measured in intensity, not duration." Similarly, Anthony Smith (1986) writes in his piece, "The Last Hour," "I will never know an hour / So precious as this. / An eternity / Gone by too fast / Every moment / A lifetime / Must last."[9]

The remarkably undertheorized notion of "love" plays a critical role in these narratives.[10] Love appears to be simultaneously measurable and uniquely elastic. Several poems suggest that love can be measured. For example, mothers like Ann Ciany assert that their love is equal to that of other mothers. "If motherhood is measured in minutes and hours, then maybe I don't qualify, but if motherhood is measured in terms of love, then I'm a mother too" (Ciany 1999:6). Mothers are also assured that they may claim "equal" love for each of their children, "that he or she was . . . equal to your other children in the love you gave, if only while inside you."

Love is also felt to be capable of transcending time and space. Love's ability to endure "forever" is a common theme in these narratives. David Nagele (1986b:4) observers, "love doesn't understand time." In a piece signed simply "Mom," a woman writes, "Your body will soon be gone, but the love goes on forever" (1985:22) and Cindy Lee Foster (1985:1) of Venice, Florida, ends her piece with a quote from M. D. Hughes, "Sorrow is not forever. Love is."

The principle that a little equals a lot is also deployed in terms of memories, where few are equated with many. "A single picture of this child will be something you can value as much as dozens of pictures of this child's brothers and sisters who survive" (Schwiebert and Kirk 1985:17).

Frequently this argument is made in terms of the conventional contrast between quality and quantity—for example, "you accomplished more in your short life than many do in their lifetimes." The quality/quantity distinction is also employed in terms of memories, "Although our time was very brief, I remember each minute clear" (Ryan 1999:9). If one had a lifetime of memories, some would inevitably fade, but in this case, these few memories are, it is asserted, indelibly imprinted on one's mind and heart.

The Replacement Child

Another way that members of pregnancy loss support groups critique consumer culture is in rejecting the oft-suggested notion of the replacement child. One of the most common ways that others encourage bereaved parents to "get over" a loss is by having another baby.[11] The support group newsletters periodically discuss the insensitive, hurtful things that well-meaning but misguided bystanders often say. Always high on this list is "Well, you can always have another." Bernadette McCauley's (1986) poem "Only a Miscarriage" illustrates this: "'It was only a miscarriage.' / That's what they all said. / 'Why are you so depressed and upset?' / 'There will be others.' . . . 'You can try again.' / 'It was only a miscarriage'— / 'Pull yourself together.'"

Parents who have subsequently born children frequently assert, rather defensively, that their new child is *not* a "replacement child" and will not erase the memory of the one(s) who died. For example, Terry Weeden's first daughter was stillborn due to Turner's syndrome. After the successful birth of another daughter, she asserts, "She won't replace our first daughter—for one person can never replace another. We will always remember our first baby" (Weeden 1985:2). Similarly, in a piece addressed to her stillborn daughter after a subsequent birth, Kelly Gonzalez (1988:4) ends with the avowal, "No on can replace you!" Writing during a subsequent pregnancy on what would have been the first birthday of a daughter who died shortly after birth while undergoing surgery, Joanne Murphy (1991:3) assures the reader and/or herself, "My new baby is not going to replace Amanda and he never will" and then switches voices and assures her daughter, "Amanda, my Forever Baby, you will always be special and never forgotten by your Mommy."

These concerns are shared by those who anticipate having another child as well. For example, Denise Lohr (1986:3), a facilitator of the Pittsburgh SHARE group wrote of the stillbirth of her first child, "someday we may have another baby, but there will never be another Daniel; he will always be our firstborn, our son." This sentiment is even more dramatically expressed by Colene Rose (1984:4), who ends her piece, "How could I forget you? My firstborn, my precious baby? I could have ten more children and still you would be special because you will always be my first." In other words, she not only rejects the one-to-one equivalency implicit in the idea of a "replacement child" but also asserts that ten-to-one would still not be an adequate rate of exchange.

These pressures and resistances resemble those experienced by parents who give birth to children with disabilities. In her contribution to this volume, "Too Bad You Got a Lemon," Landsman comments on philosopher Peter Singer's controversial position that it is not only morally acceptable but often desirable to kill disabled infants so that their parents can replace these defective children with more fulfilling ones. According to this position, "infants not only can but should be understood to be replaceable" (Landsman, this volume). Despite the similarities between these two cases there are important differences. In the case of children with disabilities, the argument is utilitarian. According to Singer, "when the death of a disabled infant will lead to the birth of another infant with better prospects of a happy life, the total amount of happiness will be greater if the disabled infant is killed (Singer, quoted in Landsman, this volume). His concern is that these children require such an extraordinary commitment of time, money, and energy that the parents are much less likely to have another child. In the case of pregnancy loss, there are no such demands on familial resources. Nevertheless, the commodified logic of replacement, and the damning evaluation of the worth of their child is staunchly rejected.[12]

Conclusions: Memory and Choice

Since the advent of the birth control pill and the legalization of abortion, having a baby in the United States has come to be understood as a matter of choice (Ginsburg 1989). Middle-class women in the United States choose when and with whom to start a family, planning the timing of their pregnancies with consideration not only of careers but also of their future children's birthdays (so as not to conflict with major holidays and other family members' birthdays). Once a pregnancy is under way, as Taylor (2000a, 2000b) has so astutely observed, a woman is intensively involved in consumption choices—what to eat and refrain from ingesting and which health care providers to use.

A third realm of consumption regards purchases for the baby-to-be. As I have described elsewhere (Layne 1999, 2000a, 2000c, 2003a), women and their social networks employ consumer goods during the course of a pregnancy to begin the process of socially constructing their "fetus" as "baby" and themselves as "mother." It is clear that mothers and members of their social networks use a great deal of care in choosing which items will be their baby's first possessions. As Peggy Swanton (1985:21) explains to her stillborn daughter, "every decision was made with such great care, What color to paint. . . ." In making choices like these, women are not only engaging in the act of "making love" (Miller 1997, 1998a) but also of making "mothers" and "babies." The qualities of these gifts communicate a great deal about the ideal personal and physical qualities the giver hopes the baby will have as well as admirable qualities of the giver (Belk 1979, 1983, 1985; Miller 1998a).

In addition, sometimes gifts are given to others in the name of the baby-to-be. One example of this is found in the personal Christmas card designed by artist Joe Kemp, in 2000, which showed a sonogram image of their baby-to-be wearing a Santa hat and read "Fetus Navidad." Inside the card read "Happy Holidays from Steph & Joe & spawn (at T-months pictured)." Such acts are an extension to fetuses of a class of distinctive North American practices by which we

FETUS NAVIDAD

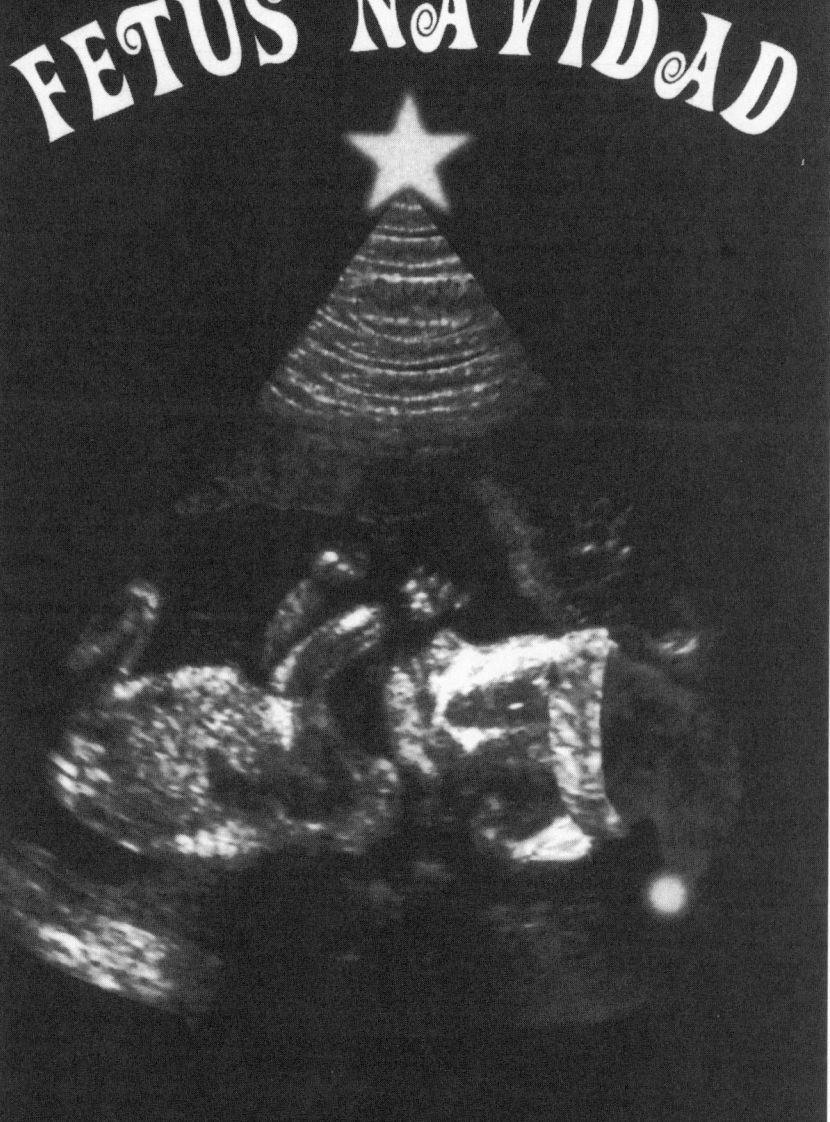

treat infants as agents. This attribution is not confined to the act of "giving" but also to that all-important marker of personhood, shopping, as summed up in the credo "I shop therefore I am." This was the advertisement for a special issue on "American Retailing" in an issue of the *New York Times Sunday Magazine*. For example, in Pat Schwiebert's poem "Please Don't Tell them You Never Got to Know Me," a dead baby reminds her mother, "[It was] I who went shopping and helped you pick out the 'perfect' teddy bear for me" (Schwiebert 1985:14). James Carrier (1991) talks of how shopping is one of the most important methods of "appropriating" consumer goods, thereby transforming mass-produced, anonymous "commodities" into personal "possessions." It would seem that an analogous process may be occurring with the fetuses as well. Shopping is one of the strategies used by mothers and their social networks to transform an anonymous mass of cells into "our precious baby."

Birth itself has become a plethora of consumer choices. Where will one give birth—at a hospital, in a birthing center, at home? Who will attend—physician, certified nurse midwife, lay midwife? Will pain medications be used? What music will one listen to during the birth? (See Davis Floyd, this volume; Klassen, this volume; and Layne 2001, 2003a).

When a pregnancy ends in death, the fallacy of control that a consumer-oriented model of pregnancy and birth engenders and perpetuates is brutally exposed. Time and time again, members of pregnancy loss support groups describe how difficult this loss of control is. To give just one example, Sue Friedeck (1995a) explains, "one of the hardest aspects of our loss of Michael was the feeling of helplessness and loss of control." And of the many moral lessons bereaved parents learn from this life-changing experience, the fact that we are not as in control of our live as we assume is one of the most frequently mentioned.

But bereaved parents do not abandon "choice." Many continue to use consumer choices to define themselves as mothers who deserve recognition and that which they lost as a baby, worthy of memory. The use of consumer goods for "singularizing" and "appropriating" the baby that begins during a pregnancy often continues after the demise. As one woman explained in answer to a questionnaire on postmortem photographs, "I wanted a picture in a dress of my choice. I want to make her a part of my life, not just a remembrance, but something I can see and show other people" (Laux 1988:12).

In addition, bereaved parents redirect choice away from the mundane, tarnished realm of consumer culture, to the superior realm of moral choices. In face of social pressure to forget, to have another child, to move on, and the fading of memory over time, memory is understood to be a matter of individual, deliberate choice. Kathy White Casey (1999), mother of four living children, ages four through twenty-two, and founder and leader of HUGSS (Help in Understanding Grief and Successfully Surviving) of Louisiana, describes in a piece entitled "I Choose to Remember" her experience of two miscarriages one year apart. "There were many choices to be made following the loss of my sweet babies, Jesse and Shelby. The one choice I made, with great determination and resolution to fulfill, was in remembering them."[13] Choosing to remember is not a neutral choice. The commitment to remember, especially in the face of subtle and not so subtle pressures to forget is clearly understood to be an honorable, moral choice—that is, as more laudatory than daily consumer choices.

In her introduction to this volume, Taylor identifies two major streams in consumption studies—one which celebrates the creative agency of consumers and one which critiques the hegemonic power of consumer culture. The case of pregnancy loss empirically illustrates both themes. As we have seen, members of pregnancy loss support groups creatively appropriate consumer goods in the social construction of the personhood of their child and as an act of resistance to the dominant social forces that would deny their experience and their child as worthy of memory. At the same time, bereaved parents reject consumer culture's standards of value that diminish the importance of their child's life and employ the standard contrast between the limited value of worldly goods and the infinitely more valuable sacred standards. In other words, the liminal case of pregnancy loss provides an excellent case for better understanding the interplay of these two ideological strands in contemporary culture.

NOTES

My research on pregnancy loss was funded by a grant-in-aid from the Wenner-Gren Foundation for Anthropological Research and a Paul Beer Minigrant and was facilitated by two one-semester sabbaticals from Rensselaer Polytechnic Institute. I would like to thank my coeditors and fellow contributors to this volume for productive intellectual exchange and to acknowledge the useful comments offered when portions of this paper were presented in 2001 at the American Ethnological Association's annual meeting in Montreal, the Committee on the Anthropology of Science, Technology, and Computing's summer workshop, USC, and at the annual meeting of the Society for Literature and Science, Buffalo, and in 2002 to the material culture seminar of the Department of Social Anthropology, University College, London, and the senior seminar of the Department of Social Anthropology, Cambridge.

1. Zorn (2001) is somewhat defensive about the importance of a photograph she has, saying that her tears as she held her grandson's "perfectly formed, robust little, still warm" body "served to imprint the moment in my mind forever. The photograph just helps me recall the details."
2. While for most the fact that so few people knew their child is seen as a problem, others cast this singularity as a privilege, akin to private, exclusive ownership of a unique object. Sue suggests that when her baby died in utero it was "as if to say, 'You're the only one who will know me.'" This not only attributes the ability to the fetus to decide on its life or death but also suggests a kind of privilege in this exclusive relationship. Another woman seems pleased that "You'll be a memory no one shares but me" (Miller 1984).
3. According to *Webster's*, technology is defined as things "by which society provides its

members with those things needed or desired," "tools used to enhance human's capacity." Because of the multivalence of material culture, the same goods are often are used to address more than one problem of memory simultaneously.
4. A recent example of this model of memory was a winter 2001 billboard for a Massachusetts local ski area that advertised, "Memories—come and get 'em."
5. See Pointon (1999) for discussion of similar issues in *Madame Bovary*.
6. In this and a related advertisement by this same group in the Arizona and New Mexico tour book, the issue of the relative durability/fragility of memory is simultaneously addressed. In this second ad, the colored photo image is of a tour boat and the header reads "Tours of Lake Powell Depart Daily. The Memories Never Leave" (AAA 2001b:51).
7. The "premiere issue" is packaged in a decorative box labeled "my memory maker" and includes along with the fictional diary of a girl who survived the *Titanic*, materials for creating and personalizing a "journal album" and instructions on how to make a memory quilt.
8. Another man explains, "The shortest moments we had together were the longest memories we shared," describing the moments after the doctors had given up hope and had asked if he wanted to hold his son in his last moments of life (Kocan 1984).
9. Pat Schwiebert ends her piece "Please Don't Tell Them You Never Got to Know Me" with the line, "It is I who was able to put a lifetime of joy into an instant" (Schwiebert 1985:14).
10. See Landsman (1999, this volume) for an analysis of the ways that love features as a transformative element in narratives of parents of children with disabilities.
11. The related difficulty of finding empathetic listeners and the cultural mandate to buck up and quit whining was vividly brought home to me when the woman I had hired to transcribe my interviews once included with the completed transcripts a copy of a poem by Brooke Astor called "Discipline." The poem begins with the author observing that in his life he has had his "share of good and bad," including "sudden death." Midway through he discovered "discipline." "I learned to take the good and bad and smile whenever I felt sad." Not only is dissimulation seen as a virtue, grief is understood to be selfish and narcissistic. "[I] began to forget both 'me' and 'I' and joined in life as it rolled by. This may not mean sheer ecstasy but it's better by far than 'I' and 'me.'"
12. The irreplaceability and uniqueness of children is sometimes addressed through analogizing children with elements from nature. For example, Linda Visconti (2001), who types the UNITE newsletter, likens her baby and all of her other "UNITE babies" to "snowflakes on a winter morning. Each unique, special, and different."
13. In another piece she reassures others that "there is no shame for those who choose to remember and make memories abide in the place of emptiness" (Casey 1997:2).

Maternal Labor in a Transnational Circuit

ANN ANAGNOST

As children adopted transnationally move from the site of reproduction to that of nurture, the question of value comes to the fore in the anxiety their new parents experience when the affective value of the child becomes entangled with commodity value. How do parents value children through the economic transactions required to rear them and what is the link between this economic "expenditure" and the affective value they represent? The question of the child's value perhaps arises, albeit less explicitly, for all families in capitalist culture, especially those of the middle class who, as Jacques Donzelot has suggested, will consume everything they can to fully "realize themselves" (1997:224). The child is therefore a site both of economic and emotional investment. In transnational adoption, we see the uncanny ways in which economy and desire map onto each other on a global scale, when capitalism's focus on the private sphere becomes expressed in the economy of desire that achieves its completion through a transnational circuit of exchanges.[1] To pursue the question of the linkage between affective and economic value, we need a concept of transvaluation that can effectively bridge regimes of economic value *and* desire as well as regimes of power in a global system complexly stratified (both within and across national borders) by conditions of economic inequality and uneven development.

Gayatri Spivak's writings on value (1987, 1988, 1990, 1994, 1999) offer a powerful frame of analysis for thinking through this problem. Value is, she suggests, a concept metaphor that has "no proper body" of its own. It is, to use Karl Marx's word, *Inhaltlos* (without content, a form of appearance) (Spivak 1990:96). This is most evident in the inability to specify what value *is* or where it resides. It emerges as an effect of an economy of relations (objects in exchange with each other). In this sense, then, Marx's idea of value is a catachresis, an ill-fitting word that must be made to make do. It appears to be naming a "substance" that is constantly changing its form. Spivak points out a structural resemblance of

Marx's concept of value to Michel Foucault's notion of power and Deleuze and Guattari's notion of desire in the shared inability of all three to be fixed to any object or location. They are *all* catachreses in the same sense—as words that attempt to name a differential in a complex set of relations. Foucault sees power as an effect of the production of subjects and objects in a discursive formation. Power is exercised through subjects discursively constituted within a particular horizon of truth. Desire, in Deleuze and Guattari's conception, is never a given but is always already captured and channeled within sedimented social relations. All three concept metaphors focus their critiques on the economies of effects we associate with modernity: capitalism, the disciplinary state, and the oedipalization of the family. By setting them up as somehow "like" each other, Spivak opens the possibility of combining them in an expanded analytic of capitalist culture that can track the transcoding of one value domain into another. In other words, Spivak uses "value" (insofar as we might define this generically: as a differential, *différance,* a textual effect emergent from a complex set of relations) as an underlying frame to conceptualize the interactions among economic, politico-cognitive, and affective value domains in a movement that would appear to "jump" the discontinuities from one domain to another. For example, how do the economic investments in the child express or even become productive of affective value and how does this process of transvaluation work the other way around? How are these economic and emotional investments in the child conditioned by the child's position within a larger political economy in which other bodies are recognized as having a lesser value? Moreover, we can use this schema to track value not just within localized social formations but across a globally heterogeneous terrain. In the postmodernization of the global economy, as Hardt and Negri (2000:292–93) suggest, affective value, in particular, may indeed have an expanded role in subsuming subjectivities and sociality to capital accumulation in the new informational economy. Indeed, the very conditions of possibility for transnational adoption and its production of affective value are most certainly contingent upon the immaterial labor of information-processing and problem-solving service economies.

Another way of posing this problem is this: If transnational adoption links together subjects inhabiting vastly different conditions of life, what sorts of transactions of value/power/desire enable infants to move across these "differentials?" The forces working on birth parents to relinquish baby girls in China are complexly constituted by economic inequality, the political imperatives of neoliberal governmentality, and the social imperatives of household reproduction. Likewise, the desire to adopt transnationally by parents in the United States is no less complexly constituted by their relatively privileged class position, the gendered production of "affectively necessary labor," and the racialized economies of multicultural identities. How in our analysis can we bring all these disparate determinations of value into relation with each other?

This essay draws primarily from Internet postings of some U.S. parents adopting infants from China to explore how cyberspace has become a medium for the formation of new kinds of subjectivity and social "space" and how these intersect with the history of family sentimentality, while reflecting global processes in which very small children are caught up in transnational flows of human capital. In this sense, Internet communications allegorize the process of globalization itself in which transnational adoption becomes a feasible means to form families and speaks to the larger issue of new formations of desire. This is perhaps all the more reason to recognize that parents who participate in Internet discussions may thereby get pulled into articulating thoughts they may not otherwise express. This essay must therefore limit itself to excavating these discussions as a specific discursive frame on transnational parenting rather than presuming to represent the sentiments of adoptive parents more generally. Yet the necessity of such an acknowledgment leads us irrevocably to the question of subjectivity itself as a historically contingent process irreducibly imbricated with the materiality of communication and how this may be transforming in the age of "web-based modes of knowing."[2] It is precisely this conjunction between communicative technologies and the production of affects that should arrest our attention.

One of the most compelling issues that surfaces most insistently in these discussions is the importance of constructing a cultural identity for the Asian adoptee, an issue that absorbs parents both on and off the Web. The politics of raced identities in contemporary U.S. society is what ultimately drives this area of parental concern.[3] However, what is particularly interesting is how the discourse of multiculturalism sets up the paradox of absorbing "difference" into the intimate space of the familial while at the same time reinscribing it, something that I have explored in more detail elsewhere (Anagnost 2000). For the purposes of this essay, I wish to pursue more deeply the question of how parenting has become a newly intensified domain for the production of middle-class subjectivity for the adult. How is it that parents imbue this privatized domain of practice as a locus for determining their social value as "good parents" and for the production of an intensified aura of sentiment surrounding family life? My interest lies with a realm of affective labor still culturally identified with "the maternal,"[4] lying within the interiority of family life but also often externalized as a practice of display. The importance of this labor becomes more urgent the more the link to the child appears to be tenuous and needing support. This is why making it an object of scholarly attention is such a sensitive issue for many parents.[5] However, in their being more highly charged, the practices of adoptive mothers can speak to those of middle-class mothering more generally. I wish, moreover, to pursue this connection in a way that speaks to the historicity of the family and its emotional life.[6]

At the same time, my approach is determinedly *noncelebratory* in the sense that it aspires to be a critical analytic of the sentimental construction of motherhood as constitutive of value for women. Exploring the formations of desire of the mother is a necessary step in opening up for analysis what Antonio Negri and Michael Hardt have called the "subjective black hole of the family" (2002:197–98; see also Hardt 1999:100) and the intertwining of the familial structures of affect with the gendered divisions of labor in capitalist culture. The labor involved in biopolitical production is an "affectively necessary labour" (here Negri and Hardt borrow a phrase from Spivak modeled after Marx's notion of "socially necessary labor") that produces affects, subjectivities, forms of life. While being a necessary foundation for capitalist accumulation and the reproduction of the patriarchal order (the biopolitical "from below"), they also see it not just as resistant to capitalist formations of value but also as carrying a potential for autonomous "circuits of valorization" and possibly liberation (Negri and Hardt 2002:198). But how to read the possibility of the latter in a way that is uncontaminated by the sentimental ensnarements of this system of affects? How might such celebration in one site of biopolitical production unwittingly feed into the structure of uneven development and the derogation of the reproductive labor of women at the opposite end of the "value chain"?

In framing my argument in terms of the historicity of the sentimental life of the family, I do not mean to imply that middle-class parents in the late-twentieth-century United States simply love their children more than parents in other places or times or to criticize them for loving "too much." I seek to explore how this structure of feeling articulates with the sociohistorical and economic transformations taking place in the larger social world in producing the specific formations of a desire for children—a manifestation of what Jacques Donzelot (1997) has referred to as the "familialization of the family" and what Lauren Berlant (1997) refers to as a more recent formation of the "intimate public sphere" in contemporary U.S. cultural politics, or what sometimes gets referenced in popular media as "boomer sentimentality about kids."[7] I would argue that the position of parent, for middle-class subjects, has become increasingly marked as a measure of value, self-worth, and citizenship in ways that beg an analysis of its specific formations in the context of late-twentieth-century capitalism, which, incidentally, fuel the desire for adoption as a necessary "completion" for becoming a fully realized subject in American life.[8]

Looking critically at multiculturalism and the intimate public sphere in a domain of practice where they appear to intersect also draws our attention to another point at which they meet. The relegation of an active citizenship within the bounds of the family effects a fragmentation of the political in ways that seem analogous to how multiculturalism (in its aestheticized form) maintains separations among ghettoized communities by obscuring immigrant histories in the United States, so that cultural difference appears uninflected by issues of class and racialized boundaries. This intersection suggests that white, middle-class parenting is as much about constituting class membership as it is about race.[9] In making this critique, my intent is not to disenable adoption, which I believe is unquestionably positive in the vast majority of cases for both parents and children.[10] Rather, my object is to explore this fragmentation of the political in a specific site where all these issues come together: the history of the family, multiculturalism as a representational regime, the formation of cybercommunities, and the service economies that enable the articulation of economic and affective value chains with a transnational spread.

Regimes of Embodied Value

Before entering into a discussion of the practices of adoptive parents in the United States, I wish to address how China's population policy has made children (especially girls) available for international adoption. In addressing this question, the immediate problem is how to untangle the issues from the representational regimes that construct China as a totalitarian state "outside" universal values of human rights and democratic freedoms.[11] A common assumption in the United States is that baby girls are abandoned (or, worse, are victims of infanticide) because, given the Chinese traditional preference for sons and the pressure of state sanctions on over-quota births, they are unwanted. While official data on the abandonment and adoption of children in China are difficult to find, there exists plenty of anecdotal evidence, supported by some recent studies, that baby girls are valued and do find adoptive homes in China, although this is done in ways that often escape official notice. One needs to be extremely skeptical of arguments that cite gender-ratio imbalance as evidence of widespread female infanticide or that a traditional preference for sons is the cause of "unwanted girls." In fact, the newly defined ideal for most families (even for those in cities, where it is for the most part unobtainable) is a desire for one child of each sex in order to be "complete." Ironically, the desire for daughters is often represented on the part of Chinese respondents in terms of the affective value they represent. In much of the Chinese countryside, the birth of a son ensures the reproduction of the household structured through patrilineal kinship, while daughters are assumed to be better caregivers for aged parents. While it is undeniable that most of the babies available for adoption in China are girls, this fact needs to be interpreted in the context of the stringency of China's birth policy and the state's economic reforms, which have set up compelling reasons for ensuring the birth of at least one son in order for the rural household to reproduce itself. Moreover, many of the baby girls in China's infant welfare homes would formerly not have had trouble finding an adoptive home domestically were it not for the state's own policies that viewed adoption as a way of circumventing the state's stringent limits on reproduction. More recently China's restrictions on domestic adoption have begun to loosen, possibly in response to domestic and foreign criticism of its "sale" of babies internationally. This may be viewed as a beneficial outcome of transnational adoption.[12] The role of the Chinese state must be emphasized in the creation of a global system of "stratified reproduction" in which the bodies of children embody a "value" that is caught up in transnational circuits of exchange.[13] However, this must also be set into the context of global discourses of population control and its role in economic development as an imperative for modernization.[14] In fact, here is where the analyst must begin to forge a linkage between the site of reproduction and the site of nurture for the China adoptee. How exactly do the determinations of the child's value in one site propel its passage to another?

China's economic reforms have produced new forms of socioeconomic inequality as the socialist economy has been reorganized around the market. Rural populations have been uprooted from what once were the bounded collectivities of the socialist economy as a mobile reserve of cheap labor for urban areas or the newly established export processing zones, mostly along China's coastal areas. The "valuing" of this labor operates according to a circular logic of value coding. Migrant labor is devalued as being of "low quality" *(suzhi di)*. It is not just that it represents a form of being that "lacks value," but its sheer massiveness, its excess quantity, also represents an almost overwhelming obstacle to the project of rapid modernization. At the same time, its quality of being undervalued is what allows the extraction of surplus value enabling capital accumulation. The coding of the migrant body as being of low quality justifies the extraction of surplus value while it also serves to legitimate new regimes of social differentiation and governmentality.

This representation of the sheer quantities of low-quality migrant and peasant bodies as a drag on China's progress to modern standards of material comfort is a powerful image that penetrates almost all aspects of daily life. Value, it would seem, is something that must be added to bodies, through capitalized inputs of education and training. It is no longer something that inheres in the powers of the body itself through its capacity for labor. For China's emergent middle class, this explains the intensity of parental investments in rearing their single child through education and through the consumption of commodities (educational toys, nutritional supplements, music lessons) that will ensure that their child will come to be recognized in the new economic order as "a body of value."[15] But in the wake of this neoliberal restructuring of economies and subject positions lies what Hairong Yan (2002) calls (following Spivak) the "spectralization" of the countryside as a devastated landscape increasingly devoid of value or hope. The rural population, subject to a reworked governmentality that increasingly makes agricultural production meaningless (without profit) and their reproduction superfluous and subject to punitive action by the state, is the reservoir of "bare life" from which the China adoptee springs.[16]

Moreover, the conditions that set up the infant as a "surplus" are precisely those of China's process of "reform and opening up" *(gaige kaifang)* to the outside (rather than the tenacious hold of "tradition" or a totalitarian state). This set of reforms are also the same conditions that set the terms for adoption as a specific set of legal and economic transactions.

Adoption from the People's Republic of China first became available somewhat fitfully in the early 1990s and has grown dramatically in recent years, reaching an annual rate of more than five thousand a year. It has also become somewhat of a media phenomenon, with cover stories in national newspapers and magazines. Because Chinese bureaucrats prefer not to deal with individual parents, a number of agencies have been established in the United States to help with the paperwork and to organize groups of parents to travel to China to receive their children.[17] While it is often noted that China adoption allows the possibility for infertile couples, gay and lesbian couples (until recently), and single parents to form families, a significant number of parents are heterosexual couples who already have biological children as well as children adopted domestically as well as from other countries. Parents and prospective parents of Asian adoptees have built up close communities via support organizations, Internet lists, and summer culture camps for their children.

The scope of this essay is mostly limited to following discussions of adoptive parents on the Internet and the issues that arise during the period that starts with referral (when an infant is assigned to waiting parents) and the months immediately following the child's arrival in her new home. However, not all adoptive parents are equally active in Internet discussions, and there are other sites that may figure with equal or greater importance in the life of their families, such as Families with Children from China (FCC), which has branch organizations all over the United States, summer culture camps, Chinese language classes, and informal parent networks. This essay addresses issues that arise in the specific context of electronic communications, a context that reflects other modes of community formed around China adoption without being necessarily coterminous with them. Most of the parents in this study are heterosexual couples who are active participants in Internet discussions, with women greatly predominating. The gendered aspect of the discussions begs for a more focused examination of maternal "citizenship" and how one defines oneself as a good parent.[18]

Technologies of the Intimate Public Sphere

The formation of a cybercommunity around the issue of China adoption exemplifies the power of the Internet to produce new forms of sociality and community.[19] The e-mail lists that figure in this study constitute a specific ethnographic site or locale for a community linked electronically rather than in terms of geographic proximity.[20] For a large number of parents, in the long months of waiting between referral and travel to China, the lists act as a prosthetic support in the transition to parenthood. Indeed, the specificity of the Internet as a technology of subject production may lie in its capacity for mutual incitement to occupy specific subject positions. Participation often begins with a period of silent observation during which the speech protocols of the list are installed. Active participation is sometimes initiated by the disclaimer one has been silently following these discussions for some time prior to entering them. Participants enter from a position of soliciting information, but as they proceed through the adoption process, they can then begin to turn more toward sharing information with others. Finally, as their attention becomes more taken up with the daily routine of parenting, participation tapers off, until the inbox overflows, and the subject unsubscribes, no longer in need of the constant circulation of signs to undergird his or her position as subject, except for moments (often of crisis) when information or sharing may be sought again.

The Internet offers a rich resource for ethnography in the sheer volume of its content and its geographical spread, but it carries with it important questions for social science methodology. The Internet's easy access appears to transgress the division between public and private. For the ethnographer, it requires no effort at all to get the subject to speak, to reveal the intimate contours of an interiorized domestic terrain. Indeed, I would go so far as to suggest that the Web enables certain modes of verbal expression and constructions of community that are not possible by any other means, although there are also clearly limits to what can be said. If ethnography as a site of knowledge production has in its postcolonial refashioning reconfigured itself around the representation of voice as the ground of its truth, then this infinitely self-disclosing subject represents for the ethnographer a hallucinatory surplus of voice. Yet the very volubility of the subject must also be raised as a problem. The figure of the self-disclosing subject eager to reveal her or his inner truth has a history that goes back to Jean Jacques Rousseau's desire to "reveal all" *(toute dire),* achieving its scientific completion in Freudian psychoanalysis and its mass mediation in Jerry Springer. The Internet has become an intimate confessional that has significant consequences for the production of subjectivity in contemporary culture. N. Katherine Hayles describes the reconfiguration of public/private in the wake of the information age in which the "home, traditionally the private space of family life, is penetrated" by wavelengths of all kinds as one in which entry is "constituted as access to data rather than as a change in physical location" (1999:41).

It seems to me that the Internet is a striking instantiation of "the intimate public sphere," which appears to promise universal access to participation in democratic debate but that may, in actuality, further segment the political in its solicitation of specific identities while also confining the political within the confines of private life. As Berlant notes, this "intimate public sphere of the U.S. present tense renders citizenship as a condition of social membership produced by personal acts and values, especially . . . originating in or directed toward the family sphere, rather than outward, "toward public life." Indeed, the growing practice of the family Web page represents perhaps the latest wave in the technologies of "middle-class familial theatricality in late capitalism" (alongside family photography and the camcorder)—a theme I discuss below in relation to the maternal archive (Berlant 1997:5).[21]

Topics in the adoption lists range from practical advice on procedural details to the sharing of emotions and ways of coping with societal noncomprehension of the wish to adopt internationally. A question that interests me particularly is how the reiterability of the exchanges appears to yield a certain performative excess in the production of the adoptive parent as a subject position unique to itself—one that opens up contradictory political possibilities in which the construction of the child's difference may be aestheticized and contained within the realm of private life or can become articulated with a more collective project of antiracism. Possible openings for the latter emerge in the lists as expressions of a certain unease that the movement of the child across national borders transforms it into a commodity bought and sold as a form of embodied value. There is also a recognition, born from the necessity of dealing with the Immigration and Naturalization Service, that adoption *is* a form of immigration and that this might potentially align the child alongside lesser valued bodies, such as illegal aliens or persons of nationalities with historically restricted quotas (of which China is one). The issue of immigration evokes an implicit comparison registered in the relative mobility and immobility of differently marked bodies that allow U.S. citizens to cross national borders to bring their children home. Yet the lists also exhibit an urgency to evade explicit confrontation with these problematic realities in favor of other kinds of narratives, often taking the form of stories of salvage and redemption, which contain the political effects of adoption within the domain of private heroic acts.[22]

Rhetorics of Disavowal

The anxiety that the child might be a commodity is aroused by the incontrovertible fact that as the child moves from one site of nurture to another, money has to change hands; agencies are established; "baby flights" are chartered; tour packages are assembled. This awareness often takes the form of a refusal and resignification of the meaning of monetary exchanges.[23]

The danger appears most explicitly in discussions of how to deal with insensitive people who ask how much the parent "paid" for the child. One mother informed a friend that the sale of babies is illegal but that the cost of adoption was approximately the same as that of a c-section, thereby aligning adoption with other reproductive technologies as a comparable means to have a child. The figure of market transaction also arises in discussions concerning the relative merits of adoption agencies, comparing the quality of service and the costs. Although prospective parents often use the Internet for referrals from other parents, in one case a parent who was new to the list and had not yet learned its speech protocols made the unfortunate mistake of suggesting that, in shopping for an agency, one should insist on getting what one pays for. This immediately incited a "flame war" that cast a shadow on the list for weeks, long after the original writer had retreated into silence. One reader wrote reprovingly that adopting a child was not the same as purchasing a dress off the rack and should not be spoken of in terms of a monetary equivalent.

Sara K. Dorow (2002) has looked at how the services of transnational adoption agencies represent a site where the ethics of care and consumption come into conflict, overlap, and mutually constitute each other. The personal care an agency offers parents and children as potential "clients" is at once what separates their services from a purely market logic while becoming a "selling point" to increase their market share. Dorow's analysis is very careful not to set up care and consumption as mutually exclusive domains. Her concern is to show how market and nonmarket sensibilities interpenetrate in the production of "needs, interests, and desires." Her exploration of these processes give us a vivid portrayal of how "affective labor" produces subjects who thereby embody the "needs, interest, and desires" that are the necessary conditions of possibility for transnational adoption. It is precisely in the sale of affective services that we see the conditions for the conversion between economic and affective value.

In Internet discussions, the figure of the commodity is quickly displaced by a rhetoric of the gift.[24] However, the language of the gift implies a personal relationship with a donor, here identified as China as a nation or the "Chinese people" as a whole. This identification of China as a benefactor puts the adoptive parent in a somewhat ambivalent relationship to the Chinese state.

Many adoptive parents bring back positive reports of their adoption journey in China; indeed, these at times verge on the euphoric, expressing a "love affair" with China and with "the Chinese people." But there are also a significant number of parents whose accounts of their experience in China are fraught with ambivalence about what they perceive as a totalitarian state in which infants, especially little girls, are "surplused."[25] The theme of salvage pervades many adoption narratives, in which the child is seen as endangered by its abandonment and its institutionalization in a Chinese orphan home. The saving of the child is portrayed as a heroic act, but one resulting in a full mutuality of affect, an exchange of love that cannot be bought. Yet, there remains an uncertainty that figures complexly in the structure of the salvage narrative. As the identity of the birth parents is quite often unknown, the adoptive parents are deprived of any direct link to the child's "origin." This loss of origin must be compensated for by a series of displacements. Some adoptive parents vividly evoke the emotional cost to the birth parents of having to give up their child. The imaginary relationship to the birth parents finds its point of connection in the shared anguish of thwarted reproductive desire. One mother wrote of how emotionally wrenched she felt when she discovered that her child had been abandoned at five months, suggesting a powerful desire on the part of the birth parents to keep her. Adoptive parents often feel a need to envision and memorialize the loss of an affective bond they would like to think had been there. Yet the severing of the child from its birth parents is a violence already enacted by the impersonal power of the state, calming the anxiety that the transfer of the child to one's care might have incurred an affective loss to another—the damage has, in a sense, already been done. The act of mourning is a compensatory act that is completed by memorializing the bond that was broken so that the infant can transfer its love elsewhere. But it is also a reassurance that affect *was* there, at the origin, that the child will be capable of delivering fully upon its promise of love.

Parents express related concerns about "reactive attachment disorder," a diagnostic category that defines a lack in the child's emotional responsiveness to others—a potential sign of the absence of nurturing contact in the early months of life.[26] Hence the anxiety about adopting an older child (beyond eighteen to twenty-four months old) produces a tremendous volume of discussion on the Internet. The quality of nurture in the orphan home is in itself an extremely sensitive issue. In the wake of the British documentary *The Dying Rooms,* which portrayed the practice of a kind of triage for infant survival in a Shanghai orphan home, agencies and parents have been quick to defend Chinese caretakers, accounting for the dour environment of nurture in terms of economic hardship.[27] Indeed, there is a desire on the part of the parent to project onto the caretaker affective feelings for the child that must also be memorialized in the adoption narrative and maternal archive. Some parents attempt to maintain this bond by sending letters and pictures of their growing child back to the orphan home. The uncertainty about early nurture, however, remains, manifested by intensive surveillance of the child's condition when it is received and of the child's subsequent physical and mental development. The results of the child's medical exam prior to adoption are sometimes scanned into family Web sites, accompanied by English translations of the Chinese text and charts plotting height and weight gain. One parent helpfully provided charts for normal growth and development curves taken from a Chinese source so that American physicians might read the child's height and weight gain in a way appropriate to the child's origin. Parents will sometimes read the signs of their child's development as affirmations that adopting the child has saved her or his life. One mother reported that she was informed by an orphanage official that her child would not have survived another three months in the orphan home.

The theme of salvage also arouses its own anxieties, however, which express themselves in feelings of guilt about the children left behind. One mother who adopted when foreign adoption was just beginning shared with me the emotional distress she felt when she was led to a crib with three infants and was asked to choose.[28] Much discussion takes place about how one can sponsor a child for fosterage in China or what one can send to the welfare home, such as boxes of used infant clothing. Concern is also expressed for how the fees for adoption collected by officials are expended, attempting to quiet the anxiety that the transfer of funds is not a sale but a way of improving the lives of children left behind. Yet there is an awareness that "donations" made to the orphan home are often required to ensure the smooth outcome of the adoption process and that funds may not always be earmarked for the care of remaining children.[29] This accounts for why some parents have moved the frontier of Asia adoption to less well trodden locales, such as Cambodia, where the procedures were perceived to be less "monetarized."[30]

The lost connection to the birth parent, while it is mourned, is also a comfort. Listing reasons why they have chosen China as their preferred adoption location, parents often include the factors that make this route relatively secure, fast, and inexpensive (when compared with domestic adoption or other international venues). However, another reason, oft noted, is that it is final. There is no danger that the birth parents will reclaim a child with whom one has already bonded, as is the fear with domestic open adoptions.[31] But if this lost connection is a comfort, it also produces a great anxiety. For once the child is truly severed from its origin, will this subvert her or his ability to cohere as an identity that can be sutured smoothly into a new site of nurture? Will the child, upon reaching adolescence, begin to question her or his own status as an object that can be bought and sold? Will the economic structures that govern this transfer of embodied value effect its own return of the repressed?

What would happen if, instead of rituals of decommodification, the specter was confronted head on? The disavowal at the heart of the fetish, "I know . . . but still . . . ," reveals that there is already an awareness of these things at some level. Perhaps we might want to consider whether commodification is necessarily a dead end. If it is one way of appropriating a sign or object, does this exhaust its possibilities?[32] Of course, the object here is a child—not an object but a subject with its own possibilities of agency—and this, of course, is the source of unease, because we can never be sure that the child will grow into what we wish it to be. The child always holds forth the possibility of indeterminacy in the contingency of social reproduction. A recognition of the terms of exchange that govern the mobility of differently valued bodies across national borders allows us to link adoption to other forms of immigration that figure importantly in how the child comes to be marked as racially other. Perhaps the difficulty of confronting the reality of these "ghostly doubles" of the child constitutes the greater problem.

The desire, increasingly acted upon, of parents to do something to help those children left behind is perhaps a beginning. It remains to be seen whether these incitements to do "something" can broaden the horizon of political possibility to articulate a critique of the global processes that work to surplus these children. Is there any connection that can be made between these parents' ability to provide superior conditions of nurture with the processes that devalue human life at the other side of the value chain?

Consuming Passions

If the figure of the smart consumer makes its appearance on these pages, it testifies to the powerful forces that position the middle-class parent as such, so that consumption becomes the means to stage middle-class domesticity as an enriched site of nurture. The entrée of any child onto the domestic scene is announced by a flurry of consumer choice-making, exemplified by the checklists that define the properly prepared parent-consumer.[33] I am interested in how these practices of consumption construct race and class for the child, even when "unmarked." One might indeed argue that the very idea of an enriched site of nurture already marks the child as middle class, hence the appeal of commodities that promise to enhance the child's early development.[34] However, consuming practices sometimes exceed this project in a jubilant flurry of shopping in which the parent-consumer becomes cathected to the ethnically marked commodity. These practices are not unlike those that enhance the adorability or "littleness" of the child with which I am all too familiar.[35] One cannot help but remark on the volume of discussion about the shopping that occurs even prior to the adoption trip and how, in the long months of waiting, the desire for the child becomes displaced onto objects that signify the child's "difference." This activity is in a sense an aspect of an imaginary relationship to the child that is already being built on the fragile ground of a tiny photograph sent from a distant orphanage.

I find it impossible to speak of the constant cultural incitements to set up the child as an object of desire and the complex relationships of this desire to commodification without appealing to a theory of the fetish—not as the marker of an individual pathology but as part of the cultural landscape we all inhabit. The notion of the fetish in relation to the child appears particularly transgressive because of its historical articulations with both psychosexual pathology and market exchange in capitalist culture. The child is an entity that is set up as needing protection from the contaminations of both sexuality (libidinal investment) and money (commodification), and yet this imperative is constantly transgressed in contemporary culture. Therefore, the fetish seems a necessary tool for understanding how the child (or the child's ethnicity) becomes a locus of desire and value.

While the search for the ethnically marked commodity might focus on the national origin of the child (such as the search for Empress Barbie, fortune cookie wallpaper borders, or anything with pandas on it), what is interesting is how the anxiety of difference is pleasurably rechanneled into the labor of hunting and gathering. For a while, participants flagged such activities as "panda sightings" in the e-mail lists. Panda appliqués on a knitted flare-style red top (with ruffle cuffs) sighted at a local Kids "R" Us were enthusiastically reported in one such sighting. Another panda sighting fortuitously made just prior to Halloween identified a "panda fleece material" that was eagerly seized on for costumes. The panda as a Chinese national totem (dating from the Mao era and resurrected as the mascot for the 1991 Asian Games in Beijing to dispel the lingering shadow of state terror) has now become the tutelary spirit of adorable little panda-suited girls plying for treats. Kwai-Cheung Lo, in a review of the history of the panda as a national symbol in China, remarks on the role it plays as a narcissistic image of beholding and recognizing oneself as a Chinese national subject. In this "animal-externalization," China is able "to see itself in a likeable image as worthy of love." The panda as an object of fantasy is attributed with the phallic power to fill in the lack in the Chinese subject (n.d.: 10, 11). It would seem that some adoptive parents have mimetically picked up on this power of the panda to fill in the gap of a national identity. At the same time, Lo notes the babylike features of the panda as contributing to the power of this fantasy-object to elicit strong emotional reactions from observers (22). Lo also juxtaposes the panda as an acceptable form of transnational circulation of Chineseness with the immigrant who may not be as welcome.[36] While these panda sightings were at times accompanied by a self-ironizing sensibility through which participants voiced objections to what they feel is an excessive focus on consumption, the lure of the panda itself was never questioned. One parent sheepishly admits that she never thought she would fall for the lure but found herself purchasing ethnically marked things for her child despite her best intentions. This suggests the productivity of the ethnic marker in articulating (in the sense of a linking together) the relationship between parent and child.

A much more serious search, however, takes place for dolls with "Asian" features (what was described in one instance as a "doll role model") as a supplement for what the parents cannot give: a surface that can mirror back to the child her or his "likeness" as a sign of the child's own difference.[37] The search for these dolls is international. China, assumed by parents as a place capable of delivering the goods "at the origin," almost always falls short. In a nation that produces more than 50 percent of the world's toys (often utilizing child labor), dolls with Asian features often prove difficult if not impossible to find. One woman wrote of her surprise at her failure to find anything but dolls with European features during her travels in China.

Yet this search, which proves so very difficult (and therefore all the more pleasurable), often founders with the child's own object choice. One mother reported that although her daughter identified with her Asian-featured doll with her own name, she still preferred her Pooh bear. Some of the parents who appear most avid in their pursuit for this inanimate double for their child do recognize that the doll is not only for their child but for themselves.[38] One mother reported her pleasure in holding the doll as if it were a real baby. Insofar as it holds the promise of completing a recursive circuit of identity, which the parent anxiously fears cannot be completed otherwise, the doll in fact becomes a supplement for what the mother feels to be lacking in herself. But there is also a sense that the doll represents a "stilled" life, a way to hold on to the infant-object in all its "littleness." For the mother, the doll, in its suspended state of infant-dependency, becomes a double displacement of the phallus (the doll replaces the child) as the sublime object of maternal desire as a child who will never grow up and leave the maternal embrace (Rose 1993).[39]

Despite the initial difficulties of this search, corporate capital is eager to seize upon this opportunity "just in time" for an emergent consumer desire. The Mattel Corporation has produced a replica of the mother-child dyad in "Coming Home" Barbie, which suddenly made its appearance in the rooms of the White Swan Hotel in Guangzhou where parents wait to receive their children.[40] "Coming Home" Barbie gives the mother an image of herself as a maternal caretaker accessorized by the baby in her arms. The doll is valued by the mother as a kind of "recognition" by the mainstream culture of her role as a mother. This recognition can take yet another form in the eagerness with which capitalism colonizes the realm of familial affect to sell its products. A television ad for Compaq computers demonstrates this quite clearly. A young, obviously nervous couple are waiting in what appears to be an adoption agency office. An African American woman sitting at a desk says something to the effect of "This ought to calm you down." The camera turns to a computer screen; she clicks on a file labeled "Asia," and the screen image reveals a newborn held up to the camera. The woman says, "Say hello to your new daughter!" The prospective parents turn to each other and smile. The camera then cuts to the Compaq logo and a slogan about Compaq changing your life.[41] On the list the reaction to the ad was immediate. One father wrote China adoption had finally made the mainstream. For him the ad represented a broader social recognition of himself as a parent with a legitimate emotional investment in the child, recognition taking the form of pulling the general viewer into the rush of affect this scene is engineered to produce. Like Advo's incorporation of the pictures of missing children into their advertisements that come by post ("Have you seen me?") or Volvo's use of ultrasound fetal images ("Something deep inside is telling you to buy a Volvo!"), the Compaq ad appropriates contemporary anxieties about the lost or endangered child to refocus desire onto the commodity.[42] I experience such ads as an involuntary welling up of emotion through my upper bodily cavity as if to seek its release in tears, resisting all the while the obvious manipulation through this deployment of the child. It is as if one's affective life had been taken over by an alien force, akin to the rays of God that Schreber described as having taken over his body to transform it into something else in service to a heteronomous desire (Santner 1996). The emotional response is overdetermined. Does every viewer feel this internal resistance to having their emotions seized up in this way?

My thoughts turn to Negri and Hardt's suggestion that the production (and manipulation) of affects is part of what drives the postmodernization of the economy. Here we have the computer (the informationalization of production), the adoption professional (problem-solving immaterial labor), and the prospective parents (affectively necessary labor) brought together within a communicational apparatus (television) that can deploy this production of affects toward consumption. One could also read this computer ad as a vivid illustration of the time-space compression of a post-Fordist regime of "just-in-time" reproduction that brings together the factors of production across vast geographic differences of unequal development. Yet this reading is overshadowed by an apparent victory in the struggle for recognition in mainstream consumer representations. Time-space compression and its linkage to cybertechnology are also reflected in the biologizing tropes of prospective parents who liken the long wait through the various stages of the adoption process to the gestational biological time of pregnancy itself, a process that culminates in the fax transmission of the agency photograph of their child's face. One mother wrote that receiving the photograph was like watching her child being born on the fax machine.

The Mirror of the Child

Parental love, which is so moving and at bottom so childish, is nothing but the parents' narcissism born again, which, transformed into object-love, unmistakably reveals its former nature.

—Freud, "On Narcissism: An Introduction"

Susan Stewart (1993) describes the recursive circuit of desire that sets up the subjective relationship between parent and child in practices such as the Tom Thumb Wedding, in which children are arrayed in the stilled tableau of the photograph as the miniature participants in a wedding ceremony. Much of the labor in staging the photograph is in the domain of maternal display, entailing the feminine detail of costumery and a maternal practice of archiving the sentimental life of the family. The photograph represents the mirroring of the adult's own moment of origin, with all the pleasure and alarm aroused by the child's potential (or failure) to replicate a self or to become a point of new beginning. For the child, it represents the mimesis of a desired adult identity that presumably sets the child on a pathway toward normative heterosexual identity. Stewart's essay suggests the importance of the practices of family photography as a technology capable of completing the subjective identification between parent and child, a technology that is contemporaneous with the intensification of family life in its modern form.[43]

At the time of referral, when a child matching the requirements and adoption status of the parents has been located, a small photograph is sent, along with the child's Chinese name, the location of the orphanage, and the child's background (insofar as it is known). The parents may share this photo with others; they may even have it scanned into the Web to share with the cybercommunity. But its primary significance is in its functioning as a token for the child itself, an object with which an unbreakable bond can be forged.[44] Mothers describe how the small photo is carried on their bodies, in a pocket, enabling frequent gazes at a tiny face, always "beautiful," inviting a love of looking that knows no limit. The photo possesses this power as a token that bears the promise of being exchanged for the original.

The tiny face is read as issuing a demand for love that promises to its prospective mother the plenitude of a love fully reciprocated. The photo-infant thus pictured and named begins to coalesce as a being whose subjectivity is already "under construction," in which the dialectic of identity and difference is already at work.[45] But this parental duty is once again exceeded in a discharge of pleasure. One mother wrote that she could already imagine her child's ethnicity. Where does this pleasure come from? We see the workings of the imaginary dimensions of subjectivity in which the parent projects herself or himself into the ego-ideal of the "educative parent" who must replicate her or his class subjectivity in the child through modern regimes of child nurture.[46] Yet here the project is expanded by the addition of the successful negotiation of ethnicity as one of the duties of the responsible parent, an added bonus on which parental worthiness can be evaluated and appraised. However, we may also wish to consider how this pleasure relates to the aestheticization of a cultural difference that appears unconnected to the history of racialized stratification in U.S. society. Is there not a curious split here in which "culture" or "ethnicity" signifies as an aestheticized difference, displacing race and class, which register as more unbridgeable frames of difference?

The strength of the imaginary relationship with the face in the photo was demonstrated in one instance when a substitution was made at the moment of the transfer of the child. The mother went into a panic when she failed to recognize the infant she was given and was informed that the baby originally referred to her was not "as good" as the one offered. The parent assumed a heroic position in her insistence on being given "her" baby and accepting no substitute. The substitutability of the infant constitutes a violation of the bond already forged between mother and child; suggesting that the mother will not "know" her own child. But for her a substitute can never be merely an abstract equivalent of the infant she has already bonded with.[47] In such moments, the shadow of the commodity once again lurks over the child and is refused.

The Problem of Naming

The child's name raises the problem of how the child is to be positioned in the realm of the symbolic. Retaining the child's Chinese name promises the eruption of "difference" in the child's positioning in language and therefore complicates the smooth suturing of the child into the symbolic order. The Chinese name presents the problem of phonemic difference and an anxiety about the unpronounceability of the child's proper name—the supreme marker of identity in a society heavily invested in the cult of the individual. This difficulty is often negotiated by giving the child a more familiar ("English") name alongside its Chinese name, or by retaining the Chinese name as a middle name. This practice sometimes results in quite a long chain of monikers. One couple named their child with three English names followed by the child's two-syllable Chinese name and a surname. One father wrote that they had changed their daughter's Chinese name to another of similar meaning that was more easily pronounced by an English speaker. They did not want the difficult pronunciation of her name to become a target of ridicule for other children.[48] Some parents seek English equivalents for the "original" meaning of the child's name (such as Jade), which seems blissfully unaware of the orientalist history of this practice (Spivak 1985). Other parents search for possible combinations of Chinese characters that bear a phonemic resemblance to an English name, using unusual spellings (Chinese pinyin) to retain the trace of a difference that can be domesticated (as in Zhuli, Judi, Wanda, Haidi, or Mali). In this sense, then, the name becomes the means to invest the child with a unique identity and a name that is "truly proper," while at the same time ethnicizing the child with a marker of cultural heritage that should not be erased in the act of renomination.[49] In one case, a parent questioned the unique signification of the proper name when she discovered that all the children adopted from an orphanage in Mao'an bore the surname Mao, with a regular occurring series of single-character given names that were reused as soon as that nominal place had been vacated by adoption. This particular practice of surnaming the child by geographical place is a comfort to some parents who feel that it strengthens the tie of the child to its point of origin. One parent expressed appreciation for the connection between place-name and the child's proper name as a supplement for her lack of "roots."[50] But the regular replication of given names threatens the unique identity of the child as having an irreplaceable value by suggesting that it is, instead, an infinitely substitutable sign (token) of value in relations of exchange that traverse national boundaries. The reiteration of names threatens to heighten the likeness of the child to a product of mechanical reproduction.

The problem of naming marks a site of anxiety about anchoring the child's identity, its ties to its place of origin, and its difference. It is an anxiety that seems to recognize the violence of renaming as the erasure of a difference that will eventually reassert itself with a vengeance when the child begins to raise the question of his or her own origin. Yet, this act of renomination also presents the possibility of reshaping the parent's identity to merge with that of the child, as when parents adopt their child's surname as their own middle name, surrendering themselves to the violence of renaming—to bear, as it were, half of that burden but also in the process announcing the presence of a "difference" in the construction of their own identities. This enunciation of a difference in parental subjectivity is also evident in the common use of teknonymy on the Internet as one's sign-off, in which the proper name alone fails to identify the speaker but is followed by "mother of . . . ," as well as all the significant dates of the adoption process, from initiating the paperwork to "gotcha day" to homecoming.

The Maternal Archive

Mary Kelly's art installation entitled *Post-Partum Document* draws our attention to the fetishizing desire of the mother toward the traces of her child's passage through infancy, a desire that the artist displaces by framing the ejecta of the nursery with the fetishizing practices of the art exhibit. Soiled diapers and pieces of her son's "blankie" were displayed in clear plastic boxes fixed to the wall as objects bathed in light and demanding the concentrated attention of the viewer. In her construction of this public document of the intimate interdependency between mother and infant (and its inevitable end with the child's entry into language), Kelly displaces her fetishization of the child onto the work of art and, in so doing, creates an ironic distance from which to understand her own desire to hold on to her child as he passes from infant dependency to an identity independent of her.

The archiving practices of adoptive parents similarly express the play of desire in relation to the child. As a parent fully implicated in the labor of sentimentalizing objects that represent a child already "lost and gone" at the various stages of his or her natural progression of growth and development, I use ethnography to provide an ironic distance from a practice with which I am myself intimately familiar. I do so not just to stave off the danger of a "maternal perversity" that remains fixated on the child long after he or she is gone, but rather to focus on the performative aspects of archiving in the production of identities (for both parents and children).[51] How does the sentimentalization of certain objects (most obviously the family photograph) constitute a realm of affect that we associate with the familial?

Here the archive is constructed proleptically in anticipation of a subject who will need a record of a past and a point of origin, readily retrievable in a form "already made up" for him or her. What catastrophic denouement does such activity forestall? Can we see here an anxiety to secure an ethnicity for the child akin to the project of securing a gender, which alongside nationality, sexuality, and race configure the coordinates of our modern identity?[52] In the film *Blade Runner*, a population of replicants is provided with a similar archive of a human childhood so that they are fooled into thinking that the identities constructed for them are "really real."[53] As Judith Williamson has noted in her essay on family photography, the narrative constructed in the family photo album is often a coercive one (something she discovered when she came across a trove of outtakes from the family album that suggest an alternative narrative about her childhood) (Williamson 1994). Similarly, the archiving practice of the adoptive mother is overlaid with an anxious anticipation of the child's search for its own origin, a chaotic possibility the mother attempts to contain in the construction of a memory book.[54]

Here again anxiety is channeled into pleasure—an aesthetic absorption in compiling a narrative for the child as a subject "under construction."[55] The archive exhibits the documents provided by the orphanage, a narrative of the adoption trip, photos of the child's introduction to his or her new home and kin, and chartings of the child's growth and development, his or her physical transformation. This "museological mania" of the mother is expressed in the search for "archive-quality" materials to assemble the child's adoption narrative into an object for display.[56] The fascination with materials—such as acid-free paper, de-acidifying chemicals, quilted boxes with plastic see-through bags to hold clothing—veers once again into the domain of a commodity fetishism that displaces onto the commodity the labor of keeping difference neatly contained. The obsession with preservation is in some cases particularly devoted to the clothing the child wore in its transfer from the orphanage to her adoptive parents, who wait in tourist hotel rooms with a new outfit brought from home, ready to complete an act of "cross-dressing" that implicitly signifies the transfer of the child from one site of nurture to another. One mother described in great detail the clothing her daughter wore, from her split-crotch pants (in lieu of diapers) to the red nail polish on her toes.

Another item sometimes mentioned is Chinese paper money, which in one case was first submerged in de-acidifying chemicals and then laminated in plastic! If the two things that prove most mysterious to the child in capitalist culture are his or her own origin (the mystery of sexual reproduction) and that of money (the mystery of value as something that circulates as a ghostly abstraction), here the two are linked.[57] Chinese money becomes a metaphoric displacement for the child. Desired because "it is pretty," its transit to the United States is fraught with anxiety because of the rules regulating the passage of Chinese currency outside national borders. The money, like the child, must be extracted from its place of origin and reinserted into a new desiring economy. This fetishization of Chinese money removes it from the circuit of economic value (which must not be allowed such promiscuous contact with the child) so that it can become resignified as affective value. Chinese money comes to bear a signifying labor as the marker of difference, a difference linked to the child in their common "origin."

These archiving practices evoke a feminist historiography of the creation of domestic space in relation to the emergence of industrial capitalism. Gillian Brown has written about the domestic ideologies of nineteenth-century America, in which the domestic sphere is constructed as a sentimentalized haven from the uncertain contingencies of the marketplace. Intrinsic to this construction are the rituals of decommodification that transform the commodity into a sentimentalized possession appropriate to a realm of affect that must be kept separate from the impersonal contract of market exchange. In this sentimental economy, the commodity is not only not recognized as fetishized but also as *not fetishized enough* in its lacking of the aura of a connectedness to family life—the very things that are familiar in the dual senses of the familial and the intimately known. New objects incorporated into this sphere must be assimilated into this realm of affect by becoming objects that are the constitutive supplements of identity, objects with a familial history (Brown 1990:50–53). I see this archiving activity to be a very similar process of constructing an affective aura around the child, whether or not he or she is adopted.

If nineteenth-century sentimentalism eschewed the promiscuous inclusion of commodities into the domestic order, however, late-twentieth-century subjects find the realm of affect completely colonized by commodity consumption. This is perhaps best illustrated in the construction of the memory books, which are lovingly made by hand but with the aid of objects prefabricated and purchased for this act of creation. The feminine pastime of "crafting" combines the notion of handicraft production with consumer capitalism in the assemblage of acid-free, "archival-quality" pages embellished with stickers, special stamps, decorative photo frames and borders as the material support for the sentimental labor of constructing this aura around the child.[58]

Although mothers take on the larger burden of affective labor within the family, fathers are not exempt. One prospective father shared with the e-mail list his "dream work" in which he saw his child adrift in a sea of complexity and difficulty. He imagined his child's biological parents and the "aunties" from the orphanage. He then pictured her giggling in the arms of his wife or sleeping in her Winnie the Pooh jammies. Yet we see his gaze at the completed image of the child in the arms of his wife as if already in the lens of a camera focused on capturing the loving touch (the realm of the haptic) between the child and the maternal body that represents so fully the most intimate core of family life (Mavor 1995).

Globalization and Its Perplexities

What is striking here is how the circuits for adopting transnationally follow alongside the articulations of spatially dispersed post-Fordist production in its endless search for cheap labor by articulating localized regimes of human capital. Adoption agencies follow in the wake of foreign investment by linking up the factors of (re)production to enable the movement of surplus value from one site to another. How bodily value is recognized in reform-era China is complexly determined by the desire for foreign capital investment. The migrant laborer is both derogated as lacking value (hence his/her labor is cheap) while also being the source from which surplus value is extracted to enable capital accumulation and the emergence of a Chinese middle class. This misrecognition of the value of migrant labor is a massive "disavowal" that I wish to link up with the disavowal of the commodification of transnational adoption. They are both necessary to the transfer of surplus value from the site of (re)production to the site of consumption. The migrant laborer is one ghostly double of the transnationally adopted child; the single child of the Chinese urban middle class is yet another.

The surplus value of the migrant travels as labor congealed in the commodity. In its travel, the commodity moves from a value regime where the "hand" of the producer is literally expendable to a value regime where it can sell at a price many times in excess of the cost of production! I cite the case of worker He Qun, who lost her hand to a stamping machine in a work environment where tens of thousands of workers are killed or maimed each year in industrial accidents (Fackler 2002). Replacing outdated machinery with equipment that can meet even minimal safety standards is less profitable than simply replacing workers. The evaluation of human capital that so cavalierly expends the "superfluity" of China's migrant workers is the same logic that "surpluses" infants for adoption. The determinations of embodied value at both ends of the value chain must be understood within the larger set of relations that connect the site of production with that of consumption.

The object world that defines a superior site of nurture—the ruffled blouse embroidered with pandas, the educational toys made of extruded plastic, the Asian-featured doll—are, more likely than not, expressions of congealed surplus value that can claim a common origin with the embodied value of the child itself. By pointing this out, I wish to reaffirm once again that I do not mean to disenable adoption and the provision of loving homes to abandoned infants, but I feel that in so doing the perplexities of the global economy need to be clearly recognized rather than disavowed.

I take this notion of "perplexity" from Priti Ramamurthy's (2003) reworking of value-chain analysis to open "the possibility of imagining globally connected lives by politicizing consumption." Ramamurthy begins with the moment of perplexity when the subjects refuse their positioning within the logics of marketing commodities. I begin, perhaps because the subjects of my study are more privileged than hers, with the moment of disavowal—a moment that elides the possibility of a refusal—in hopes of opening it up again so that it can "expand the debates on what it is people desire for themselves and others" (Ramamurthy 2003:526). Moreover, I incorporate embodied human capital into a value chain along with inanimate objects for consumption. I do this not because I want to suggest that Asian adoptees are "mere commodities," but because I see it as a means to evoke the complex interconnections between differently privileged bodies in a global circuit. Analyses of consumption need to go beyond understanding the meanings it constructs in the identity formation of consumers to elucidate the "structural elements . . . grounded in political and economic systems" (Princen, Maniates, and Conca 2002:ix).

These disjunctures do not exist just across but also *within* national borders.[59] Perhaps I should not have been so surprised when, in my field research in China in 2000, a twenty-five-year-old lawyer expressed her fantasy of adopting one child from each of China's fifty-six officially recognized national minorities and then of going to Africa to bring back a child or two to China to rear. She reasoned that her professional status gave her the economic means to give these children a better start (simultaneously recognizing the excessiveness of her desire in sheer logistical terms). But, in so doing, she is also expressing a newly imagined means of assuming a certain class privilege in which she can move effortlessly across racial and national divides—to be a new kind of citizen in the world. What this example suggests to me is the possibility of "doing good" without ever questioning one's own privilege. The critical analysis of consumption needs to query "the very idea of consumer sovereignty" whose desires and choices are shaped and conditioned by larger structural forces (Princen, Maniates, and Conca 2002:4).

This labor of confronting consumption is not reserved only for adoptive parents but properly belongs to all of us who are, often unwittingly, articulated within a complex network of exchanges that propels the commodity to us across multiple disjunctures. Such reflection is critically important if we are ever to claim a political agency that exceeds the private confines of the family and works toward a wider call to responsibility.

NOTES

An earlier version of this essay was published in *positions: east asia cultures critique* 8 (Fall 2000):389–421. It has been revised for this volume to foreground the question of value and issues of consumption. Funding support for some parts of this research was generously provided by the American Council of Learned Societies (Committee for Scholarly Communication with China), the National Foundation for the Humanities, and the Royalty Research Fund of the University of Washington. I thank Janelle Taylor for her encouragement to revisit the question of commodification for this volume. Helpful comments on earlier drafts were made by Andrea Arai, John Comaroff, Eric Diehl, Kaushik Ghosh, Lucy Jarocsz,

Victoria Lawson, Katherine Libal, Harriet Phinney, Vicente Rafael, Venkat Rao, Lorna Rhodes, Lisa Rofel, Laurie Sears, Eric Thompson, Janet Upton, Toby Volkman, and Priscilla Wald. Thanks also to Nayna Jhaveri, Priti Ramamurthy, and Yan Hairong for our ongoing discussions on questions of value. Errors of interpretation are entirely my own. I am also indebted to Marilyn Ivy and Sharon Stephens, whose critical work on the child I have found inspiring.

1. I am indebted to Kaushik Ghosh for raising this connection. In an earlier version of this argument (Anagnost 2000), I failed to develop it fully. Subsequently, my reading of Spivak's work on value enabled me to think it through more carefully.

2. I thank Lisa Rofel for helping me to clarify this issue, which is critically important for thinking through the methodological problems of using the Internet as an ethnographic resource. The ways in which Internet communications are transforming our lives has outpaced our ability to reflect on them theoretically. This makes the project of this essay all the more tentative in attempting at least to pose what appear at the outset to be critical questions. Much of the material used for this essay was gathered from e-mail discussion lists and various Web sites organized around the topic of China adoption. The two most important lists were apc (a-parents-china-digest@shore.net) and pac (post-adopt-china-digest@shore.net), both of which I followed for a period of two years. In keeping with the protocols of ethnographic protection of informants, I have not specified the issue number from which material has been cited. The question that this use of the Internet raises regarding the uncertain line between public and private in Internet communications were addressed more at length in Anagnost (2000).

3. Volkman (2003:37) points out that the Chinese authorities also ask that parents "impart respect for 'Chinese culture'" and that the right of the child to "have" a culture is part of international rights discourse.

4. Daniel Miller (1997 and in this volume) notes a similar regendering for his educated middle-class British subjects for whom motherhood is embraced as a kind of sacrifice, as if in repudiation of their former selves. Elsewhere in the same essay he suggests that motherhood displaces consumption as a "superior form of self-construction through a new social relationship" (1997:81). This nicely captures the theme of this volume in which the mother's consuming passions are redirected toward the child as an act of self-transformation. Barbara Katz Rothman (1990:45 and in this volume) proposes that the mother should be able to claim a "sweat equity" in the nurture of children that can never, in fact, be claimed in a system of capitalist patriarchy. As I argue here, in conditions of late capitalism, if not before, maternal labor is increasingly seen as producing value in the formation of human capital but under vastly unequal conditions of production.

5. I am grateful to Sara Dorow, who recently completed her ethnographically rich dissertation on China adoption, for reminding me of this point.

6. I take my inspiration here from Donzelot's attempts to trace a history of how we came to be the way "we" are (1997:8). I interpret the "we" of this statement in terms of a certain bourgeois ideology of the family that may be hegemonic, although not uncontested, in American public life.

7. Miller (1997:85 and in this volume) also interrogates what he calls "obsessive child-centredness" as related to larger social transformations.

8. If the efforts of adoptive parents to construct a cultural identity for their child seem especially charged in terms of racial difference, we could perhaps suggest that all chil-

dren are similarly constructed in terms of race and class that go unmarked because they are naturalized through the privileging of biological relatedness. Especially for middle-class parents, much of the pressure to parent in a certain way is to ensure the reproduction of class position in their child in an economic and cultural landscape that has made this outcome more uncertain.

9. I am indebted here to Berlant's (1997) conceptualization of the intimate public sphere and Lisa Lowe's (1996:84–96) critique of certain modes of aestheticized multiculturalism.

10. This is not always the case in international adoption, when children may be taken from their mothers forcibly. See Kligman (1995). One could argue this is the case in China as well, where a stringent birth policy puts pressure on parents to abandon baby girls. While this is not directly in the power of adoptive parents to change, some do express concern over the indirect ways in which adoption might support the complex justifications for an abusive policy and its "surplusing" of baby girls.

11. Eng (2003:9) asks "what cultural alibis about Chinese otherness and gender abuse must be produced" to efface the larger structural determinations of the child's value in its transfer from one place to another.

12. See Sten Johansson and Ola Nygren (1991) for a discussion of the problem of "missing girls" in Chinese demography and of how sex ratio imbalance needs to be read with a better understanding of the complex interactions of state policy and family practices. Baby girls are often strategically abandoned on the doorsteps of childless or daughterless couples who are glad to receive them. See Susan Greenhalgh (1994), on how widely a newly defined ideal family form of two children, one of each sex, has become desired, even in rural areas. My data from interviewing middle-class subjects in Nanjing in 1999 and 2000 also strongly suggests that urban residents see this family size as ideal. See Kay Ann Johnson, Banghan Huang, and Liyao Wang (1998) for a well-supported discussion of how daughters are valued as an important affective resource for parents who may resort to extralegal means to adopt one.

13. The phrase "stratified reproduction" is adapted from Shellee Colen's (1995) study of Jamaican child care workers in New York City who must leave their own children in the care of others in their place of origin as they move transnationally to care for the children of others.

14. For the politics of embodied value in China in the wake of the one-child family policy and the role of transnational discourses of population control, see Ann Anagnost (1988, 1997a, 1997b). My discussion owes much to Donzelot's (1997) discussion of the centrality of the policing of families to the emergence of a new social economy in nineteenth-century European modernities, elaborating Michel Foucault's concept of biopower in the history of the bourgeois family.

15. This discussion of the determinants of embodied value in the PRC is based on five months of field research in Nanjing, China, in 1999 and 2000. See Anagnost (2004) for a more developed discussion of *suzhi* (quality) as an inverse figure of value.

16. "Bare life" is a reference to Agamben's (1995) discussion of "unqualified life" as the substrate of modern governmentality that must be managed to produce "the good life." In reform-era China, *suzhi* becomes the figure around which bodies are recognized as having or lacking value and thereby the full rights of citizenship.

17. China is by no means the only country of origin for Asian adoptees. Adoption from Korea has a much longer history, and the community formed around Korean adoption is often appealed to by this new cohort of parents as a resource for successfully par-

enting the Asian adoptee. One adoptive mother responded to an earlier version of this essay by stating that the concern to construct a cultural identity for the child was anticipated by the issues of identity raised by an earlier cohort of Korean adoptees. While this is no doubt true, I wonder to what extent the increasing presence of multiculturalism in U.S. society has also set up new conditions for marking the child's difference.

18. Eng (2003:8) asks what it might mean when "full and robust citizenship is socially effected from child to parent and, in many cases, through the position of the adoptee, its visible possession and spectacular display."

19. There are e-mail discussions for biological parents as well, such as lists organized around the month of birth. Parents, primarily mothers, who feel isolated and anxious about issues of child nurture can compare their experiences with other mothers in North America, but also transnationally in other English-speaking communities in Europe, Australia, and other places. Similar lists exist on the Chinese-language Web as well, suggesting that the phenomenon is not limited to Anglophone cyberspace.

20. The new critical geography reconsiders the relationship between space and place, seeing the latter as a trope of spatialization that can apply to electronically linked as well as geographically proximate communities. See Morley and Robins (1989).

21. Berlant's argument usefully introduces citizenship as a central category of analysis. For work that theorizes photography as a technology not just of voyeurism but also of exhibitionism, see also Mavor (1995), McClintock (1995), and Rafael (2000). Rafael, in particular, looks at it as a technology of middle-class subject production in the Philippines.

22. An important exception to this would be the financial support collected by parent groups for Chinese orphan homes to improve conditions for children left behind.

23. See Rothman (1990:49 and in this volume) for a discussion of the uncertain line in adoption practices between a redistribution of scarce resources to parents who desire to nurture a child to profiteering in a baby market. Eng (2003:6) notes a similar perplexity in transnational adoption in its "complicating the borders between exploitation and privilege."

24. Layne (1999) suggests that parents in the United States evoke rhetorics of the gift to articulate a critique of consumer culture, especially in situations of nonnormative parenting (involving adoption, surrogacy, fosterage, and disability). In the adoption practices I am examining here, I am reading this evocation of the gift as a disavowal, rather than a critique, of capitalism. As I hope will be made clear later in the essay, my intent is to open to question the division of labor between public and private domains within capitalist culture that constitutes the family as an interiority needing protection from the contaminations of the marketplace and capitalist culture. The necessity for this critique is to help us anatomize the structure of feeling that keeps advocacy for children contained within the family.

25. The one-family policy is the enabling precondition for making Chinese baby girls so readily available for international adoption. In critiquing the "salvage" narrative, however, my intention is to comment on unreflective representations of human rights abuses that essentially "otherize" Chinese conditions of nurture. That the salvage discourse is not in itself without its own contradictions will become clear later in this essay. See also Johnson, Huang, and Wang (1998) on infant abandonment discussing how the increasing stringency of birth policy implementation in the early

1990s overloaded the underfunded network of Chinese orphan homes. International adoption was one way of relieving that pressure while raising badly needed funds. Some adoptive parents have been very vocal in defending Chinese caretakers against charges of neglect.

26. "Reactive attachment disorder" is diagnostic category No. 313.89 in the *Diagnostic Statistical Manual of Psychiatry*, 4th ed. (1994):91–93. It is characterized as "a disturbance in social relatedness ... presumed to be due to grossly pathogenic care" and resulting in "persistent failure to initiate or respond" to social interactions or, paradoxically, a tendency to "indiscriminate sociability" in the older child. Such indications are often linked to "failure to thrive" and what is called "hospitalism," due its linkage with institutional care. The anxiety that this category produces no doubt partly accounts for the projection of affect on their child's earliest caregivers, during a time in their child's life that can never be retrieved to ensure the early regime of middle-class child nurture—a time irrevocably outside of parental control.

27. The data assembled by Johnson, Huang, and Wang (1998) seem to support this more balanced picture of the conditions of Chinese orphan homes. For a more inflammatory perspective, see Human Rights Watch (1996), which presents a much more damaging picture of the state of nurture (or its lack) in Chinese orphan homes; much of the evidence in this report is from the orphan home in Shanghai featured in the BBC documentaries by filmmakers Kate Blewett and Brian Woods, *The Dying Rooms* (1995) and *Return to the Dying Rooms* (1996).

28. Since *The Dying Rooms*, adoptive parents are rarely allowed into the crib rooms of the orphan home. Most often parents wait in their hotel for their child to be brought to them.

29. Volkman (2003:46) informs that these contributions from adoptive parents have, in some cases, been substantial enough to build new orphan facilities in China.

30. This reasoning was reported by one informant, but I do not know how generalized it may be among adoptive parents who have taken that route.

31. See Clark (1998) for a discussion of how a few well-publicized cases that do not reflect the generality of adoption outcomes intensify this fear of losing one's child. Many of the issues she discusses in the context of domestic interracial adoption strikingly parallel those discussed here. She makes cogent use of Lowe (1995) in her discussion of how the family has become increasingly drawn into the realm of commodification while evoking a nostalgic longing for its inviolability from market exchanges. I am indebted to Vicente Rafael for bringing Clark's essay to my attention.

32. I am indebted to Venkat Rao for pushing me to ask this question. A similar point was raised by John Comaroff in his comments on an earlier version of this essay. The phrase "rituals of decommodification" is also his.

33. Daniel Miller notes a similar pleasure among the mothers in his study of middle-class parenting in North London (1997:71 and in this volume).

34. See Anagnost (1997) for a discussion of similar kinds of commodity appeal in Chinese urban consuming practices.

35. See Steedman (1995) for a historical genealogy of the fetishization of the child's littleness as part of the nineteenth-century cult of the child.

36. Lo is writing in the context of post-1997 Hong Kong anxieties about population movement from the PRC to the former British Crown colony.

37. This fixation on dolls parallels a similar desire for finding a Chinese nanny for the

child, someone who not only looks like her but who can talk to the child in its "native" language.
38. Miller (1997:75 and in this volume) also notes how the "stuffed toy" may become a "transitional object" for the mother and her vicarious vision of the infant as an ideal object.
39. See Yngvesson (2003:12) for a discussion of the adopted child as a "sublime object" over which "time has no power."
40. My thanks to Toby Volkman and Tom Buoye for bringing these to my attention.
41. This description of the ad is provided by Janet Upton and Eric Diehl. I have been unable to view it myself, despite repeated attempts to capture it on television.
42. See Ivy (1995) and Taylor (1992), respectively, for detailed cultural critiques of the Advo circulars and the Volvo ad. Eng (n.d.:7) cites the portrayal in a television ad for John Hancock of a white American lesbian couple and their newly adopted Chinese infant passing through U.S. customs on their way home. This ad gives a new visual normativity to lesbian families as well as families formed through adoption. Eng notes the link between the child and the selling of insurance as one that powerfully attests to the child's becoming a body of value in its transfer across national borders. See also Rothman (1990:47–48 and in this volume) for a comparable discussion of how images of needy children are used in soliciting contributions to charitable organizations.
43. Stewart elaborates this point: "If, following Lacan, we say that the recognition of the imaginary during infancy is what begins the process of the constitution of the subject, it is no less the case that the imaginary's function is to continue the process of that constitution through adult life as well. In the play of identity and difference out of which the subject 'appears' at any given point, the relation between childhood and the present, a relation which is and is not a repetition, constitutes an imaginary at either end: for the child, the mother as object of desire; for the adult, the image of the past, the dual relation before it was lost, the pure body-within-the-body, which is only approximated in reproduction. And out of this adult desire springs the demand for an object—not an object of use value, but a pure object, an object which will not be taken up in the changing sphere of lived reality but rather will remain complete at a distance. In this way, it resembles childhood, which will not change" (1993:124–25). Insofar as we can historicize this projection of desire upon the child (and childhood) as intensified in a bourgeois family formation, so must we historicize Lacan's fable of subject production via the mirror phase.
44. This is not unlike the process of constructing the personhood of an unborn child that may begin with the home pregnancy test. See Layne (2000:112).
45. Sometimes this activity anticipates the moment of referral in dreams. The dream of one prospective mother was quite detailed. The referral photo was described along with a statement of the relevant facts, including name and age. There was even a picture of the child's birth parents, in which the mother appeared thin and unhappy looking. This photo is of course the oneiric "filling in" of the gap in the child's origin, an absence imposed by the conditions of the child's abandonment (discussed elsewhere in this essay).
46. Donzelot writes: "The family's tactical withdrawal into itself and the diffusion of new norms brought about an intensification of family life. Concentrated on itself, more attentive than ever before to the least details of the children's education, the family became an avid consumer of everything that might help it to 'realize itself'.... Parents no longer have the right, as they had in the Dark Ages, to turn their children into failures" (1997:224–25). The practices of adoptive families to address the problem of

identity (constituting communities, culture camps, discussion groups) are perhaps assimilable to Foucault's concept of the technologies of the self.

47. The imaginary relation to the child is also reflected in the eager search for signs that the tie between mother and child, although not biological, was divinely ordained by God or fate. The meager facts concerning the history of the child (the circumstances of his or her abandonment, or the record of the child's fosterage), usually a list of dates, are sometimes aligned with significant dates of the parents to discover temporal linkages that resignify the arbitrary process of referral. Hence, the link between parents and child can be imagined back to the point of the child's own origin, as intended for them from the very beginning.

48. This parent also alerted listmates to the existence of a book entitled *Multicultural Baby Names* (Abadie 1993).

49. See Derrida (1976) for a discussion of the impossibility of a name that is truly proper, an impossibility that our contemporary cult of the individual hopes to evade in a renewed inventiveness in the given names of children.

50. This link to the origin is also promoted in the construction of "hometown" Web sites linking adopted children from the same orphan home with an informational node that forms a sense of place. This practice evokes the organization of "native place associations" by immigrant Chinese worldwide. See Yngvesson (2003) and Volkman (2003) for discussions of roots tourism by adoptive families. Eng (n.d.:27, 30) suggests that this obsession with origins denies the "social contingency" of kinship within a transnational frame.

51. In her work on the maternal archive work by women who have experienced pregnancy loss, Layne (2000:134–35) rejects the critical deployment of the fetish as a denigration of the cultural work of memory assigned to women in contemporary North America. I deploy it here as a means of interrogating further this division of affective labor that makes the memory work so compelling for women as mothers.

52. I thank Eric Thompson for this suggestion.

53. I am indebted to Harriet Phinney for suggesting this connection. The citation of *Blade Runner* in this way cannot avoid a certain irony in the extent to which the film portrays a dystopic American landscape overwhelmed by immigration from Asia, Africa, and Latin America (Lowe 1996:86–87).

54. This reading is inspired by the German novel by Marie Luise Kashnitz, *The House of Childhood,* as a psychoanalytic allegory for the search for the origin of the self in childhood. The childhood of Kashnitz's female protagonist is locked within an apparently impenetrable black box that reveals its contents in fragmentary screen images from which she must painfully construct a myth of origin.

55. I am indulging myself here by using the phrase for unfinished Web sites.

56. My suggestion that these objects are not solely for the child derives from the practice of some parents of posting adoption narratives, complete with photos, on family Web sites. "Museological mania" is Emily Apter's phrasing. See Kelly and Apter (1993:352).

57. See Rose (1993:102) for a discussion of this dual anxiety of childhood.

58. See Kathleen Stewart (1988) for a discussion of the linkage between "crafting" and the phantasmagoria of late-twentieth-century consumer capitalism in the nostalgic retrieval of a handicraft economy by way of the commodity form.

59. In this respect, the child waiting for a permanent home in U.S. orphanages must stand as yet another ghostly double of the Asian adoptee.

Going "Home"

Adoption, Exclusive Belongings, and the Mythology of Roots

BARBARA YNGVESSON

> An angel with no face embraced me
> And whispered through my whole body;
> "Don't be ashamed of being human, be proud!
> Inside you vault opens behind vault endlessly.
> You will never be complete, that's how it's meant to be."
>
> —Tomas Tranströmer, "Romanesque Arches"

In the world of intercountry adoption, two stories predominate: a story of abandonment and a story about roots. In the abandonment story, a baby is found in a marketplace, on a roadside, outside a police station, or in the *tour* of an orphanage; alternately, a child is left by its mother at a hospital, or is relinquished or surrendered to child welfare officials, a social worker, or the staff of a children's home. After passing through the hands of social workers, lawyers, and/or orphanage staff and perhaps in and out of hospitals, foster homes, and courts, this child may ultimately be declared free for adoption, a process that requires a second, legal separation that constitutes the child as a legal orphan. Similarly, a mother who relinquishes her child to state agents must consent to the irrevocable termination of her rights to the child. In international adoptions, the child will also be separated from its state of origin (a procedure that in some nations involves sealing the record of this severance and altering the child's birth certificate) so that it can be connected to a new family, a new name, a new nation. The child is given a new identity. It now *belongs* in a new place.

This story of separation is a story about loss and the transformation of loss into a "clean break" (Duncan 1993:51) that forms the ground for starting anew.

The clean break separates the child from everything that constitutes her grounds for belonging as a child to *this* family and *this* nation while establishing her transferability to *that* family and *that* nation. With a past that has been cut away—an old identity that no longer exists—the child can be re-embedded in a new place, almost as though she never moved at all.

Even as this legal story of separation is the official ground for constituting adoptive identities, another story competes with it in both law and adoption practice. This other story was a persistent counterpoint to the movement for "strong" adoptions that prevailed at the Hague Conference in the early 1990s (Duncan 1993) and was incorporated into the Hague Convention as children's right to preservation of their "ethnic, religious and cultural background" (Hague Convention 1993:Article 16c). The preservation story implies that there is no such thing as a clean break and underpins the search movement in domestic adoptions, the debate over sealed records, and the movement to keep adoptions open in the United States today (Yngvesson 1997; Carp 1998; Verhovek 2000). In this story, identity is associated with a root or ground of belonging that is *inside* the child (as "blood," "primal connectedness," and "identity hunger") (Lifton 1994:67–71) and unchanging. But it is also *outside* the child in the sense that it is assumed to tie her to others whom she is like (as defined by skin color, hair texture, facial features, and so forth). Alienation from this source of likeness produces "genealogical bewilderment" (Lifton 1994:68, citing Sants 1964) and a psychological need for the adopted child to return to where she *really* belongs.

The story of a freestanding child and the story about a rooted child appear to be mutually exclusive and are associated with different adoption practices. The former is associated with race and other forms of matching that are intended to produce "as if" adoptive families that mimic natural ones (Modell 1994). Even in international transracial adoptions, where race matching is impossible, adoption practices in the 1960s and 1970s emphasized complete absorption of the adopted child into the new family and nation (Andersson 1991). By contrast, the story about roots is associated with the recognition of adoption as a distinct family form (Kirk 1981) and involves acknowledging (even underscoring) the differences between an adoptee and his or her adoptive parents, constituting the adoptive family as a site of tension because of its inclusion of a child who "naturally" belongs to another person or place.

Both practices are versions of a familiar and powerful (Western) myth about identity as a matter of exclusive belongings and belonging as a matter of "an active proprietorship" (Strathern 1988:135).[1] In the clean break version of this myth, the adoptive child is set free from the past (constituted as "abandoned" or "motherless") so that he or she can be assimilated completely into the adoptive family. In the preservation story, on the other hand, the child is imagined as a part of his or her birth mother or birth nation, imagined as being constantly pulled back to that ground.

The narrative of exclusive belongings provides the rationale for legal protections in which a child's "natural" family is erased while engaging adoptive families in naturalizing practices for transforming themselves into their child's "real" parents (Yngvesson 1997; Yngvesson and Mahoney 2000:85–87). The labor of naturalization involves both legal and cultural dimensions. Legally, the child is "laundered"—money that changes hands is paid for "services" rather than for the child, the original birth record identifying the "natural" family is sealed, and the adoptive parents are legally transformed into the birth parents. In all of these ways, the material fact of the child's passage from one family, nation, mother, or world to another is canceled and the child is legally reconstituted as the natural child of his or her adoptive parents, purified of the taint that market circulation carries with it (Coutin, Maurer, and Yngvesson 2002: 820–24). Culturally, the adoptive family is rendered natural in practices such as roots trips, culture camps, and other forms of immersion through which the child's foreclosed roots and lost history can be recovered/recycled in the adoptive family environment.

As Anagnost, Wozniak, and Miller (this volume) argue, however, building on the work of Kopytoff (1986) and others, commodification and naturalization work hand in hand (see also Yngvesson 2000, 2002). The work of naturalization can *only* be accomplished in a detour through the "other" (the market, the birth mother, the "developing" nation, legal baby-laundering processes),[2] which qualify the child as a "good" (Callon, Méadel, and Raberharisoa 2001) that is my "own." Yet such detours also carry a risk of unsettling the very belongings that adoptive parents seek to secure.

In what follows, I examine this process of unsettling as it takes place on a roots trip to Chile by Swedish adoptive parents and their children. Such trips suggest how compelling the idea of a return to roots can be. But they also unsettle the idea that returns will produce "wholeness" for the adoptee (Lifton 1994) or completion for the adoptive family. Rather, as Elspeth Probyn (1996:114) suggests, "Bringing forth beginnings can result in a loss of bearings."

This loss of bearings involves the discovery of a self both familiar and strange, me and not-me, a pull to the adoptive parent at the very moment one is in the arms of a birth mother, a pull toward the birth mother at the very moment that she is embracing one's child. The identity narrative and the concept of a child or a parent as "a part of me" are inadequate for capturing the contradictions of desire that constitute this state "in-between being and longing" (Probyn 1996:35). Neither does it capture the *movement*—the "desire for becoming-other" (5)—that is part of the search for a root of belonging and that is provoked by the experience of seeing someone who "looks like me," by touching the native soil of an adopted son, or by the realization that there is a connection, not an unbridgeable gulf, between oneself and the birth mother of one's child. Each of these moments instigates "yet another journey" (Saffian 1998:301–2), an opening rather than an experience of closure.

Roots trips reveal the precariousness of "I am," the simultaneous fascination and terror evoked by what might have been and a longing for the safety of home. They materialize an unfathomable moment of choice when one life that might have been was curtailed and another life that exists now came into being: "Why just me? It feels very strange. One wonders, 'What would have become of me if I had remained there? Who was I during the time I was there?'" (Sara Nordin, interview, August 1999). Such moments interrupt the myth that the legal transformation to an "other" was free—that the child simply came home to a site of love where she always belonged—revealing instead the cost of belonging (and of love), its inseparability from the birth mother, the orphanage, the courthouse, the agency, and the histories linking nations that give children to those that receive them.[3] But they also interrupt the myth of the return as a form of completion or fulfillment in which one can find oneself in another (be consumed by an other) at a place or point of fusion, of "immanence regained." Instead, interruption "occurs at the edge, or rather it constitutes the edge where beings touch each other, expose themselves to each other and separate from one another." It is at this edge that both connects and separates, as Jean-Luc Nancy suggests, that beings "come into being" (Nancy 1991:59, 61).

The account of a roots trip that follows explores these issues, focusing on the experiences of adoptive parents as they sought to fill a gap in the belonging of their adoptive children, the complex emotions of adoptees as they were pulled between a familiar self and an unknown other, and the position of adoptive parents as witnesses to the "labor of mourning" (Benjamin 1995:113), in which their children (and the parents themselves) were involved. My analysis is based on participant observation and on interviews conducted in 1998 and 1999 with adult adoptees born in Chile, and with the Swedish parents who adopted them in the 1970s and early 1980s. I also interviewed staff of Stockholm's Adoption Centre (AC) and Chilean adoption officials. This work is part of a larger study of Swedish international adoption in which I have been engaged since 1995.

Return to Chile

> The Greek word for "return" is *nostos. Algos* means "suffering." So nostalgia is the suffering caused by an unappeased yearning to return.
>
> —Milan Kundera, *Ignorance*

In April 1998 I accompanied a group of twelve Swedish families (nineteen parents and sixteen children, ranging from ten to twenty-one years of age) to Santiago, Chile, on a roots trip organized by Stockholm's Adoption Centre. No one in the families spoke Spanish, and as I am fluent in both Spanish and Swedish, it was agreed that I would serve as one of the three interpreters for the group. I had lived in Santiago as a teenager but had not been back since that time, and in many ways the trip felt like a return to roots for me, as well as for the adopted children.

The adoptions had taken place during the middle years of the Pinochet dictatorship, and for the parents this was their first visit to Chile. Some of them had adopted other children from countries such as Thailand or El Salvador, where they had journeyed to fetch their child. As I discuss below, such trips are charged (often difficult) moments for adopting parents and many consider them a key piece in the work of transforming themselves into their adopted child's "real" parents. Tense political relations between Sweden and Chile during the 1970s and early 1980s—Sweden was a place of refuge for significant numbers of Chileans who fled their country during Pinochet's dictatorship—meant that children adopted from Chile at that time were not picked up by their adoptive parents but arrived with escorts.

To complicate matters further, Swedish adoptions from Chile ended in 1991 under strained circumstances. A new adoption law, introduced in Chile in 1988 as a result of concerns about child trafficking, changed the relationship between AC's representative in Santiago and the tribunals in southern Chile that were responsible for approving international adoptions. Chile was one of Sweden's principal "sending" or "giving" nations between 1974 and the early 1980s, with adoptions exceeding two hundred children annually in the late 1970s and remaining in excess of one hundred annually until 1985. In the late 1980s, Swedish adoptions from Chile dropped off steeply, and after 1991 they stopped completely.

Marta García, head of the adoption division of SENAME (Servicio Nacional del Menor), Chile's child welfare office, explained the ending of Chilean adoptions to Sweden in an interview in 1998:

> Before 1988, the Swedish Adoption Centre had its representative here and worked very well through an arrangement involving direct coordination with the tribunals [family courts], especially those in the south. . . . The babies were transported from the south to Santiago and in Santiago they were placed in the care of Adoption Centre, an institution which always guaranteed excellent care for the children, seriousness, transparency. No fault with the Swedish Adoption Centre, none! They had good foster mothers, good social workers who were in contact with the families, everything. But everything was very easy, also. The babies came to Santiago—almost all were from Temuco—and were entered in the civil register in Santiago with the names of the adoptive parents, with Swedish surnames. So everything was very easy for them.

When SENAME was established in 1988, I had to deal with AC's representative in Santiago and we had many clashes, trying to make her understand that things had changed and that now the business of international adoption was to be regularized. (Interview, April 1998; emphasis added)[4]

The tensions surrounding Swedish adoptions from Chile are suggested in Marta García's observation that the processing of Chilean babies for adoption in Sweden was "very easy" for Adoption Centre. Her comment hints at the complications that, in her opinion, *should* surround the conversion of a child who is assumed to be by nature Chilean into a Swedish child while tacitly acknowledging the power of state officials to effect such arbitrary conversions—the babies were simply "entered in the civil register in Santiago with the names of the adoptive parents, with Swedish surnames." The "Chilean child" in effect disappeared before it even left the country.

García's unease gestures toward the implicit assumption that underpins such transactions in children: they can only take place if the Chilean and the Swedish child are treated "as if" they are directly exchangeable for one another—that is, "as if" they are the same. Clearly, the child who might have grown up in Chile and whose mother was compelled or perhaps "chose" to relinquish, abandon, or place her child for adoption is not "the same" child who grows up in Sweden and whose mother was unable or chose not to give birth to a child, or who adopted a Chilean baby for political, humanitarian, or other reasons. The exchange is only possible, however, if this knowledge is bracketed. The adoptable child is treated "as if" it were not a material object that bears traces of its passage in the world but rather a "sublime" object that can "endure all torments with its beauty immaculate" (Zizek 1989:18). The sublime object is treated "'as if it were made of a special substance over which time has no power'" (Zizek 1989:18, quoting Sohn-Rethel 1978:59). It was this assumption and the seeming transparency of transactions that obscured it that were disturbing to Marta García, no less than the concern that some foreign adoptions were set in motion by money, or that there was a clandestine network of caring women through which the movement of babies from Chile to Sweden was occurring.[5]

By contrast, for Swedish parents who adopted from Chile at this time, the ease of the transaction was part of its appeal: there was little delay, the children were very young, and parents assumed that there was little of their child's developmental history that they were missing. The only thing needed to complete the child was his or her "culture," something that could be passed on through stories, albums, and eventually visits to a distant land with its exotic tastes, smells, and customs. For Swedish parents, the ease of the transaction eased the process of the baby becoming "my child."

García's discomfort and the satisfaction of the parents are both an effect of the power of the market in constituting *any* child—any person—as an entity that "qualifies . . . for life" in a market economy.[6] The discomfort it occasioned for García suggests how important it is to our consistency as subjects that we be blind to this truth (like the parents). Child adoption brings us face to face with this needed blindness and the myth it produces: that the circulation of children in a global economy is free, leaving no traces on the body of the child. (See Anagnost, this volume, for a related discussion of the way adoptive parents of Chinese children seek to "evade explicit confrontation with . . . problematic realities" regarding their child's adoption.)

The clashes with AC's local representative over the ease with which Chilean children were becoming Swedish disrupted this myth and in doing so brought to an end Sweden's complex relationship with Chile as a sending country for adoptive children. For Chilean adoptees and their families, this meant that there was indeed a clean break with the past, one that was no less significant than the official cut-off instantiated by adoption law. The informal relationships of communication and cooperation that tie agencies in receiving countries to orphanages, foster parents, social workers, and child welfare officials in sending countries were disbanded. These relationships, which are crucial to the movement of children from nations that give to nations that receive, are no less important (as I argue in more detail below) to the memories, desires, and (re)constructions that constitute an adopted child's identity. They provide the grounds through which adoptees (and their adoptive parents) can "seize" (Benjamin 1969:255) and "own" (Petchesky 1995) a past in which the prevailing characteristic is only fleetingly and problematically captured in the metaphor of a search for roots from which adopted children have been "cut off."

The search for roots assumes a past that is there, if we can just find the right file, the right papers, or the right person. This kind of search is part of a familiar story of belonging and of lost belongings in which an alienated self must be reconnected to a ground (an author, a nation, a parent) that constitutes its identity. By contrast, seizing the past involves not so much finding a ground as piecing one together, a process that is more material than intellectual, an active (re)inhabiting of events in order to lay claim to them (and in this sense to "own" them). Reinhabiting encompasses a broad range of processes that adopted children and their families are presently involved in, but always involves bringing the "past" into dialogue with the present rather than collapsing present into past (or privileging one over the other).[7]

In my analysis here, I am particularly interested in the revisitation of sites of involuntary displacement, separation, and (sometimes temporary) emplacement through which a child who is "abandoned" and placed for adoption undergoes the complex transformations in identity necessary to make it an *adoptable* child, a "precious resource" for the nations that receive it and that give it away (Yngvesson 2000). Laying claim to the past in this way may shake up identity in the very moment of grounding it, by revealing the interruptions, contradictions, and breaks through which the process we know as "identity" takes shape.[8] The informal relationships that bind (northern) agency to (southern) orphanage are crucial to this process of simultaneously making and shaking up identity.

In the case of Swedish adoptions from Chile, seizing the past required what Birgitta Löwstedt, the AC representative in charge of the agency's Resor och Rötter [Trips and Roots] division for South America, describes as "true detective work" (interview, May 1998). During the first months of 1996, Löwstedt received more than fifty calls from families who had adopted from Chile inquiring about adoptee backgrounds or requesting assistance in making contact with Chilean adoption officials. As a result, she renewed AC's contact with SENAME and in late 1996 made a trip to Santiago. She took with her a suitcase filled with letters and photographs from 250 adoptive families with Chilean-born children and the name and address of one of the foster mothers who had cared for the Swedish adoptees. She was cautiously hopeful that she could contact social workers and foster mothers, and possibly the doctor who had delivered many of the children.

SENAME was unexpectedly helpful in this process, in part because of its own interest in rethinking the relationship between Chile and its children adopted abroad. This rethinking of the relationship of adopted children to their birth nations has become increasingly important to officials in all of the major sending nations.[9] While SENAME had had no contact with the foster mothers, Birgitta located one whose (incorrect) address she had, with the help of a determined taxi driver. Through her, she was able to locate others, who were related as sisters, daughters, aunts, and in-laws, bringing them news of children they had been told to "forget" once the children left the country. Because the Swedish foster mother system was unofficial although not clandestine in the 1970s and 1980s, and because Sweden's activities as an adopting nation at that time were regarded with suspicion by the Pinochet government, the women had kept a low profile and had simply disappeared as a "system" when adoptions to Sweden came to an end. They had never expected to hear of the children again.[10]

The success of Birgitta Löwstedt's trip led to plans for a group tour to Chile in April 1998. The aim of the tour was in part simply to see the country, since none of the parents had been there before and the children had left when they were infants. More significant, however, Birgitta saw this as an opportunity for parents and children to visit the hospitals, orphanages, courts, foster mothers, social workers, doctor, judges, and government offices that had been involved in the adoption of the children to Sweden. For some families, there was the possibility of locating a birth parent. For all, there would be access to court records that contained details of the birth and relinquishment, key materials for piecing together a story of the early weeks or months of their child's life.

Going Back

What do you mean, go "back"? I want to travel there as if it were any other country. I want to see the *country.*"

—Nina, eighteen-year-old Chilean-born adoptee

While adoptees sometimes respond negatively to the idea that they might want to return to their birth country, insisting that they are "completely Swedish" (Clara, interview, May 1998; see von Melen 1998:116) and that for them a visit is *not* a "return," adoptive parents on the Chile trip expressed a powerful desire to go to the birth country of their children. This was especially noticeable in the stories of parents who fetched their first adopted child in his or her home country but were unable to do so for the second child. Two of these parents, who traveled to Chile with their sixteen-year-old daughter, explained why they felt this way:

MOTHER: For my part, I missed not having been in Chile. I wanted sometime in my life to come to Chile, especially because we had been in El Salvador when we adopted Daniel [their eldest child] and saw how it was there. That piece was missing, I thought, when we got Maria, because we hadn't been in Chile. But then, we have always said that the compensation was that she was so young.

FATHER: I felt that because we traveled to El Salvador we could be a means for passing on some of that to him [*förmedla något till honom*]. So we wanted to do the same for Maria, later.

MOTHER: We missed being able to pass on to her our sense of the sounds and smells, what one has experienced oneself. That's not something you see on TV, you can't experience it on the TV. And it's the same thing, being able to see the Andes from the hotel window, the busses they drive. (Interview, May 1998)

The use by these parents of the Swedish word *förmedla* (for which there is no good English translation in this context) is telling. Förmedla means "to mediate, to go between." It also means to make peace, restore harmony, bring into agreement. For them, going to Chile or to El Salvador was a way of bridging the experience gap, of restoring harmony in the experienced dissonance of having a child who belongs on (whose roots are in) the other side of the world. The parents become a bridge between there and here, become, in other words, a kind of "back" for their child by virtue of having been there to fetch the child. The album with photographs of the orphanage, the caretakers or foster mother, and other scenes from the birth country or, in more recent adoptions, a video of the arrival at the orphanage and the stay (typically lasting weeks or months) in the child's birth country are a visual prop for this "back." Because none of the parents on the Chile trip had been able to make the voyage to Chile when they adopted their children, the roots trip became, in the words of another adoptive mother, "my own life's trip [min livs resa]. It was very powerful." It provided for her (and she assumed for her daughter), something concrete to grasp on to (någonting att ta på). "If someone asks about Chile, then you can tell about it, that you have been there, you have a photographic memory of it, you have powerful experiences associated with it" (interview, May 1998).

Here, the adoptive parent becomes—like Walter Benjamin's storyteller—someone who "exchanges" experience, who "takes what he tells from experience . . . and makes it the experience of those who are listening to his tale" (1969:83, 87). In the stories told to their children by adoptive parents, "it is not the object of the story to convey a happening per se, which is the purpose of information; rather, it embeds it in the life of the storyteller in order to pass it on as experience to those listening. It thus bears the marks of the storyteller much as the earthen vessel bears the marks of the potter's hand" (159). The adoptive parents' "powerful experiences" associated with the trip to fetch (or revisit the birth country of) their child, become embedded in both parent and child through the telling of the story. By recounting experiences that might provide their adoptive children with "something concrete to grasp onto" about their native land, parents thus become engaged not only in the work of completing a child who (it is assumed) might otherwise remain fragmented, but in completing themselves as parents as well.

"Completion" here (unlike the conventional understanding of completion as fulfillment or a making "whole") is a spatial and temporal process of "infolding" (Rose 1996:43).[11] Through travel to a child's birth country and retelling the story about bringing the child home, powerful experiences associated with that distant landscape (the long journey to reach it, its associated sights, tastes, and smells) become a "part of me" for the parent, in a process that places the adoptive child "within" the parent as well. For another family on the Chile trip, this infolding of an "exterior" place was accomplished not only by stepping together with their son onto Chilean ground but also by collecting in a small plastic bag some earth from outside the hospital where he was born. The moment of gathering the earth was highly charged for the little boy's parents, who returned in tears to the bus on which we were traveling. The child himself, at ten years of age the youngest on the trip, appeared to have little interest in this event. For his parents, on the other hand, their son's past was made present in the plastic bag that they took back with them to Sweden. It contained fragments of a place and was powerfully associated with the memory of their son's birth—and would become part of the story of their return.[12]

In words that are familiar from countless stories told by adoptees, a mother on the Chile trip spoke of her daughter's need for completion in terms that applied no less (and perhaps even more) to adoptive parents. For both, adoption is a process that can never be complete. It is a response to, but continually reproduces for parent and child, a "hole in their lives that must be filled if they are to be whole people" (interview, May 1998). The trip to Chile and the memories it made possible in stories, photograph albums, and handfuls of soil were a way of attempting to fill this hole. (See Anagnost and Wozniak, this volume, for related discussions of what Anagnost terms "archiving practices.") At the same time, these embodied memories were a constant reminder of what the adoptee had left behind, of what she lacked. In the words of another adoptee who had chosen not to revisit her birthplace, this lack—which she described as "some kind of empty space"—does not go away. It remains as "some kind of pull towards an origin" *(en slags strävan mot urprunget)* (von Melen 1998:166).

As this suggests, roots trips, journeys by parents to the birth country of the child they plan to adopt, and the stories that are told about these movements that bring a child home or take her back, are not only a way of bridging a narrative gap in the relation of adoptive parent to child or completing a "break" in the child's narrative (Lifton 1994:36–37). These practices also create gaps and narrative breaks. Journeys "back" materialize a moment of abandonment by a return to the physical spaces (orphanages, foster homes, and courtrooms) in which this break was concretized. They constitute a kind of "time travel" (Saffian 1998:296) that displaces "home" (even as homes are made through such journeys) and split the present with powerful memories from the past (Aronson 1997). They reveal the impossibility of ever being fully integrated, of having anything "that constitutes both an outer and inner place where I belong" (Trotzig 1996:214).

Roots trips propel adoptees and their parents into what one Swedish social worker, in a talk about her work with adoptive parents, describes as "the eye of the storm." They bring the adoptive family and the adoptee face to face with the terror and the promise of confronting an "other" who is experienced as "a part of me" by the adoptee but who cannot be fully contained and remains irredeemably "other" for the adoptive family. In adoption practice, the birth mother embodies this "other," but the birth country is also a powerful site where the potential and the impossibility of full belonging may be experienced (Trotzig 1996; Liem 2000; Yngvesson and Mahoney 2000). Confrontation with this impossibility shakes up the idea of a coherent "I" and the illusion of autonomous families, nations, and selves on which this "I" is contingent, gesturing instead toward the dependence of receiving nations and adoptive parents on the *dis*possessed for their *self*-possession and at the irreducible distance and asymmetry involved in this relation of difference and of nonpossession. The stories below illuminate these contingencies of belonging, focusing on the ambivalence and discomfort experienced by adult adoptees while opening a space in which a more complex understanding of the relationship of self and other can materialize.

"This Is Your Country"

I don't think I had so many expectations. I didn't know what to expect of the country, except maybe that in some way I would get to know myself, but then of course one knew that one was into [*in på*] two different places, that one belongs in two different places. I already knew that before I went.

–Maria, sixteen-year-old Chilean-born adoptee

Like adoptive parents, for whom the journey to Chile was a way of placing their (unknown) child within themselves, for adoptees, coming to know Chile was a way of connecting to an unknown part of themselves, a part that they were not even sure *was* themselves. For example, Maria talked about how she had wondered, before going on the trip, "Do I really come from Chile?" By contrast to a friend from Colombia, whom she described as "having more of a Mapuche-like appearance," she herself was not obviously "from Latin America."[13] With her light skin, "I could have been something else." Maria described a ceremony held at the offices of SENAME on one of the last days of the trip, when the director said to all of them, "'This is your country.' It was, I think it was for everyone, it was a conviction that, 'OK, I am from Chile, too!' It was like a confirmation from a Chilean and from the country itself that I am from Chile. It was so big in some way. That was why we dared to respond and began to cry" (interview, May 1998).

Clara (an eighteen-year-old) described an evening gathering with the foster mothers as the moment when "I began to realize that I was really there." She had fantasized about Chile before the trip, but "it felt strange to be there. It felt as though I myself was left in Sweden although my body was in Chile and so one was somewhere in between, *where one didn't know where one was.* It was really strange. But when we met the foster mothers, I found myself" (interview, May 1998; emphasis added).

Like Maria, whose light skin made her wonder if she "really" came from Chile (as though, her father commented wryly, "we had fooled you"), Clara worried at times about who she was, but in her case it was her dark skin that occasioned doubts. She recalled a time in the second grade when people came up and began speaking Spanish to her, "and I couldn't grasp what they were saying. And then I began to think, 'they see me as an immigrant, when actually I am Swedish.'" Anti-immigrant incidents in Stockholm made her feel "scared, since it isn't obvious on the outside that one is adopted": "There is that feeling of unease [*en sådan här oroskänsla*], that others see one as though one is dark, those around you, those you know, and you know yourself that you are completely Swedish. And you know, sometimes I forget that I am dark-skinned. When I sit with friends and chat. And then when one looks in the mirror: 'Aha! That's how it is!'" (interview, May 1998).

This sudden sense of "aha!" was intensified on the roots trip to Chile and was a key element in the repeated (re)discovery by adoptees that one is *not* "completely Swedish [*helsvensk*]." This discovery was mediated, in part, by its collective dimension, and by the support experienced from other adoptees and from parents.[14] As Clara explained regarding the close bonds developed among adoptees on the trip, "one didn't need to explain how one felt, because everyone felt the same." This "same" feeling was on the one hand exhilarating. It involved a kind of grounding of an intuited self as Chilean that had always seemed just out of reach in Sweden, until one "looked in the mirror." But it was complicated by the inseparability of being Chilean (of being "dark-skinned," of being "Mapuche-like") from the experience of abandonment that was rediscovered in the physical spaces of hospitals, orphanages, and courtrooms, in the spoken words of social workers and government officials, and in the writing on "papers" that finalized the separation of each adoptee from her mother and from the country to which she (or he) was now returning in order to find or know her "self." The carefully cultivated experience of pride in being Chilean, transmitted by the Swedish parents of the adoptees and connected to their own experience of the trip as "my life's trip," was contingent on the adoptees' displacement to Sweden, on their being able to imagine Chile in the way their parents did, as part of a tour of Chile, or a temporary visit, from afar. Adoptees could share this imagined Chile with their parents, in part; but their parents could only act as witnesses to a part of Chile that their children had once experienced firsthand, up close. This complex, emotionally explosive Chile was in the rooms and beds of an orphanage, in the feel and smell of a rosary that belonged to an adoptee's birth mother, and in the written words and physical presence of a doctor or a matron who had recorded the details of a particular child's birth. As one twenty-year-old woman described her feelings after reading through a file of documents at the Temuco court, visiting the orphanage where she had spent three weeks as an infant, and driving by the house where her mother once lived, "It was the most tumultuous day of my life. I found out about everything!" [*Det var det mest omtumlande dag av mitt liv. Jag fick veta allt*] (interview, April 1998).

Two Mothers

> FATHER: How do they choose which children will be adopted? What criteria does the court have for accepting or rejecting a child?
>
> SOCIAL WORKER: There are no criteria for accepting or rejecting a child, but the mother is advised of her rights. Before the child is born, we explain what it means to place the child "in a state of abandonment" [*en*

situación de abandono]. It will be like the child is dead to her. She will never hear more about the child.

–Field notes from visit to Temuco court, April 1998

Central to the meaning of the Chile trip for each adoptee, in one form or another, was some attempt to grapple with the experience of abandonment and what Jessica Benjamin (1995:113) describes as "the labor of mourning." For some, this desire was more clearly formulated than for others. Clara went to Chile together with her adoptive mother in the explicit hope of meeting her birth mother. She had learned her name from documents in Sweden and carried with her a letter in which she wrote, "although I don't know you, I feel as though in spite of everything, you are a part of me." Clara explained how much she longed to know what her mother looked like and who she was. With the cooperation of SENAME and the assistance of a distant relative who had cared for her mother when she became pregnant and was forced to leave home, the woman was located after a week's search, and Clara's letter was delivered to her. A meeting was arranged for the day prior to our departure for Sweden. Clara explained her feelings about this meeting during an interview in Stockholm a month later:

CLARA: I felt so strange, and wondered how I would react, if I would stay in one piece [*sitta helt*], that is if I would not start to cry or if I would immediately begin to cry when she came. . . . But when she saw me, *she* began to cry and then . . . but it was as though, because I have always had a hole inside, or however one might say it, and then when I saw her, immediately I cried and then it [the hole] was filled again. I still don't understand that feeling, that it went so fast. I was almost a little scared.

BARBARA: That the thoughts were gone, you mean?

CLARA: Yes, or rather, the thoughts, the fantasy of how she would look. Now I had a picture of how she looked and how she was, how the house was. So everything fell into place in an hour. It was such a short time.

MOTHER: It was a very strong experience. I had also imagined what she would be like, that she was probably very poor and had lived a hard life and would be marked by that. But that wasn't the way it was. Well, she was poor, but not very poor. One understood how much she had suffered.

CLARA: One thing I had thought a lot about was sitting in the same room with two mothers. I thought it would feel very strange.

BARBARA: And when it actually happened?

CLARA: It felt good, partly because I could speak Swedish with my mother from Sweden, and then I had you, who could translate. I felt supported to have mamma along, someone from Sweden. It was something one could return to, that one wasn't alone in Chile. (Interview, May 1998; emphasis added)

The meeting with Clara's "mother from Chile" was held in the modest house of the woman who had cared for her eighteen years previously, and was attended by Clara's cousins, a half-sister, a nephew, and other extended kin, as well as by her adoptive mother and a social worker from SENAME. I was present at the meeting, to interpret for Clara and her birth mother. As they "cried themselves out together" and I leaned toward them to catch their whispered words, there was a kind of breathless silence. Clara's mother caressed her daughter's face and begged her forgiveness. I felt like the thinnest of membranes connecting the two women—linguistically, physically—and separating them from (joining them to) Clara's "Swedish mother," who stood nearby. I struggled to maintain my composure. Even the youngest children seemed to be suspended in the tension that caught us all up in this collective moment of recognition, in which Clara said she felt as though she were "more or less the same and yet not the same [as her birth mother], since she is mother to me and I am daughter to her."

Afterward, we all sat down to a long meal together, gifts were exchanged, addresses written down, and eventually Clara, her adoptive mother, and I left. Clara took with her a rosary that was a gift from her birth mother. She described this later as "a wonderful present. One could see that it had been used and that it had a special smell. It smelled like her." It was "something one knows about that one can make something of [later], on one's own."

This "making something of" an object surely includes moments of completion, or of "filling a hole," as in Clara's meeting with her mother. Similar moments were experienced by other adoptees in the midst of the turbulence of the return, as they walked on the street in the neighborhood where their mother once lived, visited the maternity ward of a hospital where they could "feel that my mother was here once when she gave birth to me," or held a file containing details about the time and place of their birth, the name and age of their mother, and the date on which she formally consented to their abandonment. But return trips and other efforts at recovering or confronting the past "are always double-edged" (to quote a social worker with more than twenty-five years of experience with transnational adoptions), and moments of clarity are typically that—moments—in a process of self-constitution that is ongoing, painful, and turbulent, challenging any sense of a stable ground of belonging.

One woman, elated finally to be touching the papers in her court file and overwhelmed with the sense that finally she had "found out about everything"— the hour of her birth, her mother's name, the address where her mother had lived when she was born—became distraught when she was advised not to make contact with the woman. She insisted on driving by her house, lingering on the street where she imagined she had once lived, and photographing the area. When I spoke to her a month later, she was still shaken by the experience. She had also become worried about the issue of how babies are chosen for adoptive parents. Her own parents expressed shock at the discovery that children today are carefully monitored by the agency for defects and that their adopted son, who suffers from Asperger syndrome, would surely have remained in his Thai orphanage had his affliction been known. Another adoptee, who hoped to contact her mother and brother in Chile, was told by a court social worker that this would be unwise because the woman was "extremely aggressive" and had threatened to harm herself and the baby had she not been permitted to surrender her for adoption nineteen years earlier.

These events, no less than the meeting of Clara with her birth mother, disturb the notion of return as completion or closure, revealing the distance and asymmetry separating women who give their children away and those who receive them as acts of love. They expose the work involved in producing a child who can be chosen (by the agency, by the parent) so that it can be loved as though it were "one's own," and the key role of a legal clean break in securing the ground on which exclusive belonging is forged: the freedom of the child, the adoptive parent, and the birth parent vis-à-vis one another. Returns unsettle these freedoms, revealing the powerful dependencies that underpin them. On the Chile trip, these dependencies were pieced together from fragments of a past that each person seized in an effort to make sense of an event that could *never* make sense, that would forever remain "somewhere beyond the reach of the intellect," even as it was "unmistakably present" in papers, places, and the ambiguities and silences of a court document (Benjamin 1969:158).

In each of these situations, the mediating presence of others (adoptive parents, other adoptees, AC staff, the kin of Clara's mother, the children in an orphanage, myself as interpreter) was crucial to the process of seizing the past. We became both witness and bridge, a potential space in which the complex and contradictory meanings of being "the same as me" (or "different" from me) could materialize in places that were saturated with meaning for adoptees and their families (the hospital, the maternity ward, the orphanage, the court, the house of a foster mother, and so forth). These places, perhaps more than any words that were spoken, infused present encounters with meanings that were linked to memories and fantasies of what had once taken place there. At the same time, these fantasies, and the work of constructing an account of the adoptee's abandonment, depended on her capacity to "return to [them]" in Sweden, a return that was possible because "one wasn't alone in Chile."

The Eye of the Storm

> An area like a hole or column in the center of a tropical cyclone marked by only light winds or complete calm with no precipitation and sometimes by a sunlit clear sky (the eye of a hurricane).
>
> *–Webster's Third New International Dictionary of the English Language*

Ingrid Stjerna, a Swedish social worker who works with prospective adoptive parents, speaks about how important it is to "awaken [in them] positive, warm, empathic feelings for this person who could not take care of her child. It is important for the child that they have these positive feelings." Stjerna notes that this is harder to accomplish when "you became a parent standing at Arlanda [the Stockholm airport] with money in your hands—none of this travelling to difficult countries." Meeting the mother, by contrast, "awakens anxiety. Background and country and decorations and songs, all that is fine—but the mother: no. That puts them into the eye of the storm. That forces them to come to terms with the pain and misery" (address to visiting AC representatives, Stockholm, August 1996).

Coming to terms with the fact that "there is no such thing as a motherless child—even if she is dead, she is important"—has been crucial to the transformations that have taken place in adoption over the past two decades and in international adoption during the past ten years. That the child is not motherless implies that adoptive parents must accept the fact that this is not really *their* child, Stjerna argues. What I understand her to mean by this is not that the child belongs to somebody else, but that the child is not freestanding: she came from someone and from somewhere and bears the traces of that elsewhere, just as she bears traces of the pull, the desire that links her to the adoptive parent and adoptive country. Accepting that the child belongs to no one means accepting that she is neither rooted nor freestanding, but is marked by her existential condition of thrownness into the world as much as by her need for connection, for hands to catch her, so that she can "take her place" in the world (Doyle 1994:210, paraphrasing Merleau-Ponty 1968). The return trip to Chile illuminated the contradictory truths that the adopted child—like other children—has been thrown into the world, but that she is not motherless. Thrownness is the condition that marks the child as not-me, as fundamentally other-than-me, while the condition of being "not motherless" marks the child's proximity, her openness to an encounter with a stranger who can say, "This is my child, too."[15] (For a related discussion of inclusive belonging, see Wozniak, this volume).

Ingrid Stjerna's insistence that this is not a motherless child in spite of the breaks mandated by adoption law captures (in different words) Marilyn Strathern's (1997:301) idea of the double evocatory power of the gift—the gift child of adoption has been freed for exchange and links the giver and receiver as partners in the exchange. These partners are embedded in a complex web of connections, a web that broke down when adoptions from Chile to Sweden ceased in 1991. This web binds orphanage to agency and adopting mother to abandoning mother, tying developing nations with an "excess" of children to overdeveloped nations that need these children. The physical movement of a child in adoption—the routes it takes from "there" to "here"—is a part of this interdependence and the exchanges through which it is played out. To be "in the eye of the storm" is to enter, imaginatively and in practice, the space of these exchanges.

Entering this space involves more than having warm, positive feelings about the birth mother or pride in the birth nation of a child. These benevolent feelings evoke the sense that the eye of the storm is a site of calm but ignore the relationship of this center of calm to the chaos that produces it. To enter the eye of the storm is to take risks: that a background story will be too hard to bear, that the pull "back" will be too powerful, that we will lose our boundaries, the edges that make our families complete. The challenge for international (and other forms of) adoption today is in the ways it has opened a space that is structured, but cannot be fully contained, by adoption law. This space has revealed a kind of chaos, shaking up (and opening up) families, persons, and nations in the world that created international adoption and that international adoption helped to create. While adoption is the focus of this opening up, the questions it raises reminds us that we are all, in one way or another, close to the eye of the storm, which is where life is lived.

NOTES

Research on which this paper is based was supported by the National Science Foundation (grant #SBR-9511937) and by faculty development grants from Hampshire College. It was made possible by the cooperation and generosity of adoptive parents, adoptees, staff at Stockholm's Adoption Centre, and Chilean child welfare officials. I thank Michelle Bigenho, Maureen Mahoney, Beth Notar, Jeff Roth, Janelle Taylor, Sigfrid Yngvesson, and in particular Nina Payne for their helpful comments on earlier drafts. I am grateful to Susan Coutin and Bill Maurer for insights that have emerged from our collaboration on a related project.

1. As Strathern notes (1988:158), there is no comfortable space for the presence of an "other" in this concept of identity except as supplanted authorship or proprietorship. See also Janet Farrell Smith's (1983:205, 208) discussion of the exclusion of others as fundamental to the idea of "proprietary or possessive control over another thing or person." For a discussion of the ways in which adoption policy and practice works to constitute adopted children as the adoptive parents' "own," see Ragoné (1996:359), Hoelgaard (1998:229–31), Yngvesson (1997:67–76), and Yngvesson and Mahoney (2000).
2. See Nelson (2002:310) and Fuss (1995:1–14) for a discussion of identity as produced in a detour through the Other.
3. The phrase "came home," or "will come home," is widespread in Internet chat groups for the parents of internationally adopted children and in magazines and brochures published by and for adoptive parents.
4. Interviews in this article were recorded either in Spanish or in Swedish and translated by the author.
5. The argument about the exchange value of a child is persuasively developed by Viviana Zelizer (1985) and by Igor Kopytoff (1986), both of whom build on Simmel's (1978:390–91) seminal insights about the complex relationship between desire for an object and the object being "set into motion" by money. As Zelizer (1985:14) argues, the priceless child presents a legal quandary that is no less a cultural and social quandary: "How could value be assigned if price were absent?" Kopytoff (1986:75)

points to this same paradox, noting that to be "'priceless' in the full possible sense of the term" can as easily refer to the uniquely worthless as to the uniquely valuable. To acquire value, Kopytoff argues, the "patently singular" must become part of a "single universe of comparable values"—that is, it must be placed into circulation, made "common" (Kopytoff 1986:68–72).

6. The quote is from Judith Butler (1993:2). The argument here draws on my reading of a range of works relevant to this issue, including Marilyn Strathern (1988:135–59), Igor Kopytoff (1986) and Slavoj Zizek (1989). The crucial point is that entry into the symbolic order of culture and law is an arbitrary legal process on which our "naturalization" as whole persons (as civil subjects) is contingent.

7. Here I build on Lyotard's (1984:22) insight about the "ephemeral temporality" that accompanies narrative knowledge. Lyotard argues that "the narratives' reference may seem to belong to the past, but in reality it is always contemporaneous with the act of recitation."

8. For a discussion of identity processes in adoption narratives, see Yngvesson and Mahoney (2000).

9. For a fascinating discussion of the efforts being made by the government of South Korea to reconnect to adults it sent abroad in adoption as infants or children from the mid-1950s onward, see Kim (2003).

10. While my discussion here of the work of the Chilean foster mothers is not the focus of this chapter and is necessarily brief, assumptions by Chilean state officials and by Swedish agency representatives about the insignificance of their role in the lives of foster children whom they cared for during periods that ranged from weeks to more than a year resembles assumptions made by state officials in the United States regarding foster mothers (Wozniak, this volume). In an article written for *Att Adoptera*, Adoption Centre's journal for adoptive parents, Birgitta Löwstedt described her emotional meeting with the foster mothers on her visit to reestablish contact with them in 1997. "No gift could be greater than to meet the children again," one of the foster mothers told her. "If you could only understand how much we loved the children," said another. "They were everything to us" (Löwstedt 1997:21).

11. Drawing on the work of Gilles Deleuze, Nicolas Rose describes the "fold" as indicating "a relation without an essential interior, one in which what is 'inside' is merely an infolding of an exterior" (1996:43).

12. See Benjamin's (1969:158) discussion of how "the past is 'somewhere beyond the reach of the intellect, and unmistakably present in some material object (or in the sensation which such an object arouses in us)' (quoting Proust, *A La Recherche du Temps Perdu*). Similarly, Nicholas Rose (1996:143) suggests that "memory of one's biography is not a simple psychological capacity, but is organized through rituals of storytelling, supported by artefacts such as photograph albums and so forth."

13. Note here the stereotyped linking of Latin America more generally with the "indigenous" and the use of "Mapuche" as a trope for a person of color.

14. By contrast, see Swedish adoptee Astrid Trotzig's (1996) account of her trip alone to Pusan, South Korea, where her experience of not belonging there was no less intense than in Sweden.

15. These words were spoken by an Ethiopian woman as she smoothed the bed covers over a friend of her birth daughter, during a visit of the two Swedish women to Ethiopia. Both had been adopted by families in Sweden.

A Fetish Is Born

Sonographers and the Making of the Public Fetus

JANELLE S. TAYLOR

"Evidence" shades into fantasy when the foetus is visualized, albeit through electronic media, as though removed from the pregnant woman's body, as though suspended in space. This is a form of fetishization, and it occurs repeatedly in clinical settings whenever ultrasound images construct the foetus through "indications" that sever its functions and parts from their organic connection to pregnant women.

–Rosalind Pollack Petchesky, "Foetal Images: The Power of Visual Images in the Politics of Reproduction"

[T]he fear that . . . dogs fetish discourse [is that] the observer who accuses Others of the mistake of fetishism might herself be seduced into error.

–Patricia Spyer, *Border Fetishisms: Material Objects in Unstable Spaces*

The pan-European word whose English version is "fetish" derives linguistically from the Latin *facticius* or *factitius,* an adjective formed from the past participle of the verb facere, "to make."

–William Pietz, "The Problem of the Fetish, II"

It has become commonplace in contemporary U.S. society to encounter fetuses "on screen," like a myriad other proffered objects of consumer desire. On the small screens of ultrasound devices in the context of diagnostic screening exams, many women encounter visually the fetuses that move about in their own wombs; other fetuses move about on the screens of television sets, in the context of mass media entertainment, advertising, and antiabortion propaganda. "Normal" though it has come to seem, this situation is also rife with ironies that make obstetrical ultrasound a particularly interesting vantage point from which to examine ethnographically the conjunction of motherhood with consumption that is the subject of this volume.

In this chapter, I seek to situate the ultrasound fetal images that make their way into public culture, in relation to the emergence of sonography as a new "women's" medical-technical profession, and show how they bear the traces of the social and cultural context of their making. First, I trace the emergence of the particular cultural form of the "routine" obstetrical ultrasound examination as we know it, which allows ultrasound to play the peculiar role that it does in contemporary U.S. society, in both the practices and the politics of reproduction (Taylor 1992, 1998, 2000a, 2000b). I place special emphasis, for reasons that will become clear, on the active role that sonographers (many of them women) have played in this history and on the dilemmas that it has bequeathed them. Having thus set the stage, I then indulge in a bit of "methodological fetishism" (Appadurai 1986:5) and pursue a version of what Igor Kopytoff (1986) has called a "biographical" approach to one particular commodified ultrasound fetal image, tracing its movements between different social domains and documenting the social processes through which it is both fetishized and commodified. The particular fetal ultrasound image whose "biography" I partially trace here is one that has been named (not by me!) "George" and that has probably come as close to celebrity stardom as is possible for such an entity, eventually making its way into a widely screened antiabortion television advertisement, into congressional hearings, and into pro-life "educational" videotapes. By thus tracing this "public" fetus back to the social conditions of its production, I attempt to do for fetal images what Marx suggests we must do for all commodities—and I seek, in this way, to contribute to the larger feminist scholarly work of shifting the focus of discussions of reproduction away from disembodied fetal images and back toward the lives of women.

Feminists, Fetuses, and Fetishes

Both in the case of women's visual encounters in clinical settings with the fetuses they carry and in the case of the broader viewing public's visual encounters with fetuses on television, bringing these fetuses onto the screen has arguably brought them "to life." Routine ultrasound imaging of the fetus during early pregnancy has made it possible to visualize the fetal form and document fetal heartbeats and movements long before the moment of "quickening," and in this sense has brought the fetuses that contemporary women carry "to life" in a different way, and far earlier, than the fetuses they once were would have seemed "alive" to their own mothers. Even beyond these more narrowly "medical" diagnostic functions, however, the routine ultrasound examination itself has, in contemporary U.S. society, become a scene of commodification and consumption, bringing the fetus "to life" in part by inserting it in various ways into the mass circulation of goods and images (Taylor 2000b). The "liveliness" that ultrasound helps impart to the fetuses women carry is thus not unrelated to the seeming "liveliness" of those other fetuses whose images circulate in public culture, though the latter is more obviously problematic for those concerned with reproductive rights, especially when fetal images enter our lives and our living rooms as the deputed representatives of "Life."

Rosalind Pollack Petchesky was the first to suggest, in her landmark essay "Foetal Images: The Power of Visual Culture in the Politics of Reproduction" (1987), that the public fetus is perhaps best understood as a *fetish*—that is, an object falsely endowed with powers that in reality reside elsewhere. The fetishism of commodities, according to Marx, consists in the social magic of capitalism, through which "value" is attributed to objects as if it were a power mysteriously inhering in them; this is possible only when the object's connection to the true source of its value—that is, the human labor through which it was produced—has been obscured. The challenge, then, is to "decipher the hieroglyphic, to get behind the secret of our own social products" (Marx 1978:322). Fetishism of the fetus consists in attributing to it value as "life," as if this were a property magically inhering in the fetus alone, in a manner that obscures the fact that the continued vitality of any actual fetus depends utterly and completely upon its continued sustenance by the woman who carries it. The task, for those who would contest the power of the fetishized fetus, is to reframe it in such a way as to make visible what has been rendered obscure and reveal the hidden context of social production from which it draws its seeming "life."[1]

This task, to the extent that it necessarily involves a work of making visible the invisible, revealing and unmasking what has been hidden and obscured, inevitably draws us into a rhetoric and a politics of vision. Indeed, if the Marxist concept of the fetish grants us critical leverage on "the absolute strangeness of the normal capitalist everyday" (Spyer 1997:10), it does so in large part by invoking a long cultural history of love and fear of images (Mitchell 1986), compounded by a particular fascination and revulsion with those images and objects that occupy a special place in the alien system of values of some cultural Other (Pietz 1985, 1987). It is thus perhaps overdetermined, by the theoretical apparatus we employ no less than by the phenomenon we address, that feminist scholars who have sought to critically engage the ideology of opponents of abortion in contemporary U.S. society have attributed considerable power to visual images of the fetus. In particular, Rosalind Petchesky and others have argued that obstetrical ultrasound technology enables the fetishism of the fetus, by visually objectifying it in a manner that conceals the pregnant woman from view even as it "reveals" the fetus—to the medical gaze on the one hand and to the gaze of the mass-mediated public on the other.

Unmasking fetishes is a slippery business, however. I fear that in our efforts to unmask the fetishism of the fetus, we risk being seduced into the error of fetishizing technology.[2] Reframing the fetus-as-fetish requires that we bring into view not only the technology that generates the images that seemingly grant it "life," but also the *people* who operate the technology, without whose skilled labor the technological device would be capable of nothing at all. As historians of technology remind us: "the history of technology is a history of human actions. To understand the origin of a particular kind of technological power, we must first learn about the actors. Who were they? What were their circumstances? . . . Why was the innovation made by these people and not others?" (Smith and Marx 1995:xiii). We would do well, I suggest, to revive the older meaning of *manufactured,* lying dormant within the etymology of the term *fetish* (Pietz 1985:5, 1987:24). If in our discussion of obstetrical ultrasound we focus only on the formal visual qualities of the sonogram and fail to attend closely enough to ultrasound as social practice, then we end up casting women only as the embodied objects of the technological-medical gaze—or, at best, as subjects whose relation to their own embodiment is rendered newly problematic by new technologies of visualization. In either case, we fail to recognize the full range of ways in which women have been positioned relative to this technology—and, more importantly, we miss the opportunity to document the *making* of the fetishized public fetus.

Undeleting the Image Makers

If we wish instead to seize this opportunity, one good place to begin is by interrogating the cultural form that the ultrasound examination has assumed in this country. Nothing about the physics of high-velocity sound waves, nor the medical imaging devices constructed to exploit them, *requires* that a diagnostic ultrasound procedure be performed in just the way that it has come to be in this country. Nothing about the device itself dictates, for example, that women undergoing ultrasound examinations should want and be encouraged to bring along husbands, boyfriends, or other family members or friends; that they should be shown the fetus on the screen; that seeing it should be understood as a means of effecting maternal "bonding"; that the sonographer should provide a narrative of the baby's anatomy and activities and offer to determine its sex or to give the pregnant woman a videotape or "snapshot" image to take home.

If these elements were not present in the practice of ultrasound—if, for example, an ultrasound exam were a little more like an EKG and a little less like a visit to the hospital nursery—we would still have good reason to critically question the routinization of ultrasound in obstetrics in this country. And we would doubtless still see ultrasound used for sex determination leading to sex-selective abortion, both here and elsewhere in the world, in contexts where women are under great pressure to bear male children. Yet were these elements absent, it is hard to imagine that ultrasound could occupy the peculiar position that it does in contemporary U.S. society, on the porous and contested boundaries between medicine, media, and public culture. Indeed, if we follow Judith Butler's insight that "matter" may be understood as "not a site or surface, but a process of materialization that stabilizes over time to produce the effect of boundary, fixity, and surface we call matter" (Butler 1993:9), then surely the *practice* of the routine ultrasound exam in the particular cultural form in which we know it—all these acts of showing and telling, repeated millions of times each year—must be one of the ways that the fetus has come to "matter" in the particular way that it does in contemporary American society.

How, why, and when did the ultrasound examination assume the particular cultural form that it presently takes in this country? Available historical accounts of obstetrical ultrasound, including specifically feminist accounts, have surprisingly little to say on this question. One reason for this is simply that most discussions of ultrasound that do address its history end their narrative in the early to mid-1970s, just at the beginning of what some people working in the field of ultrasound call "the sonic boom" (Blume 1992; Goldberg and Kimmelman 1988; Oakley 1984; Yoxen 1987; but see Kevles 1997; Mitchell 2001). In the early 1970s, ultrasound technology was just beginning to be produced commercially, ultrasound screening of pregnancy was just beginning to move from an experimental to a standard medical procedure, and people who worked with ultrasound were just beginning to organize themselves professionally. In other words, most of the complex, diffuse, interlocking series of transformations that led to the obstetrical ultrasound exam, in the particular form in which we now know it, becoming a taken-for-granted part of the cultural landscape of medicalized pregnancy in this country, took place *after* these narratives end.

To be sure, the difficulty of simply documenting these kinds of changes is considerable. Millions of ultrasound devices of all sorts have been sold over the past thirty years, to hospitals, imaging centers or mobile imaging services, as well as doctors in private practices. These may be operated by obstetricians, by radiologists, by midwives, or, more commonly, by sonographers (persons specially trained in the use of ultrasound technology to produce diagnostic information), though no formal education or certification in ultrasound is at present legally required. Because it involves a nonionizing form of radiation, the government does not regulate and monitor ultrasound in the way that it does, for example, X-ray and other modalities. Therefore, aside from a few lonely studies that are already long out of date, reliable national statistics on ultrasound usage are also unavailable. To write the history of obstetrical ultrasound during the period between 1970 and today, it is not entirely obvious where and how one could or should locate (or more likely, construct) one's archive—though surely this cannot be any more daunting than many other topics that creative and resourceful historians have successfully taken on.

But my own research has made very clear to me at least one point: as reproduction increasingly becomes subject to medical and technological surveillance and intervention, one woman's labor has become another woman's work. The routinization of ultrasound within obstetrics has not only meant that millions of pregnant women each year undergo ultrasound examinations, it has also meant new forms of work, for tens of thousands of other women. These include the clerical workers who type and file reports and schedule appointments, the women in developing countries who perform much of the work of assembling component parts of today's ultrasound equipment, and, in the United States, a new allied-health profession composed mostly of women, who operate ultrasound equipment and perform diagnostic procedures (Baker 1995; Mitchell 1993, 2001). Nearly forty thousand people in the United States are currently formally registered as sonographers, of whom thirty thousand have passed a registry examination in the specialized field of obstetrics and gynecology, and approximately 85 percent of these are women (although the percentage of male sonographers tends to be higher in other subspecialties such as cardiac or vascular ultrasound).[3] More than simply carrying out purely technical procedures at the request of physicians, sonographers have all along actively worked with engineers and physicians and others to develop and modify equipment, develop new medical applications, and market and repair ultrasound equipment, as well as teach others how to use the equipment and interpret the information it provides (Baker 1995).

To understand how the obstetrical ultrasound examination has assumed its present cultural form requires that we "undelete" these "image makers," to borrow Deborah Heath's phrase (Heath 1998). As Edward Yoxen (1987:303) writes: "The job of the person performing the scan has a history. The tasks involved have been designed, negotiated and defined in relation to the work of others and depend on the exercise of specific skills. Who has these skills and how they are valued by others has changed through time. Thus the experience of having an ultrasound scan depends on how various individuals are able to work, how they are intended to work, and how their constantly shifting relations with doctors are managed."[4]

From the earliest days of obstetrical ultrasound, and straight up through to the present day, obstetricians have usually relied upon other people to do the work of actually operating the equipment and performing the scans; and the contributions that these people have made to the development of the technology and its applications, though often overlooked, are hardly negligible. Indeed, although the Scottish obstetrician Ian Donald is widely acknowledged as the "father" of obstetrical ultrasound, having been the first to adapt industrial ultrasound equipment for use in detecting intrauterine tumors, the very idea of using ultrasound to visualize the fetus may fairly be credited to Marjorie Marr, a staff nurse in his employ. As Ann Oakley notes in her landmark history of prenatal care, Donald noticed with some puzzlement that Marr always seemed to know which way the fetuses were oriented in the womb—and learned that she had taken to using the ultrasound equipment that he had had installed in the ob/gyn department to locate the fetal head before Donald conducted his daily rounds. This gave Donald the idea of using ultrasound to measure the diameter of the fetal skull (biparietal diameter, or BPD), which was in fact one of the few anatomical features that early ultrasound devices could reliably measure, and which Donald believed could be useful in monitoring fetal growth through successive measurements, and in determining whether the head would fit through the pregnant woman's bony pelvis for birth (Oakley 1984:161; Mitchell 2001: 27–28).

In the early days of obstetrical ultrasound, some of the people who did the work of scanning had started out as secretaries or file clerks, while others had come to ultrasound through their prior training in allied health fields such as radiology, nursing, or nuclear medicine (Baker 1995), or were trained in the sciences and working as research assistants or in other positions within departments of obstetrics or cardiology.[5] During this period, ultrasound offered unusual opportunities for women to find employment that developed technological interests and skills. Not so uncommon among this older generation of sonographers practicing today is the type of career path described to me by Marveen Craig:

> I was living in Denver in 1966 and was bored silly once my son entered the first grade. I went looking for a part-time job to keep me occupied until school let out for the summer. Because I had both a nursing and secretarial background, I started job hunting at the University of Colorado Medical School. They offered me the job of being a "gofer" in a new research lab, the ultrasound lab. I was hired to answer phones, fetch patients, type reports and scientific papers, and so on. What began as a part-time job quickly became full-time after an unexpected divorce several months later. I was so fascinated by ultrasound . . . that I began sneaking back into the lab after hours trying to teach myself to scan. After about three months of this clandestine learning I was "caught" by one of our OB residents who kindly began teaching me what he knew. . . . Several months later when our workload began to pick up dramatically, he recommended that I be hired to scan patients as well as my "gofer" work.

Up until the late 1960s, ultrasound devices were still quite ungainly and difficult to use; some required, for example, that the patient be placed under a heavy membrane full of water, others required that the patient actually sit immersed up to the neck in a tub of water for the duration of the procedure (Blume 1992:95; Goldberg and Kimmelman 1988:11–13, 33; Yoxen 1987). The information that these devices produced was also presented in ways that were far more difficult to interpret than the sort of visual images that we associate with ultrasound today (in the form of graphed lines, for example); and in those days before computed tomography (CT) scans and magnetic resonance imaging (MRI), the way that ultrasound imaged the body, in cross-sectional "slices," was completely unfamiliar. Thus, individuals who had gained hands-on experience in ultrasound, some of whom became quite expert at it, were in considerable demand by the late 1960s, when ultrasound entered its period of rapid growth. Physician-researchers needed people skilled in the use of ultrasound to help do clinical studies; hospitals needed them to set up departments of ultrasound; and manufacturing firms needed them to test and demonstrate commercial equipment and to teach their customers how to use it (Baker 1995).

Show and Sell

As Pierre Coste (1989) has noted in his historical study of the ultrasound industry (written as a Ph.D. dissertation in executive management), selling ultrasound to physicians in the mid-1970s was a considerable challenge. The technology itself had not yet been standardized, meaning that different manufacturers were still producing equipment based upon a number of different principles, which presented quite different sorts of visual information, including "A-mode," "B-mode," and "M-mode" scanners. They thus faced the challenge of trying to persuade physicians that they needed ultrasound while also trying to make the case for a particular type of equipment. Because of the ways that their preexisting habits of practice and their perceived clinical needs intersected with the distinctive features of different models, physicians in specific specialties tended to prefer certain types of ultrasound equipment; "B-scanners remained dominant in the radiology market as did M-mode in cardiology" (Coste 1989). In this context, the advent of "gray-scale" imaging (which allowed much more nuanced images than earlier black-and-white imaging devices) and early "real-time" scanners (which made it possible to visualize movement for the first time) seemed to promise to appeal especially to obstetricians. ADR, a company that introduced early grayscale and real-time imaging equipment, focused its efforts on promoting equipment sales to obstetricians and gynecologists.

As Coste recounts, using ultrasound to "show the baby" to obstetricians' pregnant patients was an important part of their strategy: "ADR . . . focused solely on understanding the imaging needs of OBG physicians. ADR had its sales representatives spend time in hospital OBG departments to learn how to perform the examination themselves. They would bring the equipment on sales calls to OBG private practices and assist the physician in conducting the examination. The patient was delighted to be able to see her baby moving inside her body and was co-opted into advancing the sale" (Coste 1989:154). Partly because ultrasound developed on a "frontier" located at the interstices between established medical disciplines (including obstetrics and radiology), people working clinically as ultrasound technicians during this period similarly felt the need to promote the technology to physicians who for the most part did not know much about what it was, how it imaged the body, how these images were to be interpreted, and how ultrasound might be useful to them in their own practice.[6] Dave, a sonographer I interviewed who had worked clinically in ob/gyn ultrasound in the late 1960s, recalls:

> We started by taking over an unused storage room in a women's clinic, and moved in our $25,000 piece of compound scanning equipment and we were just begging people to send us patients. Doing all kinds of publicity with the different department heads, mostly the OB/GYN people, but other internal medicine areas in the hospital as well, and just wanted to try everything. And it took off from three patients a day to eventually maybe sixty or seventy patients a day, and four full-time techs and me as a chief tech, and hundreds of thousands of dollars worth of equipment. ... There was stuff going on in Europe, so we could get our hands on a clinical article and say, "Look, we should be able to do this. Give us a chance." But in OB it was a little simpler, typically they would send us somebody down with a very wild-goose-chase diagnosis of "rule out twins" or "bleeding, question placenta praevia."[7]

Clearly, this account of the process by which ultrasound gained a foothold within obstetrics (which accords substantially with recollections of this period that I have heard from other sonographers as well) hardly conforms to the usual picture of scientific "research." Sonographers were "begging for patients" and "doing all kinds of publicity" with obstetricians, then taking advantage of obstetricians' "wild-goose-chase diagnoses" to "try everything" on the patients that came their way. For them, as for ADR and other manufacturers, "showing the baby" proved a useful way of generating interest in ultrasound, among physicians and among their women patients. What we might tend to think of as the "nonmedical" aspects of the obstetrical ultrasound examination emerged, in other words, *alongside* the more narrowly "medical" applications and were indeed an important *part* of the process by which the technology and the procedure became established within medicine. These conventions, I would argue, emerged in the first instance in response to the need to promote ultrasound itself; "show and tell" was really a matter of "show and sell." Again, I quote Dave:

> DAVE: It was a tiny room, about a twelve by twelve room, had a stretcher in it and an ultrasound machine and a table and a desk and a telephone, and can you fit another body in to watch? Oh yes. And then grandmother wants to come in too, or my younger children, and I think it became not unusual

to have three or four observers, even people that weren't family members, that were on the hospital staff that had heard about ultrasound and wanted to see. So, I mean, then it turned into a real show, and I'm a ham, I'd try to make people laugh and comfortable with the situation ... you wanted good PR for the procedure anyway, because it was a fledgling, and the more people that knew about it, got a buzz going about it, the better it would be. And some places didn't allow to give away films, it was against their policy. But then eventually there was a cheaper technology, it was a thermal paper printer, each one of those costs about 8 cents. The videotape recorder didn't come along until much later. It just was natural with the obstetrical process: not sick patients, they were just here for—you know, getting the gestational age pinned down and ruling out twins or something, and not a lot of tension, not a lot of concern, nothing unsafe about the technology for them, so, give everybody a picture ...

JANELLE: Did the hospital or the clinic that you worked in have a policy on these things, the kind of not-strictly-medical part of it?

DAVE: Well, there were no policies. We were outsiders, because we belonged to radiology but we were in the women's clinic, in a part of the women's clinic where there were other X-ray procedures done, but ... I don't know, it was all alien to me, I never got to know what they did. ... So there wasn't policy. There might have been policy in the women's clinic, but I didn't have to answer to it. And radiology didn't feel ownership for me, we were like a satellite to them, I was off on my own. And we weren't rigid enough to have our own policy.

Of course, as ultrasound became more established over the course of the 1970s and into the 1980s, these conditions changed, and things became more "rigid." Ultrasound became the focus of professional "turf battles," waged on many levels between radiologists, who laid claim to ultrasound as one among many imaging modalities, and obstetricians, who claimed it as one among many ways of examining the pregnant patient (Blume 1992:109–12). Clinics became larger, with more staff and tighter workloads, and came under the more direct supervision of the departments that succeeded in laying claim to them; and conventions of practice that had been improvised on the spot came to be more or less established social forms.

The pathways that led people into work in the field of ultrasound also changed over time. Up until the late 1960s, skilled people who specialized in performing ultrasound procedures were a mixed lot, and in many European countries they remain so today: midwives, nurses, radiology technicians, and doctors of various specialties. In the United States, however, nonphysician specialists in ultrasound have organized themselves as a separate profession, beginning in 1969. Within the first decade or so, they had formed a professional society (now called the Society of Diagnostic Medical Sonography, or SDMS), and established formalized educational standards and competency exams (which are by now widely recognized and accepted, though not legally required), as well as a national registry board, and acquired other essential trappings of a profession, such as a professional journal and official recognition as a separate occupation by the Manpower Division of the American Medical Association. In addition, formal education programs designed to train sonographers for clinical practice were set up in different locations around the United States beginning in the mid-1970s, and ultrasound began to attract people drawn to it as a career, one among a number of different established allied health fields (Baker 1995). Finally, in 2002, Diagnostic Medical Sonography gained recognition from the Department of Labor as a separate occupation (U.S. Department of Labor Bureau of Labor Statistics 2002).[8]

Skill and Caring in a "Women's" Technical Profession

As obstetrical ultrasound has become widespread, routine, and familiar to the general public, many women have also decided to pursue a career in ultrasound after first encountering it during the course of an examination of their own pregnancies. Joan Baker, one of the founders of the SDMS who now teaches in an ultrasound education program in the Seattle suburb of Bellevue, explained:

> I might lecture to about five hundred people a year, and I asked them, "How many of you have had ultrasounds on yourselves?" And now, it's at least three-quarters. "And how many of you have watched an ultrasound?" And now, almost one hundred percent of the hands are up. Whereas ten, fifteen years ago, they weren't sure whether they came to listen to you to find out what the word *meant*! . . . If you ask [students today what interested them in sonography], typically they will say they had an ultrasound done on themselves or they were with somebody when they had one done. More people, it would have been an obstetrical experience.

Jane, another sonographer who has worked in obstetrics since the early 1970s, concurs:

> What interested me was the detail, the completeness of it all. . . . [But] a lot of sonographers are idealistic about obstetrics, they identify with the mother. They're women who love to be pregnant.

As a general statement, Jane's characterization of sonographers working in obstetrics as "women who love to be pregnant" is surely much too glib, and she said it half in jest. Certainly, not all sonographers working in obstetrics "love to be pregnant," and not all of them are women; Dave, quoted above, had moved into a marketing position in the ultrasound industry already by the late 1970s, but there remain approximately forty-five hundred male sonographers currently registered in the field of ob/gyn ultrasound.[9] There may nonetheless be a kernel of insight in the contrast that Jane draws between her own technical fascination with "the detail, the completeness of it all," and some other sonographers' "idealism" and tendency to "identify with the mother." We can read her statement as pointing toward tensions and debates within the community of sonographers in this country over the relationship between professional identity, gender identity, and the practice of obstetrical ultrasound. Particularly at issue in these debates are precisely those elements of the cultural form of the obstetrical ultrasound exam that we touched upon above: "showing the baby," determination of fetal sex, giving a take-home picture, and so forth.

In speaking with sonographers and in reading their publications (such as the *Journal of Diagnostic Medical Sonography*, which is the official publication of the SDMS), I have been struck by the frequency and the passion with which they exhort themselves and each other to strive to be professional. At the core of this call for professionalism is an insistence upon the high level of technical skill that ultrasound demands. Many contend that ultrasound differs fundamentally from other modalities because the production of imagery requires entirely different skills, as well as a much higher level of knowledge. The division of labor between sonographers and physicians is significantly unlike that between X-ray technicians and physicians, in that a certain degree of interpretation, or arguably even diagnosis, is necessarily involved in the very production of ultrasound imagery. Ultrasound technology images soft tissue (rather than bone); gray-scale images provide information about the density and the texture, as well as simply the shape and location, of these tissues; the internal structures that one seeks to visualize may be situated somewhat differently in the bodies of different individuals—they may be in motion (as the fetus, for example, often is)—and they must be located by moving the transducer around on the body's surface; the views thus obtained are cross-sectional, moreover, and acquiring a standard view or measurement therefore requires that one know enough cross-sectional anatomy and physiology to determine when one has found the right location and the right angle. For all of these reasons, the production of an ultrasound image is *not* just an exercise in mechanically recording a transparently available empirical reality, and in this respect it is quite *unlike* other medical imaging modalities such as X-ray—much less the visual technologies of television and photography with which most people are familiar.

Yet despite this emphasis upon technical skills, for many sonographers it is precisely the responsibility to "identify with the mother," as Jane phrased it, and more generally to provide compassionate care for the people who come to them, that distinguishes their occupation from others that they regard as being more purely "technical." One of the ways in which ultrasound is unlike other medical imaging modalities, some argue, is that it requires much more direct contact with the patient. Because no ionizing radiation is involved, the person performing the exam is not required to leave the room, as do X-ray technicians—and, indeed, the sonographer must hold the transducer in physical contact with the patient's body throughout the exam, moving it about on the body to obtain different views or in some cases inserting a specially shaped transducer into the anus or vagina. This contact is, of course, not simply physical but also social, and is further complicated by the acts of showing and telling enshrined in the cultural form that the obstetrical exam has assumed.

Ann, a sonographer that I spoke with at the annual SDMS convention in 1994, described some of the ways that her practice of ultrasound called upon her capacities beyond her merely technical skill:

> Sometimes you have girls who come from this rural area, from a real strongly fundamentalist religious community, and they just can't admit [they're pregnant]. They'll come to the doctor because of "belly pains" and get sent for an ultrasound and they're eight months pregnant.... Or women who thought they had an abortion, but then they're still gaining weight, so they come back and there's a twenty-week fetus in there and now it's too late.... I say to them, "How can I help you?" And sometimes we talk, or I've given them cab fare to get to the doctor or get home. Sometimes they just need to be held. And I'll do that.

In 1997, Sharon Durbin, a sonographer who works in an obstetrical practice, published a piece in the "Career Symposium" section of the *JDMS* titled "Words Spoken in a Dimly Lit Room." In it, she describes a number of especially emotionally charged encounters that she remembers from more than fifteen years of working with obstetrical ultrasound, and she frames these within a broad call to sonographers not to forget such moments in the rush of economic competition and technological change. Echoing Anne, she suggests that it is less her technical skill than her capacity to provide compassionate care that should be at the core of the sonographer's professional identity:

> I believe there is a need to take the time to reflect on the true humanity of our job, why we really went into this field to begin with. It is the people who come to us at a critical time in their lives.... It is the miracle and sacredness of life, not the revolution of technology or how we can become more cost effective.... It is our challenge to open our hearts and make a difference. It is in caring, it is in nurturing, it is by supporting, that we reach the very depth of our being, and give the best of ourselves to our profession. (Durbin 1997:177)

And if "caring" is what ought to be at the core of the sonographer's professional identity, this caring is manifested above all in "showing the baby" rather than in the taking of measurements or views ordered by the physician. Indeed, Durbin's essay begins thus:

> In this age of technology, let us not lose touch with the humanity of our job. Let us remember the tumbling fetus we image, with arms and legs fluttering in amniotic fluid, faces with big, dark eyes peering out at the excited parents. You hear the "oohs" and "ahs" at the commencement of life when the bondings of the strongest kind are initiated. This is truly what the core of our job is about. . . . [M]emories, faces, beginnings—images permanently etched in the corners of our minds. These emotions are enhanced in the ultrasound room, with its darkness and soft music; communication barriers are dissolved, thoughts are uninhibited, and feelings are demonstrated. (Durbin 1997:175)

There is a delicate balancing act involved in emphasizing the traditionally feminine skills of caring as properly central to the professional identity of sonographers, when at the same time it is their specialized technological skill that underwrites their claims to professionalism more generally.

Sonographers may, furthermore, more readily "identify with" some mothers than others. Some sonographers I observed at work in the Chicago clinic where my own research was based seemed to dispense "nonmedical" extras (showing the baby, giving a picture, informing of fetal sex) most readily only to women whom they perceived as *already* having demonstrated a certain seriousness about the "medical" aspects of the procedure and as more generally taking a responsible attitude toward their health and their pregnancy. Not surprisingly, perhaps, some sonographers also displayed cultural attitudes widely shared in this country (and deeply entrenched in public policy and social theory alike) in regarding the pregnancies of young, poor, unmarried African American women in their care as symptomatic of their failure to be "serious" and "responsible" about reproduction—and regarding these young women as therefore less deserving of such "extras" than mature, middle-class, married white women (Taylor 2000b:411–12; see also Mitchell 2001:135). Because ideologies of motherhood are enmeshed with ideologies of medicine, race, and class (Roberts 1997), sonographers' professional identity, to the extent that it is grounded in a particular kind of *gender* identity, is inevitably entangled with questions of *racial* and *class* identity as well.

Marjorie DeVault, writing about dieticians and community nutritionists, who like sonographers work as " 'intermediate' or 'subordinate' professionals in the health care system," has suggested that feminists ought to consider "questions about professional socialization in the 'women's' professions—about the selves that form during professional training" (DeVault 1999:167). It may be especially important to ask such questions concerning sonographers if we wish to understand how it is that the fetishized "public" fetus of the antiabortion movement emerges out of social practice.

"George" and the Cruel Commercial

The DeMoss Foundation, an evangelical organization with ties to Jesse Helms and Jerry Falwell, in 1994 produced an antiabortion television advertisement that aired on commercial stations in the Chicago area where I was living at the time.[10] In it, a split screen shows, on the left side, a white baby that looks to be several months of age, dressed in a white outfit and lying on a white crib sheet, gurgling and cooing—while on the right side it shows a real-time ultrasound image of a fetus moving around in the womb. Against a background of sentimental instrumental music, a male narrator's voice points out highly symbolic physical capabilities that they share: "The baby on the left can feel pain, so can the baby on the right. . . . The baby on the left can suck its thumb, so can the baby on the right," and so forth, then concludes: "The difference is, that the baby on the left has just been born, and the baby on the right would very much like to be." The screen then shows, in white script against a black background, the slogan "Life: What a Beautiful Choice."

For at least one woman with whom I spoke in the course of my ethnographic research in a hospital-based ob/gyn ultrasound clinic, it was this DeMoss ad that provided a reference point for her first personal experience with obstetrical ultrasound, seven months into her first pregnancy. In response to my question whether she had ever seen ultrasound pictures before she had an exam herself, Catherine, a twenty-seven-year-old African American elementary school teacher from Chicago's Near North Side, replied:

> I saw it on TV, on the abortion commercial. That was really, really cruel of them, they put people under a lot of pressure. Ultrasound makes the pregnancy more real in the earlier stages. I think that was cruel. Even though I am pro-life, I thought it was cruel, because people who are pregnant go through so many changes, so the ultrasound makes it real to you, seeing it move around makes it more difficult to decide, for someone who wants to decide to terminate. I'm pro-life pro-choice, if you can be that. It's not the decision *I* would make . . . [*Here she looked down at her big belly and laughed*] Evidently!

The ultrasound image that was featured in this ad was supplied by Shari Richard, who is a registered sonographer in Michigan and since the early 1990s has combined her professional skills with her "pro-life" activism. Richard has made antiabortion videos using the same footage that is featured in the DeMoss ad and also submitted this same footage as evidence in testimony before Congress in March 1990, when the National Right to Life requested that she testify before the Senate subcommittee opposing the "Freedom of Choice Act." We might say that Richard is to ultrasound what Lennart Nilsson is to photography: she is the one who produced the images that now circulate so widely in public culture and to a considerable extent define shared cultural imaginings of what "the fetus" looks like and what it is.

In 1990, Richard founded a company called "Sound Wave Images"; from this base she sells her videotapes and other materials, offers her services as a speaker to churches, schools, and pro-life organizations, and works to help Crisis Pregnancy Centers (what some of us know as "bogus abortion clinics") learn how they can incorporate ultrasound into their activities. On the company's website, Richard has previously posted, among other things, the following narrative account of the production and circulation of an ultrasound image of a baby she calls "George":[11]

> One evening, in 1989, while working as a sonographer, I was asked to [perform an] ultrasound on a pregnant woman in order to determine the gestational age of the baby she was carrying. I began the ultrasound without receiving any additional information regarding her history. As I placed the gel and transducer on her abdomen, a clear image of a 10 week old baby appeared on the monitor. Most babies at 10 weeks are pretty active, but will sleep during at least the last part of the procedure so that I can obtain my measurements. Not this one! The baby I nicknamed "George" waved, jumped, turned somersaults and was very active during the whole exam. I watched as the mother's sad, discouraged face suddenly changed to a glowing beam of delight. "Is that my baby moving?" . . . Look how developed it is!" . . . She couldn't believe that all this activity was going on inside of her while she couldn't feel a thing. We both laughed as I warned her that she was going to be a very busy mother.
>
> On "George's" 1st birthday, I received a call from this mother thanking me for her daughter's birthday. She told me that she had been planning to terminate the pregnancy until she saw her unborn baby through ultrasound and that this baby was God's greatest blessing to her. Then she said, "Guess what? She hasn't slowed down a bit and is still as active as she was in the womb." I was disappointed that I had nicknamed the little girl "George" and although I tried to change it to "Georgette," "George" would always slip out.
>
> "George's" mission began when I became her producer and chose her as the main character in the ultrasound videos entitled, "Ultrasound: A Window To The Womb" and "Eyewitness To The Earliest Days Of Life." These videos act as a stage permitting the voiceless unborn babies to show off their inherent beauty and humanity. Using high-frequency,

trans-vaginal sonography, I demonstrate the fetal heart beat at just 24 days and observe the babies first movements as early as 7 weeks. . . . In August of 1993 "George" was selected by the DeMoss Foundation to be used in their national commercial campaign, "Life, What A Beautiful Choice" which has now been viewed by millions and is the "picture worth a thousand words." (Sound Wave Images 1998)

I know of no reason to doubt that Richard indeed provided the DeMoss foundation with the ultrasound imagery used in this advertisement. Her story of "George" strikes me as rather implausible, however, as an actual description of the provenance of this image. Even assuming that Richard did indeed receive a call such as the one she describes from "George's" mother, it seems extremely unlikely that she would happen to have saved a videotape record of that *particular* examination, a full year after it had taken place—especially when, according to her account, the exam revealed no unusual medical conditions, and she also was not aware until much later of its profound emotional consequences.[12] Even if Richard *had* somehow kept a videotape of that examination, or (more plausibly) obtained one after the fact from "George's" mother, it seems highly unlikely that the particular videotaped examination that had figured in this transformative bonding episode would also happen to exhibit all of the very specific visual features that make an obstetrical ultrasound image suitable for use in such an advertisement.

For a sonogram to be useful as a "baby picture" in antiabortion materials (or any other mass-media venues), the image must, in the first place, be very clear and distinct—clear enough to be easily recognizable as a "baby" by the general public. This level of visual clarity in a routine ultrasound examination performed in an ordinary clinic setting is perhaps not so unusual today, thanks to the development and diffusion in recent years of equipment capable of fully digital image processing, but it would have been far more unusual in 1989 (when Richard claims to have seen "George").[13] In order for the ultrasound image to function as "baby picture" in mass-mediated public settings, the fetus must furthermore also be small enough at the time of the ultrasound examination for all or most of its body to fit into the visual frame, but at the same time developed enough that its form is easily recognizable, and must be positioned in the womb in such a way as to allow a profile view (for an image of a small round gestational sac, or a cross-sectional "slice" through the fetal abdomen, would hardly be expected to hold the same visual and emotional appeal for the general public as a facial profile, a hand, a foot), and must exhibit the right level and kind of movements to visually evoke those of a newborn baby.

While details such as these raise questions about the veracity of Richard's account as an actual account of the provenance of the ultrasound image used in the DeMoss "Life: What a Beautiful Choice" advertisement, they only add to the rhetorical force of the narrative. The footage featured in this advertisement is necessarily an image of a particular woman's particular fetus; "George" is a specific somebody and not a generic anybody. For the DeMoss ad to accomplish its aims, however, the fetus pictured must be both commodified (that is, separated from the social conditions of its production and rendered "exchangeable" with other fetuses) and fetishized (that is, falsely endowed with "life"). Some origin story for the fetus is needed to make the central antiabortion point that each fetus is a unique individual human life, but that origin story must hover somewhere between the pure abstraction of an idea and the concrete social specificity of a particular woman's particular pregnancy.

The uncertainty regarding the sex of "George"/"Georgette" is particularly telling, in this regard, given the role that sex determination plays in expectant mothers' and parents' construction of a social identity for the fetus. This deliberate obscurity, I suggest, points toward the practice of sonography as the social location at which two different kinds of commodification intersect. Reviewing anthropological approaches to the commodification of body parts, Lesley A. Sharp argues that

> two models of commodification may be at work simultaneously, one more akin to Mauss's understanding of the symbolically charged gift and reciprocity, the other to Marx's notion of commodities as goods produced under the alienating conditions of capitalism. Thus, different parties may offer competing readings of various goods of human origin. Whereas, for example, medical professionals may insist on the objectification of body parts, nonprofessionals may instead foreground understandings of kinship, body integrity, and selfhood, all of which may be embodied within an organ or other body fragment. Thus, Mauss and Marx can work in tandem. (Sharp 2000:293)

Sharp's analysis of organ donation illustrates how the two forms of commodification coincide and collide, as donor kin insist that the donated organ should not be severed from the context of its social production—that is, from social identity of the donor—while organ procurement officials work hard to accomplish and enforce just this kind of detachment (Sharp 2001).

Thanks to its cultural form, the obstetrical ultrasound examination arguably commodifies their fetuses for pregnant women, who tend to approach pregnancy to a considerable extent as a matter of consumption (Taylor 2000b). Yet this is, in Sharp's terms, a distinctly Maussian form of commodification; in the context of a diagnostic exam, or even in the context of a nondiagnostic screening at a so-called entertainment ultrasound business, the social origins of the fetus (both the social context of a particular woman's pregnancy and the social context of production of ultrasound imagery) are always known.

By contrast, Richard enacts a form of commodification more akin to Marx's notion by deliberately obscuring (even while purporting to reveal) the social context of production of "George"/"Georgette," including the identity of the pregnant woman who carried this particular fetus. It is this act of erasure, an act performed by this particular person, who took ultrasound imagery generated in the course of her work as a sonographer and made use of it in contexts far removed from (and in ways antipathetic to) the clinical medical setting, that in one movement commodified this particular fetus, fetishized it, and cast it in the role of "public" fetus.

Even thus detached from the specific social conditions of its production, however, the public fetus still retains certain crucial markers of social difference. That ultrasound imagery presents the fetus as a white figure floating against a background of black nothingness may *perhaps* be explicable in terms of the technical features of the modality (though this merits investigation). That the baby whose image is juxtaposed to this ultrasound image is specifically a *white* baby cannot be similarly attributed to any sort of technological necessity. It is, rather, the result of a decision made by the advertisement's creators—a judgment that this is what a *valued* baby looks like. As Dorothy Roberts writes of public debates surrounding the new reproductive technologies:

> The images that mark these controversies appear to have little to do with Black people and issues of race. Think about the snapshots that promote the new reproduction. They always show white people. And the baby produced often has blond hair and blue eyes—as if to emphasize her racial purity. . . . Yet it is precisely their racial subtext that gives these images much of their emotional appeal. . . . The monumental effort, expense, and technological invention that goes into the new reproduction marks the children produced as especially valuable. It proclaims the unmistakable message that white children merit the spending of billions of dollars toward their creation. Black children, on the other hand, are the object of welfare reform measures designed to discourage poor women's reproduction. (Roberts 1997:246, 269)

The visible, valued, white baby with which the fetus is equated in texts such as the DeMoss advertisement considered here takes its meaning at least in part from the implicit contrast drawn, with babies (in the United States and elsewhere) who are neither visible nor valued in the same ways. It is to this contrast that Donna Haraway points when she writes of "the *missing* representations of fetuses and babies that must trouble anyone yearning for reproductive freedom. . . . [T]his nonimage is of 'human reproductive wastage,' that is, of the dead babies and fetuses, the missing offspring, who populate the earth's off-screen worlds in unimaginable numbers" (Haraway 1998:203).

"George"/"Georgette" may be stripped of gender and all other markers of social identity but remains—at least in terms of the racial categories of contemporary U.S. society—a specific kind of valued somebody. The DeMoss advertisement, in other words, racializes the fetus even while fetishizing and commodifying it—and this is, perhaps, part of what makes it so very "cruel."

"Pro-Life, Pro-Choice, and Pro-Fessional"

Richard has publicly narrated the path that led her to her present work (Doyle 1992:4). When she was young, she says, she decided to abort two pregnancies at a time when she felt unable to cope with the responsibilities of motherhood and viewed abortion as a "sensible solution" involving the removal of "blobs of tissue." When she later pursued a career in ultrasound, Richard was shaken by her encounter with fetal imaging. She regarded the fetuses she saw as "babies she could have had years before" and felt great remorse, guilt, and also anger that she had, as she now sees it, never been properly counseled about the realities of or alternatives to abortion, became very religious, and dedicated herself to sharing her newfound vision and knowledge with women contemplating abortion by showing them ultrasound images of the fetus.

Here again, it is the practice of "showing the baby" that is at issue. Prenatal care is not the only context in which obstetrical ultrasound is used; it is also routinely used to confirm pregnancy and estimate gestational age, prior to an elective abortion. When it is known (from a notation on a woman's chart) that the purpose of an exam is dating prior to abortion, the generally accepted practice among sonographers is to allow the pregnant woman herself to decide whether she would like to see the screen or would like any other information about the fetus. Richard and her small cohort of "pro-life" sonographers argue, however, that all women considering abortion should be shown the screen for "educational" purposes before they make their decision.

In the way that she situates her antiabortion activism in relation to a difficult event in her own reproductive history, Richard is like most of the pro-life and pro-choice activists interviewed by Kristin Luker and by Faye Ginsburg in their respective studies of the American abortion debate (Luker 1984; Ginsburg 1989). One interesting aspect of Richard's story, however, is the way that her antiabortion activism also intersects with what DeVault refers to as the formation of professional selves in a "women's" profession (DeVault 1999). Shari Richard is certainly at the extreme of how sonographers understand their selves in relation to their work, and her activities have occasioned no small amount of consternation, as we'll see. Yet from another point of view, Richard is perhaps not so terribly unlike other sonographers, in that she places traditionally female skills of "caring," and what Sharon Durbin called "the miracle and sacredness of life," expressed especially in the "nonmedical" aspects of the ultrasound exam, at the center of her own sense of what her work means.

In 1993, Marveen Craig asked some twenty sonographers to respond to two questions: Do sonographers have the right to try to influence women considering abortion? And do sonographers have a duty to educate patients scheduled for an abortion? Twelve responses were collected and published in an article in *JDMS* titled "Pro-Life/Pro-Choice: A New Dilemma for Sonographers" (Craig 1993). While the contributors varied in terms of their own stances regarding abortion, all alike emphatically condemned pro-life uses of ultrasound in the clinical setting, on the grounds that they violate values of objectivity and neutrality central to the authors' understanding of what it means to be "professional." In Marveen's words, "As individuals we have the option to choose to be pro-life or pro-choice, but acting as sonographers there is no choice: we must all be pro-fessional."

Being "pro-fessional" in this sense, however, seems to require beating a hasty retreat from all of those "nonmedical" aspects of the exam that Sharon Durbin emphasized in her own vision of sonography as a caring profession, and onto the seemingly safer ground of purely technical skills. As one contributor put it: "the role of the sonographer is to collect and calculate data and to present it to the physician. It is simply not within the professional jurisdiction of sonographers to transfer their feelings to their patients" (Craig 1993:157). I doubt that most sonographers truly wish to envision themselves thus, as simple collectors and calculators of data—and even for those who do, this stance is one that the by-now firmly entrenched cultural form of the obstetrical ultrasound exam, with all its emotionally and culturally fraught rituals of showing and telling, makes it difficult to maintain in practice.

Conclusion

There is a certain irony, perhaps, in the conclusion to which this exploration into the history of obstetrical ultrasound leads us. Feminists have long insisted we must recognize that fetuses come from women; what we've discovered is that this is true in more ways than one. Not only is it pregnant women who physically bear individual fetuses, but women technological workers have also played critical roles in the *making* of the fetishized public fetus.

While this analysis complicates matters somewhat, it also has the advantage of allowing us to understand ultrasound technology and, indeed, the fetishized public fetus that this technology has helped create as *mediating relations among women*. Instead of locating their advent in relation to a grand narrative of the male medical and technological takeover of reproduction, we can locate them in relation to a narrative of the changing situations of women in this country. During the same period in which obstetrical ultrasound was becoming routinized in medical practice, and the fetishized fetus was emerging as a new feature of the public cultural landscape, women in this country were, in many ways, also being "produced" as new sorts of subjects, positioned in new ways relative to work, family, and political life, as well as relative to their sexual and reproductive bodies. Women building careers in newly emerging professions such as sonography form one thread within this broader tapestry; women learning to approach pregnancy and reproduction largely as a matter of consumption (Taylor 2000b) form another. Obstetrical ultrasound is one site among others where the two come together—and one place, perhaps, to begin the work of reweaving a different future.

NOTES

My title makes implicit and ironic reference to Lennart Nilsson's *A Child Is Born* (Nilsson 1966), which presented dramatic new photographs of "life before birth." Nilsson's photographs, initially published in *Life* magazine in 1965 (the same year I was born!), helped forge new shared understandings and imaginings into which fetal ultrasound imagery has been incorporated. Today, nearly forty years later, Nilsson's fetal photographs continue to circulate widely in antiabortion materials—they have, indeed, taken on a "life" of their own. The fact that many of them are in fact highly staged, backlit photographs of *aborted* fetuses seems not in the least to detract from their ability to function as icons of unborn "Life." For critical discussion of Nilsson's work, see Jain (1998), Michaels (1999), and Stabile (1999).

Some portions of this essay are taken from my dissertation (Taylor 1999), and the content of this essay overlaps to some extent with an article published in the *Journal of Diagnostic Medical Sonography* (Taylor 2002). Earlier versions of this argument have been presented orally to several audiences, whom I thank for their critical comments: the conference "Women and Gender in the History of Science, Technology, and Medicine," St. Louis University; the Department of Anthropology, University of Iowa; the Department of Anthropology, Wayne State University; the Department of Comparative Studies, Ohio State University; and the Society for Medical Anthropology. I am especially grateful to Linda Layne for her helpful comments.

1. See Layne (1999b) for a complementary discussion of how the concept of the fetish may apply to women's attachment to material objects associated with a desired but lost fetus in cases of pregnancy loss.
2. I now perceive this as a shortcoming in some of my own earlier writings on ultrasound as well (especially Taylor 1992).
3. As of late October 2000, the American Registry of Diagnostic Medical Sonographers (ARDMS) counted 39,339 registrants all told; 30,258 registrants with the status of passed for ob/gyn; 25,699 female registrants with the status of passed for ob/gyn; and 4,559 male registrants with the status of passed for ob/gyn. Personal communication, Gwen Henderson, Director of Registrant Services of ARDMS, October 30, 2000.

    While I know of no similarly reliable source of information on the class, race, or religious background of sonographers as a group, the Chicago clinic where I conducted research was perhaps not entirely unrepresentative in counting among its sonographers African Americans and first-generation immigrants, as well as white women born in this country. To the extent that higher education functions in the United States as both an index of class position and a primary vector of upward mobility, the structure of sonographer training programs—which are often based in community colleges, require for admission little or no education beyond high school, and offer two- to four-year specialized courses of study that combine classroom education with clinical training—might, like other allied health fields, tend to draw people who do not already belong to the most educationally and economically privileged segments of society. This is consistent with my knowledge of the routes by which sonographers with whom I have spoken (admittedly, a small sample) entered the field: via military service of one sort or another or through a personal involvement or family connection with other paramedical fields such as pharmacy, nursing, x-ray, and so forth. It is still true today, as Eliot Freidson pointed out more than thirty years ago, that

> the paramedical division of labor is a stratified system, the occupations of which are in varying degrees integrated around the work of the physician. All occupations in the system are given less prestige than the physician by society at large. Consonant with this differential prestige, the backgrounds of those recruited into all paramedical occupations are likely to be lower than those recruited into medicine itself. Furthermore, there is a hierarchy of prestige and authority among paramedical workers, with nurses, for example, being higher than attendants and technicians. This hierarchy, too, is likely to be reflected in the social origins of the workers. In the grossest comparison between physicians and paramedical workers, the latter are to a disproportionate degree women and of the less valued ethnic, racial, and religious groups in the United States. (Freidson 1970:53)

4. Yoxen ends his historical account of ultrasound on this note, with a call for research along these lines; his own account, however, ends earlier.
5. Jean Lea Spitz, personal communication, June 2002.
6. *Sonographer* is the preferred and appropriate term for people working in this capacity today. Since this term was not invented until 1980, however, I use the term "ultrasound technician" to describe people working with ultrasound to produce diagnostic information before that time.
7. See Blizzard (2000) for a parallel account of " 'building' a procedure: creating a social context in which a new procedure makes sense and identifying a means of convincing others that they should support specific developments" in the emergence of fetoscopy.
8. Thanks to Jean Lea Spitz for alerting me to this recent development.
9. See note 3.
10. This is a private organization named for Arthur S. DeMoss, who, as founder of the National Liberty Life Insurance Co., helped pioneer "the art of selling low-cost insurance by direct mail. When he died in 1979, National Liberty, which employed Art Linkletter as its spokesman, had 1.5 million policyholders, $500 million in assets, and was listed on the New York Stock Exchange. Since DeMoss' death, his wife has run the foundation, and does not grant interviews. Nor do his children, who are all active in foundation work and other evangelical Christian causes" (Apologetics Index 2003; this Web site also includes excerpts from a number of previously published newspaper articles). The DeMoss foundation supports television advertisements with an evangelical Christian orientation, but its primary activity is the advertisement and distribution (free of charge) of the book *Power for Living* (see the Web site http://powerforliving.com). Despite—or perhaps precisely because of—its extraordinarily low public profile, this organization apparently still has the capacity to inspire fear; in one instance, a fearful editor prevented me from even simply mentioning it by name in an article that I wrote.
11. I originally found this text posted on Richard's Web site in 1998. As of this writing, in July 2003, the Web site is still active and has been expanded considerably, but this

particular text is not currently posted.

12. Allen Worrall, who operates an ob/gyn ultrasound clinic in Alaska, comments that "since 1991 I have recorded all my ultrasounds (ob and gyn) on SVHS video as my official documentation of the exam. I just started my 355th ST-120 tape. I can do this because I do my own scans and do not have to watch the video after the exam unless I want to. In the conventional sonographer/radiologist setup I doubt if many practices use video for the documentation, because it would take the radiologist too long to review the case" (Joseph A Worrall, MD RDMS, personal communication, December 2002).

13. "Digital image processing" means that the ultrasound image is processed electronically at every stage of production. By eliminating the need to work with films, digital processing streamlines performance (it is no longer necessary to interrupt examinations in order to develop films), provides much higher image quality, and facilitates computerized storage and communication of images. This also opens new possibilities for teleradiology—transmission of digital images via telephone or Internet connections means that an ultrasound examination being performed at one site may be simultaneously observed or reviewed by a physician at a site elsewhere in the hospital (or indeed elsewhere in the world).

Consuming Childbirth

The Qualified Commodification of Midwifery Care

ROBBIE E. DAVIS-FLOYD

> Scholars of consumption have argued persuasively that we must understand consumption itself as a site of cultural creativity and political agency, and also (at least potentially) of subversion and resistance. Consumers are neither passive nor without agency, but rather appropriate mass-produced goods to their own projects and purposes, producing selves and making worlds in the process.
>
> –Janelle S. Taylor, "Introduction," *Consuming Motherhood*

Contemporary home-birth midwives are engaged in precisely the enterprise the editors of this book identify: by appropriating certain aspects of mass production to their own projects and purposes, they are using consumption as a site of subversion and resistance to create new selves and alternative worlds. Starting out at the margins of a consumer society they view with a jaundiced and critical eye, these midwives came to realize over time that their survival as viable practitioners requires participation in the technocracy's core processes of commodification and consumption. Their own views of these processes, while initially negative and derogatory, have subsequently expanded to encompass the ambiguity inherent in commodification. In other words, these midwives came to see that these processes can be not only agents of co-option into standardized mass markets but also forms of cultural creativity and political agency, and, indeed, also of subversion and resistance to mass standardization. The selves/identities such midwives make as they commodify in order to occupy a wider terrain in the consumer market, and the alternative realities they create through this process of commodification, are the subject of this chapter. In it, I will illustrate their appropriation of the language and strategies of the kinds of consumption and marketing that they themselves perceived as negative in what

I here identify as a process of *qualified commodification*. *Webster's New World Dictionary* (2000) gives the following as the fourth and fifth definitions of "qualify": "to modify, restrict, limit [to *qualify* one's approval]; to moderate, soften [to *qualify* a punishment]." Thus, with this term I seek to name the alchemical process through which midwives appropriate the rhetoric and core cultural characteristics of mass forms of commodification in order to move themselves into the mainstream, but modify and moderate those characteristics in an effort to simultaneously remain true to the countercultural ideals and values they have long called their own.[1]

Background and Context: Hospital Birth as Industrial and Technocratic Production

In the premodern era, midwives tended to be integral members of their communities, performing needed services within a network of reciprocal relationships and traditional lifeways. With the industrialization of the United States, including its medical services, traditional midwives often found themselves phased or pushed out of practice as birth lost its definition as a social event and moved into the hospital, where it was managed and defined through metaphors of industrial production (Davis-Floyd 1992; Martin 1987). The industrialization of birth entailed its treatment as assembly-line production and the massive use of anesthetics like scopolamine, which effectively eliminated any conscious involvement on the mother's part, thereby both justifying and facilitating her treatment by practitioners as a machine producing a product, as I have described in earlier works (Davis-Floyd 1987, 1992).

The advent of the natural childbirth movement in the 1970s, which stressed the importance of choices in childbirth (for example, Arms 1975; Hazzell 1976), was part and parcel of the simultaneous explosions of American feminism, which generated more options for women, and of American consumerism, which generated more options for everyone who could afford them. The rise of the consumer as an active agent seeking choices, high quality products, and individualized service paralleled the new feminist conversation about women's rights to agency and choice. In the cultural arena of birth, this new conversation increasingly came to include women's rights to choose to give birth at home. Reacting to the massive overmedicalization of birth and the near-complete denial of women's agency during the scopolamine era, across the nation and throughout the 1970s some women began to choose home birth. From 0.6 percent in 1970, the home-birth rate rose to 1.5 percent in 1977. This rise reflected the growth of a bona fide grassroots social movement, and it had quite an effect on hospitals, whose administrators tended to see it as both an economic and a medical threat.

Responding to the outside pressure from the home-birth movement, which by its very existence constituted a radical critique of the impersonality and technologization of hospital birth, and to direct demands from birth activists bent on getting fathers into delivery rooms and achieving more agency for birthing women, hospitals began to redefine pregnant patients as consumers and to invent marketing strategies to attract their business. New advertisements showed women blissfully laboring in Jacuzzis, Halston sheets on the double bed in the birthing suite filled with lovely oak furniture "just like home," the happy couple sipping champagne and enjoying a lobster dinner or basking with their children in the reflected glow of a joyful birth experience. Such images graphically illustrated this market redefinition of pregnant women as agentic consumers of medical care. Birth itself was redefined as a purchasable commodity: with the right obstetrician and the right health care plan, accompanied by enrollment in the right childbirth education classes and at the right hospital, a good birth seemed to become something that money and careful planning could buy. Gone were the days when women were drugged out of their minds with scopolamine during birth, gagged, slapped around, tied to their beds. Now women were "awake and aware," freed from pain by the epidural, apparently able to exercise their right to informed choice over every decision.

Concomitantly, the ways in which medical hegemony over childbirth were displayed began to shape-shift in accordance with shifts in the wider culture. In recent decades, the United States has transited from a society organized on Fordist lines around the industrial production of goods to a service economy organized around the global flow of goods and information, which I call the technocracy. In other works (Davis-Floyd 1992, 1994), I have described the central ethos of technocratic life as the supervaluation of technology and "onward and upward" technological progress. Because birth encapsulates in microcosm the core values of a culture (Davis-Floyd 1992), this shift from industrial society to technocracy was dramatically displayed in corresponding shifts in American birthways. Where the dominant symbol of industrial birth was the flat-on-the-back (lithotomy) position, which rendered women less able to push effectively and made the forceps-wielding physician the producer of the child, the dominant symbol of technocratic birth became the electronic fetal monitor. Introduced in the early 1970s to more closely monitor high-risk women during labor, within a decade this machine became pervasive in even normal births (Kunisch 1989). Its most significant contribution was information: it produces a continuous and permanent record of the fetal heartbeat and of the timing and intensity of every maternal contraction. Thus this machine brought childbirth into the Information Age, creating the information it generates both as an essential attribute of a safe birth and as a global commodity—via the Internet, it is now possible for a woman laboring in South Africa to be simultaneously monitored in real time by doctors in London and New York. This continuous flow of information intensified medical control over labor (Cartwright 1998; Kunisch 1989), helping to raise the cesarean rate from 4 to 23 percent during the 1970s, while at the same time giving women the sense that labor was a measurable, controllable, and manageable process and that *they* were making the choices based on the information the monitor gave (Davis-Floyd 1992). And the spectrum of choice generated by such technologies increased rapidly and dramatically, as ultrasound, amniocentesis, surrogacy, and the new reproductive technologies made it increasingly possible to commodify babies as well (Casper 1998; Davis-Floyd and Dumit 1998; Hartouni 1997; Layne, ed. 2000; Morgan and Michaels 1999).

The Midwifery Appropriation of Commodification Strategies

The intense commodification of reproduction has had some interesting consequences for American midwives, who are managing in some rather creative ways to appropriate it to their own ends. Effectively shut out of birth during the modernist industrial era, in the postmodern technocracy midwives have been fighting their way back (Davis-Floyd, Cosminsky, and Pigg 2001). Their numbers are growing exponentially, as is their political and legislative presence in the birth arena. Increasingly unwilling to accept their cultural marginalization, both nurse- and direct-entry (non-nurse) midwives are actively starting to think of themselves, and to present themselves to the public, as valuable health care commodities. Appropriating the notion of women as agentic consumers of maternity care (an image they helped create), midwives have added themselves to the list of birth care options from which women can now choose. Marketing has become a keystone of their strategies for success in the twenty-first century: in recent years midwives have produced advertisements, brochures, videos, and books touting the benefits of midwifery care. They have also become master politicians, successfully selling midwifery to state legislators, nursing and medical societies, and regulatory boards (Davis-Floyd and Johnson, forthcoming; Lay 2000). In some states their search is for greater representation on the boards that govern them and more beneficial rules and regulations; in others, the fight is for so basic a thing as the right to practice legally and to be licensed by the state.

Within these parameters of the commodification of American midwifery, two models and philosophies of midwifery education and practice coexist and sometimes compete for legal status and cultural recognition. The nurse-midwifery model, generally speaking, has since the 1950s encompassed hospital-based training and practice and some degree of physician supervision/ collaboration. The lay midwifery model, generally speaking, has encompassed apprenticeship and autonomous out-of-hospital practice in freestanding birth centers and homes.[2] As lay midwives professionalized, they began in the late

1980s and early 1990s to reject the appellation "lay" in favor of the more professional term "direct-entry," which they imported from Europe and adapted to mean that one enters directly into midwifery education without passing through nursing first (Benoit et al. 2001; Davis-Floyd 1998a).

Nurse-midwives have been successfully commodifying themselves for years; as a result, they are legal, licensed, and regulated in all fifty states and are reimbursed by insurance companies, Medicare, and Medicaid. They presently attend 8 percent of all births in the United States. Their national organization, the American College of Nurse-Midwives (ACNM), has approximately 7,500 members at this writing, about 5,500 of whom are in active practice. In contrast, direct-entry midwives (DEMs) still attend only 1 percent of American births; their national organization, the Midwives' Alliance of North America (MANA), has only about 800 members (one-third of whom are nurse-midwives); and they are legal in twenty-nine states but licensed, regulated, and reimbursed in only seventeen states. In Canada, nurse- and direct-entry midwives are working together in various provinces to create professional education and regulation processes that apply to all midwives. But in the United States, the historical, ideological, and practical differences between nurse- and direct-entry midwives have resulted in the fracturing of American midwifery, with each group proceeding on its own.[3]

In other works I have given equal treatment to both nurse- and direct-entry midwives (Davis-Floyd 1998a, 1998b, 1999, 2004; May and Davis-Floyd 2004). But in this chapter I will concentrate primarily on direct-entry midwives, whose efforts at professionalization and commodification contrast in fascinating ways with the ongoing value they place on their relationships with their clients and their grassroots social movement fervor. About nurse-midwives, it will suffice here to say that since 1925 they have worked hard to create a professional image and reputation in keeping with that of other health care professionals. In part these efforts were necessary to combat the negative stereotype vividly depicted in a Charles Dickens novel of the fat, lower-class, gin-swilling midwife on her way to a birth carrying a bag of dirty instruments—a stereotype that was heavily exploited in the medical campaign to eliminate midwifery in the United States. Thus one can imagine nurse-midwives' dismay at the sudden advent of the lay midwife, who went from near nonexistence in the late 1960s to attending 1.5 percent of births by 1977 (about the same percentage the nurse-midwives were attending at that time). Although these new lay midwives came from a diversity of backgrounds, including hippies, feminists, and conservative midwestern preachers' wives, their most visible public face was countercultural: long hair, long flowy skirts, and Birkenstocks constituted the visual representation they came to conjure up, along with a hippie ethos, a countercultural lifestyle and values, and a laid-back attitude. This public image was a major threat, both stylistically and professionally, to the short-haired, stockinged, and white-jacketed image of mainstream professionalism and competence that nurse-midwives had worked hard to build.

The Politics of Representing Midwives

As every anthropologist knows, ethnography is all about representation. As an ethnographer, I first became aware of how concerned direct-entry midwives are becoming about revamping their public image when I began work on a chapter (Davis-Floyd 1998a) that I was invited to write for a book being put together by *Midwifery Today* (a magazine and company dedicated to the preservation and promotion of midwifery) called *Paths to Becoming a Midwife: Getting an Education* (Tritten and Southern 1998). For that book, I had been asked to write a comparative description of "the ups and downs of nurse- and direct-entry midwifery" in nine pages or less—a task I should have known would be impossible. Yet I had been conducting fieldwork among nurse- and direct-entry midwives for four years at that point in an attempt to understand their similarities, differences, and political motivations vis-à-vis each other. I (foolishly) thought that the hundreds of interviews I had conducted with these midwives, and the dozens of midwifery conferences I had attended, would make it easy to describe them in simple, generalized terms. In the first draft of that chapter, which I wrote in a few days, I noted that direct-entry midwives are "more culturally marginalized, work longer hours, and make far less money than nurse-midwives." The direct-entry midwives who saw that first draft reacted with outrage, telling me that I made them sound like "marginalized losers" and the hospital-based nurse-midwives, who make a great deal more money and have more reasonable working hours, like winners. Aware that this *Midwifery Today* book would be read by students trying to make a decision as to whether to become a direct-entry midwife (DEM) or a certified nurse-midwife (CNM), the DEMs wanted me to represent them in the most positive light possible. I asked for suggestions for alternative wording that would be as true as what I originally had said but that would make them "look better"; putting our heads together, we came up with the following:

> Direct-entry midwives often work alone or in practices with one or two primary midwives, and are almost always on call. For some, burnout is the result of this constant availability; others find this a viable way of life. . . . Many direct-entry midwives appreciate the flexibility they enjoy as independent practitioners: should they desire more time off, they can cut down on the number of clients they take on. In areas where interest in home birth is steady or growing, they can choose to accept more clients until they build their practice to the level they desire. Thus their incomes

vary widely: those who attend only a few births a year may make only a few thousand dollars, while some direct-entry midwives make upwards of $60,000 per year....

In short, direct-entry midwives (DEMs) face the challenges and reap the benefits of being self-employed entrepreneurs. Like some MDs, they run independent practices; their earning ability is not constrained by salaries but rather depends on their level of energy and their ability to attract clients (which itself is constrained by cultural attitudes toward home birth). In states where they are licensed and regulated, they often serve as the sole proprietors of thriving businesses (at a time when many MDs are being forced to trade in their economically advantageous positions as independent practitioners for the rigid payment schedules of HMOs). Many DEMs make a good living, many do not, but all of them love their work. Most DEMs would not trade the challenges, tribulations, and rewards of their entrepreneurial practices for the constraints of working in a hospital setting. (Davis-Floyd 1998a:75)

Although I had some qualms about being made into an active agent of their marketing strategies, I felt responsible to them to describe them the way they tend to see themselves, so I was happy to find this alternative wording. But the battle was not over; they took me severely to task once again when I tried, in that same article, to describe the damaging stereotypes hospital practitioners tend to create and disseminate about direct-entry midwives. The following is what I said in that first draft:

Many medical practitioners, and some nurse-midwives, have serious concerns about the safety of direct-entry practice; they point to the fact that there are some DEMs in practice with truly inadequate training. Thus when a DEM makes a mistake, no matter what her individual knowledge and skills, most people in the medical community are only too ready to assume that she is "ignorant" and "incompetent," and go on to assume that incompetence and lack of education characterize all midwives of her ilk. (Davis-Floyd 1998a:76)

Immediately I received irate phone calls from a midwife and a midwifery advocate, both of whom asked me how dare I call direct-entry midwives "ignorant" and "incompetent"? Of course I had not done so—I had simply tried to describe the stereotypes other people held. Painful and irrational as this accusation was, it pointed up to me the extreme level of concern today's DEMs bring to public representations of their image. Fighting generations of such stereotypes applied to them by the medical profession, starting in the early 1900s with Sairy Gamp, today's professionalizing home-birth midwives react strongly to any such negative associations. Let me tell you a story that will graphically illustrate both the motivations behind their overreaction to my description of this stereotype and their drive toward commodification.

After a wonderful home birth, a mother has a retained placenta. The midwives try everything they know but they cannot get it out. They phone the obstetrician on call at the local hospital, who tells them that he will not see this woman and insists that they take her to the charity hospital, even though she has plenty of insurance. Arriving at the local hospital anyway, they are told that the only ob on call is the one who had previously refused to see this mother. Apparently irritated at having to see her after all, he takes two hours to show up. Had she hemorrhaged, this delay could have cost her life. Fortunately, she did not. He eventually put her under general anesthesia and removed the placenta, but not before telling her and her husband that it was "child abuse to risk their baby's life by giving birth at home with ignorant practitioners like midwives."

Almost every practicing DEM has several stories like this one to tell (Davis-Floyd 2003). These transport stories vivify the problematic nature of the interface between midwives and medical practitioners and the consequent deep need midwives feel for cultural legitimacy. It is one thing to proudly hold a countercultural space in which women can make alternative choices, and it is another to watch their clients suffer the effects of negative stereotyping. Thus, although many direct-entry midwives remain countercultural to the core, they are keenly aware of the necessity of making themselves more viable in the technocracy, not only to keep themselves out of jail but also to protect their clients from suffering the effects of midwives' cultural and medical marginalization. One obvious route to cultural viability would have been nurse-midwifery, but that would have meant losing the kind of independent midwifery they had worked so hard to create. How could they sell themselves without selling themselves out?

Qualified Commodification: Mainstreaming Midwives

A Certified Professional Midwife (CPM) is a knowledgeable, skilled, and professional independent midwifery practitioner who has met the standards for certification set by the North American Registry of Midwives (NARM) and is qualified to provide the Midwifery Model of Care. The CPM is the only international credential that requires knowledge about and experience in out-of-hospital settings.

–How to Become a Certified Professional Midwife

For the first three decades of their existence, direct-entry midwives were handicapped in their efforts to gain a toehold in the technocracy by several factors. These included (1) public awareness of their lack of credentials: in most states, anyone could hang out a shingle and call herself a midwife; (2) the vast variances in their educational processes, which range from pure apprenticeship to various private three-year-vocational (and two college-based) schools; (3) occasional bad outcomes at births attended by insufficiently trained practitioners; and (4) the negative stereotyping of midwives in general as less competent than practitioners. They did have a national organization, MANA, which they created in 1982 and which did develop national practice standards and core competencies during the 1980s. But full voting membership in MANA was open to anyone who called herself a midwife, and there was no obligation to abide by the standards that MANA had set. Increasingly aware that only a standardized national certification process could convince the public, including politicians, legislators, and the courts that they were safe and savvy practitioners, compensate for the variations in their educational processes, help them avoid arrest and legal persecution, and minimize the possibility of inadequately trained midwives out there doing births, the members of MANA were at the same time concerned that any kind of nationally standardized certification would compromise their ability to meet women's unique needs and requirements in out-of-hospital settings.

No one was more aware of this danger than the members of the organization created by MANA to develop an exam and later a full-fledged certification—the North American Registry of Midwives (NARM). Desiring to design a psychometrically valid testing and certification process in line with the standards set by the National Organization of Certifying Agencies (NOCA), NARM board members also and just as ardently desired not to co-opt themselves and their sisters or compromise their practices in the process. Since 1994, I have watched them struggle with the tensions generated by the often conflicting pulls to (1) enhance their public image so as to better market themselves to the public through creating a rigorous certification process; (2) preserve their ability to practice according to their own individual values and beliefs and those of their clients, which they believe constitutes the essence of out-of-hospital midwifery; and (3) establish certification requirements that work with the logistical realities of their day-to-day practices and educational processes.

As Karl Marx (1978) asserted, commodification is a transformative process, which he viewed in relatively negative terms. Since then, anthropological theories about commodification have come to encompass its many variabilities and its often creative qualities (Hebdige 1979; McRobbie 1988). MANA midwives not familiar with such writings, however, maintain deep suspicions about commodification and tend to see it in more culturally negative terms. Their view of commodification has more resonance with those of social scientists like Adorno and Horkheimer (1999), Bourdieu (1984), Baudrillard (1988), and others. In what follows I will utilize a list of the characteristics I have noted that midwives seem to associate with commodities and commodification, combining those characteristics with some thoughts of my own.

For wide success, a commodity must, among other things, be produced in a standardized way; subject to mechanisms of quality control; quantifiable, measurable; legally accessible; purchasable and user-friendly; able to tap or to create a market niche and to be marketed successfully through advertisements or other means to reach that market niche; and designed and redesigned in ways responsive to consumer desires and cultural trends. The most successful commodities, from Coca-Cola to the iMac, have in addition a brand name that gives them a unique identity and maintains consumer demand for that particular product, even in the face of clones and competitors. Inevitably, commodities are embedded in the local/global political economy—their price, availability, and symbolic worth will reflect market fluctuations, competitive pressures, government priorities, political realities and tensions, and glocal (local and global) cultural biases and beliefs.

Most of the above characteristics of commodification are antithetical to the ethos and the values that characterized lay midwives in the early days of their development (DeVries 1996; Reid 1989). They started out in resistance to the standardization of hospital birth, experienced a nonquantifiable spiritual calling to midwifery, often attended women who could not pay,[4] and would not have dreamed of marketing themselves too visibly, as they were illegal or alegal in most states. But in the early 1980s they gained legalization in Washington State, Florida, New Mexico, Arizona, Texas, and Oregon; created their national association (MANA) in 1982; started to formalize and codify their knowledge base in books, articles, and formal vocational curricula; and by the mid-1980s began to exhibit many of the characteristics of incipient professionalization, including developing various state certifications. By the early 1990s they were moving into full-scale participation in the technocracy.

But from their beginnings as a grassroots social movement, they had created a unique style of midwifery that they wanted to preserve. So their challenge in the 1990s became how to professionalize and commodify themselves without losing the essence of who they are and what, uniquely, they have to contribute. In the rest of this chapter, I will utilize the characteristics of commodities described above in order to shed light on midwives' commodifying strategies and to analyze their degree of success in achieving their primary goal: preserving the autonomous, woman-centered, and holistic style of midwifery they had created by making it viable in the technocracy, primarily through the development of CPM certification. For organizational purposes, I will address these characteristics in the following order: (1) standardized production; (2) quality control; (3) quantification, legality, and midwifery's market niche; (4) design and redesign: commodities as responsive to consumer demands; (5) commodities as embedded in the global political economy.

Characteristics of Commodification and How Midwives Fit

Standardized Production

The Certified Professional Midwife (CPM) has been educated through a variety of routes, including programs accredited by the Midwifery Education Accreditation Council (MEAC), the American College of Nurse Midwives Department of Accreditation (ACNM-DOA), apprenticeship education, and self-study.

–How to Become a Certified Professional Midwife

As the above quotation indicates, direct-entry midwifery (DEM) education takes many forms and shapes; it cannot be considered standardized. Rather, DEM training ranges along a spectrum, from the most hands-on and the least didactic (self-study and apprenticeship) at one end to highly didactic formal programs at the other. This lack of standardization has been the source of many of its public relations problems. Nurse-midwives are required to obtain basic science prerequisites, a baccalaureate degree, an RN or BSN, and to graduate from university-affiliated postgraduate programs that have been accredited by the Division of Accreditation of their national organization, the American College of Nurse-Midwives (ACNM).[5] For many years, ACNM's rigorous standards contrasted sharply with direct-entry midwives' lack of such. Some DEMs responded to this situation by creating rigorous licensure processes in a few states and/or by opening formal vocational programs, usually of three years duration. Within these formal programs, students are evaluated according to standards set by the faculty of each program. And by the mid-1990s, these programs themselves were under evaluation by a new affiliate of MANA, the Midwifery Education and Accreditation Council (MEAC).[6]

But how do you evaluate the knowledge, skills, and experience obtained through self-study or by apprenticing with a practicing midwife in a publicly convincing way? How do you standardize the unstandardizable learning process called apprenticeship? How, in other words, do you commodify an anticommodity? This was one of the most daunting challenges of developing NARM certification. Apprenticeship training is a thoroughly individualized process whose shape and nature depends on the personalities and abilities of the apprentice and the mentor(s) and most especially on the relationship that develops between them. When it is successful, the apprentice/mentor relationship provides a supportive and nurturant educational context within which the apprentice can learn about pregnancy and birth through the immediacy of touch and experience and can supplement that embodied knowledge with reading and long discussion with her mentor and others. Apprentices accompany their mentors to home births, witnessing woman after woman give birth successfully on her own and developing comprehension of the normal birth process. Where hospital training tends to focus on pathology and generate a fear-based approach to birth, home-birth apprentice training generates trust. Midwives who fundamentally trust birth are more likely to be able to create an atmosphere within which women can find their power and trust themselves to give birth. Thus, preserving apprenticeship has been and remains essential to the ethos and ethics of MANA members' philosophy and practice (Davis-Floyd 1998a, 1998b; Benoit et al. 2001).

NARM's response to the challenge apprenticeship presented was to standardize its educational *requirements* without trying to standardize direct-entry educational *processes*. NARM certification is open to midwives educated through all possible routes, including apprenticeship, self-study, formal vocational programs, university training, and all combinations of the above. NARM certification is competency based: where or how a midwife gains knowledge, skills, and experience is not the issue—that she has them is what counts. In other words, it is what midwives know and can do that matters, not how they learned it or what prerequisites they obtained (Davis-Floyd 1998a; Rooks 1997).

Thus the decisions the members of the NARM board had to make as they developed CPM certification came to center around the issue of what criteria to use for standardizing their educational requirements. The discussion quickly crystallized around three ingredients—knowledge, skills, and experience. What knowledge base did an entry-level applicant have to master, what skills did she have to learn, how much experience was enough? In establishing answers to these questions, the eight members of the NARM board[7] faced the difficult task of balancing the competent and professional public image they desired the new CPM to present against the pragmatic realities of her training and practice. Encouraged by the MANA membership not to undertake this task alone, the NARM board held five Certification Task Force (CTF) meetings around the country to seek input from the American midwifery community. Any midwife of any kind was welcome to participate in these meetings; approximately 150 did so (Alice Sammon, personal communication, May 2003); most were DEMs, some were CNMs. (Most CTF participants were members of MANA, but membership was not a requirement.) All NARM and CTF decisions were consensus based, meaning that everyone present had to agree to every major decision. Strict adherence to the consensus process carried its own set of challenges but ultimately ensured that the outcome of the process was supported by all of its creators, as it continues to be.

One of the early issues the members of the NARM board and the CTF faced was how many births to require that CPM candidates attend. They knew it would "look better" to the outside world if they required that CPM candidates attend more births as primary caregivers than the twenty births required of student nurse-midwives, but they resisted that temptation because requiring more births would, among other reasons, make achieving certification too difficult for midwives practicing in rural areas, where the births can be few and far between. Likewise, they knew it would look better, more "midwifery-like," to require that CPM candidates give large numbers of courses of continuity of care to their clients (caring for the same woman throughout the childbearing cycle), but they resisted that temptation because some of the most important midwifery training centers, such as Maternidad La Luz in El Paso, primarily serve poor Hispanic women from northern Mexico, many of whom do not show up for any kind of prenatal care or return for postpartum visits, making continuity of care extremely difficult for many students to achieve. (Wanting to require ten or more courses of continuity of care, they ultimately settled on three.)

They also knew it would "look better" to require the ability to insert IVs as an entry-level skill required of all CPM candidates—in the extensive discussion of this issue during a CTF meeting, one of the arguments repeatedly used in favor of requiring this skill was that home-birth midwives "look really good" to hospital personnel when they transport a woman who is hemorrhaging with the IV already in place. Another was that this skill is essential to safe home-birth practice. It was here, in this heated debate over whether or not to require IV insertion as an entry-level skill, that the depth of their commitment to preserving midwifery as it is understood and practiced by home-birth midwives through this new certification was put to its greatest test.

It was January 1995. The members of the NARM board and the CTF, including myself,[8] were on Captiva Island in Florida. They knew that this was about creating the future of their brand of midwifery, so a full forty of them showed up at their own expense. The sun was shining and the beach was calling on that warm and breezy day. Nevertheless, we sat in a meeting while everyone in turn spoke their mind on the important issue of which skills should be required for entry-level practice. Written on the board were "IV insertion," "catheter insertion," and "under-the-tongue pitocin administration for hemorrhage" as the skills in immediate question. From a home-birth perspective, these were highly medical skills. I listened with astonishment as midwife after midwife spoke in favor of requiring all of these skills for entry-level midwives.

Halfway into the process, I raised my hand and asked for a quick sense of the room—how many of the midwives present favored requiring all these skills? When thirty-six out of the forty sets of hands went up, I was amazed to realize that I was bearing direct witness to the professionalization of lay midwifery. Even Ina May Gaskin, an irrepressible and eternal hippie and internationally known point person for "spiritual midwifery," argued for the IV requirement. She noted that after many years of holistic midwifery practice, she realized she had been relying on EMT technicians on the Farm to insert IVs in those rare cases of severe postpartum hemorrhage and had finally taken responsibility for learning the skill herself. She felt that it was now an invaluable part of her midwifery repertoire, and she stressed not only its lifesaving potential but also its positive value in terms of the public image of midwives, saying, "When we have a hemorrhage and we transport the woman with an IV already in place, we really look good to the hospital personnel who receive our clients. It helps them to trust us as practitioners."

Only four of the midwives there were in active opposition; their primary spokesperson was Sandra ("Sandi") Morningstar, a midwife from Missouri who had been sent to the meeting with a mandate from her state midwifery association not to allow IVs to be required as an entry-level skill for CPM certification (in the consensus process used at these meetings, one person can block a proposal even if everyone else supports it). As midwife after midwife tried to get her to change her mind, Sandi held fast, insisting that requiring IV insertion as an entry-level skill sent the wrong message to student midwives. She said that IV insertion was an advanced, not an entry-level, skill because the proper first courses of action in case of a hemorrhage were, in this order, to speak to the mother, asking her to stop bleeding (an intervention that midwife/anthropologist Janneli Miller [2002] calls "magical speech"), to administer the herb shepherd's purse, to utilize bimanual compression of the uterus, to give pitocin under the tongue or a pitocin injection, and only after all that had been tried, to insert an IV and transport. Sandi herself had learned IV skills a decade ago, but she did not want student midwives thinking that they should jump straight to the IV without learning all the other techniques that home-birth midwives have rediscovered for dealing with hemorrhage, because usually those less interventionist techniques are all that is needed. And the midwives in her state, who were practicing illegally, did not want to be required to carry IV equipment, as this would open them to the serious charge of practicing medicine without a license. So steadfast was Sandi in her insistence on blocking the IV requirement that, after four hours of trying to get her to change her mind, the others gave up, put the matter in the hands of the ten members of the steering committee, of which Sandi was one, and took a break before dinner.

At dinner I was curious to see how Sandi would be treated by those who had opposed her so vehemently only an hour before. (She had been in tears at one point, openly questioning whether she should even become a CPM.) Ina May got there first, rushed over to Sandi, gave her a big hug, and thanked her for "speaking her truth" and "holding her space." Ina May said that when one midwife holds her space, it always works out better for everyone than if she had given in against her will and compromised her principles. And so the dinner went, with everyone hugging Sandi and expressing their appreciation. They still disagreed with her, but their trust in the consensus process was deep—experience had taught them that somehow it would work out.

By the time the steering committee met, everyone on it was exhausted. We sprawled around the room and tentatively started the discussion. Sandi still would not budge, until someone said, "Well, Sandi, if you knew that most of the midwives in the U.S. wanted IVs to be required, would you still hold this position?" Sandi answered, "Of course not! I'm not here to tell the majority of midwives what they should do! It's just that I don't think the forty women at this meeting [most of whom were midwifery leaders or directors of private midwifery schools] really represent the majority of practicing midwives—I'm trying to speak out for the ones who are not here, who don't think as you do." At that point, with dawning amazement, the group began to realize that they had just been handed a golden key. It occurred to all of us simultaneously that none of us could really say what the majority of practicing midwives thought about which skills should be required for entry-level practice, and it was not long before the steering committee was actively and excitedly planning what later turned out to be the largest survey of practicing midwives ever conducted in the United States.

Some months later, after hundreds of volunteer hours of work, three thousand surveys were mailed, and although they were so detailed they took over twelve hours to fill out, eight hundred of them were returned in usable form (Houghton and Windom 1996a, 1996b). As a result, the NARM process is based on midwifery as actually practiced by these eight hundred out-of-hospital midwives, not just by the forty who had been present on Captiva Island that day.[9] These grassroots midwives themselves set the standards by which they were to be judged and thereby avoided two of (what they saw as) the primary potential downsides of commodification—the many being co-opted by the rule-making few, and quality and individualized design and service giving way to mass standardization. They ultimately did standardize the production of CPMs, but the criteria they used were not arbitrarily established by an elite governing group; rather, they were consensually chosen by a majority of practicing DEMs. In other words, these midwives qualified (modified, moderated) the ways in which they commodified according to the internal standards of the larger—and still countercultural—group.

Quality Control

> The education, skills, and experience necessary for entry into the profession of direct-entry midwifery were mandated by the Midwives' Alliance of North America (MANA) Core Competencies and the Certification Task Force; were authenticated by NARM's current Job Analysis; and are outlined in NARM's *Candidate Information Bulletin* and the *How to Become a Certified Professional Midwife (CPM)* booklet.
>
> –*How to Become a Certified Professional Midwife*

As the midwives perceived it, a commodity must be subject to mechanisms of quality control. Part of the professionalizing enterprise is the inclusion of those who meet established criteria for education and practice—in other words, for quality—and the exclusion of those who do not. This simple fact was the subject of intense debate among MANA midwives during the 1980s and early 1990s. At that time, the social movement was (and remains) MANA's dominant ethos, and inclusiveness its dominant ethic. MANA's nonprofessional inclusiveness was in deliberate and direct contrast to the ACNM's professional exclusiveness. Voting membership in ACNM entailed certification as a CNM (or CM—see below). Membership in MANA entailed the simple statement that one was a midwife. When I was asked to speak at my first MANA conference in El Paso in 1991, some MANA midwives were refusing even to utter the word *professional* because of its exclusionary connotations. Nevertheless, it was clear that they were evolving themselves as professional midwives with a codified and cohesive body of knowledge and skills. Their creation of NARM certification was a strong expression of this evolving sense of professionalism.

Their motivations for seeking a more secure cultural status included not only strong desires to protect mothers and babies from the mistreatment that results from medical stereotyping of midwives, but also to protect them from mistreatment by midwives who are insufficiently educated. Although DEMs do not like to talk about it, it is a fact that in the early days of lay midwifery, when everyone was on a learning curve, occasional bad outcomes in out-of-hospital births did result from a midwife's lack of knowledge or skill. And today, although the vast majority of DEMs are now well educated and practice responsibly, they do have a named category for the "renegade midwife" (see Davis-Floyd and Johnson, forthcoming) who practices outside the protocols and parameters of her peers in her local midwifery community. Thus, a means of testing midwives to ensure that they have the necessary knowledge, skills, and experience became increasingly desirable to DEMs themselves, and NARM certification became the mechanism of quality control they chose.

It is a given that any certification process will include those who meet all requirements and exclude those who do not. This process of exclusion starts with requirements for candidacy. The desires of NARM and the CTF to minimize the exclusiveness of their certifying process led board members, in consensus with the CTF, to establish four educational categories through which student midwives can apply for NARM certification as a CPM. Applicants in all four categories must meet NARM's general education requirements, which include attendance at forty births, twenty as primary attendant under supervision; three courses of continuity of care; seventy-five prenatal exams; twenty newborn exams; forty postpartum exams; CPR (adult and neonatal) certification; and other criteria.[10] But how an applicant must demonstrate that these requirements have been met varies by the educational category through which she applies.

The first category listed in NARM's *How to Become a Certified Professional Midwife* booklet is graduation from a formal program accredited by the MEAC. Since the education of these students has already been evaluated by the faculty of the school, upon completion of their program, in general they have only to pass the NARM written exam. The second category is "certification by the ACNM Certification Council (ACC)"; its criteria represent NARM's response to the intense debate between ACNM and MANA that took place throughout the 1990s over the issue of what constitutes effective quality control in direct-entry midwifery education. While both organizations could ultimately agree that quality control in the form of national certification was a good idea, ACNM insisted that at a minimum all certified midwives should obtain a baccalaureate degree (later, they also insisted on exiting from midwifery training with a master's degree) and should be educated in university-affiliated programs; MANA insisted that good midwifery practice had nothing to do with college degrees and that safe and competent midwives could be educated through any route. Thus MANA's creation of NARM, and NARM's creation of the CPM, initially did little to allay ACNM leaders' fears that this credential would not guarantee effective quality control.

Desiring to open their profession to midwives not trained as nurses, but not trusting the validity of NARM certification, in the mid-1990s ACNM decided to go ahead with creating its own direct-entry credential, which was ultimately given the name Certified Midwife (CM).[11] (The full story of the CM's creation is too complex to tell here, but see Rooks [1997], Davis-Floyd [1998a], and May and Davis-Floyd [forthcoming] for more detail.) When NARM and MANA first got wind of ACNM's plans to create this new midwife, many of their members reacted with fury to what they perceived as an incursion into the direct-entry territory they believed they had staked out as their own.

The tensions thus generated were heightened by both organizations' use of the term *direct-entry*, which they used in radically different ways. ACNM members were using the term in what they understood as its European sense: entry directly into a formal, government-recognized midwifery training program without passing through nursing first. MANA and NARM members were using the same term to mean entry directly into any form of midwifery education, without passing through nursing. With this usage, MANA members intended to restrict use of the term *direct-entry* in the United States to professional midwives who practice out of hospital, while ACNM sought to restrict its use to midwives trained in programs accredited by the ACNM, in which students are trained primarily in hospitals. (ACNM holds the position that its students are prepared to practice in any setting and that out-of-hospital experience is not necessary for out-of-hospital practice [Reed and Roberts 2000]).

At first, and with good reason, many members of MANA and NARM perceived ACNM's creation of direct-entry certification as a gut-level challenge, most especially since the legislative legitimation and state licensing of the CM in New York was accompanied by a shift in the legal definition of unlicensed midwifery from a misdemeanor to a felony. Although many of New York's practicing direct-entry midwives came forward to apply for this new direct-entry certification after it was legalized in 1993, only two of them met the requirements and were able to achieve it. Most of the rest were effectively driven out of practice or out of the state (see Davis-Floyd 1998a and May and Davis-Floyd, forthcoming, for more detail). Thus the initial debate among the members of the NARM board over whether or not to allow ACNM certified midwives, including CMs, to apply for CPM certification was tinged with intense bitterness and exclusionary desires.

But in the end, MANA's core ethics of inclusiveness and sisterhood once again prevailed, and the NARM board decided to keep its certification open to all midwives, including both CNMs and CMs. While NARM was aware that most nurse-midwives would not want or need NARM certification, its members were also aware that some nurse-midwives would want to become NARM-certified out of a philosophical commitment to MANA and to home birth and midwifery as social movements, while others might need to become CPMs so that they could practice autonomously outside of hospitals, which in some states their nurse-midwifery certification might not allow them to do. (Many nurse-midwives are effectively prevented from attending out-of-hospital births because state regulations require them to obtain physician supervision agreements, but they cannot find any physicians willing to sign such agreements for out-of-hospital practice. If they become CPMs, they can practice autonomously in most states where CPMs are legal.) To date, four CNMs have chosen to also become NARM certified, and, as we shall see later on, NARM certification may come to have particular significance to ACNM's new CMs.[12]

Once NARM decided that CPM certification should be open to ACNM-certified midwives, there was much discussion among board members as to whether additional requirements should be established for candidates in this educational category. This discussion led to a general philosophical agreement among CTF and NARM board members that in-hospital experience, which is all that ACNM-accredited programs require, is not sufficient preparation for out-of-hospital practice. So it was decided that CNMs and CMs who apply for NARM certification must document attendance as primary midwife at a minimum of ten out-of-hospital births and three courses of continuity of care and must pass the NARM written examination. (This exam tests knowledge about birth outside the hospital, where, as one NARM member put it, "there is no button to push to call for backup and a midwife must know how to handle sudden emergencies herself.") With these requirements, NARM both kept its certification process open to and inclusive of nurse-midwives and held its own conceptual space as an organization dedicated to establishing and evaluating the knowledge, skills, and experience required to attend out-of-hospital births.

NARM's third educational category is "legal recognition in states previously evaluated for educational equivalency." This educational category was established to recognize the equivalency between some state certification or licensure processes and NARM certification. Candidates from these states can, with some exceptions, simply submit a copy of their state license and take the NARM written exam.

The most innovative category, and the most complex, is completion of NARM's Portfolio Evaluation Process, also known as NARM's PEP program. This is the route established by NARM to evaluate the education, skills, and experience of midwives trained through apprenticeship and self-study. PEP applicants are divided into two categories: "entry-level" and "special circumstances."[13] Entry-level candidates must document their fulfillment of NARM's general education requirements; provide written verification from their preceptor(s) that they have achieved proficiency in the numerous skills listed on NARM's "Skills, Knowledge, and Abilities Essential for Competent Practice Verification Form"; provide a written affidavit from their preceptor(s) that the applicant meets various other requirements; provide three professional letters of reference; and pass the NARM Skills Assessment. This hands-on skills assessment is a unique feature of NARM certification. ACNM does not require a hands-on skills assessment, as the skills of nurse-midwives are verified by the various preceptors in their educational program. But since an apprentice-trained midwife may have only one or two preceptors during her entire training, who may be her friends, CTF and NARM board members identified the need to establish a mechanism for testing the actual skills she obtains.[14] Ideally, such an exam would evaluate the skills demonstrated by the student midwife at a birth, but that would have required the exam administrator, called a NARM Qualified Evaluator, to travel to wherever the midwife lived and wait there until her client went into labor. Cost and logistical and liability difficulties made this impossible for NARM to afford. So instead they utilized the list of required skills that stemmed from the survey results, emphasizing those that could be demonstrated on a pregnant volunteer and an infant. For each exam, the skills that will actually be tested are randomly chosen from this list by a computer; the Qualified Evaluator asks the applicant to demonstrate each skill and grades her according to performance. This skills exam has formed an essential part of NARM's success in establishing the CPM as a valid credential, as it helps to resolve the issue of how apprentice-trained midwives can prove that they have obtained the skills that were identified as required for entry-level practice on the large-scale survey that NARM conducted (Houghton and Windom 1996a), thus ensuring the requisite degree of uniformity in quality among CPMs.

Within a profession, another major aspect of quality control is what mechanisms exist for taking disciplinary action against members who are accused of malpractice. The creation of an effective peer review process has been a major challenge for the NARM board, as it requires them to sit in judgment of their own, a painful position for midwives operating under an ethos of sisterhood and inclusivity. Due to space limitations, I will not discuss the complexities of this process here, as to date there have been very few cases in which the peer review process has had to be activated (only two CPM certifications have had to be revoked). More important for the issue of quality control is birth outcome, which for midwives is the ultimate litmus test of quality control.

Quantification, Legality, and Midwifery's Market Niche

QUANTIFICATION. A commodity must be quantifiable and measurable. How many are produced, how many are sold, how many are used, how well do they work? And a commodity must be able to tap into an existing market niche, or, like the personal computer, create one where none previously existed. Lay midwifery in the United States arose in response to the desires of some women to avoid hospital birth. In other words, the market niche existed, and lay midwifery arose to fill it. But as long as midwifery remained primarily a social movement, the numbers of women utilizing lay midwives' services remained miniscule. In the United States, throughout the 1990s home births accounted for less than 1 percent of all births (Rooks 1997). While many have decried this low figure, Ina May Gaskin, former president of MANA, has come up with a reinterpretation of its meaning. This reinterpretation exemplifies midwives' discursive trend toward conceptualizing themselves in the quantifying terms of marketing strategies. Ina May insists that that the low percentage of home births can be seen as an accomplishment, given the highly financed, highly organized efforts that American physicians over the course of this century have made toward stamping out home birth altogether.

> We have not only maintained that steady rate, but we have begun to experience what happens when a struggle such as this takes place over a generation. Given the opposition the medical profession has directed against midwifery, we in MANA believe that it has been an accomplishment for us to have survived at all! As more studies are carried out on the safety and efficacy of DEM practice, we believe that the percentage of home births will rise, not fall, during the years to come. We see the six-fold increase in home births in Oregon, where midwifery has long been legal, as significant. We are still in the stage of being a "best-kept secret" when it comes to mainstream culture. (Personal communication 1998)

Direct-entry midwives have long contended that more women want home birth than are able to achieve it because of the limitations on their accessibility imposed by lack of legalization, licensure, and/or insurance reimbursement. Where they are illegal, they are accessed only by the tiny minority of women so committed to the philosophy and spirit of the home-birth movement that they are willing to go outside the law to achieve it. Where they are legal but unlicensed, they are accessed only by women who can pay out of pocket for their services. Where they are legal, licensed, and insurance reimbursed, their accessibility to a much wider clientele is reflected in the higher home-birth rates Ina May mentions in Oregon, which are paralleled by rising home-birth rates in Florida, New Mexico, Arizona, and Washington State. In certain areas of Seattle, for example, where licensed midwives are easily accessible to large numbers of women and fully insurance reimbursed, home-birth rates have risen to 8 percent or more, reinforcing Ina May's point that the "1 percent barrier," as it used to be known, was a reflection not of women's lack of interest in home birth, but rather of its culturally imposed inaccessibility.

Over the past decade, this inaccessibility, which was near-universal in the United States in the 1960s, has given way to wild variation in the legal status of (and thus consumer access to) DEMs from state to state. DEMs are legal and regulated, and licensed, registered, or certified in nineteen states; legal through judicial interpretation or statutory inference, or alegal (not legally defined but not specifically prohibited from practice) in thirteen states; legally or effectively prohibited in twelve states; and of ambiguous status in others.[15] They can obtain insurance reimbursement from private companies in most states where they are licensed, and Medicaid (and sometimes managed care) reimbursement in Arizona, Oregon, Florida, Washington, New Mexico, South Carolina, and Vermont. (In many other states licensed midwives are fighting for Medicaid and managed care reimbursement, with varied results. In most states, home birth attended by direct-entry midwives is still an out-of-pocket expense.) The ultimate goal is to become legal, licensed, regulated, and third-party reimbursed in all fifty states without losing their autonomy as practitioners and without compromising their ability to offer their particular brand of holistic, out-of-hospital, woman-centered care.

For midwives, issues of quantification, measurability, and marketability in terms of their public image center primarily on outcome. The database MANA had accumulated of fourteen thousand births was not considered epidemiologically valid because the data were voluntarily submitted, leaving the results open to the charge that midwives had simply not sent in any bad outcomes they may have had. In 1999 the NARM board decided to address this problem by requiring that every CPM submit a prospective form for every client she accepted in the year 2000 and then account for the outcome of those births. Participation in this endeavor, which became known as the CPM 2000 project, was made mandatory for recertification (which must be done every three years). The outcome forms had to be verified by the client whose birth they describe. In this way, the members of the NARM board and the MANA statistics committee intended to generate outcome data for CPMs that meets epidemiological standards for validity. In a sense, they "bet the company" that the outcomes would be good; if they were not, the public image of the CPM and her value as a health care commodity would suffer accordingly.

The results of the CPM 2000 project were presented at the 2001 meetings of the American Public Health Association (Johnson and Daviss 2001) and the 2001 and 2002 MANA conventions, and are being written up for publication in medical journals. Three hundred and fifty CPMs sent in data on more than seven thousand courses of care. The transport rates from home to hospital were 8 percent, meaning that out of every hundred women who started out intending to give birth at home, ninety-two did so successfully; eight were transported; six of these transports were preventative; two were emergencies. (When a home-birth mother lives thirty minutes away from a hospital, if the hospital immediately begins preparing for the cesarean, the time from start of transport to cesarean is that same thirty minutes. Inside the hospital, the time from "decision to incision" is also about thirty minutes.) (See Davis-Floyd 2003 for an analysis of midwives' transport stories.) The cesarean rate was 4 percent. And the perinatal mortality rate (PNMR), which is the most critically scrutinized figure, was two to three per thousand, exactly what it is for nurse-midwives attending home births and for physicians attending low-risk births in hospitals. This study definitively shows that there is no added risk to planned home birth attended by a CPM. These good outcomes, which demonstrate safe and effective care, will now be included in every legislative package and will become a major marketing tool.

As I have tracked the evolution of the CPM, I have wondered with fascination at what point, if ever, MANA would evolve into a professional organization requiring CPM certification for voting membership.[16] Conversations about creating a separate organization representing CPMs began around 1997 but were usually squelched with the argument that such an organization would generate a further fracturing of an already too-fractured midwifery community. With only eight hundred members, MANA could hardly afford to lose a third or more of them to a separate organization. In 1999, yet another problem became visible. While ACNM's membership was growing by five hundred or more a year, as new students graduating from the forty-five existing nurse-midwifery programs became full voting members, MANA's membership had hovered between seven hundred and one thousand for years. Part of the problem, it turned out, was that only about half of the new CPMs belonged to MANA. All the members of the NARM board are longtime members of MANA and were concerned by this trend. So the NARM board decided to run an ad in the spring 2000 edition of the *CPM News*; here is how it read:

NUMBERS MATTER!

MANA is the only national organization that is open to all midwives. The ACNM's membership has surpassed 8000 while MANA's membership has held steady at around 1000 for nine years. In order to continue to provide an effective counterbalance to the medicalization of midwifery, and to promote the Midwifery Model of Care and the CPM,
MANA must grow!
Only half of all CPMs currently belong to MANA.
JOIN MANA, SO THAT WE CAN STAND TOGETHER AND BE COUNTED!
Benefits of membership include:
The MANA News—a primary source of information about political issues affecting CPMs.
Ensuring that MANA represents the interests of CPMs
Being part of the Sisterhood of Midwives
Fostering midwifery as a social movement
Helping to preserve out-of-hospital birth
Being counted in the national tally of direct-entry midwives
ASK NOT WHAT MANA CAN DO FOR YOU—
ASK WHAT YOU CAN DO FOR MIDWIFERY BY JOINING MANA!!

It is an ironic twist that its concern with numbers has placed MANA, whose members created CPM certification, in the position of having to market itself to CPMs. Querying those who hesitate to join MANA, I found that many of them preferred to pay membership dues to their state associations, which represented them as regulated professionals or were lobbying to make them so; they did not perceive membership in MANA as relevant to their concerns as professionals. This situation represents a further transformation in American direct-entry midwifery, demonstrating that a significant portion of CPMs are more committed to the professionalizing enterprise than to the social movement.[17]

Potential need for a separate organization for CPMs became clear during the attempt that nurse- and direct-entry midwives are currently making for legislation in Massachusetts that will heal the breach created in New York by regulating both types of midwives under the same state midwifery board. Legislators understand professional organizations and the standards they set. The Massachusetts CNMs could point to national practice standards set by ACNM, but the CPMs could not, because although MANA had set practice standards similar to those of ACNM, MANA is not a professional organization that requires certification for membership. So the direct-entry midwives of Massachusetts felt the need to create a national organization requiring CPM certification for membership that could set specific standards for CPMs. (Such standards are not only reassuring to legislators; they are also helpful to midwives in retaining control over their profession—a better situation than having standards set for them by regulatory agencies with nonmidwife members.) A new task force meeting was held at MANA 2001 in Albuquerque; the discussion revolved around whether the new CPM organization should be independent or should be a section of MANA, albeit with its own independent governing board. The consensus at the time crystallized around the latter option. The thirty or so midwives at the task force meeting wanted to honor the need of CPMs for their own organization and representation, without fracturing MANA, which as they termed it would be "matricide"—killing the organization that gave them birth. But many interested parties were not present at that meeting (it occurred shortly after the attacks of September 11, 2001), so the discussion continued, ultimately resulting in the creation of a CPM section within MANA *and* an independent CPM organization, the National Association of CPMs (NACPM). Their strong and inclusive consensus tradition led them to form both and then see which one would ultimately receive the most grassroots support. This complicated development reflects the identity struggles of the new CPMs—are they primarily invested in the professionalizing/commodifying enterprises of certification, legalization, and licensure (which the NACPM represents) or in the social movement of midwifery and its traditional inclusivity, which MANA represents? Or will they accomplish and support both simultaneously?[18]

LEGALITY, ILLEGALITY, AND THE PRICE OF LICENSURE. The multibillion dollar international drug trade makes it clear that it is not absolutely necessary for a commodity to be legal to be successful in creating and reaching its market niche. Where consumer demand exists, entrepreneurs will try to fill that demand even if it means breaking the law and risking jail. In most such cases, there is nothing noble about this enterprise; it is simply about money and power. In contrast, the early "lay" and contemporary "direct-entry" (many of whom are the same people) midwives flouted the law and continue to do so in some states, not out of a quest for money and power but out of the moral imperative they feel to keep the home birth option open to the women in their communities. Members of social movements regularly break the law in the name of their cause; part of the point is to get the laws changed to reflect the realities the social movement is trying to generate. Commodification forms a major part of the strategy midwives and their consumer allies employ to obtain legality.

In many such states, consumer groups, often called Friends of Midwives (as in Massachusetts Friends of Midwives or Maryland Friends of Midwives), work to help direct-entry midwives gain legal status. At the national level, a consumer group called Citizens for Midwifery (CfM) has generated a number of helpful publications, from brochures on the Midwives Model of Care to information on lobbying and working with media to help consumers and midwives work for favorable state legislation.[19] CfM focuses on networking, sharing information and resources, promoting the Midwives Model of Care, encouraging public education efforts, and helping state organizations with legislative initiatives. CfM's stated vision is "to see that the Midwives Model of Care is recognized as the optimal kind of care in all settings and available to all women" (Susan Hodges, personal communication 2003). Through such consumer support groups, direct-entry midwifery's market niche loudly proclaims its existence in highly public ways. For example, when DEMs are arrested or persecuted, or are actively promoting legislation or trying to change an unfavorable bill, they are often helped to win their cases by the public demonstrations consumer groups sponsor and the press coverage they obtain.

When lay practitioners become professionals and obtain the benefits of legalization and licensure (which include not only insurance reimbursement but also not having to worry about being arrested), there is usually also a price to be paid. Licensure means regulation, and regulation means restrictions on one's decision-making power and thus on one's autonomy. When DEMs practiced illegally or alegally, they did pretty much everything they wanted to do—it was all illegal so what was the difference? Thus their practices often included attending women choosing home birth who would be classified in the hospital as high risk, most especially women with babies in the breech position and women giving birth to twins. While most entry-level DEMs would themselves consider these to be high-risk conditions meriting transport, some experienced DEMs have gained special expertise in attending such births and are often more skilled at it than most physicians. (Increasingly, vaginal birth after cesarean [VBAC] is considered high risk in hospitals; most DEMs do not consider them so and often attend them at home.)

Nevertheless, getting state legislatures to legalize DEMs and state boards to regulate them in ways that actually allow them to continue to practice almost always requires certain compromises; most often, it is these three kinds of births that midwives have to give up the right to attend out of hospital. Before regulation, attendance at such births was a matter of a midwife's individual choice; after, they would be breaking the law to do so and in danger of losing their license. So midwives seeking commodification have had to decide which is more important: full autonomy or being able to sleep at night instead of lying awake in fear of the knock on the door.[20] Most of the time, they compromise and accept these sorts of restrictions in return for the benefits of licensure; in other words, most of the time they are willing to pay the price of commodification.

But some midwives refuse to pay that price. In Pennsylvania and other states, such midwives call themselves "plain midwives," to differentiate themselves from the professionalizing direct-entry midwives. Few such midwives belong to MANA. Often they are members of religious groups; in general, they just want to be left alone to serve their communities according to their particular customs and beliefs, preferring to remain completely outside of the system. Although they often run the risk of being arrested for practicing medicine without a license, in actuality they are so few in number and so adept at avoiding publicity that they are usually left alone; to them, that seems better than the closer scrutiny that comes with legalization and regulation. In other words, content to remain in the cultural margins, the plain midwives reject both professionalization and commodification, while their direct-entry colleagues actively seek through both of these strategies to enter the mainstream. After sometimes bitter rhetorical battles with plain midwives in their states, DEMs often decide to accept or actively generate a fissioning of their social movement by clearly differentiating themselves from midwives who do not want any kind of licensure or regulation. Mary Lay has documented this process in detail for Minnesota, a state in which the professionalizing DEMs formed a midwifery guild and eventually won state licensure based on NARM certification, in part by actively distancing themselves from their nonprofessionalized colleagues. Lay (2000:78) notes that during the legislative hearings, "the Minnesota direct-entry midwives made clear that the midwifery community was divided and to some extent took advantage of that division. As those involved in the hearings struggled to define the 'good midwife,' they did so by acknowledging an 'other' midwife who seemed not to rely on medical knowledge to screen her home-birth clients and who was in essence silenced in the hearings."

Such silencing is not atypical of the results of successful commodification processes. Midwives who succeed in professionalizing and obtaining licensure often find it both ironic and intensely distressing that their mainstream status results in the establishment of exclusionary hierarchies in a community where before there were none. In Washington State, for example, in the early 1980s, DEMs succeeded in gaining legalization and licensure via an old law on the books that allowed for midwives to be licensed if they graduated from a formal vocational school. The Seattle Midwifery School thus became the first and is by now the best-known three-year DEM vocational program. Its founders were countercultural self-help feminists who thought they were going to end up in jail for practicing midwifery but ended up founding a school instead. The downside was that no DEM could become legal and licensed in Washington without graduating from this school, which takes three years and costs approximately $25,000 in tuition. The result has been the hierarchization of non–nurse-midwifery in the state: SMS graduates, who call themselves direct-entry midwives, are legal, licensed, regulated, and insurance-reimbursed. The "other midwife" thus created is called a lay midwife; she can practice legally only if she does not accept any money in payment for her services. Thus the victory of some has been the defeat of others. Since this result was never their intention, the directors and staff of SMS have been trying for years (and have recently succeeded) to get the legislature to open other routes to licensure in Washington State. In one sense, opening such routes is like shooting themselves in the foot, as it may limit the number of applicants they receive. But their commitment to the spirit and inclusive ethos of the social movement remains strong, and they would prefer to qualify, even compromise, the success of their commodification rather than continue to live with the exclusions and hierarchies it has created.

This respect for and appreciation of nonprofessionalizing lay or "plain" midwives is one of the primary reasons MANA members voted at their Florida convention in 2000 to keep their membership open to all midwives. Licensed midwives responsible to the state often find themselves torn between parents' wishes and regulatory protocols. They stand to lose their licenses if they accept out-of-protocol home-birth clients (for example, VBACs, breeches, or twins). Sometimes licensed midwives take the risk and accept those cases anyway; at other times they refer such clients to the unlicensed, illegal or alegal "lay" midwives nearby (if they respect those midwives' skills), who are often termed "renegade midwives" because they do not follow peer group protocols but rather consider the wishes of the parents to be primary. The professionalizing members of MANA, who used to have the same priorities, regard these lay midwives with an odd combination of distrust and wistfulness, but they would never want to exclude such midwives from membership in MANA. Having to turn away certain clients one has the skills to attend is the price many pay for licensure, and there is a great deal of respect within MANA for skilled and responsible unlicensed midwives who are unwilling to pay that price and so will serve the clients licensed midwives are supposed to refuse. (For a deeper discussion of "renegade midwives," see Davis-Floyd and Johnson, forthcoming.)

PURCHASABILITY, MARKETING, AND BRAND NAME RECOGNITION

> Certified Professional Midwives (CPMs) are skilled professionals qualified to provide the Midwifery Model of Care, which is appropriate for the majority of births.
>
> –"The Certified Professional Midwife (CPM)," NARM brochure

Commodities are sold and bought. This kind of purchasability came after the fact to many lay midwifery pioneers who began their work out of an ethic of service to women. Over time and across the country, these early pioneers evolved into seasoned professionals with set fees, bookkeeping systems, and a desire for insurance reimbursement. But to be bought, commodities must be readily available. In states where direct-entry midwifery remains illegal, their practice is very much underground and they can be extremely hard to find. In contrast, in states where they are fully legal, licensed, and regulated, midwives' advertisements often appear in bold letters in the yellow pages. For example, an ad for the Austin Area Birthing Center in Austin, Texas, reads as follows:

> Create an Ideal Birth for You and Your Baby . . . 346-3224
> With Gentleness and Individual Care in a beautiful, warm, homelike environment!

Staffed with Certified Professional Midwives and Licensed Nurses
Medical backup
Covered by most insurance
Spacious birthing rooms with fire place & waterbirth tub
Complete care from prenatal through birth
Over 1800 successful births since 1981
Childbirth the Way It Should Be!

Fees for midwifery services vary widely from rural to urban areas. For a quick example, in Austin, direct-entry midwives charge three thousand dollars for one entire course of care, including prenatal care, labor and delivery, and postpartum follow-up. Although their fees are markedly lower in most areas than those charged by obstetricians and CNMs, DEMs remain at a disadvantage because in most states their fees must still be paid out of pocket, a fact that often limits their client base to the middle class. Lack of insurance reimbursement has in some places been a powerful motivator for midwives to obtain NARM certification and to drive for legislation recognizing the CPM as a legitimate health care provider. In this endeavor, cost-effectiveness is one of their major supporting points. Because DEMs employ few technological interventions and practice out of hospital, from a governmental perspective they are a cost-effective alternative to highly expensive obstetrical care. But the costs of state testing and licensure are high, so the expenses of the boards that must regulate licensed midwives can be prohibitive. Thus one of NARM's most effective marketing strategies has been pointing out to state agencies how much money it can save them to let NARM do the testing and credentialing, instead of the state. A fact sheet developed by NARM, dated August 12, 1999, reads as follows:

> HOW CAN THE CERTIFIED PROFESSIONAL MIDWIFE (CPM) CREDENTIAL SAVE GOVERNMENT AGENCIES MONEY?
> When the CPM is used as the state credential for midwives practicing in out-of-hospital settings, government agencies can:
> 1) Avoid expending valuable staff time to validate the education of direct-entry midwives who practice in primarily out-of-hospital settings;
> 2) Avoid test construction and maintenance costs associated with the creation of a licensure examination;
> 3) Save the costs of test administration;
> 4) Save the costs of continuing education monitoring for re-licensure.
> IT'S A GOOD DEAL FOR THE MIDWIVES! IT'S A $$ SAVER FOR THE STATE!

Through such promotional literature, NARM seeks to demonstrate not just its cost-effectiveness, but also its user-friendliness to state agencies, whose beleaguered workers are often delighted to be relieved of some of their administrative burdens.

Of course, "user-friendliness" has become a buzzword for accessibility in technology; likewise, brand name recognition is often an essential ingredient of a commodity's success. User-friendliness has been a central distinguishing feature of midwives' practices from the beginning, one that they have long branded "woman-centered care" in order to contrast their approach to that of physicians, who often place their own needs or the requirements of the institution above those of the mother. Another identifying phrase, a sort of generic label adopted by all American midwives, has been "the midwifery model of care." These two phrases are universally used by both nurse- and direct-entry midwives. But as NARM crystallized its certification, its members and many others worked for months to develop and copyright their own "brand name," which turned out to be a definition of what they originally called the "Midwifery Model of Care" (adding the capitalization to distinguish its wording as uniquely theirs).

This focus on the model of care rather than the midwife was a contribution from consumers, as Susan Hodges, president of the national consumer group Citizens for Midwifery, recounts:

> When representatives of MANA, MEAC, and NARM began having regular phone calls (in the spring of 1996), one of the first things that came up was the need for some way to succinctly describe what we were all working for. The idea was to come up with a definition of a "midwife." It was Citizens for Midwifery that suggested a definition of a kind of care rather than of a midwife. As consumers, we were very aware that the kind of care you get is much more important than the letters after someone's name. [We knew] that there was tremendous variation among midwives in terms of how they practice. So it was the consumers who strongly suggested a definition of the model of care, which has turned out to be much more useful than a definition of "midwife." (Personal communication 2003)

As these direct-entry midwives organized their marketing strategies around this model, they were increasingly disconcerted by the fact that the word *midwifery* was not user-friendly: many people, including legislators, had a problem pronouncing it, which often resulted in embarrassment and a general turnoff on the legislator's part. On the advice of a professional marketing organization they had hired to help them revamp their public image, they changed the name to "Midwives Model of Care," trademarking the label and the description of that model on which they had all agreed:

> Midwives Model of Care™
> The Midwives Model of Care is based on the fact that pregnancy and birth are normal life events.
> The Midwives Model of Care includes:

monitoring the physical, psychological, and social well-being of the mother throughout the childbearing cycle;

providing the mother with individualized education, counseling, and prenatal care, continuous hands-on assistance during labor and delivery, and postpartum support;

minimizing technological interventions;

identifying and referring women who require obstetrical attention.

The application of this woman-centered model has been proven to reduce the incidence of birth injury, trauma, and cesarean section. (NARM, *How to Become a Certified Professional Midwife* [2002]:2)

This description was originally copyrighted in May 1996 by the Midwifery Task Force (a nonprofit corporation) under the title "Midwifery Model of Care." It was recopyrighted in 2000 with the new title "Midwives Model of Care." This brief description of the MMOC appears in all NARM literature, including its consumer brochures and legislative lobbying packets. A much more detailed description of what a woman should expect from a practitioner promising this kind of care was published in a CfM brochure in 1998; many thousands of copies have been distributed in the United States and around the world. As the brochure points out, any practitioner, including MDs, can provide this model of care. This focus on a user-friendly and consumer-oriented brand name—the Midwives Model of Care—instead of on midwives themselves, is an intentional strategy suggested by consumers and agreed on by midwives. This consensus arose to keep more attention focused on the pregnant woman as the deserving recipient of a special kind of care and less on the self-promotion of midwives who seek to provide that kind of care (even though the ultimate effect may be the same). Through this brand-name choice, CPMs remind themselves, even through their self-marketing, that their primary mission is to mothers.

Design and Redesign: Commodities as Responsive to Consumer Demands and Market Trends

The term "midwifery consumer".... implies a certain agency and choice on the part of women having midwifery care that has always been important to midwifery. Indeed, the consumer-based campaign for choices in childbirth was a key factor that fueled midwifery as a social movement over the last several decades. The idea of the midwifery consumer, however, is not simply a result of the self-conscious feminist agenda of woman-centred care and the critique of biomedicine. It also speaks to the political economy of reproduction ... in the context of late capitalism and demographic transition, specifically, the trend towards having fewer children later in life and the trend towards treating pregnancy and childbirth as valuable experiences.

–Margaret MacDonald, "The Role of Midwifery Clients in the New Midwifery in Canada: Postmodern Negotiations with Medical Technology"

Successful commodities in today's market frequently shape-shift in response to technological advances, consumer trends, and market demands. Computers were beige and boxy until the iMac set new standards for attractiveness in computer design, reshaping consumer expectations for how computers should look. The ugly but functional toaster from Target is elegantly redesigned; the software upgraded; the dishwasher computerized. The "redesign" of direct-entry midwives in response to consumer trends has to date been most obvious in Ontario, where the legalization of midwifery in 1993 was accomplished through an alliance of nurse- and lay midwives who united behind a model of midwifery practice based on the principle that "the midwife follows the mother." In other words, women select their site of birth—home, birth center, or hospital—and the midwife will attend them there. As a result, Ontario's former lay midwives, who practiced only outside of the hospital for two decades when midwifery was a social movement and not yet a profession, have had to familiarize themselves with hospital protocols and technologies. And, as documented by MacDonald (2001), Sharpe (2004), and Daviss (2001), Ontario midwives' client base has shifted from homebirthers dedicated to the holistic principles of the midwifery and home-birth movements to consumers who have had no involvement in these movements and may simply want more personalized care.

In particular, Margaret MacDonald's recent work (2001) points to the agentic role midwifery consumers are playing in reshaping the nature of Ontario midwifery. North American consumers display increasing familiarity with and respect for information obtained through high technology; when they choose midwifery care, they add to this familiarity the midwifery principle of fully informed choice. The result is that even when midwives themselves do not recommend certain technologies, such as repeat ultrasounds or genetic testing, consumers often choose them anyway, and midwives find themselves the go-betweens in a game they are very uncomfortable playing. As Canadian midwife and social scientist Mary Sharpe (2004) expressed it:

> Midwives felt that the requirement to offer testing shifted their care towards a focus of *verifying* rather than *assuming* that pregnancy is normal, and were concerned that midwives themselves might be moving away from a wellness model towards a pathology-oriented model, relying on ultrasounds and an increased use of the system and spending less time on woman-generated discussions relating to the woman's feelings, questions and circumstances.

In addition to the shape-shifting they are undergoing in response to consumer demands, Ontario midwives find themselves changing even more as they attend more births in hospitals. In other words, the market for midwives to attend hospital births, which is larger than the home-birth market, is slowly but inexorably reshaping the nature of Ontario midwifery. As Sharpe (2004) describes it, at the beginning of their entry into the hospital,

> midwives ... were on a steep learning curve with respect to orientation to hospital procedures, protocols, equipment and paperwork, as well as client admission and discharge. While attending their first hospital births as primary caregivers following legislation, it would take two midwives up to four hours following the birth to accomplish the usual post partum care and the new paperwork. . . . Comments from midwives expressed how they felt their practices were ruled by these new procedures:
>
> > The hospital is the most disturbing situation to me because I'm finding it difficult to feel like I'm both fulfilling my expected role as a health care professional in the hierarchy of the system in the hospital as well as just being with someone which is what I feel my primary role is. (Anna)

Some midwives felt closely monitored and scrutinized in hospital, and that the hospital staff was testing them, waiting to assess their level of competence. There was great pressure to be very careful about what they did. . . . In exchange for hospital privileges, some midwives felt compromised, now required to comply with certain hospital rules with which they didn't agree. Some midwives implied that they had to "behave like good girls" and "move into line" in order to get what they wanted for their clients in the hospital setting and to maintain their credibility. . . . The definition of being a good midwife in the hospital had changed for one midwife: before the legislation it had to do with her labour supporting skills, now, with her clinical care and charting. Another noted that experiences in the hospital were influencing how she worked at home births in that she didn't have as much hands on caring for the woman in either setting. . . . The client of one midwife who previously appreciated the spiritual aspect of her work, hired a "spiritual midwife." She wondered if she was now the "clinical midwife."

Decades of hospital practice have also clearly had their effect on American nurse-midwives; an examination of birth certificate data shows that many CNMs now use some technological interventions, such as electronic fetal monitoring, at the same rates as physicians (Curtin 1999). My interview data indicate that nurse-midwives' use of hospital technologies is influenced by the degree to which they are taught to rely on such technologies during their midwifery education, by pressures placed on them by other hospital personnel to utilize high technologies, and by the choices and demands of their clients, many of whom feel reassured by the application of high technologies to their births and actively choose their use (see Davis-Floyd 2003). This brief glance at the influence of hospital practice on Canadian midwives and American nurse-midwives clearly illustrates how the market and its consumers can reshape the nature of the commodity.

Predictably, American DEMs are often heard to suggest that CNMs have sold out to or have been co-opted by the medical system, noting that while out-of-hospital practice limits DEMs' accessibility as a health care commodity, it also significantly limits the extent to which they can be co-opted into overmedicalization. While they have certainly done some shape-shifting themselves in response to market trends and consumer demands, as long as they remain outside of hospitals, DEMs may be able to successfully limit the degree of change they undergo as they professionalize and commodify.

Commodities as Embedded in the Global Political Economy

American DEMs respect Ontario's former lay midwives for their success at achieving full integration into the Canadian health care system and American nurse-midwives for being there for women who choose hospital birth. But U.S. DEMs are simultaneously aware that their purely out-of-hospital independent midwifery system is unique. Recently I coauthored, with a group of international scholars, a chapter comparing midwifery education in the United States, Canada, and Europe (Benoit et al. 2001), which we organized around the three basic models of midwifery education that exist: apprenticeship, vocational training, and university education. As I worked on the sections on the United States, I was fascinated to note that because of the American DEMs, the United States is the only Euro-American country in which all three basic models of midwifery training are alive and flourishing. All over the developed world, I have heard American direct-entry midwives extolled as examples of "holistic midwifery," "pure midwifery," and "real midwifery." Many long-professionalized midwives in the United Kingdom, Italy, Australia, and other Western countries consider American direct-entry midwives to represent the heart or essence of what midwifery should be and engage in long discussions about how they might try to recapture some of the spirituality and woman-centeredness that, in their professionalism, they feel they have lost. Thus American midwives feel a special responsibility not only to themselves but also to the world to preserve what they have created. Their sense of the value of their independent midwifery system and out-of-hospital knowledge base, in relation to midwives everywhere, has led the members of the NARM board to make the CPM an international certification, available to midwives in any country who might choose to adopt it. Some beginnings have been made: the Canadian province of Manitoba recognizes NARM certification, and four Mexican midwives have become CPMs.

Conclusion

With legislation, midwives are learning new texts and engaging in new rulings. Are these rulings slowing us down, fixing us gradually and inexorably into new relationships and new ways of acting and being? Or do these rulings provide structure and support and free us?. . . . The bottom line for midwives is: can legislation enhance creativity and expand possibilities for women and midwifery or limit them? . . . We need continuously to hold our behaviour in question. . . . We require a tireless vigilance to maintain what some would say are midwifery's gains, and others would call our compromises. And we must continue to examine our practices in order to recognize how we, for better or for worse, are implicated in the rulings of our profession.

—Mary Sharpe, "Exploring Legislated Ontario Midwifery"

I have often heard members of NARM and MANA echo Sharpe's words as they work to maintain a tireless vigilance over the gains they achieve and the losses they suffer in their professionalizing and commodifying enterprises. What I have observed over and over is that every time these midwives face a choice between enhancing their public image as health care commodities and compromising their values, their practices, or their training programs, they let go of image and concentrate on what works and what, in their eyes, preserves the essence of who they are. Speaking for all those who participated in the development of CPM certification, during a 1997 panel discussion direct-entry midwives Pam Weaver, Elizabeth Davis, and Alice Sammon exclaimed, "We did it! We actually managed to develop a certification that encompasses everything we hold dear!"

To be sure, many midwives who have struggled to fill out NARM's detailed forms, to come up with the required documentation, or to generate enough income to pay NARM's fees, have done their share of complaining about the number and complexity of the hoops they are asked to jump through, as have those who failed the NARM exam on their first and even second attempts and have had to take it again. But I have watched this process long enough to be awed by the lack of controversy now surrounding it among MANA members, who have moved from initial deep suspicion of any standardizing moves to acceptance of the CPM as a credential that supports them far more than it gets in their way. As longtime home-birth midwife Sharon Wells put it recently, "the CPM is the only ground we have to stand on." Even the thirty direct-entry students I have interviewed, instead of complaining about NARM requirements, are happy to have specific goals to work toward. Several of them noted to me that apprentice-trained midwives are often not sure at what point during their training they can actually start to call themselves midwives instead of students. The arrival of their CPM certificate in the mail has become a concrete marker for them that they have earned the right to say "I am a midwife."

Debates continue in various states between midwives willing and unwilling to compromise in order to gain a toehold in the technocracy, with one group accusing the other of selling out to get in. Many midwives mourn some of their lost freedoms to serve their clients as they saw best at the same time as they rejoice in their legal status and the many new clients who are seeking them out because they are legal and insurance-reimbursed. When I focus on the big picture, what I see, all things considered, is that American direct-entry midwives, even as they professionalize and commodify, are simultaneously striving to maintain themselves as the woman-centered, family-serving, intuition-honoring, birth-trusting, and system-flouting guides and guardians of birth that they have always been. Clearly, commodification can be more than a means of selling out to capitalism. When qualified according to the values of a particular group newly perceiving itself as a commodity, it can also be a creative way of generating needed services that offer consumers a rich array of alternatives, precluding homogenization and facilitating the heterogenization of individual choice.[21]

NOTES

I wish to thank CPMs Shannon Anton, Elizabeth Davis, Abby J. Kinne, Carol Nelson, Holly Scholles, and Alice Sammon; consumer advocate Susan Hodges; and sociologist Christina Johnson, as well as the editors of this book, for their helpful comments and suggestions, and two anonymous reviewers for their supportive and encouraging comments.

1. Funded by the Wenner-Gren Foundation for Anthropological Research Grants #6015 and #6247, between 1996 and 2000 I carried out research on "The Development of Direct-Entry Midwifery in North America: Politics and Professionalization." My methodology has involved attending international, national, and local midwifery and childbirth conferences, participation on one midwifery board and in a national coalition, and conducting seventy interviews with leaders and educators in nurse- and direct-entry midwifery, focusing on their motivations for developing two new direct-entry certifications, the practical and philosophical issues that divide them, and the legislative processes in several states. In addition, I interviewed seventy-five midwifery students (thirty direct-entry and forty-five nurse-midwifery students) about their educational processes, seeking to understand the relative benefits and disadvantages of each. Some of the results of this research have been published in Davis-Floyd (1998a, 1998b, 1999, 2001) and in Benoit et al. (2001). More will be forthcoming in Davis-Floyd and Johnson.

2. As with everything in this postmodern era, the boundaries between these models have long been blurred: about two hundred nurse-midwives practice in freestanding birth centers and homes, and fifteen direct-entry midwives (all of whom are CPMs) practice in hospitals or work for large health care institutions.

3. See Rooks (1997) and Davis-Floyd (forthcoming) for descriptive and analytical histories of this fracture.

4. As Margaret Reid put it in "Sisterhood and Professionalization: A Case Study of the American Lay Midwife" (1989:229): "The first transformation to occur was often an internal one, a change in self-perception or self-image. . . . It was always a significant change, as one midwife's comments illustrate: "it took me a long time [to realize], 'I want some money for this. I'm spending maybe sixty hours a week, I'm away from my family . . . and I want to be compensated.' And with that grew the birth of a professional."

5. The ACNM's Division of Accreditation can accredit programs that either grant the baccalaureate degree upon exit or require it for entry. But there are no nurse-midwifery educational programs that grant the degree upon exit. So for all practical purposes, the baccalaureate is a requirement for entry, and all nurse-midwifery education is postgraduate.

6. Like NARM, MEAC is part of MANA's professionalizing enterprise. Created in 1991, MEAC's members consist of MANA's most experienced and most accomplished midwifery educators. In an effort to maintain clarity and consistency for midwifery students, MEAC members kept their educational requirements in line with those established by NARM; often, details were worked out jointly by both groups. To date, MEAC has accredited eleven direct-entry programs around the United States. In November 2000, the U.S. Department of Education granted MEAC full status as a government-recognized accrediting body. In November 2002 that status was reaffirmed.

7. At that time, the members of the NARM board, who held primary responsibility for developing CPM certification, included Sondra Abdullah-Zaimah, Shannon Anton, Robbie Davis-Floyd (since 1994 I have served as the consumer representative on the NARM board; my role has been largely advisory), Alice Sammon, Suzanne Suarez, Ruth Walsh, Sharon Wells, and Pam Weaver. Key committee heads included Ann Cairns, Sandi Morningstar, Abbey Kinne, and Susan Hodges.

8. I was invited to become a member of the NARM board in 1994, in the position of consumer representative. Before I accepted the invitation, I made it clear that if I accepted, I would want to be studying NARM's work even as I participated in it, a request that was approved by the board members at the time. The members of the NARM board and the Certification Task Force have always been tolerant of and helpful with my dual roles as participant and observer, and I would like to express my appreciation to them for accepting me in both capacities.

9. Reviewers of this chapter have asked that I include the results of the IV question on this survey. A large majority of respondents indicated that IV insertion should not be required for entry-level practice, and so it was not. Another fascinating result of the survey was in the category of "Well-Woman Care." Respondents indicated that they did not wish the category as a whole to be required; however, they did wish all the skills listed under it to be required. At first puzzled by this response, the NARM board eventually ascertained that its meaning was that practicing midwives wanted entry-level midwives to be able to perform all these skills, but not to be required to offer general well-woman (gynecological) care.

10. See NARM's *How to Become a Certified Professional Midwife (CPM)* booklet for more details. The booklet is available at http://www.narm.org/htb.htm or from Debbie Pulley, 5257 Rosestone Dr. N.W., Lilburn GA 30047.

11. While ACNM members who had favored "Certified Professional Midwife" as the title for their new direct-entry certification were deeply angered by what they perceived as NARM's preemption of that name, others within ACNM had not liked it in the first

place, as the side-by-side listing of Certified Nurse-Midwives with Certified Professional Midwives might be read as implying that CNMs were less professional. Those who took this latter position were quite happy to choose Certified Midwife (CM) as their new direct-entry name. It is simple and straightforward, and has the additional ideological advantage of reaffirming that members of the ACNM are primarily midwives, not nurses.

The identity issues generated by being "nurse-midwives" have been problematic for ACNM members for years. Because most states define nurse-midwives as advanced practice nurses, they are usually regulated by nursing boards that do not recognize their desires to be autonomous and independent practitioners. Most members of ACNM would prefer to be midwives first and nurses second and to be regulated by midwifery boards so they can "get out from under the thumb of nursing," as many have expressed it to me. The mere existence of the CM and her admission in 1996 to full voting membership in the ACNM allowed ACNM members to rapidly change the name of their primary textbook from *Varney's Nurse-Midwifery* to *Varney's Midwifery* and the name of their journal from the *Journal of Nurse-Midwifery* to the *Journal of Midwifery and Women's Health*, and to start an as-yet-unsuccessful movement to change the organization's name from the American College of Nurse-Midwives (ACNM) to the American College of Midwifery (ACM). These moves are unlikely to do anything to increase nurse-midwifery's value as a public commodity; indeed, they may decrease it, as many consumers appreciate the combination of nursing and midwifery upon which ACNM was founded. Rather, such moves directly reflect the social movement ideology that many nurse-midwives still retain, the fact that many of them still experience a strong spiritual calling to midwifery just as many MANA midwives do, and their passionate desire for more autonomy and less subordination to physicians, with whom they desire not "supervision" but "collaboration" (Reed and Roberts 2000).

12. In an interesting twist, Linda Shutt, the first direct-entry midwife certified by ACNM as a CM, was a CPM who had been practicing illegally in New York for years (see Davis-Floyd 1998a for the whole story).

13. NARM's inclusivity is perhaps best demonstrated by the special circumstances category, which is designed to allow midwives trained in other countries, "grand midwives" who began practice before 1965, or midwives trained through other unusual circumstances to apply. Special circumstances applicants must document attendance at a minimum of seventy-five births in the past ten years (ten of which must have occurred in the preceding two years) and fulfill an extensive set of further requirements; they are individually evaluated by a special NARM committee. In addition, for the first two years of CPM certification, NARM held open an "Experienced Midwife" category as a mechanism to quickly evaluate and certify experienced practicing midwives. Qualification for the "Experienced Midwife" category required being in practice for more than five years and attending a minimum of seventy-five births as primary caregiver. Although this move was criticized by some members of ACNM and others as an easy way of granting certification to the "members of the club," it proved to be a critical and viable transitional strategy for creating a base of qualified midwives who could then mentor student midwives through their educational and certification processes.

14. For more information about apprenticeship training, see Davis-Floyd (1998a, 1998b) and Benoit et al. (2001).

15. For the most up-to-date information about the legal status of direct-entry midwifery in all fifty states, go to http://www.narm.org/.

16. CPMs are not required to belong to MANA. CNMs and CMs are not required to belong to the ACNM, but they are intensively socialized during their educational processes to think of ACNM as their professional organization, and the vast majority of them do. In contrast, MANA remains aprofessional, trying to meet the needs of both professionally licensed or certified midwives and those who are not, an increasingly difficult task.
17. For a fascinating comparison of the alternative birth and midwifery movements in the United States and Canada, see Daviss (2001).
18. My thanks to Susan Hodges, president of Citizens for Midwifery, for helping me to achieve deeper insight into these issues.
19. Information about Citizens for Midwifery can be obtained from www.cfmidwifery.org or 1-888-236-4880.
20. Ohio midwife Abby J. Kinne, CPM, points to another crucial issue regarding midwifery autonomy even where state regulations do not exist (in Ohio, direct-entry midwifery is not legally defined but not prohibited):

    It is not just fear of the knock on the door—for many of us, it is the trade-off for making the midwifery model of care more accessible to the home-birth community at large. Although Ohio has yet to institute regulations (which are quite likely, in the end, to restrict our ability to attend VBACs, twins, and breeches) some of us already are limited in such special circumstances in order to maintain good relations with supportive backup physicians. You can choose to help these moms and risk losing good backup, or you can make a concession to your backup doc so that you can continue to provide good backup to the vast majority of our clients who do not face these rare circumstances. It is a major dilemma for us. (Personal communication 2003)

21. At press time (April 2004), nine hundred midwives have received CPM certification.

Mothers between God and Mammon

Feminist Interpretations of Childbirth

PAMELA E. KLASSEN

The language of the market—of production and reproduction, of commodities and exchange—is a language that seems to invite religious glosses. From Karl Marx's "commodity fetishism" to Marshall Sahlins's "cosmologies of capitalism," theorists have long realized that the workings of the market demand a certain faith—a faith often hidden within the scientific metaphor of the "laws" of the market (Marx 1977; Sahlins 1994). In turn, as this volume demonstrates, language about reproduction borrows in obvious and more subtle ways from the language of the market and from scientific metaphors for the birthing body. But like all languages, the terms of science and of the market have their gaps; they cannot articulate all there is to say about the experience of childbirth. For many contemporary North American feminists, religious language bridges this gap by offering a powerful vocabulary to describe and analyze the experience of childbirth (see Kahn 1995 and Rabuzzi 1994).

Aside from the word *reproduction* itself, the most obvious conjunction between discourses of the market and of childbirth is in the stress on choice. Especially in middle-class North America, women choose from a large array of childbirth options in deciding how best to bring forth new life. Women make choices as consumers selecting from a range of birthing services, including doctor-attended "patient choice cesarean" (Harer 2000) and midwife-attended home birth. Not all choices are equally sanctioned by the market or the state, however, since in several states and provinces midwife-attended home birth is neither legal nor covered by insurance (Rooks 1997). As the more politicized discourse of choice in terms of abortion shows, a woman's individual choice about reproductive issues is circumscribed by legal, religious, and economic conditions. In childbirth, as well, the free market of birth choices is shaped by various forces, including the state's interest in the health of "its" children, medical opinions about safety and appropriate technology, and women's convictions about the nature of birth and their bodies.

The market metaphors of production and consumption, and their correlate, commodification, can be very helpful theoretical tools to make sense of the social, cultural, and economic relations guiding women's choices about childbirth. However, birthing women who live within the capitalist economy of North America adopt notions of production, consumption, and commodification to describe the conditions of childbirth only with considerable ambivalence. As terms so infused with the history and legacies of market capitalism, *production* and *consumption* tend to be viewed as reductive terms, not fully capable of expressing the complexities of important human relationships, like that between a mother and her emerging child. In the midst of this ambivalence is the irony that commodities—the things that circulate within cycles of production and consumption—themselves reveal much about human relationships, in terms of what people value both materially and morally (Comaroff and Comaroff 1990:196). How the ambiguous language of the market both illuminates and obscures the experience of childbearing women, and how that language intersects with religious understandings of childbirth, is what I treat here.

Many scholars have already written convincingly on the history and influence of metaphors of production regarding childbirth (Martin 1987; Taylor 2000a). In what follows I explore both the adoption of and the resistance to metaphors of consumption among a particular group of North American childbearing women, namely home-birthing feminists. I find that in simultaneously borrowing and disavowing the language of the market, especially in conjunction with their assertions about home birth as a spiritual act, home-birthing feminist women are part of a wider cultural attraction to and repulsion from metaphors and practices of consumption.

I explore the ambiguous interpretive virtues of consumption via three main perspectives. I begin by focusing on home-birthing women's direct adoption or critique of consumption in terms of childbirth, drawing from my larger ethnographic project on religion and home birth.[1] After considering these explicit discussions of consumption, I turn to an analysis of how notions of sacrifice shape home-birthing women's understanding of their labor as childbearing women. Here I am writing in response to the work of Daniel Miller, especially his focus on feminist women's devotion to their babies in what he calls "the cult of the infant" (Miller, this volume, 1997). Miller's distinction between women's self-sacrifice and self-realization in mothering then leads me to a discussion of feminist analyses of women's subjectivity in pregnancy and childbirth, and of opposing views within some medical circles. Finally, I conclude with an analysis of what I am calling the purchase of experience, asking how religion, childbirth, and consumption coalesce and conflict.

This essay, then, asks how home-birthing women negotiate their religiously based criticisms of the "business of birth" in the midst of their own location within a culture of consumption in which nothing, not even religion, is sacred. That is, religion itself is commoditized in complex ways, especially in a North American marketplace of faiths where *choice* of one's religion is enshrined in law. Religion no longer holds, if it ever did, the status of a noncommodity, or what Igor Kopytoff has called the "non-saleability [that] imparts to a thing a special aura of apartness from the mundane and the common" (Kopytoff 1986:69; see also Moore 1994 and Schmidt 1996). Relationships of exchange, whether in the form of sacrifice, tithing, or theologies of divine/human reciprocity, have always been part of religious practice. Nevertheless, within most religions there is lively debate about how those relationships of exchange should be structured (Brown 1997; Davis 2000). When childbirth is considered a religious or spiritual act its relations of exchange are also scrutinized with a spiritual lens, leading many home-birth advocates to root their criticisms in an idealized view of spirituality that does hold birth "apart," as they call their society to respect the "essential mystery of birth" (MANA in Davis-Floyd and Davis 1997:322).

"Buying the Best Birth Care": Stories of Critical Consumption

Based on their own experiences and, for some, on their readings of feminist anthropological texts that have developed the "birth as production" analogy, many home-birthing women have developed a critique of medicalized childbirth that draws from consumer analogies. In this view, women need to challenge the system through exercising their consumer power. That is, they need to turn from obstetricians and hospital birth to midwives and home birth. Their embrace of consumer activism, however, sits in uneasy tension with what for some is a religiously informed critique of the commodification of birth—a critique that sees a commodity as "the symbol of contamination, which a purifying religiosity . . . needs to reject" (Miller 1995:145). This religiosity is not necessarily tethered to specific religious traditions but might be a more eclectic sense of a spirituality—or perhaps a cosmology, as used by both Miller (1998a:20) and Sahlins (1994)—guiding one's choices.

In my study, feminist women were not alone in their sense of the spirituality of birth.[2] Women ranging from Orthodox Jews and conservative Christians to spiritual feminists, "new age Jews," and even a few self-described nonreligious women, asserted to me that for them childbirth was not a medical event but a physical event infused with spiritual meaning. Their criticisms of the medical model of birth (of which many of them had direct experience) were similar to the ways Marx described his notion of alienated labor: "it alienates man [*sic*] from his own body, nature exterior to him, and his intellectual being, his human essence" (Marx 1977:83). Unlike Marx, however, these women would not limit the notion of human essence to their "intellectual beings" but would argue that the essence of being human must also include the "spirit." The spirit, of course, means different things to different people, but for the purposes of this chapter, I use the terms *spirit* and *spirituality* in a somewhat generic way to refer to a force external to the human will often contained in the terms *God, Goddess*, or, for some, *nature*.[3] The alienation of the spirit, then, is just as serious a consideration for these women as the alienation of their own physical labor—in fact, many would argue that the two are inseparable.

Rejecting the alienation of the labor of their birthing bodies brings home-birthing women and other home-birth advocates to employ a range of arguments that both draw from and resist the language of consumption. In keeping with the commercialized model of health care in the United States, home-birthing advocates, including midwives and birthing women, make recourse to a variety of economic arguments to vouch for home birth. Scholar-midwives write articles in their scholarly journals detailing the "cost-effectiveness" of home birth, and their clients and supporters write newsletters encouraging women to be wise consumers of birth-related services (Anderson and Anderson 1999). Alongside these sorts of pragmatic economic arguments is a noticeable discomfort with applying discourses of consumption to the act of birth. As one midwifery advice book phrased it, in the case of home birth, "cost should not be the primary basis for your choice" (ACNM and Jacobs 1993:237). Part of this discomfort, as I will show, stems from a larger unease in American culture with pairing religion and money—if birth is ideally a spiritual experience then its ties to a consumer economy must be severed, or at least reduced. The unease with consumer metaphors also stems from a strand within home birth discourse that considers midwifery and home birth to be "revolutionary" forces that challenge not only biomedical conceptions of female bodies but also the economic and political structures supporting biomedicine itself (Rich 1986).

Of all the women I spoke with, Larisa Marquez had one of the most pointed critiques of the "business of birth" in the United States, in which she argued that the market system was inappropriate as an environment or metaphor for the relations of childbirth.[4] Larisa lived with her husband and baby on a busy urban street in a second-story apartment decorated with Guatemalan fabrics and posters celebrating Che Guevara. She came to the United States from Venezuela at the age of ten. Though she had attended Episcopalian youth groups all through high school, she was no longer affiliated with any religious institution. Her primary source of community was now an alternative food co-op, where most of the members were vegetarian, and a weekly women's group that focused on spiritual and political issues. In these environments her questioning of the institutions of her society grew. Accordingly, when Larisa became pregnant at twenty-three, she knew the hospital was not the place for her: "I don't believe in the 'system' . . . I'm not into banks, hospitals, anything that's basically the norm. I don't really agree with it because I see a lot of flaws, a lot of things wrong with it. Like medicine and stuff like that, that's not even my thing. I don't believe in even taking a Tylenol, even if I had a headache. I'd rather take the headache, and not work. I think that American society is too quick to jump and say they want a quick out." Larisa's criticisms went beyond an alternative view of health and illness to include harsh words for the economics of the medical system: "When I found that I was pregnant, I wouldn't have it any other way but a home birth, because I don't really believe in the hospital. I see the hospital view as . . . a business. The amount of money that a lot of doctors . . . get paid to [do] what they do, it's ridiculous." For Larisa, the hospital represents a larger system that requires, or expects, its users to believe in it. Although Larisa, after a three-day labor, did end up going to the hospital to have her baby—vaginally and with an epidural—she still maintains that the hospital is not the place for normal birth. Larisa chose direct-entry midwives in part because a woman she knew from her co-op recommended them, but also because they were more distanced from the medical system she disavowed. In her state, direct-entry midwives were forced to practice underground, since they were not regulated, which meant Larisa was also transgressing the legal system in her choice of birth attendants.

Another significant factor influencing her choice, however, was the very pragmatic issue of cost. Direct-entry midwives were less expensive than were the nurse-midwives in the area. Money was an issue for Larisa and her husband, a craftsperson, since they did not have health insurance. Despite the cost and even after her difficult labor, she said she would plan to give birth at home for any subsequent births and, if still in the area, would probably use the same midwives. To Larisa, these midwives were more like friends than professionals, to the extent that she was considering inviting one midwife, who was about thirty years her senior, to her weekly women's gathering.

While cost was a factor for many women I interviewed—home birth being much less expensive than hospital birth—many had to pay out-of-pocket for their births due to the strictures of medical insurance. Those who opted for care from a certified nurse-midwife were often covered by insurance, at least partially, but the fees of direct-entry midwives were never covered. Hence, while home birth may often be understood as a challenge to the dominant economic system, just as frequently it requires a substantial outlay of money, approximately $750 to $3000. Even though many direct-entry midwives use a sliding scale to set their fees, for those who cannot afford this expense, home birth is generally not an option. Not all certified nurse-midwives who attend home births choose to or are able to accept Medicaid reimbursement, and many direct-entry midwives, due to their unlicensed status, cannot interact with state or private health insurance even if they choose to.[5] The economics of birth in the United States—like the economics of all kinds of health care—are affected by the structure of the insurance system no matter what mode of birth is chosen.

Larisa was aware of her necessary embeddedness in a political, ritual, and economic system that she did not endorse. She criticized the "commercialization" of religious holidays that were "all focused on people spending money" and evidenced a sort of pragmatic but critical resignation about her ties to capitalist consumer culture. In her words: "we live here, in the belly of the beast. And we kind of have to do stuff that we don't really want to do, because we don't have an alternative. We don't have money to go buy some land and live completely out of the system." However, Larisa reserved some agency for herself, as she tied her decision to give birth at home with her critique of "patriarchal religion" and her embrace of alternative views of health and nutrition. Admitting that she was unable (and apparently unwilling, given her trip to the hospital) entirely to abandon capitalist institutions in the case of childbirth, Larisa's critique of dominant modes of childbirth both acknowledged and decried the ironies of consumption in the practices of home birth in America.

For Larisa, decisions about the economics of birth care were tied to larger frameworks of belief about just societies. Natalie Ruppolo, a Christian Scientist practitioner, also contended that giving birth was an occasion in which a woman endorsed a particular belief system, whether implicitly or explicitly. Natalie found the resources in her faith in God to resist what she saw as an incompatible belief system, namely medicine. For Natalie, however, the commodification of birth was not central to her critique. Coming from a religious tradition founded by a woman, Mary Baker Eddy, who developed her following through selling her services as a religious healer, Natalie's religious commitment to home birth was not predominantly shaped by a critique of consumption (Gill 1998). She did root her choice, however, in a conviction that the state did not have the final say in how her baby should be born.

Following the Christian Science emphasis on the power of Mind or God over the flesh, during her pregnancy Natalie felt God was in control and exempted her from some state-sanctioned medical guidelines. Though she hired a certified nurse-midwife, her first way to deal with difficulties such as anemia was to turn to Christian Science modes of healing (namely prayer) instead of taking iron supplements as her midwife suggested. Natalie drew a parallel between her choice to put her faith in a Christian Science view of the body and other women's choices to put their faith in the medical view of the body:

> I felt that at home, having this home birth, that God was my primary caregiver. I was fulfilling the laws of the land by having the midwife. I felt supported by having someone who was experienced at this there, but I didn't feel that she was in charge of the case. I felt that God was in charge of the case, and I think that would apply if someone were in the hospital. On one hand, they're trusting the physician who is delivering, but ultimately they are trusting the system that's governing the physician. So you've got to have faith in what you're doing. And one way or the other

there's got to be some higher power, if it's medicine or if it's God. You've got to have trust in the system that you've turned to, trust enough to then leave the individual responsible for taking the human footsteps that they'll do what they have to do, because they're governed by that higher system. The doctor is governed by medicine, and that midwife was under God's authority in our home.

While Natalie, and other Christian Scientists, rejects medical authority and to a certain degree state authority, her rejection is not primarily a critique of consumerism. Opting out of the medical system, however, also entails opting out of insurance systems and acts as an implicit critique of the commodification of childbirth.

Tessa Welland is a home-birth activist who merged the two strands of Larisa's predominantly economic analysis and Natalie's predominantly religious one. Tessa also saw the choice of home birth as embedded in wider systems of belief and practice that included an ambiguous rejection of the commodification of birth and the embrace of spirituality. Tessa, now in her late thirties, has given birth at home three times. She is a middle-class, Euro-American woman who grew up Catholic but is now, like Larisa, drawn to more eclectic, less institutionalized, "woman-friendly" spirituality. For Tessa, giving birth at home influenced her developing sense of spirituality in complex ways. Thinking in terms of Robbie Davis-Floyd's categories of holistic and technocratic approaches to birth, Tessa would be considered holistic—that is, she would agree that "the human body is a living organism with its own innate wisdom, an energy field constantly responding to all other energy fields" (Davis-Floyd 1992:156). In fact, Tessa, like several other women I interviewed, had read Davis-Floyd's anthropological study of childbirth as an American rite of passage and explicitly identified with the notion of holistic childbirth in which the needs of the mother and of the baby are considered to be harmonious.

For Tessa, choosing to birth at home was not simply a rejection of a medical model of birth but an assertion of a different value system: "What do we value in our culture? We value technology and science and we value money. And I don't want to live in a culture and be a member in a culture where that's what is the major value. I think that the values should be much more of a holistic thing, and that technology is necessary and good when it's used appropriately, but the value of the society should be on the family, and it should be on the spirituality of the infant."

Tessa did not keep this criticism to herself. Instead, she was active as a home birth advocate through working as a doula, childbirth educator, and aspiring direct-entry midwife, and through participating in a legal case attempting to make direct-entry midwifery legal in her state. In her work as a doula and childbirth educator, Tessa considered herself to be involved in a spiritual vocation. In the course of her work, Tessa has created "Blessing Way" ceremonies for some of the women with whom she has worked.[6] For one of her own births, Tessa's women friends organized a Blessing Way for her in which ritual practices attributed to Native Americans, like lighting candles, singing songs, and washing the feet in blue corn meal prepared her to give birth. Tessa regretted that a Blessing Way ceremony marked only one of her births, since for her other births no friends initiated the process, and, like a baby shower, "it wasn't something that you put on for yourself." Now she puts on Blessing Way ceremonies for certain clients and friends, doing about one per month.

The ceremonies do not fit with every client, though, and she does them based on her "inclinations" toward a client. Tessa feels that a client's receptivity to the ceremony is connected not with "personality, but with what I perceive as spiritual development." Using herself as an example, Tessa pointed to choices like home birth and home schooling as ways to discern such development. For Tessa, seeing beyond specific religious traditions by being open to a wider form of spirituality and creating new syncretic rituals within home-based communities were also signs of spiritual development. Tessa seemed to have little concern about the politics of appropriating from Native American cultures in creating her Blessing Way ceremonies. Instead, she evidenced a somewhat pragmatic approach to ritual borrowing, feeling that symbols, perhaps like commodities, were extractable from their contexts and available for circulation.

Tessa's approach to ritualizing shares much with that of Jeannine Parvati-Baker, a self-described "shamanic midwife" from Utah. Parvati-Baker also draws liberally from Native American culture, seemingly without concerns about appropriation (Parvati-Baker 1992).[7] Tessa's and Parvati-Baker's Blessing Way services are a reinvention of traditions that, while espousing a countercultural model of birth, operate within a market system. They both offer their services for a fee, so their rituals, while home based, do not function as reproductions of an earlier time when women came together to aid each other freely in community, in expectation of similar aid when they themselves would need it (Smith-Rosenberg 1985:70).[8] While this view of an earlier era of midwifery in the community may itself be idealized, reinvented ritual specialists like Tessa and Parvati-Baker have constructed home birth within a consumer economy in ways quite different from other contemporary home-birthing women.

For example, in the context of their birth businesses, Tessa and Parvati-Baker do not attend their clients' births as "friends," as was the case with many women I interviewed who sought the support of friends in their communities. Nor do they offer their prayers without a fee, as did women who were part of religious communities with strong traditions of prayer. The commodification of religion and birth is not new or "bad." As in the case of Christian Science, alternative, women-led religions often develop as small-scale businesses of a sort, given that they do not have the institutional resources and finances of long-established churches, where offering plates and other ritual gestures obscure the financial transactions on which churches depend. Even when women's rituals of birth are cast as honoring women, family, and home in a new and radical way, however, they often remain tied to the very economic and social structures they mean to disrupt, in this case commodification, whether of services, rituals, or blue cornmeal.

The plethora of paid services that have grown up around home birth—from magazines to doulas to ritual specialists—are evidence that even alternative visions of health and spirituality are tied into the consumption-oriented society that is North America, and that women have changed the practices of childbirth by embracing the consumer model (Burst 1983). Despite Tessa's embrace of holistic living and her concomitant disapproval of the way her society values money, she was also quite forthright in her assertion that women needed to act as consumers of childbirth options. In an article written for the newsletter of a local network of home-birth supporters, Tessa declared: "Consumerism and birth care must go hand in hand. We can only be responsible parents if we begin parenting with the intention of buying the best birth care our consumer dollars can buy." However, she cautioned, "spending more money is not necessarily better." While being a responsible parent is part of her argument, Tessa also considered that good birth care involved honoring a woman's bodily and emotional needs and required the building of complex relationships between midwives and their clients. Substantial amounts of time, openness to exploring psychological or spiritual issues, and ritual experimentation were all part of this relationship in her view, in addition to checking blood pressure, measuring fundal height, and testing urine.

The mix of roles taken on by midwives—spiritual and emotional confidante during pregnancy, bodily supporter during birth, and paid professional, to name a few—was sometimes an awkward combination. For most of the women I spoke with, their relationships with their midwives were infused with morality, spirituality, and physical care, and then tied to economic aspects in ways that were not always comfortable. For example, many women experienced a sense of loss once their baby was born and they no longer had regular hour-long visits with their midwives. The hazy cross between professional and friend that often obtains in the midwife-client relationship seemed to obscure the economic dimension of the relationship for many women and strained the process of making the transition out of a midwife's care. Putting a dollar value to birth services, from those provided by a midwife to those offered by a doula, is at once a necessary and discomforting practice (see Davis-Floyd, this volume).

A few women dealt with the discomfort of employing a midwife—a cross between caregiver, specialist, and in the case of registered midwives, the eyes of the state—by opting for no midwife at all. While one of these women made her choice for explicitly religious reasons as a conservative, evangelical Christian, the other two were "unassisted birthers" who made their decision in part on feminist principles. Like Laura Kaplan Shanley, the author of *Unassisted Childbirth*, they believed that childbirth was "an event that should ideally reinforce a woman's sense of power and autonomy" and that, for them, the best way to do that was to give birth without medical or midwifery care (Shanley 1994:xvi). One of these women, Miriam Shonovsky, a self-proclaimed New Age Jew, echoed Natalie's conviction that birth demanded faith, which for Miriam meant a faith in her instinct and the ability of her body to give birth (see Shanley 1994:71).

For Miriam, giving birth to her fifth and last child without a caregiver present truly embodied her contention that childbirth was "revolutionary." Giving birth with only her husband there to help allowed her to follow her "instinct" and to take full responsibility for the birth of her baby: "Somehow I thought to make sure the bonding was okay, for this birth I had to take charge . . . I didn't want to answer to anybody. This was going to be my thing." Trying to extricate herself simultaneously from the medical system, the state, and her doubts about the workings of her birthing body, Miriam also exempted herself from the role of a consumer of birth care and claimed a radical autonomy in the process. She felt that her baby's birth—like her earlier home births—was a profoundly spiritual experience in which a "love for the universe" washed over her. For Miriam, home birth in general was her "first feminist act—this is the crux, taking charge of your own body and your own birth." Pushing that autonomy even further, Miriam positioned herself, at least temporarily, outside of relationships of authority and exchange. She considered her unassisted childbirth to be a transformative event in personal terms and a revolutionary event in social terms. Miriam's choice of unassisted birth would provoke the harshest condemnations from opponents of home birth—what for them would be a foolish and selfish act was for her a means to step outside, at least for a few hours, of the authority of medicine, the state, and the market.

Sacrifice and Labor

Home-birthing women in North America are struggling—to borrow a phrase from Marx—to retrieve their "alienated labor" (Marx 1977:83). That they have done so both as consumers and as people struggling against the commodification and medicalization of birth suggests the intractable ironies of life under capitalism. In their ambivalent relationship to childbirth as the consumption of midwifery and ritual services and to childbirth as a spiritual event, many feminist home-birthing women in North America parallel the British National Childbirth Trust (NCT) women that Daniel Miller has described. Detailing the NCT women's devotion to their babies, and to their experiences of pregnancy and childbirth, Miller distinguishes a "virtual cult of the infant" that may, for some women, have "replaced religion as the main experience in life within which the sense of transcendence of one's individuality is felt and avowed" (Miller, this volume, 34). While somewhat ironically and reluctantly drawing from psychoanalytic theory, Miller goes on to define a "cosmology" subscribed to by these mothers, in which "the goodness of the child is a biological projection of her own original nature and goodness, and is only corrupted when outside materialistic forces come and wrest the child away from its biological roots" (Miller, this volume, 50).[9] Many U.S. home-birthing mothers share this sense that their society's materialistic drive for commodification—in which things and services gain their value through their exchange value or their monetary worth—threatens the sacrality of birth and early childhood.

Before I delve into my argument in this section I should disclose, similarly to Daniel Miller in his relationship to the NCT, that I locate myself at least partially within the group I have defined here as North American feminist home-birthing women. I, too, have considered childbirth a profoundly transforming experience on many levels, and I, too, struggle to mediate my young children's interaction with what I believe is a potentially "corrupting" consumer culture. Reading Miller's article provoked a tension in me between laughing at the acuity with which his anecdotes reflected some of my own experiences and being perturbed that something was not quite right with his picture. I came to the conclusion that the lenses of psychoanalysis and consumption helped him to see the cosmological aspects of the NCT women's approaches to mothering in very interesting ways, but as a pair these lenses limited his depiction to a caricature of women that he conscientiously strove to respect.[10] From my work, I would maintain that taking seriously what women describe as the religious aspects of their experiences of childbirth and mothering demands a consideration of these aspects with more than the potentially reductive views of consumption and psychoanalysis.[11]

One of the primary oppositions in Miller's description of the NCT mothers could be glossed as a struggle between self-sacrifice and self-realization. He argues that throughout the process of pregnancy, childbirth, and caring for her baby, an NCT mother negates her previous feminist "skills of self-construction through agency" (including "skills of consumption") in order to devote all her attention to her baby, whom she views as part of a "dual persona of mother-infant" (Miller, this volume, 37). Miller contrasts this repudiation of feminist self-realization with a new mother's embrace of self-sacrifice, using religion to make the comparison: "In many religions the most effective way of establishing a relationship that is ontologically privileged (that is, which transcends the separation of the two entities) is through acts of sacrifice. Here, too, mothers will construct acts of self-sacrifice. For example, women who frequently went out at night for entertainment may refuse to go out even once for more than a year after the infant's birth" (Miller, this volume, 38). That choosing not to go out at night without one's baby is a repudiation of feminism seems an unfounded conclusion to which I will return later. What I am more interested in here is the ways that Miller utilizes religion to make his point. Miller seems to be using religion as an analogy for emphasis, not necessarily because he considers mothering to be religious in itself. Perhaps, however, the line between mothering as analogical to a religious experience and mothering as a religious experience is much fuzzier than he implies. Reconsidering the distinction between religion as analogy and religion as experience also prompts a reconsideration of Miller's distinction between self-realization and self-sacrifice in mothering. Perhaps the two are not so distinct—self-realization itself, at least in North America, is rooted in a cultural, religious, and economic milieu that once privileged self-denial and self-sacrifice as the paths to salvation (Lears 1983:4).

Although Miller's argument does not rule this out, I would argue more forcefully than he that sacrifice is not always a threat to female subjectivity but in some cases a creative venue for that subjectivity. As Alison Lindt-Marliss, a self-proclaimed feminist mother of three children, phrased it to me: "I'm giving love, and raising people, so that they will grow to be secure and confident to do what they want to do. I'm also fulfilling myself.... I don't buy that how motherhood is a place that has no intellectual stimulation, I think it's there for you ... I feel that your world does not have to close when you have children, I feel it can be just the opposite, that it opens up." Like Miriam, Alison felt equally sure that experiencing the "power of pain" in childbirth, while at home in the company of her family and caregivers, was an empowering experience that evoked a "spiritual connection to other women, a connection to what was within me, and what is beyond." She acknowledged that both childbirth and motherhood were difficult endeavors that asked a lot of women but that accepting the responsibility of giving birth and raising children had the potential to transform a woman's sense of self, and even her cosmology. Self-realization could occur—and must occur, in part—within relationships of motherhood.

Who decides what constitutes sacrifice and whether sacrifice carries a positive or negative valence are questions crucial to any analysis of women's subjectivity. Pregnancy and modes of childbirth are increasingly chosen experiences, especially for middle-class North American women, yet no woman can fully determine how her birth will progress (Gallagher 1995:349; Taylor 2000a). In its simultaneously willed and involuntary status, the childbearing body itself challenges notions of agency and of sacrifice; it is a bodily act in which women give of their bodies and undergo pain on behalf of another. The agency mixed with sacrifice in the choices of childbirth can be read many ways, whether a woman opts for the biomedical model of birth or an alternative method like home birth.

In a climate where biomedical approaches claim to offer the safest environment for controlling the uncertainties—the risks—of birth, women who do opt for home birth are often portrayed as abusing both agency and sacrifice.

According to opponents of home birth, these women assert too much agency—too much power over the circumstances of their births while sacrificing the safety of their child for a "good experience" and making insufficient sacrifice of themselves. In this argument, home-birthing women turn what is a force of nature ideally tamed by medicine into a consumer decision in an inappropriate way. In a curious inversion, these anti–home birth arguments use the discourse of consumption as an alienated realm of crass disenchantment against home-birthing women. Women seeking a fulfilling birth experience are said to be indulging their individual desires at the expense of the greater good—the health of their baby. As legal scholar John Robertson commented: "A woman's interest in an aesthetically pleasing or emotionally satisfying birth should not be satisfied at the expense of the child's safety" (Robertson in Overall 1987:98). Or, as one man opposed to home birth put it to me more forcefully: "Childbirth is not about an experience; it's about procreating a new life into the world. If you want an experience, ride a roller coaster." Sacrifice is volatile, especially for feminist mothers it seems: on the one hand, they draw criticism for not sacrificing enough of themselves for their children and, on the other, they are erased as feminist subjects if they sacrifice too much.

The resistance to home birth as an irresponsible and selfish act is linked to another discourse that again merges religious and market metaphors and influences: the theory of procreation described by Carol Delaney in which the child is viewed as the product of the father's seed and his "property" (Delaney 1998). It is not for a woman, as vessel for the seed, to decide how she will birth the baby—the baby is not hers to risk, let alone sacrifice. In Delaney's analysis, women's ability to give birth is seen as a transgressive kind of production that men cannot do—and perhaps can never fully reciprocate (see also Jay 1992). In the act of bearing a child a woman gives a great gift to both her family and her society—but if the societal value of this gift is to be realized, then she must do her job right and produce a healthy baby. Though a child is the product of her parents, she is also a concern of the state.

In contrast to the view of the child as property of the father and/or the state, many feminist theorists and birthing women emphasize the dyadic relationship between mother and child engendered by pregnancy and birth—that dyadic relationship that Miller described as "obsessive child-centeredness" (Davis-Floyd 1992:205; Miller, this volume; Petchesky 1995). In this alternate "theory of procreation," pregnancy and birth are moral acts that call forth an ethics of responsibility in which differentiating between a birthing woman's experience and her baby's "safety" becomes a very difficult, if not hazardous, endeavor. I would agree with Miller that the relationship of a birthing woman to her fetus/baby is a complicated relationship of self and other, in which the boundaries between the two are not clearly drawn. But this blurry boundary need not mean a repudiation of feminist principles—it could be a different model for human relationships in which attending to others in need and situating oneself within connections to others does not necessarily mean forsaking one's subjectivity (see Ruddick 1994).

The meaning of subjectivity in the context of embodiment has been a topic of great debate, especially in feminist circles (for example, Butler 1993). "Reproductive subjectivity" is an especially fraught concern, and it is one that is key to any understanding of how consumption, religion, and reproduction interrelate (Bordo 1993:93). With the repercussions for abortion legislation always lurking as a backdrop, debates about the relationship between female subjectivity and "fetal subjectivity" have grown increasingly intense (see Morgan and Michaels 1999). Some legal and medical interpretations seem to insist that pregnant women should not be allowed to consider their bodies their own. Instead, in these interpretations the rights of a woman's fetus exceed her own as cases of forced caesarean and imprisonment for fetal abuse show (Annas 1982; Gallagher 1995).

In her essay "Are Mothers Persons?" Susan Bordo describes the fetal rights position as a "construction . . . in which pregnant women are not subjects at all (neither under the law nor in the zeitgeist) while fetuses are *super*-subjects" (Bordo 1993:88). This denial of female subjectivity is also evident in the rhetoric of opponents of home birth, who argue that childbirth is not primarily about a woman's subjective experience but about her "safety" and the safe delivery of a healthy baby—where safety is a highly contested term (Goodwin 1997; Zander 1981).[12] As a woman's subjectivity is increasingly stripped away from what is thought to be "essential" to reproduction, she becomes more akin to a "carrier" of a child on behalf of society and seems less of a subject who experiences pregnancy and birth through her own particular embodied history.

Despite the anomalous and privileged status that religious choices sometimes have in the case of health care decisions, even religiously based choices for home birth are criticized from a standpoint that denies women's reproductive subjectivity, similarly to other religiously based maternal refusals of obstetrical interventions (Epstein 1995). Writing of the view of a judge who ordered a woman to undergo a caesarean despite her religiously based refusal, Bordo contended: "Religious scruples are on a par with the flightiest of personal whims when they come into conflict with the supreme role the pregnant woman should be playing: that of incubator to her fetus. In fulfilling that function, the pregnant woman is *supposed* to efface her own subjectivity, if need be. When she refuses to do so, that subjectivity comes to be construed as excessive, wicked" (Bordo 1993:79).

In this case religion, far from being an attunement with transcendent forces larger than the self, becomes another personal choice in a world of hyperindividualized choices, tearing at the fabric of an orderly society. This critical view of individualism voiced in the name of the fetus has deep yet ambivalent roots in broader critiques of individualism and consumption in American society (see Schmidt 1997). Ironically, this anticonsumption critique of home-birthing women is used against women who themselves view society as demeaned by an overly individualized and consumption-driven ethos.

Spirituality and the Purchase of Experience

The spirituality attributed to home birth, in tandem with its usually necessary economic aspects, offers an intriguing lens onto the dilemmas provoked when consumption, bodily experience, and reproduction are combined. Pregnancy and birth are consumer events for all women in the North American context, in which "a woman demonstrates her power and her talents as a consumer, and engages in the construction of her identity by the manner in which she consumes her pregnancy and birth" (Taylor 2000a:157).[13] Pregnancy constructed as consumption is framed as a moral question of how to be the best "fetal environment" one can be, causing a woman to ponder carefully everything from what she eats to what prenatal tests she decides to have.[14]

While the practices of pregnancy are an important concern for home birth advocates, their critiques are more keenly focused on practices of childbirth itself. They argue that the medical model has made a business of birth, as shown by the unnecessary rise in costly caesarean sections (Cohen 1991:23). But what exactly is being commoditized in the medicalization of birth? If we understand a commodity as "a thing that has use value and that can be exchanged in a discrete transaction for a counterpart" (Kopytoff 1986:68), what is it that is being exchanged?[15] From one perspective the fetus/baby is the product/commodity (Taylor 2000a). Some home-birthing women adopted this metaphor when criticizing biomedical versions of childbirth in which a woman was too drugged to recall or sense her birth.[16] According to one woman, her mother-in-law bought her babies at "the Stork Club as she called it." Some critics of home birth have come close to advocating the model of baby as product more in earnest. For example, Nova Scotia doctor James W. Goodwin, writing in opposition to the approval his Ontario colleagues have given to home birth, suggested that the risks of home birth are too great to allow a home birth midwife to practice: "With the public expectation of the perfect perinatal outcome, unless one can prove beyond a shadow of a doubt that home birth is absolutely and completely safe, then to advise the client to participate in a home birth is a gamble. Is it ethical or conscionable for the midwife herself to recommend such a course to the client woman if this definition holds true? I think not" (Goodwin 1997:1187). Perfect perinatal outcomes, otherwise known as healthy babies, are the bottom line for Goodwin and are of utmost importance to midwives and home-birthing women as well. However, midwives and home-birthing women are not as convinced that any kind of technology, be it fetal monitoring or the Gaskin maneuver, can guarantee such an outcome.[17] At the same time, Goodwin argued that obstetricians should adapt some midwifery practices as a response to the consumer consciousness midwifery has generated. For example, Goodwin argued that "the woman must feel that she is in control and that she can decide." To this end, after "informing" women of the risks of birth, obstetricians "must allow the woman to choose"—but this tolerance does not extend to allowing her to choose her place of birth (Goodwin 1997:1186).

Goodwin's assessment preferring perfect perinatal outcomes to women's desired experiences of childbirth sets up a dichotomy not unlike Miller's distinction between self-sacrifice and self-realization. Just as many feminist mothers would argue that self-sacrifice and self-realization are not always mutually exclusive, many birthing women would argue that in most cases a woman's experience of childbirth and the health of her baby are not competing goods. When they make their choices about childbirth care, then, they are shopping not only for someone who will help bring their baby safely into the world but also someone who will honor their needs, desires, and experience. To put it one way, they are trying to purchase an experience that will be uncomplicated and profound.

Focusing on the birth experience itself as that which is commoditized raises some intriguing theoretical questions. The (at least rhetorical) resistance to commoditizing experiences like childbirth, emotions like love, and dispositions like spirituality is deeply engrained in North American culture. With what Robert Wuthnow calls a "legacy of ambivalence," North Americans at once condemn materialism as a threat to spiritual values while embracing the fruits of consumption (Wuthnow 1995:4, 8). The pairing of this ambivalent, religiously rooted critique of consumption with a conviction that childbirth is a religious experience crystallizes one of the most basic tensions in American capitalist culture. Namely, that bodies are at once the site of profound and perhaps ineffable sacredness and the recipients of the very material goods and services that consumption brings to them.

Considering an experience—whether of birth, of sacredness, or of gastronomic delight—as commoditized brings us to what Arjun Appadurai describes as the understudied "service dimension of commoditization," a dimension that Appadurai (1986:55) contends is particularly dominant in postindustrial economies. The commoditization of spiritual and ritual services, in particular, raises visceral reactions in a society in which historically spirituality and material consumption have been slated as polar opposites and where an accusation of simony or hucksterism is one of the most damning critiques that can be launched at a religious practitioner (Brown 1997; Marty 1995:239; Schmidt 1999). Tessa's sale of her ritual services together with her reluctance to "purchase" or arrange for a Blessing Way for herself demonstrate both the fact of the commoditization of ritual services and experiences, as well as the discomfort with this reality.[18]

An important part of the legacy of ambivalence concerning the relationship between consumption and religion is rooted in the very language of theories of consumption themselves, which put religion to rhetorical use without necessarily considering it in itself. *Commodity, fetish, cosmologies*—all of these words are critical to the study of consumption and are defined via religious metaphors. For example, when defining commodities, Marx insisted that "to find an analogy, we must have recourse to the mist-enveloped regions of the religious world. In that world the productions of the human brain appear as independent beings endowed with life and entering into relation both with one another and the human race. So it is in the world of commodities with the products of men's hands. This I call the Fetishism which attaches itself to the products of labor, so soon as they are produced as commodities" (Marx 1977:436). The fetish in Marx's commodity fetishism is itself a hybrid term encompassing the religious artifact and the commodity, which historically emerged out of the encounters between Portuguese traders and West Africans. William Pietz argues that fetishes, whether in the Marxist sense or the psychoanalytic sense, have been defined in part by their "untranscended materiality" (Pietz 1985:7). That is, a fetish was not thought to hold the more exalted status of icon (or even idol); it was a thing in and of itself, not pointing to a greater sense of the transcendent. In some ways, Daniel Miller's discussion of NCT mothers evokes a sense of the child and the experience of childbirth as fetish in its untranscended materiality when he speaks of "obsessive child-centeredness" and the way women "highlight the specific experience of childbirth, and . . . dwell upon it both before and after the event" (Miller, this volume, 50, 30). Perhaps this is the root of my discomfort with Miller's analysis, for all that I found it insightful and provocative: he uses religious metaphors not to understand the profundity of motherhood for the women he studies, but to make them seem strange, fetishistic, temporarily unhinged from their feminist selves, as they "radically negate a feminist project of autonomy in mothering" (Miller, this volume, 50). Perhaps if Miller's starting point had been mothering, and not shopping, his conclusions would have been different; perhaps if he had used religion as a tool of analysis and not simply analogy, his portrait of the significance of love, children, relationships, and autonomy for these women would also have transformed.

Thinking about feminist mothering also requires an expanded sense of what counts as autonomy—or at least what counts as women's right to own or control their bodies—that market metaphors of consumption or property do not fully explain (Petchesky 1995:387).[19] African American feminists have advanced some of the most important theorizing about the ways mothering can promote self-realization through relationships while also sometimes "extract[ing] high personal costs" (Collins 1992:235; Hooks 1990). Paraphrasing feminist theorist Patricia Hill Collins, Rosalind Petchesky writes: "Black women . . . have forged a sense of self and bodily integrity that is rooted in strong dyadic relationships with their children. Motherhood becomes here a source of self-determination that is integrative, extended, communal" (Petchesky 1995:397). Feminist autonomy need not be at odds with attending to the needs of the other; feminism is not necessarily defined as the satisfying of the pleasures and desires of the consuming woman unencumbered by relationships to children, lovers, neighbors, and in some cases deities. Furthermore, at least in North America, religion is not only a tool of mystification; it can also be the ground of feminist subjectivities that attempt the unending task of attending to responsibilities for others and commitments to self, whether in reproducing children or society (Collins 1992:234).

In the discomfort that many home-birthing women feel over the commoditization of childbirth lie the traces of a conflict between viewing the body as thing that can be possessed and scientifically explained and the body as a site of mysterious generativity and potential spiritual awakening. Some home-birthing women, like Tessa, combine these views by strategically employing models of consumer activism to maintain the "essential mystery of birth." In the words of Igor Kopytoff, they remove childbirth from the realm of commodities by "singularizing" it and thus conferring upon it a sacralized status (Kopytoff 1986:87). In the view of home-birth advocates, each woman's birth is unique and must be treated as such—the mystery of birth lies partly in its unpredictability and singular trajectory for each woman, an unpredictability that biomedical models of birth have sought to overcome in their attempts to standardize and routinize patterns of labor (Rothman 1983).

Home-birthing women attempt this singularization and sacralization of childbirth within a culture shaped by a scientific worldview that, as Evelyn Fox Keller remarked, has ruptured "the residual sense of sublimity" formerly attached to the notion of "life" (Keller 1997:217). According to Keller, the sublimity of life in Western culture was closely attached to the "secrets of nature"—the mysteries of genesis and generation. As long as such secrets were veiled, women and the category of nature retained some ineffable power. With their unveiling, the ambivalent power derived from the "mystery of birth" began to wane (Keller 1997:216). While neither the mystery of birth nor the sublimity of life are certain paths to empowerment for women, it does seem to be the case that transforming childbirth from women's work to (mostly) men's expertise disempowered many women (Leavitt 1986).

Today, ironically, as some frontiers of reproductive technology work toward making the female body (let alone any kind of god or goddess) incidental if not irrelevant to the process of creating life,[20] home-birthing women are struggling to return a sense of the sublime to the experience of childbirth. In the process, they turn to the tools of their consumer culture while also challenging its premises. Harnessing the many legacies of ambivalence in their culture—the uneasy pairing of materialism and spirituality, the coupling of reproductive subjectivity with an invocation of the essential mystery of birth, the unavoidable tension (or creativity?) within the self-sacrifice and self-realization embedded in motherhood—feminist home-birthing women simultaneously embrace and resist the ironies of consumption and spirituality engendered in the practices of giving birth.

NOTES

For their very helpful comments on this article, I am grateful to Janelle Taylor, Danielle Wozniak, Linda Layne, the anonymous reviewers, and John Marshall. This work was supported by the Fulbright Canada/U.S. Scholars Program, the Louisville Institute for the Study of Religion, and the Social Sciences and Humanities Research Council of Canada.

1. This chapter offers a new argument drawn from my ethnographic study of religion and home birth in the northeastern United States. For this study, I interviewed forty-five home-birthing women from across a range of religious identities, visited midwifery clinics, went to various home birth-related events, read home birth literature, and attended a home birth, over the course of two years, from 1995 to 1997 (Klassen 2001).

2. Although all of the women I interviewed were affected by feminism in some way, because of my later discussion of sacrifice and self-realization, I focus here on women who considered themselves feminists.

3. I explore the uses of the term *spirituality* in the context of home birth in Klassen (2001).

4. I have given pseudonyms to all the women with whom I spoke.

5. Insurance is a troublesome issue for certified nurse-midwives, as the insurance industry and medical authorities have tried to restrict the ability of certified nurse-midwives to take out their own liability insurance. They have also ostracized or levied insurance premiums on doctors who have agreed to work with midwives and have made it difficult for midwives to be reimbursed directly instead of through a doctor. Certified nurse-midwives who attend home births sometimes do not even take out insurance, because suits against them are rare (ACNM and Jacobs 1993:250; Norsigian 1996:88; Rooks 1997).

6. Blessing Way ceremonies are traditionally Navajo, but in Navajo communities they can be protective rituals for anyone from a pregnant woman about to birth to a man about to leave the community to join the army. Euro-American adaptations or appropriations of the Blessing Way may have little to do with the tradition as practiced among Navajos (Kluckhohn and Leighton 1974:212; Lamphere 1977:28).

7. I wrote to Jeannine Parvati-Baker asking her how she understood her borrowing from native culture. She responded by offering to send me more of her writings or for me to call her for a phone consultation, at ninety dollars per hour. For more on the ethics of cross-cultural borrowing within the feminist spirituality movement, see Eller (1993:74–82).

8. Of course, even in eighteenth-century New England, midwives charged fees (Ulrich 1991:198–99).

9. For other instances where anthropologists have adopted the term *cosmology* as a kind of substitute for *culture,* see Sahlins (1994, 1996) and Applbaum (1998).

10. I want to emphasize that though I have criticisms of some of Miller's conclusions, I

find his work, especially in *A Theory of Shopping* (1998), to be innovative and insightful and provocative for both feminist theory and religious studies.

11. Miller himself notes that he is using psychoanalytic theory somewhat jokingly and awkwardly and that he is concerned to avoid its universalizing tendencies (1997:68, 80).
12. As well, see the interview with Dr. Yvonne Thornton and midwife Ina May Gaskin on National Public Radio's "Talk of the Nation," on March 31, 1999.
13. I am grateful to Margaret MacDonald for coining this latter phrase.
14. For example, most home-birthing women elect to forgo obstetrical ultrasound testing both out of a concern about its safety and a desire to maintain the "mystery" of birth (Declercq, Paine, and Winter 1995:480).
15. For other perspectives on the definition of the term *commodity*, see Appadurai (1986) and Comaroff and Comaroff (1990).
16. Another way that some home-birthing women used a metaphor of exchange occurred when they spoke of difficult births that caused them to exchange their desires for a low-intervention home birth for a healthy baby. For example, one woman who received a very hostile reaction at the hospital when she had to go there due to complications during her first planned home birth reflected at the end of her story: "But, you know, she's here and she's healthy and she's safe and that's the important thing. And that's what I really care about. That was the point of having a baby. . . . The point of getting pregnant was to have a baby and I got this beautiful little girl. If that's what it took—that's what it took."
17. The Gaskin maneuver is a manual technique for shoulder dystocia named after its inventor, Ina May Gaskin, a prominent home birth midwife. For other perspectives on evaluations of the risks of childbirth among midwives and medical doctors, see Sarah (1987) and Kaufert and O'Neil (1993).
18. The Blessing Way is not unique here—Tessa would probably feel the same kind of discomfort if she were to hold her own baby shower. Baby showers, however, are not usually arranged by a paid host, although services like catering might be paid for, as are most of the gifts.
19. Ironically, from the point of view of home birthers, the president of the American College of Obstetricians and Gynecologists recently suggested that "patient choice cesarean" was a feminist breakthrough for reproductive choice (Harer 2000).
20. For example, see Valerie Hartouni's discussion of the extraction of uteruses from dead women for the experimental purposes of housing fertilized eggs (Hartouni 1991:48).

Commentaries

Commoditizing Kinship in America

IGOR KOPYTOFF

The issue with which this volume is centrally engaged is the interaction, in American society, between kinship relations (involving such matters as reproduction, parenthood, adoption, and childhood) and "economistic" principles of behavior, including the commoditization of these kinship relations. I shall use here the cover term *economism* for assigning a primary role to the bundle of features rendered by such terms as *industrialism, capitalism, the market, commoditization, consumerism,* and so on. The larger issue is an old one, rather recently expressed by the unease of both conservatives and radicals in the nineteenth century with the impact of the market on social relations. Within the anthropological tradition, this unease has been expressed most strongly in Karl Polanyi's *The Great Transformation* (1944), which dealt with the historical process by which "society" came to be subordinated by the "economy" under modern capitalism.

Empirically, the issue is especially problematic in America and the West in general. Modern Western culture (and one must stress "modern") insists on drawing a categorical and moral distinction between persons and things, between the world of people regarded as social and the world of goods regarded as economic. Each of these worlds, it is felt, must be governed by a different ethos, and this modern consecration of the difference taps some deep cultural roots (out of which have also sprung, in the distant past, the granting of souls to humans and to humans alone and the Cartesian separation of mind and matter and, later, of mind and brain). Recently, however, the distinction between persons and things—and between the social and the economic—has come under a great deal of pressure with the development of new technologies of reproduction. The social and economic repercussions have undermined the supposedly clear cultural boundaries between the world of persons and the world of things (for a discussion of these conundrums, see Taylor 2000b). And these difficulties, in turn, have spilled over into the legal realm (see, for example, Kopytoff 1988).

Historically, of course, Western culture was not always adamant about drawing a clear distinction between persons and things. It is not so very long ago that, in the West, some people were legally treated as objects and traded as slaves, much as they were and had been in most human societies. Indeed, a case can be made that the increasingly uncompromising insistence in the late nineteenth and the twentieth century on the distinction between persons and things has partly arisen in the shadow of slavery and the historical guilt over it, since abolition was argued precisely by invoking the moral difference between persons and things. Contemporary Americans are strikingly sensitive to the morality of any social arrangement that may be taken to be reminiscent of slavery. Thus, they insist that, to be legal, the adoption of children should scrupulously avoid any hint of material profit; and American courts have generally been hostile to overly binding employment contracts—notably in sports and movies and recently even to rules of employment imposing certain clothes, headgear, or hairdo—because they remotely imply involuntary servitude.

In the modern American and general Western perspective, then, there is a moral threat in the commoditization of children and, by extension, of human reproduction; the threat lies in the possible invasion of the human and sacralized world of kinship by economistic principles deemed appropriate only to the world of things. Anthropology is especially qualified to analyze this modern Western stance in light of its familiarity with the range of ethnographic variations. And this volume presents a number of analyses of these issues by way of case studies within American society itself.

The first noteworthy ethnographic observation that suggests itself is that many, indeed most, human societies have found the invasion of kinship by economics rather congenial. In some cases, this invasion appears to have been extreme, as, for example, among the Yurok of northern California (Erikson 1943). Innumerable societies have framed various social arrangements—such as inheritance, co-residence, marriage, reproduction, rights over children, and adoption—in terms of concrete rights-in-persons, rights transacted through payments in things, animals, commodities, and money. The sheer ubiquity of these commoditizing arrangements tempts one to ask, Is there something that makes kinship relations plausibly, perhaps even "naturally," liable to an economistic approach? After all, kinship touches upon the production and acquisition of human capital and resources such as rights over people's bodies and sentiments, rights to their services, rights to their sexuality and labor, and rights to their reproductive capacities; these rights all involve material gains and losses. It is thus not surprising that what lies at the very core of kinship—rights in the newborn—is quickly allocated in some way upon birth in nearly all societies. There is thus a certain logical intertwining between kinship and economism (inevitably expressed, as Alison Clarke argues in this book, in the material and consumerist provisioning of children by parents). However, the precise relationship between kinship and economism remains indeterminate since it is open to other influences, not least the varying cultural interpretations that are imposed on it.

If we proceed, then, with the assumption that a degree of economizing is, in some primordial sense, a "natural" tendency in kinship as in all social relations, certain questions can be asked: To what extent can this natural tendency be overcome culturally? Do qualms, such as Polanyi's, spring from a peculiarly strong Western cultural sensitivity to the interpenetration of cultural values and "natural" economistic tendencies, seeing it as an invasion by the "economy" of "society"? In modern America, the answers to these questions may appear to be inconsistent.

As most of the papers in this volume show, American culture tends on the one hand to encourage a certain rationalistic and economistic worldview, and this cannot but shape the cultural construction of all social relations, including those of kinship. But on the other hand, there is a very visible and often very successful opposition to this economistic tendency. In most modern industrial societies, material affluence allows unprecedented wide choices in personal as well as in societywide expenditure (such as in welfare programs). On the personal level, this allows Westerners to purge relations with kinsmen of much economic content and make them almost entirely "social." Kinship relations in these affluent societies have very few obligatory economic correlates (and even these often have to be enforced by a legal system rooted in the past). This disjunction between kinship and economics is apparent even in the most intimate kin relations, such as those of parents and children. Parents can permit themselves the moral luxury of treating their children as vessels of purely sentimental investment and of spending resources on economically unproductive offspring without any expectation of future returns—even though, as Ann Anagnost shows in her article, this calculus comes under strain in cross-national adoption, which raises very starkly the question of the balance between economic investment and expected sentimental returns. But in most cases, affluence allows the social sphere to be relatively unconstrained and endows it with considerable autonomy; this opens the social sphere to an unproblematic play of contradictory values. All this is in stark contrast to peasant and "primitive" societies that can ill afford a purely sentimental treatment of children and where basic material needs impose a different calculus on kinship relations. Hence the widespread institutions that put material transactions, such as bridewealth and childwealth, at the core of kinship relations in these societies.

A culture may simply accept some aspects of the coexistence of kinship and economism as unproblematic, or at least as a balanced and untroubling duality of attitudes. Both Pamela Klassen and Robbie Davies-Floyd show in this book how this duality expresses itself among modern American midwives. On the one hand, the midwives play the New Age card by "spiritualizing" their occupation.

On the other hand, they simultaneously engage in economistic practices by collecting fees, engaging in advertising, and, in general, appealing to consumerist values.

The balance between seemingly contradictory values may be maintained by resorting to equally powerful cultural rhetorics. In the West, market talk has its appeal, but so does humanistic antimarket talk. Debates over the legalization of surrogate motherhood have often exhibited this duality of approaches. For surrogacy can be damned as a species of baby selling and praised as a method of providing childless couples with children. We are now entering a similar duality of argument in the case of human cloning.

As Barbara Yngvesson stresses in this volume, in her analysis of adoption and the material transactions around it, this duality is indeed subject to cultural evaluation, and in the West it is not always simply taken for granted. Westerners prefer to create and preserve, if only rhetorically, a distinction between "gifts" and "deals" in these transactions—that is, a distinction between the social and the economic. And, as Anagnost points out in her article, adopters strive to see any given adoption in either an affective or an economic light—but not both. For all the deep penetration of society by economism, Westerners tend to deplore the integration of the two and feel uncomfortable with thinking about kinship in economistic terms. The result is that antieconomism coexists with economism in a problematic, delicately stable relation.

Commoditization carries with it the equalization of items as commodities. And equalization means their de-individualization; and, as Yngvesson points out, de-individualization is something that child adoption inevitably confers upon the child and makes it potentially liable to commoditization. What is notable here, again, is that modern Westerners generally find this de-individualization deplorable. In many "primitive" societies, child substitution is taken to be logical—the party responsible for a child's death is required to give another child in its stead. Westerners find this unsatisfactory, given their emphasis on rights to children's sentiments. Even adoption, let alone substitution, is a second best solution to childlessness; it is a kind of substitution by another child for the "real" child that actually never came into being. The other side of this unresolved conundrum appears, one suspects, in the recent trend to grant access to various records to adult adoptees who wish to search for their personal origins and thus to re-individualize themselves. But most societies have been quite comfortable with the de-individualization that accompanies changes in social roles. Inspired by these societies, Van Gennep saw it as being at the root of the nearly universal and unabashedly de-individualizing rites of passage.

One wonders whether the very awareness of de-individualization—an awareness psychologized into an existential problem and a philosophical concern in the modern West—is even possible in societies that do not hold individual uniqueness to be a precious human right. In traditional African societies, for example, adoption is seen as being obviously a transaction in socially recognized legal rights in a person; it involves tangible gains and losses that call for material compensation as a matter of equity. Whether the adoptee knows or does not know his or her origins is given little existential importance, though it may be of practical import: knowledge of one's origins may dilute the adoptee's loyalty to the adopters, putting the transaction at a potential risk.

If we insist that the interpenetration of kinship and economism is inherently contradictory, we might interpret its occurrence in the modern West as a case of a triumphant consumerism invading the realm of kin reproduction. But we might, on the other hand, resort to another interpretation by assuming (as I have suggested above) that kinship relations plausibly and "naturally" lend themselves to economism. What contradiction there is is not a matter of analytical or structural fact but a matter of cultural perception. The perception derives from the strongly felt Western and American view—a view shared by social analysts no less than by ordinary people—that kinship belongs to the world of sentiment and spirituality and that economism belongs to materialism, and that their integration is somehow contradictory and morally inappropriate. This view is, of course, ethnocentric and, in its more uncompromising forms, relatively modern.

The ethnographic record shows that materialistic attitudes easily coexist with what modern Westerners regard as spirituality. The record is full of cases in which relations with spirits are governed by economic and consumerist principles. Diviners and ritual specialists regularly charge fees for their services. People's relations with protective spirits are often formed on a quid pro quo basis, like economic relations. And ritual formulae and personal guardian spirits are often bought and sold like commodities. The premodern West also often conformed to this pattern in its spiritual endeavors. Medieval religious plays given in cathedrals involved careful financial calculations; the organization of pilgrimages exhibited many features of modern tourism; and the sale of indulgences coexisted with theological condemnations of simony. Modern Christianity, too (from the perspective, say, of a Sicilian village rather than of the Vatican), countenances many quid pro quo interactions with saints and the Deity. It says something about the complexity of Western attitudes in these matters that Protestantism (which has been so often given a role in the development of capitalism) began with theological objections to indulgences in what may be seen as a harbinger of a particular kind of intolerance of economism. Thus, the modern commoditization of body parts (such as blood or semen), analyzed by Barbara Katz Rothman, reflects historically not so much a change in attitude as a shift in focus from some objects to others.

I would submit that the hostility to the expansion of commoditization into previously untouched spheres is in fact a measure of the strength of the anticonsumerist values in Western culture. This explains the exaggerated nature of the hostility by Western intellectuals who are modern secular society's clerics. And the expansion and even the very emergence of commoditization is then made part and parcel of a bigger bundle of deplorable socioeconomic forces of rather recent origin—the bundle of capitalism, industrialism, consumerism, the market, and so on. We must therefore examine the place of the idea of commoditization in the dynamics of recent Western intellectual history.

Certainly, the socioeconomic forces in the bundle need some deconstruction, for they are not inextricably interdependent. Industrialism, since its appearance in the West a few centuries ago, has by now operated in many noncapitalist societies, including the now defunct "socialist" societies where it was in fact extolled as a great shining goal. Industrialism with its values can thus be safely detached from capitalism and the values that it is purported to encourage. For regardless of whether or not industrialism is connected to capitalism, it imposes its own constraints: factory management, hierarchy of decision making, work discipline, calculations of costs, consumer demand, efficiencies in the production and distribution of goods and services (including medical, obstetric, and social services), and so on. The various elements of the bundle do not appear to be analytically interdependent variables. Their association is a historically contingent nineteenth-century phenomenon.

In this perspective, the nature of consumerism itself cries out for elucidation, if it is to be of analytical usefulness. At present, it seems to be merely a descriptive term in Western social analysis for a phenomenon that, as Colin Campbell (1987) has suggested, arose in the seventeenth century. Is consumerism to be regarded, then, as a universal cross-cultural possibility, a systemic emergent under certain conditions that takes on local cultural colors? Or is it quite simply a kind of greed for certain material goods—goods whose marginal utility approaches zero in the eyes of the intellectual speaker. Simply put, is the desire for better televisions consumerism, but not the desire for better encyclopedias? Do tendencies inherent in commonplace greed become consumerism only when they provoke marketlike exchanges, as among the Kapauku of Papua New Guinea described by Leopold Pospisil (1963). Is this greed usually hidden but ever ready to blossom forth if given a chance—among hunters-gatherers no less than among American suburbanites? One of the difficulties with establishing the relationship between consumerism and capitalism lies in that capitalism is most visible at the production point of the economic process. By contrast, phenomena such as greed and consumerism are embedded at some distance from production, at the consumption end.

Connections among elements within American culture also pose special interpretive problems. As the articles in this volume indicate, there are many strands within American culture that are often contradictory, yet each of them may be endowed with its own cultural legitimacy. Whether and when these varied strands are merely coexistent or actively antagonistic is a matter of American cultural perception. Gail Landsman's article shows how such strands coexist in the alternative American models of disabled children: the consumer model of the imperfect baby as a kind of defective product, as opposed to the quasi religious model of the imperfect baby as a special gift that spiritually ennobles its parents. Culturally, both models resonate equally persuasively—for a working-class Christian no less than for a secular intellectual.

Finally, there is the historical dimension. One has the impression that, before the late nineteenth century, Westerners were culturally more comfortable than now with an "economizing" model of kinship relations, that they were not as ready to be shocked by any suggestion of commoditization in the treatment of children. One thinks, for example, of our modern uneasy reaction to that notorious late-nineteenth-century train from New York that peddled orphans for adoption at successive railroad stations in the western frontier lands; only a purely cultural explanation can account for our discomfort with what another (and not so distant) age saw as a rational philanthropic way of rescuing homeless orphans.

In sum, modern Americans are indeed prone, on the one hand, to surrender to the economistic and consumerist forces in kinship as in other spheres of life. On the other hand, they also exhibit a sincere cultural dislike of these forces, and this lends the intellectuals' critique of consumerism its persuasiveness and legitimacy. They hold on to a sentimental model of kinship affectivities, consecrate it by dubbing it "traditional," and worry that the new reproductive technologies risk commoditizing children into designer products. And these worries are compounded by the fear that in the end we shall all succumb to the temptations of the new technology. All this involves contending, contradictory, and vague values of different historical depths and varied powers of compulsion. As Daniel Miller points out in his article reprinted in this book, even the progressivist anticonsumerist members of the middle class in North London resort to consumerist techniques in child rearing.

A common cultural solution to the clash between contradictory values is to subordinate one value to the other. This approach to contradiction is examined in this volume by Janelle Taylor, Linda Layne, and Danielle Wozniak.

Taylor describes elsewhere how the imaging of the fetus by ultrasound technology contributes to mother-fetus bonding and how the fetus gradually acquires personhood as various baby goods are bought in advance of birth (Taylor 2000b). Here consumerism is not so jarring because it is made to serve the higher value of endowing the mother-child tie with culturally appropriate sentiments. Taylor sees this, however, as a kind of "commodity fetishism." Indeed, in the chapter included in this volume, she shows how ultrasound images of the fetus that circulate in public culture come to be endowed with tremendous powers that verge on the magical. Like the classic fetishes of "primitive" societies, they perform powerful sociological feats.

Similarly, Layne shows how, in cases of pregnancy loss, some parents acquire commodities as a way of conferring personhood on the lost child and motherhood on the mother. And Wozniak speaks of a parallel logic when a departed foster child is memorialized in a quasi kinship position by the former foster parents through the use of material goods. In both cases, sociological and psychological purposes are achieved by what we are likely to call a "symbolic" manipulation of goods, reminiscent of similar uses of goods in magic and sacrifice, thus overcoming the Western cultural barrier between commodities and kinship.

What strikes one about the articles in this volume is their reversal of the common anthropological procedure. Usually, we look to the ethnographies of non-Western societies to give us a perspective on our own. Here, by contrast, thick ethnographic analyses of our own society give us a key to the social efficacy of classic anthropological phenomena, such as the endowment of things with power—as in fetishism, kinship relations, motherhood, adoption, fosterage, and surrogacy. The foray of anthropology out of what used to be its "primitive" preserve into the wider world has come a full and productive circle!

May I now summarize the main points I have made?

1. Economism in kinship relations, including commoditization, is, I suggest, a "natural" phenomenon, as seen in the fact that it occurs in innumerable societies. What varies is the cultural perception of the phenomenon.
2. In Western culture, as in others, there are two coexisting strands: (I) the "natural" commoditizing, economistic strand and (2) the strand opposed to it. These two strands, though logically antagonistic, were culturally balanced in the precapitalist West.
3. Capitalist development and industrialization undermined this balance. On the one hand, they reinforced the economistic strand, and, on the other, they raised the ethical sensitivity and opposition to what appeared to be the "invasion" of the society by economism.
4. The result, at present, is a very uneasy balance, marked by a conscious resistance (so far, relatively unsuccessful) to the economistic invasion of more and more spheres of life.

Caught in the Current

BARBARA KATZ ROTHMAN

If this book can be thought of as the intersection of two streams of critical, scholarly work, work on consumption and work on motherhood, then I, paddling along in the one stream, feel quite sideswept by the other. Twenty-five years and more of scholarly, feminist, critical work on motherhood, even thinking long and hard about motherhood under capitalism, did not fully prepare me for the insights of critical scholarly work on consumption. I felt myself drowning, splashing, struggling against the current as I read. It was, I told the editors, terrifying to see all of this put together this way. What do I mean by "all of this"? The consequences of capitalism for motherhood, what it really means for mothers to be doing the work, living the lives of mothers, in a capitalist system.

One would have thought that I, of all people, would understand this. My words, I am proud to say, are used as one of the introductions to this volume. But knowing this as an intellectual abstraction and seeing the consequences spread out before me here are two very different experiences.

When I first began writing about the ways that capitalism shaped motherhood, I did not even have a vocabulary available to me. I struggled for a word to describe what was happening to fetuses and to babies and came up with *commodification*. A copyeditor rejected it: not a word, not acceptable. I insisted, as have others, and it is a word that now sails right through copyediting. And cuts right through our lives and our bodies.

The editors use the work of Daniel Miller on infants growing mothers and my own work on women growing products called babies to introduce the book. It is a sensible choice of alternatives. I have focused on women as producers; he focuses on women as consumers. Taken together, we have a more rounded understanding of women as mothers today in the United Kingdom, the United States, and probably much of Europe and, increasingly, other places as well.

Women under capitalism, I have argued, have found that the babies they grow are commodities, and the only real question being asked is, "Whose commodity?" To whom does the baby belong? Who has rights of ownership? In struggling to (re)claim their own babies and their own bodies, women have drawn upon the same language of ownership, the "rights talk" that makes so much sense in America. And this is what we—women in the home-birth movement, the midwifery movement, the women's health movement—have done. On issues as varied as abortion, adoption, home birth, surrogacy, breastfeeding, sterilization, and more, we have invoked "rights," and, by implication, ownership. A woman has, we declare, a right to do as she wills with her body. It is her baby she produces with that body, and she has rights over that baby as well. We have defended these rights, rights which are repeatedly threatened, under constant attack, until perhaps a callous has built up over the argument. We cannot hear, we cannot afford to hear, the limitations, the potential threats of the "rights" and "ownership" language itself.

But what does it mean to "own" a body when that body itself is disvalued? What does it mean to have a baby of one's "own" when the word *own* is defined by others? What does it mean to have a "right" to services when those services are fundamentally human relationships? These are the questions raised and sometimes answered in this disturbing and powerful book.

Miller shifts our focus and looks at women as consumers, and does so in ways that I find sad, troubling, and sometimes maybe funny, too. I think we're supposed to find this funny, to share the "ironic distance" on these losing battles against the consumerist tide that swallows our children. Maybe I lack perspective. Maybe I lack a sense of humor. But when he talks about mothers seeing the television as a "corruption of the child by an external force acting against its own welfare," well, excuse me while I turn down the sound of my kid watching MTV, but, well, yeah. My thirteen-year-old daughter and I have been watching DVDs of the old "Howdy Doody Show," the kids' TV of the 1950s that I grew up on. And so I have been watching Buffalo Bob sell Wonderbread, which "grows strong bodies twelve ways, boys and girls, just tell your mother to look for the red, yellow, and blue balloons!" and Twinkies, "just have your mother look in the store near the checkout counter for the familiar 'Hostess' lady on the wrapper" (a nice set of clues not requiring literacy of me as a kid in the grocery store). Watching this now as a middle-aged woman, remembering how much I just loved Howdy Doody Time, I do feel a bit, oh, corrupted? used? duped?

That was me the child being turned into the consumer that me the mother now is, the consumer that Miller analyzes. And, yes, he is looking at women younger than I, and in London, not Brooklyn, but I know who he means, I recognize myself, as he recognizes himself, in these mothers. The process that Miller talks about in the development of these mother-consumers is a move from the radical student, to "people with taste," to mothers who exercise that "taste" in the construction of their babies and children, transferring the "skills and pleasures" of consumption from themselves to their children. Allow me to think through each step.

As students, Miller explains, their individuality was mainly expressed in the formation of left-of-center political opinions. That psychologizes away any of the issues that might have been involved for these mothers in their politics. The civil rights movement in the United States, the varied international antiwar movements, the feminist movement—were these only about expressing "individuality"? I heard Talcott Parsons once, late in his life, comparing the student movements of the 1960s and 1970s, right while they were still happening, to the "panty raids" of frat boys of the 1950s. I cannot take such an analysis seriously.

As these women grew up, became employed, entered the "mainstream," and as a cohort faced a very different political climate, they may well have shifted their emphasis into developing themselves as "consumers" and "people with taste." And then, yes, they do turn that to the infant, producing a particular kind of child by consumption, buying to create an appropriately presentable child. That change does not negate the political work they did or values that they held.

As mother/consumers though, I see, or I think I see—or maybe, after all, I only want to see—these mothers looking at the child with a double vision, negotiating two sets of demands. There are those demands, those needs, presented by the child. Miller seems rather astonished by the emphasis on the needs of the child, on the "child centeredness" of the enterprise. I think we need a bit of context here. The various childbirth movements, including the NCT in the United Kingdom that he refers to, grew in response to the medicalization of birth and early motherhood. In the medical model, the baby was not seen as a being with human or even animal needs. In some of the more flagrant disregards of the needs of the child, physicians routinely did surgery on infants without anesthesia—they wouldn't feel it, and if they felt it, they wouldn't remember it, doctors claimed. Not remembering seemed highly significant to the doctors, who also developed pain relief regimens for mothers in birth, such as scopolamine, that did nothing to remove pain but did remove memory. Or conscious memory. Less dramatically, doctors dismissed the contented smile of the newborn, one of motherhood's greater rewards, as "gas." And the frantic crying of a hungry baby was to be ignored until the clock rang for the next feeding. It was in this context that the needs of the child were reintroduced. I can see the excesses; but I also see the historical context, the reasons for insisting on taking the needs of the babies as real and actual needs, not arbitrary "demands" of insensate beings. So one eye of the mother/consumer is on the baby, consuming services, from midwifery to lactation consultation, to perhaps some infant products, in the interests of the needful baby.

The other eye, the one not on the baby itself, is on the way the world sees that baby, and, too, the way the world sees the woman as the mother/producer of the baby. So babies are indeed dressed and "styled" to represent a particular type of mother(ing), to identify the competence and style and taste of the mother, much the way her own dress or her home furnishings identify her. In that context, the child's development as an independent consumer threatens the mother's identity. Two highly gendered examples come to mind: girls and Barbies; boys and guns. To take the awful Barbie battle: the mother (her possible feminist credentials, her sense of the "kind of person" she is) is threatened by the child as a Barbie owner. I am not—she feels, I feel, probably most of us feel—the kind of mother whose kid plays with Barbies. And, yet, apparently I am; apparently most of us are. Just as my own mother found herself to be the kind of mother who lets her kids eat Wonderbread and Twinkies!

Thus one aspect of this book is the work on the mother as consumer for her child and the child as a developing consumer itself. I will return to this theme. But another theme is the way that mothers become consumers of pregnancy and birth services. This is what Klassen addresses in her work on home-birth feminists, what Davis-Floyd talks about in the "qualified" commodification of midwifery care, and to some extent what Taylor describes in her work on sonographers. I turn now to the history of the home birth, alternative birth, and midwifery movements, the larger social frame in which the NCT style of mothering developed.

Now and Then

There is a full body of research on the stages of social movements, how they develop, coalesce, institutionalize, and, sometimes, pass on. One very small piece of that history of social movements, but a piece that has great resonance for some of us, is the way that social movements relate to scholarship and the academy.

In the early days of a social movement, we often draw upon the academy for justifying arguments. Scholarship and academic work are used to buttress social movements, to provide the intellectual scaffolding on which to build a movement. We—those of us seeking to make social change with our burgeoning movement—draw upon available scholarship to show that change is necessary or at least desirable. We use anthropology to look at how other societies have organized themselves on the issue, psychology to look at how the social management of the issue affects the individual, history to look at how the issue has come to its current form, and my own discipline of sociology to look at the structural concerns, the way the problem is institutionalized. When we have drawn upon the available literature, we go on to do new research, research stimulated by the concerns raised in the social movement. One of the products of many a social movement, probably a more predictable product than social change, is research.

Later on in a social movement, the academy comes to have a very different role. Rather than being used to support the movement, scholarship develops to evaluate, analyze, and critique the movement itself. The movement itself becomes the object of study, that which is subject to discussion and analysis. The changes brought by the movement become the new institutions to be studied. And it may well come to pass that new social movements grow out of that new understanding, that new activists draw upon that scholarship to create yet newer social movements.

You know you are getting old when your work moves from the former to the latter—from the work being used to buttress a social movement to the work that is analyzed by the scholars constructing the current wave of the movement. And that has been the case with me of late. My earliest work on the home-birth movement in the United States—my dissertation and first book and other pieces of my earlier work that were part of the home birth movement, and, more generally, "the childbirth movement" and, even more generally, "the women's health movement"—is now ripe for analysis. Newer scholars, with ideas and approaches never thought of in the early days of the movement, are now taking an appropriate critical stance toward what we have—and have not—accomplished.

It seemed important, for example, at a certain point in the women's health movement, to adopt the language of "consumers and providers" rather than patients and doctors. We were, I can assure you, no longer patient. The roles of both patient and doctor had become so embedded in a particular paternalistic, gendered scheme that the vocabulary itself had to go. A "consumer," believe it or not, was a role with more dignity, more power, than that of "patient." Now why is that? It has, presumably, a great deal to do with the development of capitalism. But if your focus is on improving the position of women receiving services—and sometimes we meant that quite literally, "off our backs," up from the lithotomy position—then the reason *why* consumer seems better than patient doesn't really come up. You grope around for a different model, a better way of thinking about a woman seeking assistance in her birth or in her abortion, with her breastfeeding or with her contraception, and you use what is available. In a capitalist system, in a fully consumerist world, consumption and the language of consumers is what comes to hand.

Klassen demonstrates the more recent consequences of this in her work on "home-birth feminists"—once again, people I probably overidentify with—who borrow and simultaneously disavow the language of the market. When you try to choose a better place and way to give birth, you do end up talking about "shopping around." When you choose one type of practitioner over another, you are indeed comparing services on a marketplace. And, as Robbie Davis-Floyd and I have discussed endlessly, with each other and with midwives, when midwives offer their services, paid or unpaid, they inevitably, for good or ill, become part of the marketplace of services.

It is hard not to laugh at the "plethora of paid services surrounding home birth" these days, as Klassen points out. It struck me first with breastfeeding—the first time I spoke at a lactation conference and saw a huge room full of marketers selling special pumps, pillows, nipple creams, breastfeeding teddy bears, every imaginable and some unimaginable objects one could insert between a breast and a baby. The claim that breastfeeding was simple, direct, and out of the marketplace of baby formula became laughable as I saw the array of goods and services that had grown to surround, prop, and intervene in breastfeeding (see Linda Blum [1999] for a fuller discussion). And so, too, with home birth. I myself own a nice collection of midwifery and home-birth T-shirts!

But Klassen does not dismiss the politics, the values, the morality of the issues these women are confronting, carefully placing herself in some opposition to the "psychoanalyzing away" that Miller does. There is something there, this call to spirituality, this religious aspect to birth. I've always presented myself as "spiritually tone deaf".... and have always defended the right to not think of birth in "spiritual" terms. I'm known at midwifery meetings for easing my way out the back of the room, off to have coffee with a few likeminded friends, when the spirituality stuff gets too heavy, when the meditation sessions start, the earth goddesses get invoked too often. But, while I know absolutely that it is not the only reason women want home births, and for some of us not the reason at all, the spiritual and/or the religious is indeed a driving force for many and maybe most women in choosing home birth.

Of course, in this world the spiritual itself enters into the marketplace, and goddess necklaces, blessing rites, all kinds of goods and services come to be for sale. (Buffalo Bob would be OK with that—after selling Wonderbread, he reminded the children each Saturday morning that tomorrow they should go to the Sunday school or church of their choice to practice their freedom of religion).

And just as Klassen cannot dismiss the very powerful drive for meaning that women value in birth, Robbie Davis Floyd and I value the very real work midwives do in offering alternative meaning for birth. If birthing women stand outside of the system and choose, as intelligent critical consumers, the best birth, midwives stand in the system, negotiating between institutions and the needs of women. One of the fundamental moral dilemmas to be faced in life is how to do good in an evil system. And make no mistake: for some of us, the highly medicalized, contemporary American hospital birth is indeed evil. The overly high cesarean section rate literally kills women; the punishing treatment of their bodies, their souls, and their babies does damage.

Anyone can figure out how to be good in a good world. How can you be good, do good, in a bad world? Midwives have been debating this throughout the whole reemergence of midwifery and home birth. Some declare you must go where the women are, and if that means walking into the belly of the beast, so be it. They become hospital-based midwives, trying their hardest to treat women respectfully in a deeply demeaning institution, trying to offer spirituality in settings that deny the possibility, trying to teach women to trust themselves in systems set up not to trust women. Others stay outside of the worst of the institutions and seek to create alternative institutions. All struggle with their relationship with the state on the one hand and the women on the other.

The Woman Consumer

The story is perhaps the clearest with the midwives, but echoes abound in other birth-related services. Lactation consultants, doulas, even the sonographers, as Taylor shows, are trying to help women, trying to reach out as women to women, with respect and sometimes even awe. Yet each works within a larger system and ultimately faces corruption by that system. The sonographer strives to be "professional," to offer a high level of technical skill, the only thing for which she will be valued in the marketplace. And yet she also offers her "human skills," her highly gendered skills of understanding, relating, mediating between the machinery and the woman. In the case of the sonographer, she ends up, I would argue, placing herself between the woman and her own body, the very stance the midwives try so hard to avoid, creating for, and with the active participation of the willing woman, the fetal commodity.

The sonographer, in her eagerness to "show the baby," to (re)present the baby to the mother, participates in the erasure of the mother's own body. To make the fetus visible, the mother becomes invisible, even to herself. She turns away from her own body, away from her lived experience of the fetus, and watches it on the screen. The erasure of inconvenient mothers and the glorification of much-wanted fetuses/babies is very much the ongoing story of contemporary motherhood, with ever more sophisticated technologies being used to reify the patriarchal concept of the woman as vessel.

Sonographers participate in this erasure with their technology, but adoptive mothers do it as well, with their stories. We have here stories of two types of adoption, the Swedish adoption of children from Chile and the American adoption of children from China. In both cases the children are perhaps less valued but not racially disvalued. They are "a discrete shade of off-white," not white, perhaps, but most assuredly not black. Anagnost describes the "panda sightings," the attempts to capture "ethnicity" or "culture" with consumer goods. A baby or child is removed from its country of origin—what one of my City University of New York graduate students, Hosu Kim, has pointed out to me is another form of forced migration—and the parent/purchasers work on turning that into something cute. Something vaguely identified as "culture" or "ethnicity" displaces race and class, Anagnost claims—but that is not true for black children—and speaks primarily to the "whitening" of Asian Americans that students of whiteness have observed. It is that almost-whiteness that makes Asian children, first the Korean cohort and now the Chinese, so appealing for American would-be adopters, unlike children from Africa. Or the Bronx.

It is not only their almost-whiteness that draws Americans to China for babies, but also the almost-complete erasure of the mother. The children appear to come from orphanages, not mothers. Yngvesson quotes the Swedish social worker Stjerna, who recognizes this tension: a "roots" journey to the country is one thing, a journey to the mother would be something else again. Background and country and decoration are all fine—they are the sanitized "ethnicity" we find so charming. But the reality of a grieving mother, a woman who birthed and bled and lost, is far more than most adoptive parents want. Some, perhaps particularly the lesbian mothers drawn to Chinese adoption because it rescues girls qua girls, have particular reason to feel vulnerable, to fear that whatever power a birthmother might have might be used in conjunction with the state to threaten their already threatened families. And some adoptive families do actually seek out birthmothers. But most do not, and adoptions that promise anonymity are marketed for their reassurance to adopters.

In that way, by denying the mother herself, many adoptive parents participate in this erasure of mothers and simultaneous glorification/commodification of children. Adoptive parents, and I myself am one of those, too, bristle and feel genuine anger and revulsion when people ask about the "costs" of adoption, implying the "cost/worth" of the child. But only a comparative few of us have taken that to its logical conclusion and opened up adoptions, acknowledging and even celebrating the complicated tangle of relationships between the child, the birth mother, the adoptive parents, the other children of both sets of parents, the extended family on all sides. For most parents, by birth or by adoption, the image of the child as a product and a commodity is indelible and ownership inevitable.

Anagnost concludes with the rather chilling story of the young American lawyer who wanted to collect a complete set of Chinese children, one from each ethnic group and a couple of African ones besides. Not that it hasn't been done before. Josephine Baker in the 1950s set out to adopt one black, one white, one yellow, and one red child, what she called a "Rainbow Tribe." She ended up with twelve children from around the world, working at filling in the hard-to-collect specimens of a "red," or Indian, child and a little Jew. It is not a new thing for women of privilege to enjoy the pleasures of consumption, even in their "reproduction," and at who knows what cost to other women.

And Now What?

What I found so depressing, so distressing in reading this book is that there seems no way to think beyond consumerism. One can consume differently, but almost whatever one does as a mother becomes just one more cog in the consumer wheel. In a capitalist, consumerist system, motherhood and its defenses, its reinterpretations, the very battles of motherhood, will take this form. This is a level of analysis that could not have been done twenty-five years ago, when we were struggling to find alternatives to the medicalization of motherhood and found consumption a useful tool. And it was, and continues to be, a useful tool.

Now *that*, the editors of this volume remind me, is the other, less depressing side of this problem of commodification. In working on this piece, Janelle Taylor clarified for me that "commodification is not always or only about devaluation of people; it can also sometimes be about creating/asserting/claiming value for people." This is obviously what Wozniak shows that "foster" mothers are doing when they claim their children are children, not foster children, and consume on their behalf to so mark them. It is there also when, as Landsman shows, mothers of disabled children use consumption as a conscious strategy, "normalizing" their children as much as possible with the objects and accessories of normal childhood. They use consumption while at the same time they come to utterly reject the conceptualization of the child itself as a "commodity," let alone a flawed commodity. And it is perhaps most poignantly there, Layne shows, when mothers of babies who have died "curate" the few items of babyhood to create enough of a person out of their lost baby so that others can share in the mourning. In each case, the "foster" child, the disabled child, and the child who has died, consumption is used to claim value for a profoundly disvalued child.

In the human struggle to create meaning, to live meaningful lives, we all use the tools we have to hand. The battle is to use those tools and not be used by them. That is the action, the struggle, the work that we see going on by these mothers so richly portrayed here. As foster mothers, as adoptive mothers of racially disvalued children, as mothers of the various "rejects" of the consumer hierarchy, and even as the ordinary mothers of ordinary children in their most ordinary moments, mothers use the very consumerist language and practices to fight for their children. And it is those same tools that midwives use to fight for mothers. We speak the language of consumption, but we aim to achieve meaning and value.

We fight the good fight from within and from without, as part of the market, when as consumers, as cogs in that wheel, we try to turn it to a different purpose. My dear friend and colleague Eileen Moran reminds me that in a market economy even the critics point to the gaps between the ideology of fair and open, response markets and the reality we face, to "show how the fix is in." In other words, they buy into the ideology of the market to show how its reality does not even live up to that standard. Similarly, Eileen reminds me, if we were living in the middle ages, our critiques of the establishment would most likely be offered in religious terms, accepting at some level the religious perspective while critiquing it. "But does it matter?" she asks, ever the pragmatist and activist. "It's still resistance." Of course there is no place of purity, no "outside" to stand, and yet, to accept the religious point of view, or to accept the market point of view, does damage even while we argue against it. It is the loss of language itself that troubles and saddens me: the inability to get outside of the system even in our thoughts. If I feel that birth is something more, more than a service offered or purchased, more than a moment of consumption or production, how am I supposed to talk about that? In the language of spirituality and religion? That works for most of the women that Klassen interviewed, but it does not satisfy my needs to move outside of that system of oppression as well. How can we speak of that which we value?

The language of consumption itself cheapens the language of value, reducing it to cost. In this language, good value is a bargain! And so I, perhaps given to a rather dour view of the world anyway, come back to the depressing part of this work. We each take that which we hold sacred and try to hold it out of the marketplace. Mothers do it with their babies; I find I am tempted to do it with some abstracted, romanticized, sentimentalized idea of "motherhood." Midwives often want to do it with birth. Yet we all are functioning within a system that takes the language out of our mouths, turns it around, and pushes us further into the world of consumerism. Midwifery becomes yet another service, a purchasable commodity; a better birth, a better baby, a better midwife, a better mother, all there to be purchased in whole or in part.

I am writing this in Germany, spending a sabbatical semester talking about genetics, bioethics, and related things with German students. I am immersed at the moment in the way other systems, nonconsumerist systems, have tried to use motherhood in the service of evil. Nationalism, racism, patriarchy—those are not systems that do well by mothers either.

The relationships between human beings are something I value. They are something I think we ought to value—as individuals, as societies, as a world community. Motherhood is a, and maybe *the* prime relationship: primary in the life span of the person being mothered, primary in establishing our understandings of what it is to be connected with another human being. If motherhood is or can be a force for good in the world, one of the ways that we can learn and teach the interconnectedness of our lives, then how can we understand motherhood outside of the systems, often systems of evil, in which we live? What tools can we reach for?

REFERENCES CITED

Abadie, M. J. 1993. *Multicultural Baby Names*. Stamford, Conn.: Longmeadow.
Abold, D. 2001. "I Will Hold You in Heaven." *SHARE Newsletter* 10 (3): 5.
Adorno, T., and M. Horkheimer. 1999. *Dialectic of Enlightenment*. New York: Continuum.
Agamben, G. 1995. *Homo Sacer: Sovereign Power and Bare Life*. Stanford: Stanford University Press.
Albion, M. 1997. *Tuesdays with Morrie: An Old Man, a Young Man, and Life's Greatest Lesson*. New York: Doubleday.
Albom, M. 2002. *Tuesdays with Morrie*. New York: Doubleday.
American Academy of Pediatrics, Committee on Children with Disabilities. 2001. "Developmental Surveillance and Screening of Infants and Young Children" (RE0062). *Pediatrics* 108 (1): 192, 196.
American Automobile Association (AAA). 2001a. *Tour Book: Colorado and Utah*. Heathrow, Fla.: AAA Publishing.
———. 2001b. *Tour Book: Arizona and New Mexico*. Heathrow, Fla.: AAA Publishing.
American College of Nurse-Midwives (ACNM) and S. Jacobs. 1993. *Having Your Baby with a Nurse-Midwife*. New York: Hyperion.
Anagnost, A. 2004. "The Corporeal Politics of Quality *(Suzhi)*." *Public Culture* 16 (2).
———. 2000. "Scenes of Misrecognition: Maternal Citizenship in the Age of Transnational Adoption." *positions: east asia cultures critique* 8 (2): 390–421.
———. 1997a. "Children and National Transcendence in China." In *Constructing China: The Interaction of Culture and Economics*, ed. K. Lieberthal, S. Lin, and E. Young, 195–222. Ann Arbor: University of Michigan Center for Chinese Studies.
———. 1997b. *National Past-Times: Narrative, Representation, and Power in Modern China*. Durham, N.C.: Duke University Press.
———. 1988. "Family Violence and Magical Violence: The Woman as Victim in China's One-Child Birth Policy." *Women and Language* 9 (winter): 16–22.
———. n.d. "Maternal Perversities."
Anderson, R. E., and D. A. Anderson. 1999. "The Cost-Effectiveness of Home Birth." *Journal of Nurse-Midwifery* 4 (1): 30–35.
Andersson, G. 1991. *Intercountry Adoption in Sweden—The Experience of Twenty-five Years and 32,000 Placements*. Sundbyberg, Sweden: Adoption Centre.
Annas, George C. 1982. "Forced Cesareans: The Most Unkindest Cut of All." *Hastings Center Report* 12 (3): 16–17, 45.
Antze, P., and M. Lambek, eds. 1996. *Tense Past: Cultural Essays in Trauma and Memory*. New York: Routledge.
Apologetics Index. 2003. http://www.apologeticsindex.org/ accessed July 28.
Appadurai, A. 1996. *Modernity at Large: Cultural Dimensions of Globalization*. Minneapolis: University of Minnesota Press.

———. 1986. "Introduction: Commodities and the Politics of Value." In *The Social Life of Things: Commodities in Cultural Perspective,* ed. A. Appadurai, 3–63. Cambridge: Cambridge University Press.

———, ed. 1986. *The Social Life of Things: Commodities in Cultural Perspective.* Cambridge: Cambridge University Press.

Applbaum, K. 1998. "The Sweetness of Salvation: Consumer Marketing and the Liberal-Bourgeois Theory of Needs." *Current Anthropology* 39 (3): 323–49.

Arms, S. 1975. *Immaculate Deception.* New York: Houghton Mifflin.

Aronson, J. 1997. "Not My Homeland." Senior thesis, Hampshire College, Amherst, Mass.

Asch, A. 1999. Comments made at "Ethics, Health Care, and Disability" Forum, Princeton University, Princeton, N.J., October 12, 1999.

Austin, R. 1994. "'A Nation of Thieves': Consumption, Commerce, and the Black Public Sphere." *Public Culture* 7 (1): 225–48.

Baker, B. 1996. "A Case for Permitting Altruistic Surrogacy." *Hypatia* 11 (2): 34–48.

Baker, J. 1995. *Society of Diagnostic Medical Sonographers Focus on the Future: The History of SDMS's First Twenty-five Years.* Philadelphia: Lippincott-Raven Publishers.

Baudrillard, J., ed. 1988. *Selected Writings.* Stanford: Stanford University Press.

Beck, U., and E. Beck-Gernsheim. 1995. *The Normal Chaos of Love.* Cambridge: Polity.

Belk, R. 1985. "Trait Aspects of Living in a Material World." *Journal of Consumer Research* 12:265–79.

———. 1983. "Worldly Possessions: Issues and Criticisms." In *Advances in Consumer Research,* vol. 10, ed. R. Bagozzi and A. Tybout, 514–19. Ann Arbor, Mich.: Association for Consumer Research.

———. 1979. "Gift-Giving Behavior." In *Research in Marketing,* vol. 2, ed. J. Sheth, 95–126. Greenwich, Conn.: JAI Press.

Bell, L., and J. Ribbens. 1994. "Isolated Housewives and Complex Maternal Worlds—The Significance of Social Contacts between Women with Young Children in Industrial Societies." *Sociological Review* 42 (2): 227–62.

Benjamin, J. 1995. *Like Subjects, Love Objects: Essays on Recognition and Sexual Difference.* New Haven: Yale University Press.

Benjamin, W. 1969. "The Storyteller." In *Illuminations: Essays and Reflections,* ed. H. Arendt, trans. H. Zohn, 83–109. New York: Schocken Books.

Benoit, C., R. Davis-Floyd, E. van Teijlingen, S. Wrede, J. Sandall, and J. Miller. 2001. "Designing Midwives: A Transnational Comparison of Educational Models." In *Birth by Design: The Social Shaping of Maternity Care in Euro-America,* ed. R. DeVries, E. van Teijlingen, S. Wrede, and C. Benoit. New York: Routledge.

Berlant, L. 1997. *The Queen of America Goes to Washington City: Essays on Sex and Citizenship.* Durham, N.C.: Duke University Press.

Bierman-van Eedenburg, M. E., A. D. Jurgens-van der Zee, A. A. Olinga, H. Huisjes, and B. C. Touwen. 1981. "Predictive Value of Neonatal Neurological Examination: Follow-up Study at Eighteen Months." *Developmental Medicine and Child Neurology* 23:296–305.

Biskupic, J. 2000. "'Crack Babies' and Rights." *Washington Post* (February 29): A3.

Blizzard, D. 2000. "Building Collectivities and Enrolling Allies: A Fetoscopy Collective-in-the-Making." Chapter 4 in *The Socio-cultural Construction of Fetoscopy.* Ph.D. diss., Rensselaer Polytechnic Institute, Troy, N.Y.

Blum, Linda. 1999. *At the Breast.* New York: Houghton Mifflin.

Blume, S. 1992. *Insight and Industry: On the Dynamics of Technological Change in Medicine.* Cambridge, Mass.: MIT Press.

Bongaarts, J., and R. Potter. 1983. *Fertility, Biology, and Behavior: An Analysis of the Proximate Determinants.* New York: Academic Press.

Bordo, S. 1993. *Unbearable Weight: Feminism, Western Culture, and the Body.* Berkeley: University of California Press.

Bourdieu, P. 1984. *Distinction: A Social Critique of the Judgment of Taste.* Cambridge, Mass.: Harvard University Press.

Bourgeault, I., C. Benoit, and R. Davis-Floyd, eds. 2004. *Reconceiving Midwifery: The New Canadian Model of Care.* Toronto: McGill Queens University Press.

Bourgeault, I., and M. Fynes. 1997. "Integrating Lay and Nurse-Midwifery into the US and Canadian Health Care Systems." *Social Science and Medicine* 44 (7): 1051–63.

Boyette, K. 1996. "No Vacation." *SHARE Newsletter* 5 (3): 15.

Bricker, S. 2000. "It's Mother's Day." *UNITE Notes* 19 (1): 1.

Brison, S. 1997. "Outliving Oneself: Trauma, Memory, and Personal Identity." In *Feminists Rethink the Self,* ed. D. Meyers, 12–39. Boulder, Colo.: Westview Press.

Brown, G. 1990. *Domestic Individualism: Imagining Self in Nineteenth-Century America.* Berkeley: University of California Press.

Brown, M. 1997. *The Channeling Zone: American Spirituality in an Anxious Age.* Cambridge, Mass.: Harvard University Press.

Bruner, J. P., S. Drummond, A. Meenan, and I. M. Gaskin. 1998. "All-Fours Maneuver for Reducing Shoulder Dystocia during Labor." *Journal of Reproductive Medicine* 43:439–43.

Buchli, V., and G. Lucas. 2000. "Children, Gender, and the Material Culture of Domestic Abandonment in the Late Twentieth Century." In *Children and Material Culture,* ed. J. S. Derevenski, 131–38. London: Routledge.

Burman, E. 1995. "'What Is It?': Masculinity and Femininity in Cultural Representations of Childhood." In *Feminism and Discourse,* ed. S. Wilkinson and S. Kitzinger, 49–67. London: Sage.

Burst, H. 1983. "The Influence of Consumers on the Birthing Movement." *Topics in Clinical Nursing* 5 (3): 42–54.

Butler, J. 1993. *Bodies that Matter.* New York: Routledge.

Callon, M., C. Méadel, and V. Raberharisoa. 2002. "The Economy of Qualities." *Economy and Society* 31 (2): 194–217.

Campbell, C. 1987. *The Romantic Ethic and the Spirit of Modern Consumerism.* Oxford: Basil Blackwell.

Cannell, F. 1990. "Concepts of Parenthood: The Warnock Report, the Gillick Debate, and Modern Myths." *American Ethnologist* 17 (4): 667–86.

Carp, E. 1998. *Family Matters: Secrecy and Disclosure in the History of Adoption.* Cambridge, Mass.: Harvard University Press.

Carrier, J. 1990. "Reconciling Commodities and Personal Relations in Industrial Society." *Theory and Society* 19:579–98.

———. 1991. "Gifts, Commodities, and Social Relations: A Maussian View of Exchange." *Sociological Forum* 6 (1): 119–36.

Cartwright, E. 1998. "The Logic of Heartbeats: Electronic Fetal Monitoring and Biomedically Constructed Birth." In *Cyborg Babies: From Techno-Sex to Techno-Tots,* ed. Robbie Davis-Floyd and Joseph Dumit, 240–254. New York: Routledge.

Casey, K. 1997. "How Early Is Too Early? Mourning a Baby Lost through Miscarriage." *Sharing* 6 (2): 1–2.

Casper, M. J. 1998. *The Making of the Unborn Patient: A Social Anatomy of Fetal Surgery.* New Brunswick: Rutgers University Press.

Chaidez, S. 1985. "Lacy." In *When Hello Means Goodbye: A Guide for Parents Whose Child Dies before Birth, at Birth, or Shortly after Birth,* ed. Pat Schwiebert, RN, and Paul Kirk, MD, 16. Portland, Ore.: Perinatal Loss.

Chin, E. 2001. *Purchasing Power: Black Kids and American Consumer Culture.* Minneapolis: University of Minnesota Press.

Chodorow, N. 1995. "Individuality and Difference in How Women and Men Love." In *Psychoanalysis in Contexts,* ed. A. Elliot and S. Frosh, 89–105. London: Routledge.

Ciany, A. 1999. "I'm a Mother Too." *Sharing* 8 (3): 6.

Clark, D. 1998. "Mediadoption: Children, Commodification, and the Spectacle of Disruption." *American Studies* 39 (2): 65–86.

Clarke, A. 2002. "The Aesthetics of Social Aspiration." In *Home Possessions,* ed. D. Miller. Oxford: Berg.

——. 2000. "'Mother Swapping': The Trafficking of Nearly New Children's Wear." In *Commercial Cultures: Economies, Practices, Spaces,* ed. P. Jackson, M. Lowe, D. Miller, and F. Mort, 85–100. Oxford: Berg.

——. 1998. "Window Shopping at Home: Catalogue, Classifieds, and New Consumer Skills." In *Material Cultures,* ed. D. Miller. Chicago: Chicago University Press.

Clarke, A., and D. Miller. 2003. "Fashion and Anxiety." *Fashion Theory* 6 (2): 191–214.

Cohen, N. 1991. *Open Season: Survival Guide for Natural Childbirth and VBAC in the 90s.* New York: Bergin and Garvey.

Coleman, D. 2001. Diane Coleman, President of Not Dead Yet, to Michael D. Jenkins, Executive Director of the New Hampshire Governor's Commission on Disability, August 6.

Colen, S. 1995. "'Like a Mother to Them': Stratified Reproduction and West Indian Childcare Workers and Employers in New York." In *Conceiving the New World Order: The Global Politics of Reproduction,* ed. F. Ginsburg and R. Rapp, 78–102. Berkeley: University of California Press.

Collins, P. 1992. "Black Women and Motherhood." In *Rethinking the Family: Some Feminist Questions,* ed. B. Thorne and M. Yalom, 215–45. Boston: Northeastern University Press.

——. 1994. "Shifting the Center: Race, Class, and Feminist Theorizing about Motherhood." In *Mothering: Ideology, Experience, and Agency,* ed. E. N. Glenn, G. Chang, and L. R. Forcey. New York: Routledge.

Comaroff, J., and J. L. Comaroff. 1990. "Goodly Beasts, Beastly Goods: Cattle and Commodities in a South African Context." *American Ethnologist* 17 (2): 195–216.

Conklin, B., and L. Morgan. 1996. "Babies, Bodies, and the Production of Personhood in North American and Native Amazonian Society." *Ethos* 24 (4): 657–94.

Cook, D. 2003 "Spatial Biographies of Children's Consumption: Market Places and Spaces of Childhood in the 1930s and Beyond." *Journal of Consumer Culture* 3 (2): 147–70.

——. 1995. "The Mother as Consumer: Insights from the Children's Wear Industry, 1917–1929." *Sociological Quarterly* 36 (3): 505–22.

Cooksey, T. 1992. "The Aesthetics of Natural Theology: Charles Bucke and the Sublimities of Nature." Paper presented at the Society for Literature and Science's annual meeting, Atlanta.

Corea, G., ed. 1987. *Man-Made Women: How New Reproductive Technologies Affect Women.* Bloomington and Indianapolis: Indiana University Press.

Coste, P. 1989. "An Historical Examination of the Strategic Issues Which Influenced Technologically Entrepreneurial Firms Serving the Medical Diagnostic Ultrasound Market." Ph.D. diss., Claremont College Graduate School.

Coutin, S., B. Maurer, and B. Yngvesson. 2002. "In the Mirror: The Legitimation Work of Globalization." *Law and Social Inquiry* 27 (4): 801–43.

Coward, R. 1989. *The Whole Truth.* London: Faber and Faber.

Craig, M. 1993. "Pro-Life/Pro-Choice: A New Dilemma for Sonographers." *Journal of Diagnostic Medical Sonography* 9 (3): 152–58.

Cross, J. 1988. "I Must Go On." *SHARE Newsletter* 11 (1): 1.

Curtin, S. 1999. "Recent Changes in Birth Attendant, Place of Birth, and the Use of Obstetric Interventions." *Journal of Nurse-Midwifery* 44 (4): 349–54.

Dally, A. 1982. *Inventing Motherhood: The Consequences of an Ideal.* London: Burnett Books.

David, M., R. Edwards, M. Hughes, and J. Ribbens. 1993. *Mothers and Education: Inside Out? Exploring Family-Education Policy and Experience.* Basingstoke: Macmillan.

David, M., A. West, and J. Ribbens. 1994. *Mothers' Intuition? Choosing Secondary Schools.* London: Taylor and Francis.

Davis, E. 1997. *Heart and Hands: A Midwife's Guide to Pregnancy and Birth.* 3d ed. Berkeley, Calif.: Celestial Arts.

Davis, N. 2000. *The Gift in Sixteenth-Century France.* Madison: University of Wisconsin Press.

Davis-Floyd. 2003. "Home Birth Emergencies in the United States and Mexico: The Trouble with Transport." In *Reproduction Gone Awry,* ed. Gwynne Jenkins and Marcia Inhorn, a special issue of *Social Science and Medicine* 56 (9): 1913–91.

———. 2002. "The Technocratic, Humanistic, and Holistic Models of Birth." *International Journal of Gynecology and Obstetrics* 75, supplement 1:S5–S23.

———. 2001. "*La Partera Professional:* Articulating Identity and Cultural Space for a New Kind of Midwife in Mexico." In *Daughters of Time: The Shifting Identities of Contemporary Midwives,* ed. Robbie Davis-Floyd, Sheila Cosminsky, and Stacy Leigh Pigg, a special issue of *Medical Anthropology* 20 (2–3): 185–243.

———. 1999. "Some Thoughts on Bridging the Gap between Nurse- and Direct-Entry Midwives." *Midwifery Today* (March).

———. 1998a. "The Ups, Downs, and Interlinkages of Nurse- and Direct-Entry Midwifery: Status, Practice, and Education." In *Getting an Education: Paths to Becoming a Midwife,* 4th ed., ed. Jan Tritten and Joel Southern, 67–118. Eugene, Ore.: Midwifery Today.

———. 1998b "Types of Midwifery Training: An Anthropological Overview." In *Getting an Education: Paths to Becoming a Midwife,* 4th. ed., ed. Jan Tritten and Joel Southern, 119–33. Eugene, Ore.: Midwifery Today.

———. 1992. Birth as an American Rite of Passage. Berkeley: University of California Press.

———. 1987. "Obstetric Training as a Rite of Passage." *Medical Anthropology Quarterly* 1 (3): 288–318.

———. "The History, Ideology, and Politics of American Midwifery." Chap. 1 in *Mainstreaming Midwives: The Politics of Change,* ed. R. Davis-Floyd and C. Johnson. New York: Routledge, forthcoming.

Davis-Floyd, R., Sheila Cosminsky, and Stacy Leigh Pigg, eds. 2001. "Daughters of Time: The Shifting Identities of Contemporary Midwives," a special issue of *Medical Anthropology,* Nos. 2–3/4.

Davis-Floyd, R., and E. Davis. 1997. "Intuition as Authoritative Knowledge in Midwifery and Home Birth." In *Childbirth and Authoritative Knowledge: Cross-Cultural Perspectives,* ed. R. Davis-Floyd and C. Sargent, 315–49. Berkeley: University of California Press.

Davis-Floyd, R., and Joseph Dumit, eds. 1998. *Cyborg Babies: From Techno-Sex to Techno-Tots.* New York: Routledge.

Davis-Floyd, R., and C. Johnson, eds. *Mainstreaming Midwives: The Politics of Change.* New York: Routledge, forthcoming.

Davis-Floyd, R., and C. Sargent, eds. 1997. *Childbirth and Authoritative Knowledge: Cross-Cultural Perspectives.* Berkeley: University of California Press.

Daviss, B. A. 2001. "The Alternative Birth Movement in the U.S. and Canada: A Compari-

son." In *Birth by Design: Pregnancy, Maternity Care and Midwifery in North America and Europe*, ed. Raymond DeVries, Edwin van Teijlingen, Sirpa Wrede, and Cecilia Benoit, 145–67. New York: Routledge.
de Certeau, Michel. 1984. *The Practice of Everyday Life*. Berkeley: University of California Press.
Declercq, E., L. Paine, and M. Winter. 1995. "Home Birth in the United States, 1989–1992: A Longitudinal Descriptive Report of National Birth Certificate Data." *Journal of Nurse-Midwifery* 40 (6): 474–82.
de Grazia, V., and E. Furlough, eds. 1996. *The Sex of Things: Gender and Consumption in Historical Perspective*. Berkeley: University of California Press.
Delaney, C. 1998. *Abraham on Trial: The Social Legacy of Biblical Myth*. Princeton: Princeton University Press.
Deleuze, G. 1992. *The Fold: Leibnitz and the Baroque*. Minneapolis: University of Minnesota Press.
Derevenski, J. S., ed. 2000. *Children and Material Culture*. London: Routledge.
Derrida, J. 1976. *Of Grammatology*. Trans. G. Spivak. Baltimore: Johns Hopkins University Press.
DeVault, M. 1999. "Whose Science of Food and Health? Narratives of Profession and Activism from Public-Health Nutrition." In *Revisioning Women, Health, and Healing: Feminist, Cultural, and Technoscience Perspectives*, ed. A. Clarke and V. Olesen, 166–83. New York: Routledge.
———. 1991. *Feeding the Family: The Social Organization of Caring as Gendered Work*. Chicago: Chicago University Press.
DeVries, R. 1996. *Making Midwives Legal: Childbirth, Medicine, and the Law*. 2d ed. Columbus: Ohio State University Press.
di Leonardo, M. 1998. *Exotics at Home: Anthropologies, Others, American Modernity*. Chicago: University of Chicago Press.
———. 1987. "The Female World of Cards and Holidays: Women, Families and the Work of Kinship." *Signs* 12: 440–58.
Dirks, J. 1988. "Her Picture." *SHARE Newsletter* 11 (3): 12.
Disability Rights Education and Defense Fund (DREDF). 2002. "Against the Philosophy of Peter Singer: Statement of the Disability Rights Education and Defense Fund." Circulated on the Internet.
Doherty, M. 1991. "The Keepers of the Flame." *UNITE Notes* 10 (3): 1.
Donzelot, J. 1997. *The Policing of Families*. Baltimore: Johns Hopkins Press.
Dorow, S. 2002. "'China 'R' Us'? Care, Consumption, and Transnationally Adopted Children." In *Symbolic Childhood*, ed. D. Cook, 149–68. New York: Peter Lang.
Douglas, M. 1966. *Purity and Danger*. Harmondsworth: Penguin.
Doyle, E. 1992. "Window on the Womb." *RT Image* 5 (30): 4–6.
Doyle, L.1994. *Bordering on the Body: The Racial Matrix of Modern Fiction and Culture*. New York: Oxford University Press.
Dubowitz, L. M. S., V. Dubowitz, P. G. Palmer, G. Miller, C-L. Fawer, and M. I. Levene 1984. "Correlation of Neurologic Assessment in the Preterm Newborn Infant with Outcome at One Year." *Journal of Pediatrics* 105: 452–56.
Duncan, W. 1993. "Regulating Intercountry Adoption: An International Perspective." In *Frontiers of Family Law*, ed. A. Bainham and D. Pearl, 46–61. London: John Wiley & Sons.
Durbin, S. 1997. "Words Spoken in a Dimly Lit Room." *Journal of Diagnostic Medical Sonography* 13:175–78.
Eller, C. 1993. *Living in the Lap of the Goddess: The Feminist Spirituality Movement in America*. New York: Crossroad.

Eng, D. 2003. "Transnational Adoption and Queer Diasporas." *Social Text* 74, 21 (3): 1–37.
Epstein, J. 1995. *Altered Conditions: Disease, Medicine, and Storytelling.* New York: Routledge.
Erikson, E. 1943. "Observations on the Yurok: Childhood and World Image." *University of California Publications in American Archaeology and Ethnology* 35 (10): 257–301.
Everingham, C. 1994. *Motherhood and Modernity: An Investigation into the Rational Dimension of Mothering.* Buckingham: Open University Press.
Fackler, M. 2002. "China's Workers Pay Price in Death and Injury for Country's Export Success." Associated Press (September 9).
Fadiman, C., ed. 1985. *The Little, Brown Book of Anecdotes.* Boston: Little, Brown and Co.
Farrell Smith, J. 1983. "Parenting and Property." In *Mothering: Essays in Feminist Theory,* ed. J. Trebilcot, 199–212. Totowa, N.J.: Rowman & Allanheld.
Ferber, M., and J. Nelson, eds. 1993. *Beyond Economic Man: Feminist Theory and Economics.* Chicago: University of Chicago Press.
Fiedler, D.C., and R. Davis-Floyd. 2001. "Midwifery as a Reproductive Right." In *The Historical and Multicultural Encyclopedia of Female Reproductive Rights in the United States,* ed. J. A. Baer. New Haven, Conn.: Greenwood.
Finch, J., and D. Groves, eds. 1983. *A Labour of Love: Women, Work, and Caring.* London: Routledge and Kegan Paul.
Finch, J., and Mason, J. 2000. *Passing On: Kinship and Inheritance in England.* London: Routledge.
Finger, A. 2002. "A Modest Proposal for Preventing Disabled Children from Being a Burden to Their Parents and Society, and for Making them Beneficial to the Public, by Peter 'Stinker.'" *Ragged Edge Magazine Online,* 1.
Finnegan, J. 1993. *Shattered Dreams—Lonely Choices: Birthparents of Babies with Disabilities Talk About Adoption.* Westport, Conn.: Bergin and Garvey.
First, M., A. Francis, and H. Pincus. 1995. *Diagnostic and Statistical Manual: Handbook of Differential Diagnosis.* 4th ed. Washington, D.C.: APA Press.
Foley, B. 1985. "Our Grandparents' Day—Grief and Memories." *Unite Notes* 4 (3): 1–3.
Forty, A. 1999. "Introduction." In *The Art of Forgetting,* ed. A. Forty and S. Kuchler, 1–18. Oxford: Berg.
Foster, C. 1985. "Baby Things." *SHARE Newsletter* 8 (5): 1.
Franklin, S. 1997. *Embodied Progress: A Cultural Account of Assisted Reproduction.* New York and London: Routledge.
Franklin, S., and S. McKinnon, eds. 2001. *Relative Values: Reconfiguring Kinship Studies.* Durham, N.C.: Duke University Press.
Freidson, E. 1970. *Profession of Medicine: A Study in the Sociology of Applied Knowledge.* New York: Dodd, Mead and Co.
Freud, S. 1984. "On Narcissism: An Introduction." In *On Metapsychology,* 59–97. Harmondsworth: Penguin.
Friedeck, S. 1995a. "Milestone or Millstone." *SHARE Newsletter* 4 (5): 5.
———. 1995b. "When Remembering Becomes More Sweet Than Bitter." *SHARE Newsletter* 4 (4): 1–2.
———.1995c. "Caring for Those Special Photos." *SHARE Newsletter* 4 (4): 11.
Frye, A. 1995. *Holistic Midwifery: A Comprehensive Textbook for Midwives in Home Birth Practice.* Vol. 1, *Care during Pregnancy.* Portland, Ore.: Labyrs Press.
Fuss, D. 1995. *Identification Papers.* New York: Routledge.
Gabbe, S. 1994. "Routine versus Indicated Scans." In *Diagnostic Ultrasound Applied to Obstetrics and Gynecology,* ed. R. Sabbagha. Philadelphia: J. B. Lippincott Co.
Gailey, C. 2000. "Ideologies of Motherhood and Kinship in U.S. Adoption." In *Ideologies and*

Technologies of Motherhood: Race, Class, Sexuality, Nationalism, ed. H. Ragoné and F. Twine, 11–55. New York: Routledge.

Gallagher, J. 1995. "Collective Bad Faith: 'Protecting the Fetus.'" In *Reproduction, Ethics, and the Law: Feminist Perspectives,* ed. J. Callahan, 343–79. Bloomington: Indiana University Press.

Gardener, M. 1914. *Nursery Management.* London: Eveleigh Nash.

Gaskin, I. M. 1990. *Spiritual Midwifery.* 3d ed. Summertown, Tenn.: Book Publishing Co.

Gell, A. 1986. "Newcomers to the World of Goods: Consumption among the Muria Gonds." In *The Social Life of Things: Commodities in Cultural Perspective,* ed. Arjun Appadurai, 110–38. New York: Cambridge University Press.

Gill, G. 1998. *Mary Baker Eddy.* Cambridge, Mass.: Perseus Books.

Gilligan, C. 1982. *In a Different Voice: Psychological Theory and Women's Development.* Cambridge, Mass.: Harvard University Press.

Ginsburg, F. 1989. *Contested Lives: The Abortion Debate in an American Community.* Berkeley: University of California Press.

Ginsburg, F., and R. Rapp. 1999. "Fetal Reflections: Confessions of Two Feminist Anthropologists as Mutual Informants." In *Fetal Subjects, Feminist Positions,* ed. L. Morgan and M. Michaels, 279–95. Philadelphia: University of Pennsylvania Press.

———, eds. 1995. *Conceiving the New World Order: The Global Politics of Reproduction.* Berkeley: University of California Press.

Glenn, E., G. Chang, and L. Forcey. 1994. *Mothering: Ideology, Experience, and Agency.* London: Routledge.

Goffman, E. 1961. *Asylums: Essays on the Social Situation of Mental Patients and Other Inmates.* Garden City, N.Y.: Anchor Books.

Goldberg, B., and B. Kimmelman. 1988. *Medical Diagnostic Ultrasound: A Retrospective on Its Fortieth Anniversary.* Eastman Kodak.

Gonzalez, K. 1988. "Tears for Alycia." *UNITE Notes* 7 (4): 4.

Goodwin, J. 1997. "Where to Be Born Safely: Professional Midwifery and the Case against Home Birth." *Journal of the Society of Obstetricians and Gynecologists of Canada* 19 (11): 1179–88.

Gordon, L. 1994. *Pitied but Not Entitled: Single Mothers and the History of Welfare.* Cambridge, Mass.: Harvard University Press.

Greenhalgh, S. 1994. "Controlling Births and Bodies in Village China." *American Ethnologist* 21 (1): 3–30.

Groce, N., and J. Marks. 2000. "The Great Ape Project and Disability Rights: Ominous Undercurrents of Eugenics in Action." *American Anthropologist* 102 (4): 818–22.

Grosskurth, P. 1985. *Melanie Klein.* London: Masresfield Library.

Gullestad, M. 1986. *Kitchen Table Society: A Case Study of Family Life and Friendships of Young Working-Class Mothers in Urban Norway.* Oslo: Universitetsforlaget.

Hacking, I. 1996. "Memory Sciences, Memory Politics." In *Tense Past: Cultural Essays in Trauma and Memory,* ed. P. Antze and M. Lambek, 67–87. New York: Routledge.

Hague Convention. 1993. "Hague Conference on Private International Law, Final Act of the Seventeenth Session," May 29, 32 I.L.M. 1134.

Handwerker, P., and D. Wozniak. 1997. "Sampling Strategies for the Collection of Cultural Data." *Current Anthropology* 38 (5): 869–75.

Haraway, D. 1998. *Modest_Witness@Second_Millenium.FemaleMan©_Meets_OncoMouse™: Feminism and Technoscience.* New York and London: Routledge.

———. 1989. "A Manifesto for Cyborgs: Science, Technology, and Socialist Feminist in the 1980s." In *Coming to Terms: Feminism, Theory, Politics,* ed. E. Weed. New York: Routledge.

Hardt, M. 1999. "Affective Labor." *Boundary 2* 26 (2): 89–100.
Hardt, M., and A. Negri. 2000. *Empire.* Cambridge, Mass.: Harvard University Press.
Hardyment, C. 1983. *Dream Babies: Child Care from Locke to Spock.* London: Jonathan Cape.
Harer, W. B. 2000. "Patient Choice Cesarean." *ACOG Clinical Review* 5 (2): 1–3.
Harmon, C. 1988. "Memories." *SHARE Newsletter* 11 (3): 11.
Harris, S. 1987. "Early Detection of Cerebral Palsy: Sensitivity and Specificity of Two Motor Assessment Tools." *Journal of Perinatology* 3 (1): 11–15.
Hartouni, V. 1997. *Cultural Conceptions: On Reproductive Technologies and the Remaking of Life.* Minneapolis: University of Minnesota Press.
———. 1991. "Containing Women: Reproductive Discourse in the 1980s." In *Technoculture,* ed. Constance Penley and Andrew Ross, 27–56. Minneapolis: University of Minnesota Press.
Hayles, N. K. 1999. *How We Became Posthuman: Virtual Bodies in Cybernetics, Literature, and Informatics.* Chicago: University of Chicago Press.
Hazzell, L.D. 1976. *Commonsense Childbirth.* New York: Berkeley Medallion Books.
Heath, D. 1998. "Locating Genetic Knowledge: Picturing Marfan Syndrome and Its Traveling Constituencies." *Science, Technology, and Human Values* 23 (1): 71–97.
Hebdige, Dick. 1979. *Subculture: The Meaning of Style.* London: Melthuen.
Heil, J. 1989. "My Journey." *UNITE Notes* 9 (1): 3.
Hendon, J. 2000. "Having and Holding: Storage, Memory, Knowledge, and Social Relations." *American Anthropologist* 102 (1): 42–51.
Heringshaw, D. 1988. "My Baby's Picture." *SHARE Newsletter* 11 (1): 1.
Hermann, G. 1997. "Gift or Commodity: What Changes Hands in the U.S. Garage Sale?" *American Ethnologist* 24 (4): 910–30.
Hershey, L. 1994. "Choosing Disability." *Ms.* 5 (1): 26–32.
Hill, M. 1989. "The Role of Social Networks in the Care of Young Children." *Children and Society* 3 (3): 195–211.
Hintz, C. 1988. "Rainbows." *UNITE Notes* 7 (3): 3.
Hirsch, E. 1993. "Negotiated Limits: Interviews in South-East London." In *Technologies of Procreation,* ed. J. Edwards, S. Franklin, E. Hirsch, F. Price, and M. Strathern, 67–95. Manchester: Manchester University Press.
Hoelgaard, S. 1998. "Cultural Determinants of Adoption Policy: A Colombian Case Study." *International Journal of Law, Policy, and the Family* 12 (2): 202–41.
Hooks, B. 1990. *Yearning: Race, Gender, and Cultural Politics.* Boston: South End Press.
Houghton, P., and K. Windom. 1996a. *1995 Job Analysis of the Role of Direct-Entry Midwives.* North American Registry of Midwives.
———. 1996b. *Executive Summary of the 1995 Job Analysis of the Role of Direct-Entry Midwives.* Copies can be obtained from the NARM Education and Advocacy Department (1-888-842-4784) or see www.mana.org/NARM.
Hrdy, S. 1999. *Mother Nature: A History of Mothers, Infants, and Natural Selection.* New York: Pantheon Books.
Human Rights Watch/Asia. 1996. *Death by Default: A Policy of Fatal Neglect in China's State Orphanages.* New York: Human Rights Watch.
Ivy, M. 1995. "Have You Seen Me? Recovering the Inner Child in Late Twentieth-Century America." In *Children and the Politics of Culture,* ed. Sharon Stephens. Princeton: Princeton University Press.
Jain, S. 1998. "Mysterious Delicacies and Ambiguous Agents: Lennart Nilsson in *National Geographic."* *Configurations* 6 (3): 373–94.

James, A. 1979. "Confections, Concoctions, and Conceptions." *Journal of the Anthropological Society of Oxford* 10:83–95.
James, A., C. Jencks, and A. Prout. 1998. *Theorizing Childhood*. New York: Teacher's College Press.
James, A., and A. Prout, eds. 1990. *Constructing and Reconstructing Childhood*. London: Falmer Press.
Jay, N. 1992. *Throughout Your Generations Forever: Sacrifice, Religion, and Paternity*. Chicago: University of Chicago Press.
Jeffries, L. 1998. "Remembering." *UNITE Notes* 17 (2): 5.
Jenkins, M. 2001. Michael Jenkins to Diane Coleman, August 14.
Jewell, S. 1993. *From Mammy to Miss America and Beyond: Cultural Images and the Shaping of U.S. Social Policy*. New York: Routledge.
Johansson, S., and O. Nygren. 1993. "The Missing Girls of China: A New Demographic Account." *Population and Development Review* 19 (2): 35–51.
Johnson, H. 2003. "Unspeakable Conversations." *New York Times Sunday Magazine* (February 16).
Johnson, K. 1997. "Randomized Controlled Trials as Authoritative Knowledge: Keeping an Ally from Becoming a Threat to North American Midwifery Practice." In *Childbirth and Authoritative Knowledge: Cross-Cultural Perspectives*, ed. R. Davis-Floyd and C. F. Sargent, 350–65. Berkeley: University of California Press.
Johnson, K., and B. A. Daviss. 2001. "Results of the CPM Statistics Project 2000: A Prospective Study of Births by Certified Professional Midwives in North America." Abstract presented at the annual meeting of the American Public Health Association, Atlanta, Georgia.
Johnson, K., B. Huang, and L. Y. Wang. 1998. "Infant Abandonment and Adoption in China." *Population and Development Review* 24 (3): 469–510.
Johnson, M. 2001. "'A Kick in the Face,' Says Not Dead Yet," *Ragged Edge Magazine Online Extra* (October).
Kahn, R. 1995. *Bearing Meaning: The Language of Birth*. Urbana and Chicago: University of Illinois Press.
Kaplan, A. 1994. "Look Who's Talking, Indeed: Fetal Images in Recent North American Visual Culture." In *Mothering: Ideology, Experience, and Agency*, ed. E. Glenn, G. Chang, and L. Forcey, 121–37. London: Routledge.
Kashnitz, M. 1990. *The House of Childhood*. Trans. Anni Whissen. Lincoln: University of Nebraska Press.
Kaufert, P., and J. O'Neil. 1993. "Analysis of a Dialogue on Risks in Childbirth: Clinicians, Epidemiologists, and Inuit Women." In *Knowledge, Power, and Practice: The Anthropology of Medicine and Everyday Life*, ed. S. Lindenbaum and M. Lock, 32–54. Berkeley: University of California Press.
Keller, E. 1997. "Secrets of God, Nature, and Life." In *The Gender/Sexuality Reader*, ed. R. Lancaster and M. di Leonardo, 209–18. New York: Routledge.
Kelly, M. 1983. *Post-Partum Document*. London: Routledge and Kegan Paul.
Kelly, M., and E. Apter. 1993. "The Smell of Money: Mary Kelly in Conversation with Emily Apter." In *Fetishism as Cultural Discourse*, ed. E. Apter and W. Pietz, 352–62. Ithaca, N.Y.: Cornell University Press.
Kevles, B. 1997. *Naked to the Bone: Medical Imaging in the Twentieth Century*. New Brunswick: Rutgers University Press.
Kim, E. 2003. "Wedding Citizenship and Culture: Korean Adoptees and the Global Family of Korea." *Social Text* 74, 21 (1): 57–81.

Kirk, D. 1981. *Shared Fate: A Theory of Adoption and Mental Health.* New York: Free Press.
Kirmayer, L. 1996. "Landscapes of Memory: Trauma, Narrative, and Dissociation." In *Tense Past: Cultural Essays in Trauma and Memory,* ed. P. Antze and M. Lambek, 173–98. New York: Routledge.
Kittler, F. 1997. *Literature, Media, Information Systems: Essays,* ed. J. Johnston. Amsterdam: Overseas Publishers Association.
Klassen, P. 2001. *Blessed Events: Religion and Home Birth in America.* Princeton: Princeton University Press.
Klein, M. 1975. *Envy and Gratitude and Other Works.* London: Delacourte Press.
Kligman, G. 1995. "Political Demography: The Banning of Abortion in Ceausescu's Romania." In *Conceiving the New World Order: The Global Politics of Reproduction,* ed. F. Ginsburg and R. Rapp, 234–55. Berkeley: University of California Press.
Kluckhohn, C., and D. Leighton. 1974. *The Navaho.* Cambridge, Mass.: Harvard University Press.
Knopf, B. 1999. "My Journey . . . My Memories." *SHARE Newsletter* 8 (4): 1.
Kocan, Ron. 1984. "My Life Starts as the Suffering Ends." *SHARE Newsletter* 7 (3): 4–5.
Kopytoff, B. 1988. "Surrogate Motherhood: Questions of Law and Values." *University of San Francisco Law Review* 22 (2/3): 205–49.
Kopytoff, I. 1986. "The Cultural Biography of Things: Commoditization as a Process." In *The Social Life of Things: Commodities in Cultural Perspective,* ed. A. Appadurai, 64–91. Cambridge: Cambridge University Press.
Kundera, M. 2000. *Ignorance.* Trans. L. Asher. New York: HarperCollins.
Kunisch, J. 1989. "Electronic Fetal Monitors: Marketing Forces and the Resulting Controversy." In *Healing Technology: Feminist Perspectives,* ed. K. S. Ratcliff, 41–60. Ann Arbor: University of Michigan Press.
Ladd-Taylor, M., and L. Umansky, eds. 1998. *"Bad" Mothers: The Politics of Blame in Twentieth-Century America.* New York and London: New York University Press.
Lambek, Michael. 1996. "The Past Imperfect: Remembering as Moral Practice." In *Tense Past: Cultural Essays in Trauma and Memory,* ed. P. Antze and M. Lambek, 235–54. New York: Routledge.
Lamphere, L. 1977. *To Run After Them: Cultural and Social Bases of Cooperation in a Navajo Community.* Tucson: University of Arizona Press.
Landsman, G. 2003. "Emplotting Children's Lives: Developmental Delay vs. Disability." *Social Science and Medicine* 56:1947–60.
———. 2000. "'Real' Motherhood, Class, and Children with Disabilities." In *Ideologies and Technologies of Motherhood,* ed. H. Ragoné and F. Twine, 169–90. New York: Routledge.
———. 1999. "Does God Give Special Kids to Special Parents? Personhood and the Child with Disabilities as Gift and as Giver." In *Transformative Motherhood: On Giving and Getting in a Consumer Culture,* ed. L. Layne, 133–66. New York: New York University Press.
———. 1998. "Reconstructing Motherhood in the Age of 'Perfect' Babies: Mothers of Infants and Toddlers with Disabilities." *Signs* 24 (1): 69–99.
Lang, R. 1972. *The Birth Book.* Palo Alto: Genesis Press.
Larson, E. 1992. *The Naked Consumer: How Our Private Lives Become Public Commodities.* New York: Henry Holt.
Latour, B. 1993. *We Have Never Been Modern.* New York: Harvester Wheatsheaf.
Laux, J. 1988. "Baby Questionnaire—Part II." *SHARE Newsletter* 11 (4): 10–12.
———. 1985. "Untitled." *SHARE Newsletter* 8 (4): 1.

Lay, Mary. 2000. *The Rhetoric of Midwifery: Gender, Knowledge, and Power.* New Brunswick N.J.: Rutgers University Press.

Layne, L. Forthcoming a. "Birth, Death, and Materiality." *Sage Handbook of Material Culture,* ed. C. Tilley, W. Keane, S. Kuechler, M. Rowlands and P. Spyer.

———. Forthcoming b. "'Your Child Deserves a Name': Names, Naming, and the Meropolitics of Pregnancy Loss." In *Tropes of Entanglement: Towards an Anthropology of Names and Naming,* ed. G. vom Bruck and B. Bodenhorn. Cambridge University Press.

———. Forthcoming c. "Unintended Consequences of New Reproductive and Information Technologies on the Experience of Pregnancy Loss." In *Women, Gender, and Technology,* ed. S. Rosser, M. Fox and D. Johnson. Champaign: University of Illinois Press.

———. 2003a. *Motherhood Lost: A Feminist Account of Pregnancy Loss in America.* New York: Routledge.

———. 2003b. "Unhappy Endings: A Feminist Reappraisal of the Women's Health Movement from the Vantage of Pregnancy Loss." In *Reproduction Gone Awry,* ed. M. Inhorn and G. Jenkins, special issue of *Social Science and Medicine* 56:1881–91.

———. 2001. "'In Search of Community': Tales of Pregnancy Loss in Three Toxically-Assaulted Communities in the US." *Women's Studies Quarterly* 29 (1/2): 25–50.

———. 2000a. "'He was a Real Baby with Baby Things': A Material Culture Analysis of Personhood and Pregnancy Loss." *Journal of Material Culture* 5 (3): 321–45.

———. 2000b. "'The Cultural Fix': An Anthropological Contribution to Science and Technology Studies." *Science, Technology, and Human Values* 25 (4): 355–77.

———. 2000c. "Baby Things as Fetishes? Memorial Goods, Simulacra, and the 'Realness' Problem of Pregnancy Loss." In *Ideologies and Technologies of Motherhood,* ed. H. Ragoné and F. Twine, 111–38. New York: Routledge.

———, ed. 2000. *Transformative Motherhood: On Giving and Getting in a Consumer Culture.* New York: New York University Press.

———. 1999a. "'True Gifts from God': Of Motherhood, Sacrifice, and Enrichment in the Context of Pregnancy Loss." In *Transformative Motherhood,* ed. L. Layne, 167–214. New York: New York University Press.

———. 1999b. "Introduction: New Directions in EuroAmerican Gift Exchange." In *Transformative Motherhood,* ed. L. Layne, 1–27. New York: New York.

———. 1999c. "'I Remember the Day I Shopped for Your Layette': Goods, Fetuses and Feminism in the Context of Pregnancy Loss." In *Fetal Subjects, Feminist Positions,* ed. L. Morgan and M. Michaels, 251–78. Philadelphia: University of Pennsylvania Press.

———. 1998. "'He Was a Real Baby with Baby Things': A Material Cultural Analysis of Personhood and Pregnancy Loss." In *Ideologies and Technologies of Motherhood,* ed. H. Ragoné and F. Twine. New York: Routledge.

———. 1997. "Breaking the Silence: An Agenda for a Feminist Discourse of Pregnancy Loss." *Feminist Studies* 23 (2): 289–315.

———. 1996. "'Never Such Innocence Again': Irony, Nature, and Technoscience in Narratives of Pregnancy Loss." In *Comparative Studies in Pregnancy Loss,* ed. R. Cecil, 131–52. Oxford: Berg Publishers.

———. 1992. "Of Fetuses and Angels: Fragmentation and Integration in Narratives of Pregnancy Loss." Special issue of *Knowledge and Society,* ed. D. Hess and L. Layne, 9:29–58. Hartford, Conn.: JAI Press.

Lears, T. J. J. 1983. "From Salvation to Self-Realization: Advertising and the Therapeutic Roots of Consumer Culture, 1880–1930." In *The Culture of Consumption,* ed. R. W. Fox and T. J. J. Lears, 3–38. New York: Pantheon.

Leavitt, J. 1986. *Brought to Bed: Childbearing in America, 1750–1950.* New York: Oxford University Press.
Liem, D. 2000. *First Person Plural.* Ho-Ho-Kus, N.J.: Mu Films.
Lifton, B. 1994. *Journey of the Adopted Self: A Quest for Wholeness.* New York: Basic Books.
Lo, K. n.d. "Welcome to Theme Park Hong Kong: Giant Panda, Mickey Mouse, and Other Transnational Objects of Fantasy." Unpublished manuscript.
Lohr, D. 1986. "In Memory of Daniel Lohr Elbling." *SHARE Newsletter* 9 (2): 3.
Longhurst, R. 1999. "Pregnant Bodies, Public Scrutiny: 'Giving' Advice to Pregnant Women." In *Embodied Geographies: Space, Bodies, and Rites of Passage,* ed. E. K. Teather. London: Routledge.
Löwstedt, B. 1997. "Möte med rötter (Meeting with roots)." *Att Adoptera* 28 (2): 20–21.
Lowe, D. 1995. *The Body in Late-Capitalist USA.* Durham, N.C.: Duke University Press.
Lowe, L. 1996. *Immigrant Acts: On Asian American Cultural Politics.* Durham, N.C.: Duke University Press.
Luker, K. 1984. *Abortion and the Politics of Motherhood.* Berkeley: University of California Press.
Lury, C. 1996. *Consumer Culture.* New Brunswick, N.J.: Rutgers University Press.
Lyotard, J-F. 1984. *The Postmodern Condition: A Report on Knowledge.* Trans. G. Bennington and B. Massumi. Minneapolis: University of Minnesota Press.
MacDonald, M. 2001. "The Role of Midwifery Clients in the New Midwifery in Canada: Postmodern Negotiations with Medical Technology." *Medical Anthropology* 20 (2–3): 245–57. Special issue, *Daughters of Time: The Shifting Identities of Postmodern Midwives,* ed. R. Davis-Floyd and S. Cosminsky.
MacDorman, M., and G. Singh. 1998. "Midwifery Care, Social and Medical Risk Factors, and Birth Outcomes in the U.S.A." *Journal of Epidemiology and Community Health* 52:310–17.
Macklin, R. 1996. "What Is Wrong with Commodification?" In *New Ways of Making Babies: The Case of Egg Donation,* ed. C. Cohen. Bloomington: Indiana University Press.
Marshall, G., H. Newby, D. Rose, and C. Vogler, eds. 1988. *Social Class in Modern Britain.* London: Hutchinson.
Martin, E. 1987. *The Woman in the Body: A Cultural Analysis of Reproduction.* Boston: Beacon Press.
Marty, M. 1995. "Materialism and Spirituality in American Religion." In *Rethinking Materialism,* ed. R. Wuthnow, 237–53. Grand Rapids, Mich.: Eerdmans.
Marx, K. 1978. "Capital." In The Marx-Engels Reader, ed. R. Tucker. New York: W. W. Norton.
———. 1977. "Economic and Philosophical Manuscripts." In Karl Marx: Selected Writings, ed. David McLellan, 75–112. Oxford: Oxford University Press.
Massey, D. 1994. *Space, Place, and Gender.* Minneapolis: University of Minnesota Press.
Mauss, M. 1990. *The Gift: The Form and Reason for Exchange in Archaic Societies.* New York: W. W. Norton, 1990.
Mavor, C. 1995. *Pleasures Taken: Performance of Sexuality and Loss in Victorian Photographs.* Durham, N.C.: Duke University Press.
May, M., and R. Davis-Floyd. "Dreams and Nightmares: Midwifery in New York." In *Mainstreaming Midwifes: The Politics of Change,* ed. R. Davis-Floyd and C. Johnson. New York: Routledge, forthcoming.
McCannell, K. 1988. "Social Networks and the Transition to Motherhood." In *Families and Social Networks,* ed. R. M. Milardo. Newbury Park: Sage.
McCauley, B. 1986. "Only a Miscarriage." *UNITE Notes* 5 (5): 4.
McClintock, A. 1995. *Imperial Leather: Race, Gender, and Sexuality in the Colonial Context.* New York: Routledge.

McNeal, J. 1999. *The Kids' Market: Myths and Realities.* New York: Paramount.

McRobbie, Angela. 1988. *Zoot Suits and Second Hand Dresses: An Anthology of Fashion and Music.* Boston: Unwin and Hyman.

Meredith, J. 1988. "God's Will." *SHARE Newsletter* 11 (2): 2.

Merleau-Ponty, M. 1968. *The Visible and the Invisible.* Evanston, Ill.: Northwestern University Press.

Michaels, M. 1999. "Fetal Galaxies: Some Questions About What We See." In *Fetal Subjects, Feminist Positions,* ed. L. Morgan and M. Michaels, 113–32. Philadelphia: University of Pennsylvania Press.

Miller, A. 1984. "You're Not Here." *SHARE Newsletter* 7 (4): 1.

Miller, C. 1988. "Shoes Never Worn." *SHARE Newsletter* 11 (2): 1.

Miller, Daniel. 2000. *The Dialectics of Shopping.* Chicago: Chicago University Press.

———. 1998a. *A Theory of Shopping.* Ithaca: Cornell University Press.

———. 1998b. "John Lewis and the Cheapjack: A Study of Class and Identity." In *Shopping, Place, and Identity,* ed. D. Miller, P. Jackson, N. Thrift, B. Holbrook, and M. Rowlands. London: Routledge.

———. 1997. "How Infants Grow Mothers in North London." *Theory, Culture, and Society* 14 (4): 67–88. Reprinted in this volume.

———. 1995. "Consumption and Commodities." *Annual Reviews in Anthropology* 24: 141–61.

———. 1987. *Material Culture and Mass Consumption.* Oxford: Blackwell.

———, ed. 1995. *Acknowledging Consumption.* London: Routledge.

Miller, Janneli. 2002. "Midwives' Magical Speech." Unpublished manuscript.

Mitchell, L. M.. 2001. *Baby's First Picture: Ultrasound and the Politics of Fetal Imaging.* Toronto: University of Toronto Press.

Mitchell, W. J. T. 1986. *Iconology: Image, Text, Ideology.* Chicago: University of Chicago Press.

Modell, J. 1994. *Kinship with Strangers: Adoption and Interpretations of Kinship in American Culture.* Berkeley: University of California Press.

Mom. 1985. "Hello, Little Son." In *When Hello Means Goodbye: A Guide for Parents Whose Child Dies before Birth, at Birth, or Shortly after Birth,* ed. P. Schwiebert and P. Kirk, 22. Portland, Ore.: Perinatal Loss.

Moore, R. 1994. *Selling God: American Religion in the Marketplace of Culture.* New York: Oxford University Press.

Morgan, A., and J. Aldag. 1996. "Early Identification of Cerebral Palsy Using a Profile of Abnormal Motor Patterns." *Pediatrics* 98 (4): 692–97.

Morgan, L. 1996. "Fetal Relationality in Feminist Philosophy: An Anthropological Critique." *Hypatia: A Journal of Feminist Philosophy* 11 (3): 47–70.

Morgan, L. M., and M. W. Michaels, eds. 1999. *Fetal Subjects, Feminist Positions.* Philadelphia: University of Pennsylvania Press.

Morley, D., and K. Robins. 1989. "Spaces of Identity: Communications Technologies and the Reconfiguration of Europe." *Screen* 30 (4): 10–34.

Murphy, J. 1991. "Remembering . . . Looking Forward." *UNITE Notes* 10 (2): 2–3.

Myers-Ciecko, J. 1999. "Evolution and Current Status of Direct-Entry Midwifery Education, Regulation, and Practice in the United States, with Examples from Washington State." *Journal of Nurse-Midwifery* 44 (4): 384–93.

Nagele, D. 1986a. "For Jonathan." *UNITE Notes* 6 (1): 3.

———. 1986b. "Untitled." *UNITE Notes* 6 (1): 4.

Nancy, J-L. 1991. *The Inoperative Community.* Minneapolis: University of Minnesota Press.

Narayan, U. 1995. "The 'Gift' of a Child: Commercial Surrogacy, Gift Surrogacy, and Motherhood." In *Expecting Trouble: Surrogacy, Abuse, and New Reproductive Technologies*, ed. P. Boling, 177–201. Boulder, Colo.: Westview Press.

Nelson, D. 2002. "Indian Giver or Noble Savage: Duping, Assumptions of Identity, and Other Double Entendres in Rigoberta Menchú Tum's Stoll/en Past." *American Ethnologist* 28 (2): 303–31.

Nelson, K., and J. Ellenberg. 1982. "Children Who 'Outgrew' Cerebral Palsy." *Pediatrics* 69 (5): 529–36.

Nelson, M. K. 1994. "Family Day Care Providers: Dilemmas of Daily Practice." In *Mothering: Ideology, Experience, and Agency*, ed. E. N. Glenn, G. Chang, and L. R. Forcey, 181–209. New York and London: Routledge.

Negri, A. 1999. "Value and Affect." *Boundary* 2 26 (2): 77–88.

Negri, A., and M. Hardt. 2002. "'Subterranean Passages of Thought': Empire's Inserts." *Cultural Studies* 16 (2): 193–212.

Niehoff, M. 1994. "Healing Memories." *SHARE Newsletter* 2 (4): 1, 4.

Nilsson, L. 1966. *A Child Is Born: The Drama of Life before Birth in Unprecedented Photographs: A Practical Guide for the Expectant Mother*. Photos: L. Nilsson. Text: A. Ingelman-Sundberg and C. Wirsén. Trans.: B. and C. Wirsén and A. MacMillan. New York: Delacorte Press.

Norsigian, J. 1996. "The Women's Health Movement in the United States." In *Man-Made Medicine: Women's Health, Public Policy and Reform*, ed. K. Moss, 79–97. Durham: Duke University Press.

Oakley, A. 1984. *The Captured Womb: A History of the Medical Care of Pregnant Women*. London: Basil Blackwell.

Ortron, L. 2000. *The Vermont Country Store Holiday Catalogue*. Weston, Vt.

Overall, C. 1987. *Ethics and Human Reproduction: A Feminist Analysis*. Boston: Allen & Unwin.

Page, H. 1953. *Playtime in the First Five Years*. London: Allen and Unwin.

Paine, L. L., C. M. Dower, and E. O'Neil. 1999. "Midwifery in the Twenty-first Century: Recommendations from the Pew Health Professions Commission/UCSF Center for the Health Professions 1998 Taskforce on Midwifery." *Journal of Nurse Midwifery* 44 (4): 341–48.

Parker, R. 1995. *Torn in Two: The Experience of Maternal Ambivalence*. London: Virago.

Parvati-Baker, J. 1992. "The Shamanic Dimension of Childbirth." *Pre- and Perinatal Psychology Journal* 7 (1): 5–20.

Pavlak, F. 1984. "Sarah's Secret Life." *SHARE Newsletter* 7 (3): 3.

Petchesky, R. 1995. "The Body as Property: A Feminist Re-vision." In *Conceiving the New World Order: The Global Politics of Reproduction*, ed. F. Ginsburg and R. Rapp, 387–406. Berkeley: University of California Press.

———. 1987. "Foetal Images: The Power of Visual Images in the Politics of Reproduction." In *Reproductive Technologies: Gender, Motherhood, and Medicine*, ed. M. Stanworth. Minneapolis: University of Minnesota Press.

Pietz, W. 1987. "The Problem of the Fetish, II." *Res* 13:23–46.

———. 1985. "The Problem of the Fetish, I." *Res* 9:5–17.

Pointon, M. 1999. "Materializing Mourning: Hair, Jewellery and the Body." In *Material Memories: Design and Evocation*, ed. M. Kwint, C. Breward, and J. Aynsley, 39–57. Oxford: Berg.

Polanyi, K. 1944. *The Great Transformation*. New York: Rinehart.

Pospisil, L. 1963. *Kapauku Papuan Economy*. Yale University Publications in Anthropology, No. 67. New Haven: Yale University.

Press, N., C. Browner, D. Tran, C. Morton, and B. LeMaster. 1998. "Provisional Normalcy and 'Perfect' Babies: Pregnant Women's Attitudes Toward Disability in the Context of Prenatal Testing." In *Reproducing Reproduction: Kinship, Power, and Technological Innovation,* ed. S. Franklin and H. Ragoné, 46–65. Philadelphia: University of Pennsylvania Press.

Princen, T., M. Maniates, and K. Conca, eds. 2002. *Confronting Consumption.* Cambridge, Mass.: MIT Press.

Probyn, E. 1996. *Outside Belongings.* New York: Routledge.

Rabuzzi, K. 1994. *Mother with Child: Transformations through Childbirth.* Bloomington: Indiana University Press.

Rafael, V. 2000. "The Undead: Photography in the Philippines, 1988–1920s." In *White Love and Other Events in Filipino History.* Durham, N.C.: Duke University Press.

Ragoné, H. 1999. "The Gift of Life: Surrogate Motherhood, Gamete Donation, and Construction of Altruism." In *Transformative Motherhood: On Giving and Getting in a Consumer Culture,* ed. L. Layne, 65–88. New York: New York University Press.

———. 1996. "Chasing the Blood Tie: Surrogate Mothers, Adoptive Mothers, and Fathers." *American Ethnologist* 23 (2): 352–65.

———. 1994. *Surrogate Motherhood: Conception in the Heart.* Boulder, Colo.: Westview Press.

Ragoné. H., and F. W. Twine, eds. 2000. *Ideologies and Technologies of Motherhood: Race, Class, Sexuality, Nationalism.* New York and London: Routledge.

Ramamurthy, P. 2003. "Material Consumers, Fabricating Subjects: Perplexity, Global Discourses, and Transnational Feminist Research Practices." *Cultural Anthropology* 18 (4): 524–50.

Rapp, R. 1999. *Testing Women, Testing the Fetus: The Social Impact of Amniocentesis in America.* New York: Routledge.

Reed, A., and J. E. Roberts. 2000. "State Regulation of Midwives: Issues and Options." *Journal of Midwifery and Women's Health* 45 (2): 130–49.

Reid, M. 1989. "Sisterhood and Professionalization: A Case Study of the American Lay Midwife." In *Women as Healers: Cross-Cultural Perspectives,* ed. C. McClain, 219–38. New Brunswick: Rutgers University Press.

Ribbens, J. 1994. *Mothers and Their Children.* London: Sage.

Rich, A. 1986. *Of Woman Born: Motherhood as Experience and Institution.* New York: Norton.

Roberts, D. 1997. *Killing the Black Body: Race, Reproduction, and the Meaning of Liberty.* New York: Vintage.

———. 1991. "Punishing Drug Addicts Who Have Babies: Women of Color, Equality, and the Right of Privacy." *Harvard Law Review* 104: 124–55.

Romero, M. 1992. *Maid in the U.S.A.* New York and London: Routledge.

Rooks, J. 1997. *Midwifery and Childbirth in America.* Philadelphia: Temple University Press.

Rooks, J. P., and S. H. Fishman. 1980. "American Nurse-Midwifery Practice in 1976–1977: Reflections on Fifty Years of Growth and Development." *American Journal of Public Health* 70:990–96.

Rose, C. 1984. "To My Darling Erin, On Her Birthday." *SHARE Newsletter* 7 (5): 4.

Rose, J. 1993. *The Case of Peter Pan, or, the Impossibility of Children's Fiction.* Philadelphia: University of Pennsylvania Press.

Rose, N. 1996. "Identity, Genealogy, History." In *Questions of Cultural Identity,* ed. S. Hall and P. du Gay, 128–50. London: Sage Publications.

Rothman, B. K. 1992. "Not All That Glitters Is Gold." *Special Supplement, Hastings Center Report* (July–August): S12–15.

———. 1989. "Motherhood under Capitalism." In *Recreating Motherhood: Ideology and Technology in a Patriarchal Society,* 39–50. New York: Norton. Reprinted in this volume.

———. 1983. "Midwives in Transition: The Structure of a Clinical Revolution." *Social Problems* 30 (3): 262–71.

———. 1982. *In Labor: Women and Power in the Birthplace*. New York: W. W. Norton and Co.

Rowland, R. 1992. *Living Laboratories: Women and Reproductive Technologies*. Bloomington and Indianapolis: Indiana University Press.

Rozin, P., C. Nemeroff, M. Wane, and A. Sherrod. 1989. "Operation of the Sympathetic Magical Law of Contagion in Interpersonal Attitudes among Americans." *Bulletin of the Psychonomic Society* 27: 367–70.

Rubinstein, I. 2001. "Storytelling with Our Hearts." *UNITE Notes* 19 (4): 3.

Ruddick, S. 1994. "Thinking Mothers/Conceiving Birth." In *Representations of Motherhood*, ed. D. Basin, M. Honey, and M. Kaplan, 29–45. New Haven: Yale University Press.

———. 1982. "Maternal Thinking." In *Rethinking the Family: Some Feminist Questions*, ed. B. Thorne and M. Yalom. New York: Longman.

Ryan, J. 1999. "Memories." *SHARE Newsletter* 8 (4): 9.

Saffian, S. 1998. *Ithaka: A Daughter's Memoir of Being Found*. New York: Basic Books.

Sahlins, M. 1996. "The Sadness of Sweetness: The Native Anthropology of Western Cosmology." *Current Anthropology* 37 (3): 395–428.

———. 1994. "Cosmologies of Capitalism: The Trans-Pacific Sector of 'The World System.'" In *Culture/Power/History: A Reader in Contemporary Social Theory*, ed. N. Dirks, G. Eley, and S. Ortner, 412–55. Princeton: Princeton University Press.

Saigal, S., B. L. Stoskopf, D. Feeny, W. Furlong, E. Burrows, P. L. Rosenbaum, and L. Hoult. 1999. "Differences in Preferences for Neonatal Outcomes among Health Care Professionals, Parents, and Adolescents." *JAMA* 281 (21): 1991–97.

Sampson, D. 1998. "Rejecting Zoe Baird: Class Resentment and the Working Mother." In *"Bad" Mothers: The Politics of Blame in Twentieth-Century America*, ed. M. Ladd-Taylor and L. Umansky, 310–18. New York: New York University Press.

Sandelowski, M. 1993. *With Child in Mind: Studies of the Personal Encounter with Infertility*. Philadelphia: University of Pennsylvania Press.

Santner, E. 1996. *My Own Private Germany: Daniel Paul Schreber's Secret History of Modernity*. Princeton, N.J.: Princeton University Press.

Sants, H. J. 1964. Genealogical Bewilderment in Children with Substitute Parents. *British Journal of Medical Psychology* 37:133–41.

Sarah, R. 1987. "Power, Certainty and the Fear of Death." *Women and Health* 13 (1–2): 59–71.

Sautman, B. 1996. "Theories of East Asian Intellectual and Behavioral Superiority and Discourses on 'Race Differences.'" *positions: east asia cultures critique* 4 (3): 519–68.

Savage, M., J. Barlow, P. Dickens, and T. Fielding. 1992. *Property, Bureaucracy, and Culture: Middle Class Formation in Contemporary Britain*. London: Routledge.

Scanlon, J. 2000. *The Gender and Consumer Culture Reader*. New York: New York University Press.

Scheper-Hughes, N. 1990. "Difference and Danger: The Cultural Dynamics of Childhood Stigma, Rejection, and Rescue." *Cleft Palate Journal* 27 (3): 301–6.

Schlinger, Hilary. 1992. *Circle of Midwives*. Layfayette, N.Y.: author.

Schmidt, L. 1999. "Trust and Confidence in American Religious History." In *Perspectives in American Religion and Culture*, ed. P. Williams, 366–77. Malden, Mass.: Blackwell.

———. 1997. "Practices of Exchange: From Market Culture to Gift Economy in the Interpretation of American Religion" In *Lived Religion in America*, ed. D. Hall, 69–91. Princeton: Princeton University Press.

———. 1996. *Consumer Rites: The Buying and Selling of American Holidays*. Princeton: Princeton University Press.

Schmidt, M., and L. J. Moore. 1998. "Constructing a 'Good Catch,' Picking a Winner." In

Cyborg Babies: From Techno-Sex to Techno-Tots, ed. R. Davis-Floyd and J. Dumit, 21–39. New York: Routledge.

Schneider, D. 1980. *American Kinship: A Cultural Account.* 2d ed. Chicago: University of Chicago Press.

Schor, J., and D. Hope, eds. 2000. *The Consumer Society: A Reader.* New York: New Press.

Schwaegler, S. 1989. "Pink Roses." *SHARE Newsletter* 12 (1): 1.

Schweibert, P. 1985. "Please Don't Tell Them You Never Got to Know Me." In *When Hello Means Goodbye: A Guide for Parents Whose Child Dies before Birth, at Birth, or Shortly after Birth.* Portland, Ore.: Perinatal Loss.

Scoggin, J. 1996. "How Nurse-Midwives Define Themselves in Relation to Nursing, Medicine, and Midwifery." *Journal of Nurse-Midwifery* 41 (1): 36–42.

Segura, D. A. 1994. "Working at Motherhood: Chicana and Mexican Immigrant Mothers and Employment." In *Mothering: Ideology, Experience, and Agency,* ed. E. N. Glenn, G. Chang, and L. R. Forcey, 211–33. New York and London: Routledge.

Seiter, E. 1993. *Sold Separately: Parents and Children in Consumer Culture.* New Brunswick, N.J.: Rutgers University Press.

Shanley, L. K. 1994. *Unassisted Childbirth.* Westport, Conn.: Bergin and Garvey.

Sharma, U. 1986. *Women's Work, Class, and the Urban Household: A Study of Shimla, North India.* London: Tavistock.

Sharp, L. A. 2000. "The Commodification of the Body and Its Parts." *Annual Reviews in Anthropology* 29 (1): 287–328.

———. 2001. "Commodified Kin: Death, Mourning, and Competing Claims on the Bodies of Organ Donors in the United States." *American Anthropologist* 103 (1): 112–33.

Sharpe, M. 2001. "Exploring Legislated Ontario Midwifery: Texts, Ruling Relations, and Ideological Practices." In *Reconceiving Midwifery: The New Canadian Model of Care,* ed. I. Bourgeault, C. Benoit, and R. Davis-Floyd. Toronto: McGill Queens University Press.

Sharpe, S. 1999. "Bodily Speaking: Spaces and Experience of Birth." In *Embodied Geographies: Space, Bodies and Rites of Passage,* ed. E. K. Teather. London: Routledge.

Shue, V. 1999. "Sublime Sacrifices: Three Texts on Charity and Nationalism in Twentieth-Century China." Paper presented at the conference on "Nationalism: The East Asian Experience," Academica Sinica, Taipei, May 25–28.

Simmel, G. 1978. *The Philosophy of Money,* ed. D. Frisby, trans. T. Bottomore and D. Frisby. New York: Routledge.

Singer, P. 1995. *Rethinking Life and Death: The Collapse of Traditional Ethics.* New York: St. Martin's Press.

———. 1993. *Practical Ethics.* 2d ed. New York: Cambridge University Press.

Sirota, R. 1998. "Les copains d'abord. Les anniversaries de l'enfance, donner et reçevoir." *Ethnologie Française* 4: 457–72.

Smith, A. 1986. "The Last Hour." *SHARE Newsletter* 9 (3): 2.

Smith, J. 1984. "Parenting and Property." In *Mothering: Essays in Feminist Theory,* ed. J. Treblicot. Totowa, N.J.: Rowman and Allenheld.

Smith, M. R., and L. Marx. 1995. "Introduction." In *Does Technology Drive History? The Dilemma of Technological Determinism,* ed. M. Smith and L. Marx, 2–35. Cambridge: MIT Press.

Smith, R. T. 1996. *The Matrifocal Family: Power, Pluralism, and Politics.* New York: Routledge.

Smith-Rosenberg, C. 1985. *Disorderly Conduct: Visions of Gender in Victorian America.* New York: Oxford University Press

Sohn-Rethel, A. 1978. *Intellectual and Manual Labor.* Atlantic Highlands, N.J.: Humanities Press.

Sound Wave Images. 1998. http://www.unborn.com.

Specter, M. 1999. "The Dangerous Philosopher." *New Yorker* (September 6): 46.

Spigel, L. 2001. *Welcome to the Dreamhouse: Popular Media and Postwar Suburbs*. New Brunswick: Rutgers University Press.

Spivak, G. 1999. *A Critique of Postcolonial Reason: Toward a History of the Vanishing Present*. Cambridge, Mass.: Harvard University Press.

———. 1994. *Outside in the Teaching Machine*. New York: Routledge.

———. 1990. "Practical Politics of the Open End." In *The Postcolonial Critic*, ed. S. Harasym, 95–112. New York: Routledge.

———. 1988. "Scattered Speculations on the Question of Value." In *In Other Worlds*, 154–78. New York: Routledge.

———. 1987. "Speculations on Reading Marx: After Reading Derrida." In *Post-Structuralism and the Question of History*, ed. D. Attridge, G. Bennington, and R. Young, 30–62. Cambridge: Cambridge University Press.

———. 1985. "Can the Subaltern Speak? Speculations of Widow-Sacrifice." *Wedge* 7/8:120–30.

Spyer, P. 1997. "Introduction." In *Border Fetishisms: Material Objects in Unstable Spaces*, ed. P. Spyer, 1–11. New York and London: Routledge.

Stabile, C. 1999. "The Traffic in Fetuses." In *Fetal Subjects, Feminist Positions*, ed. L. Morgan and M. Michaels, 133–58. Philadelphia: University of Pennsylvania Press.

———. 1998. "Shooting the Mother: Fetal Photography and the Politics of Disappearance." In *The Visible Woman: Imaging Technologies, Gender and Science*, ed. P. Treichler, L. Cartwright, and C. Penley, 171–97. New York: New York University Press.

Stacey, J. 1986. "Are Feminists Afraid to Leave Home? The Challenge of Conservative Pro-Family Feminism." In *What Is Feminism?* ed. J. Mitchell and A. Oakley. Oxford: Basil Blackwell.

Stacey, M. 1985. "Commentary." *Journal of Medical Ethics* 11 (4): 193.

Steedman, C. 1995. *Strange Dislocations: Childhood and the Idea of Human Interiority, 1780–1930*. Cambridge, Mass.: Harvard University Press.

———. 1987. *Landscape for a Good Woman*. New Brunswick: Rutgers University Press.

Steffgan, K. 1999. "The Brown Star Story." In *When Hello Means Goodbye: A Guide for Parents Whose Child Dies before Birth, at Birth, or Shortly after Birth*, ed. P. Schwiebert, RN, and P. Kirk, MD. Portland, Ore.: Perinatal Loss. Reprinted in *SHARE Newsletter* 8 (4): 7.

Steiner, J. 1998. *Look-Alikes*. Boston: Little, Brown and Co.

Stewart, K. 1988. "Nostalgia: A Polemic." *Cultural Anthropology* 3 (3): 227–41.

Stewart, S. 1993. *On Longing: Narratives of the Miniature, the Gigantic, the Souvenir, the Collection*. Durham, N.C.: Duke University Press.

Strathern, M. 1997. "Partners and Consumers: Making Relations Visible." In *The Logic of the Gift: Toward and Ethic of Generosity*, ed. A. Schrift, 292–311. New York: Routledge.

———. 1992. *Reproducing the Future: Essays on Anthropology, Kinship, and the New Reproductive Technologies*. Manchester: Manchester University Press.

———. 1988. *The Gender of the Gift*. Berkeley: University of California Press.

Swanton, P. 1985. "Micaelee." In *When Hello Means Goodbye: A Guide for Parents Whose Child Dies before Birth, at Birth, or Shortly after Birth*, ed. P. Schwiebert, RN, and P. Kirk, MD, 21. Portland, Ore.: Perinatal Loss.

Taylor, J. S. 2002. "The Public Life of the Fetal Sonogram and the Work of the Sonographer." *Journal of Diagnostic Medical Sonography* 18 (6).

———. 2000a. "An All-Consuming Experience: Obstetrical Ultrasound and the Commodification of Pregnancy." In *Biotechnology and Culture: Bodies, Anxieties, Ethics*, ed. P. Brodwin, 147–170. Bloomington: Indiana University Press.

———. 2000b. "Of Sonograms and Baby Prams: Prenatal Diagnosis, Pregnancy, and Consumption." *Feminist Studies* 26 (2): 391–418.

———. 1999. "Mediating Reproduction: An Ethnography of Obstetrical Ultrasound." Ph.D. diss., Department of Anthropology, University of Chicago.

———. 1998. "Image of Contradiction: Obstetrical Ultrasound in American Culture." In *Reproducing Reproduction: Kinship, Power, and Technological Innovation*, ed. S. Franklin and H. Ragoné, 15–45. Philadelphia: University of Pennsylvania Press.

———. 1992. "The Public Fetus and the Family Car: From Abortion Politics to a Volvo Advertisement." *Public Culture* 4 (2): 67–80.

Thurer, S. 1994. *Myths of Motherhood: How Culture Reinvents the Good Mother*. Boston: Houghton Mifflin.

Tivers, J. 1985. *Women Attached: The Daily Lives of Women with Young Children*. London: Croom Helm.

Triano, S. 1999. "Reading Peter Singer —and Protesting Him." *Electric Edge: Online Edition of Ragged Edge Magazine*, October extra edition.

Tritten, J., and J. Southern. 1998. *Getting an Education: Paths to Becoming a Midwife*, 4th ed. Eugene, Ore.: Midwifery Today.

Trotzig, A. 1996. *Blod är tjockare än vatten* (Blood is thicker than water). Stockholm: Bonniers.

Ulrich, L. 1991. *A Midwife's Tale*. New York: Vintage.

Umansky, L. 1996. *Reconceiving Motherhood: Feminism and the Legacies of the 1960s*. New York: New York University Press.

Urwin, C. 1985. "Constructing Motherhood: The Persuasion of Normal Development." In *Language, Gender, and Childhood*, ed. C. Steedman, C. Urwin, and V. Walkerdine, 164–202. New York: Routledge and Kegan Paul.

U.S. Department of Labor, Bureau of Labor Statistics. 2002. *Health Technologists, Technicians, and Healthcare Support Occupations*. Bulletin 2540–9, http://www.bls.gov/oco/reprints/ocoroo9.pdf.

Van Gennep, A. 1960. [1908]. *The Rites of Passage*. Chicago: University of Chicago Press.

Van Keulen, P. 1991. "A Poem for Kirstie." *SHARE Newsletter* 14 (4): 1

van Mens-Verhulst, J., K. Schreurs, and L. Woertman 1993. *Daughters and Mothering*. London: Routledge.

Varney, H. 1997. *Varney's Midwifery*, 3d ed. Sudbury, Mass.: Jones and Bartlett Publishers.

Verhovek, S. 2000. "Debate on Adoptees' Rights Stirs Oregon." *New York Times* (5 April).

Visconti, L. 2001. "Winter's Beauty/Spring's Sustenance." *UNITE Notes* 19 (4): 6.

Volkman, T. 2003. "Embodying Chinese Culture: Transnational Adoption in North America." *Social Text* 74, 21 (1): 29–55.

von Melen, A. 1998. *Samtal med vuxna adopterade* (Conversations with adult adoptees). Stockholm: Raben Prisma/NIA.

Weeden, T. 1985. "Sharing from Terry." *SHARE Newsletter* 7 (4): 2.

Weiner, A. 1992. *Inalienable Possessions: The Paradox of Keeping-While-Giving*. Berkeley: University of California Press.

Weiss, Meira. 1994. *Conditional Love: Parents' Attitudes toward Handicapped Children*. Westport, Conn.: Bergin & Garvey.

Werbner, P. 1990. *The Migration Process: Capital, Gifts, and Offerings among British Pakistanis*. Oxford: Berg.

Whyte, S. R., and B. Ingstad. 1995. "Disability and Culture: An Overview." In *Disability and Culture*, ed. B. Ingstad and S. R. Whyte, 3–37. Berkeley: University of California Press.

Williamson, J. 1994. "Family, Education, Photography." In *Culture/Power/History: A Reader in*

Contemporary Social Theory, ed. N. Dirks, G. Eley, and S. Ortner, 236–44. Princeton: Princeton University Press.

Wilt, M. 2003. Personal Interview. July 9, 2003.

Winnicott, D. 1980. *Playing and Reality.* Harmondsworth: Penguin.

Woollett, A., and A. Phoenix 1991. "Psychological Views of Mothering." In *Motherhood: Meanings, Practices, and Ideologies,* ed. A. Phoenix, A. Woollett, and E. Lloyd, 28–46. London: Sage.

Wozniak, D. 2002. *They're All My Children: Foster Mothering in America.* New York: New York University Press.

———. 1999. "Gifts and Burdens: The Social and Familial Context of Foster Mothering." In *Transformative Mothering: On Giving and Getting in a Consumer Culture,* ed. L. Layne, 89–131. New York: New York University Press.

———. 1997a. "Twentieth Century Ideals: The Construction of U.S. Foster Motherhood." Ph.D. diss., University of Connecticut.

———. 1997b. Foster Mothers in America: Objectification, Sexualization, Commodification. *Women's History Review* 6, no. 3:357–66.

Wuthnow, R. 1995. *Rethinking Materialism.* Grand Rapids, Mich.: Eerdmans.

Yan, H. 2002. "Development, Contradictions, and the Specter of Disposability: Rural Migrant Women in Search of Self-Development in Post-Mao China." Ph.D. diss., Department of Anthropology, University of Washington.

Yngvesson, B. 2002. "Placing the 'Gift' Child in Transnational Adoption." *Law and Society Review* 36 (2): 227–56.

———. 2000. "Un Niño de Cualquier Color: Race and Nation in Intercountry Adoption." In *Globalizing Institutions: Case Studies in Regulation and Innovation,* ed. J. Jenson and B. de Sousa Santos. Aldershott, England: Ashgate.

———. 1997. "Negotiating Motherhood: Identity and Difference in 'Open' Adoptions." *Law and Society Review* 31:31–80.

Yngvesson, B., and M. Mahoney. 2000. "'As One Should, Ought and Wants to Be': Belonging and Authenticity in Identity Narratives." *Theory, Culture, and Society* 17 (6): 77–110.

Young, Allan. 1996. "Bodily Memory and Traumatic Memory." In *Tense Past: Cultural Essays in Trauma and Memory,* ed. P. Antze and M. Lambek, 89–102. New York: Routledge.

Young, J. 1993. *The Texture of Memory: Holocaust Memorials and Meaning.* New Haven: Yale University Press.

Young, James E. 1997. "Suffering and Origins of Traumatic Memory." In *Social Suffering,* ed. A. Kleinman, V. Das, and, M. Lock, 245–60. Berkeley: University of California Press.

Yoxen, E. 1987. "Seeing with Sound: A Study of the Development of Medical Images." In *The Social Construction of Technological Systems: New Directions in the Sociology and History of Technology,* ed. W. Bijker, T. Hughes, and T. Pinch, Cambridge, Mass.: MIT Press.

Zander, L. I. 1981. "The Place of Confinement—A Question of Statistics or Ethics?" *Journal of Medical Ethics* 7: 125–27.

Zeches, M. 1989. "Dustin Michael, Child of My Heart." *SHARE Newsletter* 12 (1): 2.

Zelizer, V. 2003. "Intimate Transactions." In *Economic Sociology for the Next Millennium,* eds. R. Collins, M. Guillen, P. England, and M. Meyer. Russell Sage Foundation.

———. 1985. *Pricing the Priceless Child: The Changing Social Value of Children.* New York: Basic Books.

Zizek, S. 1989. *The Sublime Object of Ideology.* London: Verso.

Zorn, C. 2001. "The Picture of Joseph." *SHARE Newsletter* 10 (1): 8.

CONTRIBUTORS

ANN ANAGNOST is associate professor of anthropology at the University of Washington and editor of the journal *Cultural Anthropology*. She is the author of *National Past-Times: Narrative, Representation, and Power in Modern China* (Duke University Press, 1997) and numerous articles addressing questions of gender, modernity, and governmentality in China. She is currently at work on a comparative study of the construction of maternal subjectivities in China and the United States.

ALISON J. CLARKE is professor of design history and material culture at the University of Applied Arts, Vienna, Austria. She is coeditor of a forthcoming journal dealing with the domestic, titled *Home Cultures*, and is a project supervisor at the AHRB Centre for the Study of the Domestic Interior, Royal College of Art, London. Her publications include *Tupperware: The Problem of Plastic in 1950s America* (Smithsonian Institution Press, 1999); "Mother Swapping: Trafficking Nearly New Children's Wear," in *Commercial Cultures: Economies, Practices, Spaces*, edited by Peter Jackson, Michelle Lowe, Daniel Miller, and Frank Mort (Berg, 2000); "Taste Wars and Style Dilemmas," in *Contemporary Art in the Home*, edited by C. Painter (Berg, 2002); and "Fashion and Anxiety," with Daniel Miller, *Fashion Theory* 6, no. 2 (2002): 191–214.

ROBBIE E. DAVIS-FLOYD serves as senior research fellow in the Department of Anthropology, University of Texas, Austin, and as adjunct associate professor in the Department of Anthropology, Case Western Reserve University, Cleveland. Her many articles and books on trends and transformations in health care, childbirth, obstetrics, and midwifery include *Birth as an American Rite of Passage* (University of California, 1992), reissued in a revised second edition in fall 2003, and, with Gloria St. John, *From Doctor to Healer: The Transformative Journey* (Rutgers, 1998). She is coeditor of *Childbirth and Authoritative Knowledge: Cross-Cultural Perspectives*, with Carolyn Sargent (University of California, 1997); *Cyborg Babies: From Techno-Sex to Techno-Tots*, with Joseph Dumit (Routledge, 1998); and *Daughters of Time: The Shifting Identities of Contemporary Midwives*, with Sheila Cosminsky and Stacy Leigh Pigg, in *Medical Anthropology* 20, no. 2–4 (2001).

PAMELA E. KLASSEN is associate professor in the Department for the Study of Religion at the University of Toronto. She is the author of *Blessed Events: Religion and Home Birth in North America* (Princeton University Press, 2001) and of several articles on religion and childbirth in North America, as well as other works on women and religion in North America. She is currently working on a book on the intersection of Christianity, healing, and medicine in twentieth-century North America.

IGOR KOPYTOFF, professor of anthropology at the University of Pennsylvania, specializes in cultural anthropology and African ethnology. He has written about the African frontier, African indigenous and world slavery, commoditization, and various topics in cultural anthropology. His article "The Cultural Biography of Things: Commoditization as Process" appeared in *The Social Life of Things: Commodities in Cultural Perspective*, edited by Arjun Appadurai (Cambridge University Press, 1986). He also edited, with Suzanne Miers, *Slavery in Africa* (University of Wisconsin Press, 1977) and *The African Frontier* (Indiana University Press, 1987).

GAIL LANDSMAN is associate professor of anthropology at the University at Albany, State University of New York. She has carried out research on Native American political activism, the woman suffrage movement, activism to pass family and medical leave legislation, and mothers of children with disabilities. She is the author of *Sovereignty and Symbol: Indian/White Conflict at Ganienkeh* and numerous articles on motherhood and disability and was a member of the independent panel to develop the New York State Health Department's *Clinical Practice Guideline for Motor Disabilities: Assessment and Intervention for Young Children*. She serves on the New York State Early Intervention Coordinating Council's Parent Involvement Committee. She is currently preparing a manuscript based on her research, tentatively titled " 'There Is No Normal': American Mothers of Disabled Children in the Age of 'Perfect' Babies."

LINDA L. LAYNE is Hale Professor of Humanities and Social Sciences at Rensselaer Polytechnic Institute in Troy, New York, and the mother of two boys. Her books include *Home and Homeland: The Dialogics of Tribal and National Identities in Jordan* (Princeton University Press, 1994); *Transformative Motherhood: On Giving and Getting in a Consumer Culture* (New York University Press, 2000); and *Motherhood Lost: A Feminist Account of Pregnancy Loss in America* (Routledge, 2003).

DANIEL MILLER is professor of material culture studies in the Department of Anthropology at the University College London. Recent books include *The Sari*, with Mukulika Banerjee (Berg, 2003); *The Dialectics of Shopping* (University of Chicago Press, 2001); and *A Theory of Shopping* (Routledge, 1997). Recent edited volumes include *Home Possessions: Material Culture behind Closed Doors* (Berg, 2001) and *Car Cultures* (Berg, 2001).

BARBARA KATZ ROTHMAN is professor of sociology at the City University of New York and, most recently, a Leverhulme Professor at Plymouth University in the United Kingdom. Her books include *The Book of Life: A Personal and Ethical Guide to Race, Normality, and the Implications of the Human Genome Project* (Beacon, 2001); *Recreating Motherhood: Ideology and Technology in a Patriarchal Society* (Rutgers, 2000); *The Tentative Pregnancy: How Amniocentesis Changes the Experience of Motherhood* (W.W. Norton, 1993); and *Laboring On: Birth in Transition in the United States*, with Wendy Simonds and Bari Meltzer (Routledge, forthcoming).

JANELLE S. TAYLOR is assistant professor of anthropology at the University of Washington. Her writings on obstetrical ultrasound have appeared in numerous publications, including *Feminist Studies, Public Culture, Science as Culture, Techniques et culture,* and the *Journal of Diagnostic Medical Sonography*. Recent articles raising critical questions about the ways that "culture" is conceptualized and taught within medical education have appeared in *Medical Anthropology Quarterly* and *Academic Medicine*.

DANIELLE F. WOZNIAK is a research scientist and adjunct professor at the University of Connecticut. Her research interests are constructs of motherhood and kinship in the United States as well as women's sexuality and reproductive health. She is the author of *They're All My Children: Foster Mothering in America* (New York University Press, 2002) and is currently working on her fourth book, *The Naked Truth: Women, Sexuality, and Desire in America*.

BARBARA YNGVESSON is professor of anthropology at Hampshire College. She is the author of *Virtuous Citizens, Disruptive Subjects: Order and Complaint in a New England Court* (Routledge, 1993) and coauthor of *Law and Community in Three American Towns* (Cornell University Press, 1994). Her current research focuses on transnational movements of children, the power of law in constituting these movements, and the hierarchies of belonging and exclusion (racial, familial, national) that they produce.

INDEX

abandonment, 143, 148–149, 168, 169, 173, 174, 178, 180–183
abortion, 5–6, 21–22, 24, 108, 206, 249; activism against. *See* activism, antiabortion; alternatives to, 206; debate, 206; failed, 199; forced, 23; versus infanticide, 102; legal issues of, 134, 262; rights, 12; selective, 23, 101, 108–109, 114, 190, 206. *See also* pro-choice; pro-life
activism: antiabortion, 8, 57, 187, 188, 189, 201–206, 208, 209n10; antiwar, 281; consumer, 249, 266; disability rights, 100–102, 112–113, 115–119
Adams, John Quincy, 22
adoption, 4, 8, 26, 28, 72–73, 89, 94–96, 98n2, 110, 117, 120n3, 164n24, 168–186, 272, 274; in Africa, 274–275; agencies, 145, 147, 148, 153, 154, 160, 171, 174, 175, 183, 184; black market, 28, 164n23; commodification of, 160; as completion, 142; cost of, 286; and "doing good," 161; domestic, 143, 150; extralegal, 163n12; as forced migration, 285; forcible, 163n10; gay and lesbian, 145; and gender, 140; as heroic, 148, 155; interracial, 165n30; law, 170, 172, 173, 184, 185; narratives, 148–149, 158, 167n56, 170, 285; open, 150, 169, 286; of orphans, 277; as positive, 143; private, 28; support groups, 145; surrogacy, 184; transformation of, 184; transnational, 8, 105, 139–167, 173, 285, 286; trips, 158
Adoption Centre (AC), 171, 172, 173, 174, 183, 184, 186n10
advertising, 45, 56, 129, 153, 166nn41, 42, 187, 201, 205–206, 209n10, 214, 220, 237, 274; critique of, 166n42, 188
agency, 11–12, 120n5, 137, 254, 260; excessive, 261; of fetus, 137n2; of infant, 34, 48, 135; political, 161
alternative medicine, 33, 41
American College of Nurse-Midwives (ACNM), 21, 226, 233, 246n5, 247n11, 248n16; Certification Council (ACC), 227; Department of Accreditation (DOA), 221
American Medical Association, Manpower Division of, 197
American Public Health Association, 232
American Registry of Diagnostic Medical Sonographers (ARDMS), 208n3

American Society for Reproductive Medicine, 28
amniocentesis, 5, 23, 214
Anagnost, Ann, 8–9, 105, 165n34, 170, 174, 178, 273, 274, 285, 286
animal liberation, 100, 120n2
antenatal care, 67. *See also* prenatal care
anthropology, 31, 32, 55, 71, 102, 129, 204, 255, 267n9, 271, 272, 278, 282; feminist, 251; and psychoanalysis, 31, 49
Appadurai, Arjun, 15, 108, 264, 268n15
archives, 191; and domestic space, 159; maternal, 147, 149, 157–159, 167n5, 178
artificial insemination, 27. *See also* reproduction, assisted
Asch, Adrienne, 102–103, 113, 115
Asperger's syndrome, 115, 183
assimilation, 169
Association of Recognizing the Life of Stillborns, 124
Austin, Regina, 7
authenticity, 59–60
autism, 115, 117

babies: commodification of, 1, 19, 25, 29, 214; as "organic," 40; valued, 205–206. *See also* children; infant
baby books, 58
Baby Doe rules, 100
baby selling, 24, 104, 144, 147, 274
baby showers, 56, 68–69, 268n18
Barbie, 44–47, 152, 153, 282
Benjamin, Jessica, 181
Benjamin, Walter, 177, 186n12
bereavement, 74, 92–95, 97, 123–133, 136, 137. *See also* grieving; mourning
Berlant, Lauren, 142, 147
bioethics, 100–102, 113, 288
biomedical technology, 2. *See also* new reproductive technology
biomedicine, critique of, 240
biopolitics, 142
birth. *See* childbirth
birth centers, 214, 241. *See also* childbirth
birth control, 12; pill, 134. *See also* contraception
birthday parties, 41, 67, 70
birth mothers. *See* birth parents
birth order, 42

315

birth parents, 140, 148–149, 159, 169, 170–171, 178, 181, 183; locating, 175; lost connection to, 150; power of, 286
Blake, William, 131
body, the, 22; ownership of, 21–23; and religion, 22; views of, 21–23, 254, 266
Bordo, Susan, 262
brand names, 220. *See also* advertising
breastfeeding, 34, 38, 40, 283; prolonged, 38
Brison, Susan, 124
Brown, Gillian, 159
Buchli, Victor, 57–58
Butler, Judith, 186n6, 191

Cambodia, 150
Canada, 215
capitalism, 1, 2, 4, 7, 8, 19–29, 73, 110, 131, 139, 142, 147, 151, 153, 158, 164n24, 240, 245, 250, 253–254, 258, 264, 271, 276, 279, 283, 287; alienating conditions of, 204; cosmologies of, 249; emergence of industrial, 159; globalizing, 12; and industrialism, 276; ironies of, 258; magic of, 189; and motherhood, 1, 4; and nostalgia, 167n58; and patriarchy, 20, 162n4; and Protestantism, 275; and technology, 20
caregivers. *See* childcare
Carrier, James, 136
cerebral palsy, 112, 115, 117
cesarean section, 33, 147, 232, 235; forced, 262; "patient choice," 249, 268n19; rates of, 214, 240, 263, 284
charity, 5, 27, 166n42
childbirth, 249–268; activists, 213; and agency, 213, 260–266; ambivalence about, 250; breech, 235, 237, 248n20; "business of," 250–251, 252–253, 263; choices in, 136, 212, 213, 214, 218, 231, 234, 240, 241, 243, 245, 249, 250, 255, 257, 260–264; classes, 33; commodification of, 4, 136, 211–248; complications in, 102; costs of, 231; and culture, 212, 213; economics of, 253; education, 213, 255; as empowering, 258, 260, 266; experience of, 33, 56, 213, 241, 249, 258, 264, 265–266; and fathers, 213; and feminism, 212, 249–268; high-risk, 213; holistic, 255; at home. *See* home birth; hospital, 212, 213, 241, 242, 243, 249, 251, 252–253, 254, 268n16; marketing of, 213; medical interventions of, 37, 51n4, 213, 251, 262, 263, 281; metaphors of, 249, 250; movements, 218; "mystery of," 251, 266, 268n14; natural, 33, 34, 212, 222; normal, 239, 253; outcomes, 219, 226, 230, 231, 232, 263, 268n17; out-of-hospital, 226, 230–231, 233, 238, 249; pain, 33, 51n4, 136, 212, 213, 260, 281; planning, 213; and religion, 249–268, 284; as revolutionary, 258; risk, 33, 235, 237, 260, 262–264, 268n17; as rite, 33, 255; as sacred, 4, 259, 288; as social event, 212; as spiritual, 250, 251, 258, 261, 262, 264, 288; statistics, 212; technocratic, 255; and technology, 212, 213, 255; of twins, 235, 237, 248n20; unassisted, 258;

vaginal, 253; vaginal after cesarean (VBAC), 235, 237, 248n21
childcare, 2, 4, 32, 72, 165nn25, 26; paid, 2, 4, 41, 61, 78, 163n12
childrearing: economic transactions of, 139; and gender, 38, 63; literature, 38, 61
children: abandoned, 143, 148–149; commodification of, 27–28, 74, 77, 81–82, 106, 108, 110–111, 114, 117, 119, 139–168; as consumers, 280–282; as designer products, 277; desire for, 142; and difference, 147, 151–152, 155, 156, 159, 164n17, 169; as endangered, 148, 153; fetishization of, 157; foster, 72–99; "littleness of," 151; lost, 153; "making of," 74; motherless, 169; "normal," 108–109, 114, 115; ownership of, 75–76, 261; "real," 74, 77, 83–84, 97, 98n2; replacement of, 133–134, 138n12; sacralization of, 84; sentimental value of, 126; singularization of, 77–78, 114, 119, 136, 137n2; "state," 77–84; substitution of, 274; "temporary," 74; "unwanted," 143; value of, 139, 144
Chile, 170–186, 285
Chin, Elizabeth, 7
China, 105, 139–167, 286; demography of, 163n12; population policy of, 143, 144, 163nn10, 14, 164n25
Chodorow, Nancy, 32
Christian Science, 254, 255, 256. *See also* religion
Citizens for Midwifery (CFM), 239, 248nn18, 19
citizenship, 142, 145, 147; new kind of, 161, 164n18
civil rights, 112, 281. *See also* activism
Clarke, Alison, 8
cloning, 274
clothing, 39, 43, 59, 69, 74, 83–84, 150, 158
Collins, Patricia Hill, 265
commodification, 12, 103–104; of adoption, 160; ambiguity of, 211; anthropological theories of, 219; anxieties about, 147; of bodies, 19, 104, 204; of childbirth, 4, 249–268; of children, 7, 28, 74, 77, 81–82, 105, 106, 108, 110–111, 114, 117, 119, 139–168, 147, 150; and contamination, 251; and ethnicity, 151; of experience, 250; of fetal sonograms, 8, 57, 188–210; of humans, 1, 104; and marketing, 220; of midwifery, 211–248; of motherhood, 4; qualified, 211–248, 282; of religion, 251; of reproduction, 103, 105, 214; rhetoric of, 212; and standardization, 220; as transformative process, 219
commoditization. *See* commodification
computed tomography (CT) scans, 194
Consortium for Citizens with Disabilities, 102
consumerism: activism, 249, 266; anti-, 65, 110, 253, 275, 277, 280, 288; assumptions of, 122; critique of, 114, 116–117, 130, 137, 164n24, 259; culture, 2, 7, 8, 71, 73, 76, 122, 130, 212, 251, 253, 266; groups, 234–235, 239; hierarchy, 287; power, 251

INDEX

consumption, 2, 4, 8, 9, 11–12, 58, 144, 150; and agency, 11–12, 211, 212, 213, 245, 259; of childbirth, 211–248, 249–268; and children, 4, 47; and choice, 151; critical, 251, 284; critique of, 254, 255, 263, 277; and ethics of care, 148; and fetishism, 14; ideologies of, 7, 10; ironies of, 254; language of, 252; and memories, 8; metaphors of, 10–11; moralities of, 66; options of, 14; pleasures of, 286; scholarship of, 11, 211, 265, 279; as subversive, 211; theory, 122
contraception, 24, 283. *See also* birth control
Coste, Pierre, 194
CPM News (newsletter), 232–233
CPM 2000 project, 231–232. *See also* midwives, Certified Professional
"crack babies," 105
Crisis Pregnancy Centers, 202
c-section. *See* cesarean section
culture, 3, 68, 75, 272, 285; alibis, 163n11, 173; camps, 145, 167n46, 170; Chinese, 162n3; of consumption, 4; and cosmology, 267n9; counter, 45, 212, 215, 218, 225, 256; creativity, 211; and difference, 142; and heritage, 156; and identity, 8, 141, 162n8, 164n17; and legitimacy, 276; material, 11, 14, 55, 60, 70–71; and memory, 124–125; North American, 5, 8, 105; and Other, 189; and perception, 275; and power, 9; public, 191; rhetoric of, 273; right to, 162n3, 169; and value, 255
cybercommunities, 143, 155, 164n19. *See also* Internet

daughters, desire for, 143
Davis-Floyd, Robbie, 4, 255, 273, 282, 283, 284
Delaney, Carol, 261
Deleuze, Giles, 140
DeMoss, Arthur, 209n10
DeMoss Foundation, The, 201, 203, 204, 205, 206, 209n10
depressive position, 31, 39–44
desire, 139–142, 151, 153, 184, 185n5, 261; for children, 142, 143, 151; contradictions of, 170; discourses of, 154; economy of, 139, 159; objects of, 187
DeVault, Marjorie, 200, 206
development, 139, 142, 144
diagnostic screening exam, 187. *See also* prenatal testing
diagnostic tests. *See* prenatal testing
disability, 5, 164n24; children with, 5, 6, 23, 27, 100–120, 133, 138n10, 277, 287; and personhood, 100–120; prejudice, 103; rights activism, 100–102, 112–113, 115–119; scholarship, 116
Disability Rights Education and Defense Fund (DREDF), 113
discipline, of children, 38–39, 50
discrimination, 113
doctors. *See* physicians
Donald, Ian, 192, 193
Donzelot, Jacques, 139, 142, 162n6, 163n14, 166n46

Dorow, Sara K., 148, 162n5
Douglas, Mary, 45
doulas, 255, 257, 285
Down syndrome, 112, 114, 115, 117, 118
duty, parental, 155
Dying Rooms, The (documentary film), 149, 165nn27, 28

ecology, 20
economism, 271–278; anti-, 274, 275; and kinship, 271–278
Eddy, Mary Baker, 254
education, 35, 66–67, 70, 72, 144, 155; and childbearing, 35
eggs. *See* ova
electronic fetal monitor, 213–214, 242. *See also* childbirth; fetus
employment, 2
epidural, 213, 253. *See also* childbirth, pain
ethnicity, 9, 60, 68–69, 71n1, 80, 151, 155–156, 285, 286; aestheticization of, 155; and commodities, 151, 152; negotiation of, 155; sanitized, 286; securing, 158
ethnography, 3, 9, 12, 14, 32, 51n6, 98n1, 145, 146, 157, 162n2, 188, 201, 250, 266, 272, 275, 278; postcolonial, 146
eugenics, 101
euthanasia, 108. *See also* infanticide
exchangeability of children and persons, 77, 101, 104–105, 107–115, 133–134, 147, 150, 155, 159, 173, 185n5, 204, 259, 263

Falwell, Jerry, 201
Families with Children from China (FCC), 145
family, 7, 22, 72, 77, 168; belonging, 169; breakdown of, 7; confines of, 161; constraints of, 33; critique of, 12; emotional life of, 141; extended, 66, 286; female headed, 6; historicity of, 141, 142, 143; life, 159; -making, 75; modern, 155; as "natural," 104, 170; nuclear, 58, 74, 77; origins, 48; sentimentality of, 141, 142, 154; varieties of, 14; Web pages, 147, 167n56
family planning, 101, 163n12. *See also* contraception
Farm, the, 223
Farrell Smith, Janet, 21, 23, 185n1
fathers, 42; rights of, 29, 261
feminism, 3, 4, 14, 15, 16, 21, 35, 41, 44, 50, 57, 188, 200, 207, 259, 260, 261, 262, 264, 265, 266, 267n2, 281, 282; African American, 265; and autonomy, 36, 42, 265, 266; and childbirth, 212, 215, 240, 249–268, 282, 283; and childrearing, 42; and ethos of individualism, 23; historiography, 159; North American, 249; and scholarship, 10–14, 57, 64, 70, 105, 189, 250, 251, 261, 268n10, 268n10
fetal abuse, imprisonment for, 262
fetal environment, 263
fetal monitoring, 163. *See also* electronic fetal monitor
fetal subject, 8, 13, 262; emergence of, 122
fetal surgery, 130

INDEX

fetal ultrasound images, 5, 8, 153; and advertising, 163. *See also* prenatal testing; sonograms; ultrasound
fetish, 150, 187; definition of, 189; Marxist concept of, 189; theory of the, 151
fetishism, 14, 265; of child, 157; commodity, 158, 159, 189, 249, 265, 277; methodological, 188
fetus, 10, 23; abnormalities of, 102; agency of, 137n2; commodification of, 57, 188–210; consumption of, 70; cultural imaginings of, 202; history of, 8; "liveliness" of, 189; as object of desire, 187; "on screen," 187; origin story of, 204; photographs of, 202; public, 8, 187–210; racialized, 206; as removed from pregnant woman, 187; as social person, 8, 57, 110, 204, 277; as supersubject, 262; visibility of, 56, 189, 192, 202, 285. *See also* fetal subject
foetus. *See* fetus
Foley, Bernadette, 130
food, 10, 46
fostering, 4, 27, 72–99, 150, 164n2, 172, 174, 175, 176, 179, 186n10, 278; stigma of, 80, 99n4, 104, 297
Foucault, Michel, 140, 163n14, 166–167n46
"Freedom of Choice Act," 202
Freud, Sigmund, 37, 146, 154
Friends of Midwives, 234

Gaskin, Ina May, 223, 230, 231, 268nn12, 17
Gaskin maneuver, 263, 268n17
gender, 38, 143, 145; abuse, 163n11; and babies, 41; and childrearing, 38, 51n1, 63–64; concepts of, 32; constructions of, 41; eruption of, 41; ideology, 42, 66; securing, 158
genetic testing, 120n4, 241. *See also* amniocentesis; prenatal testing
"George," 188, 201–204. *See also* activism, antiabortion; The DeMoss Foundation
Germany, 50, 288
"ghostly double," 150, 160
gift, 48–49, 56, 59, 63–64, 69–70, 81, 85–86, 91, 95, 129, 135, 182, 186n10, 268n18, 274, 277; power, 184; and reciprocity, 204; rhetoric of, 148, 164n24; symbolically charged, 204
Gilligan, Carol, 30
Ginsburg, Faye, 9, 206
globalization, 12, 141, 160; perplexities of, 160
God, 22, 154, 202, 254, 255
Goodwin, James W., 263–264
governmentality, 144, 163n16
Governor's Commission on Disability, 119–120n1
grandchildren, 39, 49
grandparents, 39, 48–49, 99n5, 124
grieving, 89–90, 92–95, 136, 286. *See also* bereavement; mourning
Groce, Nora Ellen, 101
Guattari, Felix, 140
guilt, 32, 33, 36, 38–39, 49, 150, 206

Hague Conference, 169
Hague Convention, 169
Haraway, Donna, 205
Hardt, Michael, 140, 142, 154
Hayles, N. Katherine, 146
health care: professionals, 115; resources, 101
Heath, Deborah, 192
Heil, J., 124
Helms, Jesse, 201
Help in Understanding Grief and Successfully Surviving It (HUGSS), 136
herbal medicine, 224
HMOs, 217
home birth, 4, 26, 211, 222, 230, 231, 232, 235, 237, 241, 244, 249, 284; advocacy, 251, 252, 255; commodification of, 4, 249–268; "cost-effectiveness" of, 252; cultural attitudes towards, 217, 218, 249–268; as feminist act, 258, 282, 283; legal issues of, 231, 235, 248n20, 249; limits on, 231; movement, 212, 280–281; opposition to, 258, 260–264; as "revolutionary," 252, 258; rituals, 13. *See also* childbirth; midwives
"human nature," 20
human rights, 143, 165n27; abuses, 164n25
hunger, 10

identity, 7, 8, 13, 48, 58, 60, 73, 81, 83, 98n1, 150, 153, 155, 157, 167n46, 175, 185nn1, 2, 186n8, 211; adopted, 169; and "blood," 169; class, 200; of commodities, 220; of consumer, 160; coordinates of, 158; cultural, 8, 141, 162n8, 164n17; gender, 198, 200, 205; "hunger," 169; and memory, 123; of mother, 282; multicultural, 140; myth about, 169; and naming, 156–157; narratives of, 170; national, 152, 158, 174; new, 168, 174; normative, 154; and objects, 159; of organ donor, 204; of pregnant woman, 205; production of, 157; professional, 8, 13, 198–200, 211–248; racial, 158, 200; religious, 267n1; sexual, 158; and shopping, 32, 117; transformations in, 174; transitory, 73
ideology, 21; dominance of, 68; of market, 287; of medicine, 200; "pro-life," 189; of race, 200; of technology, 19
immigration, 13, 109, 142, 147, 152, 167nn50, 55, 172; anti-, 179; illegal, 147; quotas, 147, 179. *See also* labor, migrant
Immigration and Naturalization Service (INS), 147
individualism, 23, 63, 71; cult of, 156
infant: "cult of the," 34, 165n35, 250, 258; spirituality of, 255
infanticide, 101–102, 108, 113, 118, 143. *See also* euthanasia
infertility, 4, 27, 145, 274; research, 27; treatments, 27
Internet, 102, 113, 116, 141, 145, 146–148, 155, 157, 159, 164n19, 167n50, 210n13, 213; as ethnographic resource, 162n2; and social space, 141
"intimate public sphere," 142, 146–147, 163n9

in vitro fertilization (IVF), 27–28; success rates of, 28. *See also* new reproductive technology; reproduction, assisted; reproductive technology; technology, procreative
IVF. *See* in vitro fertilization

James, Alison, 45
Johnson, Harriet McBryde, 102, 103, 115, 118
Journal of Diagnostic Medical Sonography (JDMS), 198, 199, 208

Keane, Noel, 29
Keller, Evelyn Fox, 266
Kelly, Mary, 157
Kevorkian, Jack, 102
kinship, 15, 55, 59, 64, 96, 204; and "blood," 75; claims to, 90–91; cultural interpretations of, 273; and economism, 271; extended, 182; legal, 75; patrilineal, 143; quasi-, 278; rhetoric of, 76; and sacrifice, 78; sentimental model of, 277; social contingency of, 167n50; symbols of, 94
Klassen, Pamela, 4, 273, 282, 283, 284, 288
Klein, Melanie, 31–51n2; on "good" and "bad" breast, 34, 36–39
Kopytoff, Igor, 14–15, 103–104, 170, 185–186nn5, 6, 188, 251, 266
Korea, 163n17, 164n17, 186nn9, 14, 286
Kundera, Milan, 171

labor, 10, 19–20, 74, 75, 79, 144, 265, 266; "affective," 9, 140, 141, 142, 148, 153, 159, 167n51; alienated, 251–252, 258; cheap, 160; child, 152; divisions of, 142, 159, 164n24; and gender, 142, 159, 209; and hierarchy, 209n3; maternal, 2, 19, 72–99, 104, 162n4; migrant, 144, 160; of mourning, 171, 181; of naturalization, 170; and objects, 189; and sacrifice, 258; signifying, 159; "socially necessary," 142
lactation: conference, 284; consultation, 281, 285
Landsman, Gail, 5, 277, 287
Lay, Mary, 236
Layne, Linda, 8, 55, 56, 93, 120n5, 164n24, 166n44, 167n51, 208n1, 277, 278, 287
"lemon law," 109–110; cultural, 114
liminality, 75, 137
Lo, Kwai-Cheung, 152
London, North, 1, 2–3, 8, 14, 31–51, 55, 59–70, 165n33, 277
Look-Alikes (Joan Steiner), 1
loss, as "clean break" in adoption, 168–169. *See also* pregnancy loss
love, 37, 50, 88, 105, 109, 117–119, 132, 138n10, 142, 148–149, 171, 186n10, 260, 264, 265; demand for, 155; enactment of, 126; history of, 189; making, 134; and money, 3, 4, 15, 77–88, 104; mother, 117; and objects, 1, 81–82, 92, 117, 152
Lucas, Gavin, 57–58
Luker, Kristin, 206

MacDonald, Margaret, 241, 268n13
magnetic resonance imaging (MRI), 194
Marks, Jonathan, 101
Marr, Marjorie, 192
Marx, Karl, 2, 10, 139–140, 142, 188, 189, 204, 219, 249, 251, 258, 265
Marxist scholarship, 11
masculinity, 41
materialism, 40, 50, 264, 266, 275; anti-, 51n6; as pollution, 45–46
Mattel Corporation, 153
"matter," 191
maturity, 35, 48; concepts of, 32
Mauss, Marcel, 204
media, 107, 145, 187, 189, 191, 234, 235
Medicaid, 117, 215, 231, 253
Medicare, 215
Melanesia, 32
memory, 8, 13, 58, 73, 74–75, 77, 94, 97, 183, 186n12, 200; of birth, 177; boxes, 127; as choice, 136; and culture, 124–125, 138n11; durability of, 138n6; embodied, 178; and gender, 130; and identity, 123; making of, 8, 92–93, 122–138; problem of, 125, 138n3; retrieving, 125; scholarship on, 122; and time, 129
methodology, 146
middle-class, 3, 35, 41, 59–70, 99n7, 108, 142, 151, 162n4, 165n26, 238, 249, 255, 260, 277; Chinese, 160, 163n12; cultural values of, 3, 7, 35–36, 41, 66, 69, 139, 147; and educational expectations, 35; mothers, 32, 126, 200; subjectivity, 141, 164n21. *See also* social class
midwifery, 211–248; brand name of, 237, 239, 240; in Canada, 215, 241, 242, 243, 263; commodification of, 211–248; consumption of, 240, 258, 281; ethos of, 215, 220, 222, 226, 228, 230, 233, 236, 237; European, 227, 243; fees for, 238; and feminism, 215, 240; fracturing of, 215, 232; history of, 212; holistic, 220, 223, 231, 241, 243; insurance reimbursement for, 215, 231, 235, 236, 237, 238, 245, 249, 253, 267n5; legalization, of, 220, 236, 238; mainstreaming, 218; marketing of, 214, 217, 230, 232, 233, 234, 237, 238, 239, 241; in Massachusetts, 233, 237; medicalization of, 233, 243; meetings, 284; in Mexico, 243; in Minnesota, 236; models of, 214; in New York, 228, 233, 247n12; in Oregon, 230, 231; peer review, 230, 237; in Pennsylvania, 235; professionalization of, 214, 215–216, 219, 226, 232, 233, 234, 235, 236, 237, 238, 241, 243, 246nn4, 6; quality control of, 220, 226, 227, 229, 230, 231; quantification of, 230, 231; regulation of, 215, 217, 219, 234, 235, 236, 237; and religion, 235; as "revolutionary," 252; and risk, 232; as social movement, 215, 220, 226, 228, 230, 233, 234, 236, 240, 241, 247n11, 280; "spiritual," 223, 243, 247n11; support groups for, 235, 239; woman-centered, 220, 231, 237, 239, 240, 243, 245, 285. *See also* childbirth; home birth; midwives

Midwifery Education Accreditation Council (MEAC), 221, 227, 239, 246n6
Midwifery Model of Care (MMOC), 218, 233, 234, 235, 237, 239, 240; as brand name, 239, 240
Midwifery Task Force, 240
Midwifery Today (magazine), 216
midwives, 4, 13, 283, 284, 285, 287, 288; and agency, 225, 241; and apprenticeship, 219, 222, 229, 243, 245, 247n14; autonomy of, 231, 235, 247n11; and birth outcomes, 219, 231, 232; certification of, 219, 220, 222, 223, 225, 227, 230, 232, 234, 236, 238, 244, 245; Certified (CM), 226, 227, 228, 247nn11, 12, 248n16; Certified Professional (CPM), 218, 220, 221, 225, 227, 228, 229, 230, 231, 232, 233, 234, 237, 238, 243, 245, 247nn11, 12, 248nn16, 20; "clinical," 242; as commodities, 214; consensus of, 223, 224, 234; credentials of, 218, 226, 229; direct-entry (DEM), 214, 215, 216, 217, 218, 221, 222, 225, 226, 227, 230, 231, 233, 234, 235, 236, 238, 239, 241, 243, 245, 246n11, 247nn12, 15, 248n20, 253, 255; education of, 214, 215, 216, 218, 219, 221, 225, 226, 227, 229, 232, 239, 242, 243; evaluation of, 221, 222, 229; "grand," 247n13; hierarchies of, 236, 237, 242; and home birth, 211, 222, 228, 230, 231, 232, 235, 237, 241, 244, 251, 263, 284; and hospital births, 220, 227, 230, 231, 232, 233, 238, 241, 242, 243, 284; idealization of, 256; "lay-," 214, 215, 226, 230, 234, 236, 237, 241, 243, 246n4; legal issues of, 218, 220, 224, 228, 229, 230, 231, 232, 233, 234, 235, 236, 237, 244, 245, 247nn12, 15, 248n20, 249, 253, 255, 267n5; licensing of, 215, 217, 228, 229, 234, 235, 237, 238, 253; lobbying of, 234, 238, 240; marginalization of, 212, 214, 215, 216; medical skills of, 223, 224, 235, 246n9; nurse- (CNM), 214, 215, 216, 218, 222, 226, 228, 232, 233, 238, 239, 241, 242, 243, 247n11, 248n16, 253, 254, 267n5; pay of, 216, 236, 238, 253, 267n8, 274, 283–284; and physicians, 218, 230, 239, 242, 247n11, 248n20, 264; "plain," 235, 236, 237; public image of, 216, 217, 218, 219, 221, 223, 231, 235, 237, 243, 244; "renegade," 226, 237; representing, 216; roles of, 257, 273; rural, 223; scholar-, 252; in Seattle, 213, 236; self-employed, 217; "shamanic," 256; spiritual calling of, 220, 242, 255; stereotypes of, 215, 217–218, 219, 226; survival of, 211. *See also* childbirth; home birth; midwifery
Midwives' Alliance of North America (MANA), 215, 219, 225, 226, 227, 228, 230, 232, 233, 235, 239, 244; and certification, 219, 220, 222, 225, 227; conferences, 226, 237; database, 231; statistics committee, 232; task force meeting, 234
migration, 9; forced, 285. *See also* labor, migrant
Miller, Daniel, 3, 14, 60, 79–80, 88, 105, 162nn4, 7, 165n33, 166n37, 170, 250, 251, 258, 259, 260, 261, 264, 265, 267–268n10, 281; critique of, 259, 260–261, 264, 265, 267–268n10, 277, 279, 280, 284
mind-body dualism, 24
miscarriage, 122, 123, 125, 128. *See also* pregnancy loss
modernity, 140, 271; critique of, 11
modernization, 144
money, 3, 12, 45, 81, 86–88, 147, 170, 173, 184, 185n5, 213, 216, 236, 253, 257; contamination of, 151; fetishization of, 159; and love, 3, 4, 15, 77–78, 88, 99n4; as metaphor, 158; and religion, 252, 254; "state," 80, 104
Moran, Eileen, 287
"mother development," 32
motherhood: "alternative," 32; and capitalism, 1, 4; constructing, 56, 65, 68, 142; and difference, 32; foster, 72–99; ideologies of, 3, 10, 200; and labor, 2, 19, 72–99, 104; lesbian, 13; as "natural," 104; as oppressive, 12; politics of, 71; and poverty, 6, 13; proletarianization of, 19; as relationship, 2, 3; as sacrifice, 38, 106, 250, 259, 260, 266; as self-realization, 250, 259, 260, 266; as service, 86–87; single, 6, 13, 65; styles of, 32, 61; teenage, 105; "unfit," 58. *See also* adoption; fostering; parenthood
"motherhood club," 55
mother-infant relations, 31–51, 61–62, 157, 250, 259, 261, 265–266
Mother's Day, 125
mourning, 149, 150; labor of, 171, 181, 287. *See also* bereavement; grieving
multiculturalism, 140, 141, 142–143, 163n9, 167n48; discourses of, 141; as representational regime, 143
"museological mania," 167n56

naming, 155, 167nn47, 48; problem of, 156–157
Nancy, Jean-Luc, 171
nannies, 61. *See also* childcare, paid
narcissism, 43, 45, 49, 154
narrative, 147, 204; of adoption, 148–149, 158, 167n56; of belonging, 170; gaps, 178; of identity, 170; knowledge, 186; of pregnancy loss, 131; of "salvage," 164n25; of trauma, 124
nation, and belonging, 169
National Association of CPMs (NACPM), 234
National Childbirth Trust (NCT), 32, 33, 34, 41, 42, 50, 51n4, 62, 67, 258, 259, 265, 281–282
National Council of Jewish Women (NCJW), 122
nationalism, 288
National Organization of Certifying Agencies (NOCA), 219
National Right to Life, 202. *See also* activism, antiabortion; pro-life
natural childbirth. *See* childbirth
natural theology, 131
nature: ideology of, 41, 44; images of, 131; models of, 50

INDEX

Negri, Antonio, 140, 142, 154
neoliberalism, 140, 144
neonatal intensive care, 115
Newborn Followup Program, 120n3
new reproductive technology, 45, 70, 205, 214, 266, 271, 277; debates around, 205; naturalizing of, 104; public acceptance of, 104; and race, 205; temptations of, 277. *See also* cloning; electronic fetal monitor; infertility; in vitro fertilization; ova; prenatal testing; reproductive technology; sex determination; sex selection; sperm donors; surrogacy; technology, procreative; ultrasound
Niehoff, Michael, 128, 130
Nilsson, Lennart, 202, 208
North America, 5, 8, 68, 74, 105
North American Registry of Midwives (NARM), 218, 219, 223, 225, 227, 228–229, 231–232, 239, 243, 244, 246nn6, 7, 10, 247n13; and certification, 219, 221, 222, 223, 227, 232, 236, 237, 238, 239, 240, 246n11; Certification Task Force (CTF), 222, 223, 226, 229, 246n8; Portfolio Evaluation Process (PEP), 229; Qualified Evaluator, 229; Skills Assessment, 229; survey, 225, 229
Not Dead Yet (disability rights group), 102, 116, 119n1
nurseries, 8, 157; decorating, 56, 59–70; provisioning of, 8, 56, 59–70
nurture, 139
Nygren, Ola, 163n12

Oakley, Ann, 192
object relations, 31; theory, 32
objects, 1, 2, 11, 55, 161; and desire, 46, 185n5, 187; as fetish, 189; and identity, 159; and labor, 189; and love, 1, 37, 81–82, 91; and meaning, 83; and memory, 126–128; power of, 2; secondhand, 83–85; and value, 189; world of, 160
obstetrical ultrasound. *See* prenatal testing; ultrasound
obstetricians, 192, 194, 196, 238, 251, 264. *See also* physicians
organ donation, 204
orientalism, 156
origins, 154, 156–159, 168, 178, 275, 285; search for, 158; stories, 204
orphanage. *See* orphan homes
orphan homes, 148, 149, 151, 155, 156, 158, 159, 164n22, 165nn25, 27, 29, 167nn50, 59, 171, 175, 178, 180, 183, 184, 286; contributions to, 165n29, 168
"other," the, 170, 171, 178, 185nn1, 2, 189; cultural, 189
ova, 104, 268n20; auctioned, 104

pain, 184; of childbirth, 33, 34, 260; of loss, 89, 124; power of, 260
paranoid-schizoid position, 31, 34–39
parenthood, 25, 75; adoptive, 9, 73, 140, 141, 143, 149, 286, 287; artificial, 79; commodification of, 1; co-, 76; and duty, 155; foster, 72–99; gay and lesbian, 145, 166n42, 286; Jewish, 31, 40; and narcissism, 37; nonnormative, 164n24; as practice, 48; property model of, 21, 27; "responsible," 257; single, 145; stages of development in, 31–51; standards for, 77; strategies of, 48; transition to, 146; transnational, 141; value of, 141. *See also* birth parents; motherhood
parents. *See* parenthood
Parker, Rozika, 51n2
Parsons, Talcott, 281, 285; and capitalism, 20, 24, 162n4; ideology of, 19, 24–25, 59; marketing of, 29; and rights of fathers, 29; and technology, 20
patriarchy, 19, 20, 24, 29, 68, 288
Perinatal Mortality Rate (PMR), 232. *See also* childbirth, outcomes
personhood, 100–101, 136, 166n44; cross-cultural concepts of, 101; and disability, 100–120; mainstream view of, 103; Western views of, 104–105
Petchesky, Rosalind Pollack, 187, 189, 265
philosophy: Cartesian, 271; utilitarian, 100–101
photographs, 74, 91–92, 95, 123, 126–127, 129, 130, 132, 147, 149, 151, 154, 164n21, 166n45, 167n56, 173, 175, 178, 182, 198, 202; family, 155, 157, 158; postmortem, 136, 137n1
physicians, 111–112, 192, 194, 195, 207, 209n3, 213, 217, 230, 240, 248n20, 253, 254, 281, 283
Pietz, William, 187
pitocin, 223, 224
play, 39, 61, 65
playgroups, "alternative," 38
Polanyi, Karl, 271, 273
political economy, 140, 240
political theory, liberal, 5
pollution, 40, 45
Popisil, Leopold, 276
population control, 163n14; discourses of, 144
Post-Partum Document (Mary Kelly), 157
poverty, 6–7, 23, 181, 205
power, 9, 140; and culture, 9; of objects, 2, 278
pregnancy, 55, 59, 63; and consumption, 106, 134, 204, 208; control of behavior during, 24, 64, 105–107, 114, 134, 200; cultural attitudes about, 200; disclosing, 68; experience of, 26–28, 33, 241, 258; guidebooks, 106; as normal, 239; "responsible," 200; as work, 24
pregnancy loss, 8, 13, 55, 56, 120n5, 122–138, 167n51, 208n1, 278; narratives, 131; support groups, 8, 57, 122–127; as traumatic experience, 122–138. *See also* miscarriage; reproductive mishaps
prenatal care, 107, 206; history of, 192–193. *See also* antenatal care
prenatal diagnosis. *See* prenatal testing
prenatal testing, 5, 106–108, 188–210, 214, 241, 263; and disability, 5, 23, 108–109; implications of, 5–6, 23, 102, 108–109, 114,

prenatal testing (*cont.*)
  120n4, 190. *See also* amniocentesis; genetic testing; ultrasound
Princeton University, 100, 102, 112, 115
privacy, 21, 23
Probyn, Elspeth, 170
pro-choice, 201, 206, 207. *See also* procreative choice
procreative choice, 23
pro-life, 57, 188, 201, 206, 207; "educational video," 188, 201–206, ideology of, 189. *See also* activism, antiabortion
property, 21–23, 66; baby as, 24; body as, 21–23; rights, 24
psychoanalysis, 31, 32, 45, 49–50, 51n2, 146, 167n54, 259, 265; and anthropology, 31, 49, 268n11, 284

race, 4, 19, 28, 59, 76, 108, 120n3, 123, 140, 142–143, 163n8, 169, 200, 201, 205, 206; construction of, 151; and difference, 155, 162–163n8, 205; and reproduction, 205
racism, 7, 285; anti-, 147, 287, 288
Ragged Edge (online journal), 113
Ramamurthy, Priti, 169–170
rape, 23, 125
Rapp, Rayna, 5, 9, 108–109, 120n4
"reactive attachment disorder," 149, 165n26
rebirthing, 33, 46, 50
Reid, Margaret, 246n4
religion, 4, 22, 34, 38, 48, 64, 260, 275, 277, 287–288; and childbirth, 235, 249–268, 284; choice in, 251, 284; commodification of, 251, 265; and money, 252, 254, 256, 275; patriarchal, 254; women-led, 256
reproduction: as analogous to production, 11, 56; assisted, 5; commodification of, 103, 105, 214; household, 140; language of, 249; political economy of, 240; politics of, 188; "stratified," 9, 144, 163n13
reproductive mishaps, 8, 122; taboos regarding, 122. *See also* miscarriage; pregnancy loss
reproductive rights, 6, 21, 189
reproductive subjectivities, 262
reproductive technology, 11, 20, 23, 27–29, 148; controversies surrounding, 11. *See also* cloning; electronic fetal monitor; infertility; in vitro fertilization; new reproductive technology; ova; prenatal testing; reproduction, assisted; sex determination; sex selection; surrogacy; technology, procreative; ultrasound
resistance, 12, 137, 211, 278, 288
Richard, Shari, 201–202, 206
rights, 21, 23; talk of, 289
rites of passage, 34, 274
ritual, 13, 14, 47, 56, 79, 92, 97, 126; appropriation of, 256, 267nn6, 7; birth, 13, 257; Blessing Way, 256, 264, 267n6, 268n18; borrowing, 256; commodification of, 257; consumption of, 258; cycle of, 128; of decommodification, 150, 159, 165n32; experimentation, 257; formulae, 275; gestures, 257; Native American, 256; reinvented, 256; sale of, 264; of showing and telling, 207; specialists, 256; of storytelling, 186n12; syncretic, 256
Roberts, Dorothy, 7, 205
Robertson, Jon, 261
Rofel, Lisa, 162n2
"Ron's Angels" website, 10. *See also* ova
"roots," 156; mythologies of, 168–186; return to, 170; tourism, 167n50; trips, 9, 170, 171
Rothman, Barbara Katz, 4, 14, 15, 55, 162n4, 164n23, 275
Rousseau, Jean-Jacques, 50, 146
Rubinstein, Iris, 125

sacrifice, 38–39, 47, 49, 62, 78–80, 85, 88, 106, 162n4, 250, 251, 258, 260–261, 264, 266, 267n2, 278
Sahlins, Marshall, 249, 251
Santiago, 172, 173, 175
Saussure, Ferdinand de, 73
school. *See* education
scopolamine, 212, 213, 281. *See also* childbirth, pain
self-realization, 139, 250, 260, 264, 265, 266, 267n2
sentiment, 141, 142, 154, 157, 159, 201, 273, 274, 277
Servicio Nacional del Menor (SENAME), 172, 173, 175, 179, 181–182
sex determination, 190, 198, 200
sexism, 7, 44–45; non-, 66
sex selection, 105, 143, 163n12, 190
sexual abuse, 125
sexuality, contamination of, 151
Shanley, Laura Kaplan, 258
Sharp, Lesley, 204
Sharpe, Mary, 241, 242, 244
shopping, 14, 32, 39–40, 47, 49, 59, 60, 85, 151, 265; for babies, 45, 59, 64, 106, 114, 134, 268n10, 277; and identity, 32, 136; and love, 105; pleasure of, 36
Singer, Peter, 100–120, 120n2, 133–134; protests against, 100, 102, 113, 115–119, 120–121nn1, 3
single mothers. *See* motherhood, single
skin color, 169, 179, 180
slavery, 272
Smith, Adam, 7
Smith, Raymond T., 7
social class, 2, 3, 4, 7, 19, 24, 32, 41, 49, 59–60, 66, 68, 71n1, 78, 80, 99n7, 123, 142–143, 155, 163n8; construction of, 151; privilege, 161; switching, 60. *See also* middle class; working class
socialism, 144, 276
sociality, 62, 67, 140, 145
social justice, 16
social movements, 282; and the academy, 282–283
social theory, 2; critical, 11
social welfare institutions, 6, 72–99, 168
social workers, 81–84, 95, 99n6, 130, 168, 172, 174, 175, 178, 180, 182, 183, 184, 286

INDEX

Society of Diagnostic Medical Sonography (SDMS), 197, 198, 199
sonograms, 8, 57, 126, 134. *See also* fetal ultrasound images; prenatal testing; ultrasound
sonographers, 8, 13, 188–210; against abortion, 187, 188, 189, 201–206, 208; active roles of, 188, 285; contact with patients, 198–200; dilemmas of, 188, 207; professional identity of, 198–200, 206, 207, 208n3; relations with physicians, 192, 196, 207, 282. *See also* sonography; ultrasound
sonography: as caring profession, 207; educational standards for, 197; as female profession, 188, 192, 197–198, 206; as separate profession, 196. *See also* prenatal testing; sonographers; ultrasound
Source of Help in Airing and Resolving Experiences (SHARE), 122, 127, 130, 131, 133
South America, 68–69
speciesism, 100
sperm donors, 29
Spivak, Gayatri, 139, 140, 142, 144, 162n1
Springer, Jerry, 146
Spyer, Patricia, 187
Stacey, Margaret, 20
stages of development, 31, 32, 37; "natural," 38–39; of parents, 31–51
state, 249, 258, 261, 285, 286; authority, 254; control, 23, 74, 77–78, 80, 143, 145, 148, 152, 163n12, 173
statistics, 7
Steiner, Joan, 1, 2
sterilization, 24
Stern, William, 29
Stewart, Susan, 154
stillbirth, 122, 124, 125, 132, 133. *See also* pregnancy loss
Stockholm, 170, 179
Strathern, Marilyn, 3, 32, 184, 185n1, 186n6
style, 36, 43–44, 49, 59, 61, 65, 280, 282
subjectivity, 146, 155
sublime, the, 131, 166n39, 173, 266
sugar, 40–41, 45
surrogacy, 4, 24, 28–29, 164n24, 214, 274; commercial versus altruistic, 104; contracts, 28
surveillance: medical, 192; technological, 192
Swanton, Peggy, 134
Sweden, 9, 170–186, 285, 286

Taylor, Janelle, 56, 71, 166n42, 211, 277, 282, 287
technology: and capitalism, 20, 21; ethos of, 213; fetishizing, 190; history of, 190; ideology of, 19; and patriarchy, 20; people who operate, 190; procreative, 20; of visualization, 190. *See also* reproductive technology
teenagers, 36–37, 48, 105
television, 45, 153, 154, 166n41, 188, 198, 201, 280

toys, 9, 44–46, 51n7, 58, 61–66, 71, 73, 74, 93, 95, 144, 165n37; educational, 160; and ethnicity, 152–153, 160; gendered, 42, 44–45, 66; as mass commodities, 46, 152; as transitional objects, 166n38
Tranströmer, Tomas, 168
transvaluation, 139, 140
trauma, 125; narratives of, 124; scholarship on, 122; survivors of, 124; victims of, 124

ultrasound, 8, 188, 214, 241, 268n14, 277; and antiabortion, 187–210; cultural form of, 190, 191; as educational, 206; as entertainment, 204; feminist accounts of, 191; of "George," 188; growth in use of, 194; history of, 191–194, 209n4; images, 187, 188; industry, 194; for monitoring fetal growth, 193; narratives about, 191; "nonmedical" aspects of, 195, 207; policy on, 196; routinization of, 188, 189, 190, 192, 197, 207; as social practice, 190; standardization of, 194, 197; technician, 209n6. *See also* prenatal testing; sonographer; sonography
Umanski, Lauri, 12
UNITE, 122, 124, 125, 127, 128, 130, 138n12
United Kingdom, 20, 31–51, 55, 59–70, 162n4
United Parents Protesting Singer (UPPS), 102, 112, 115–116, 118, 120n3

value, 139, 140, 142, 151, 162n4, 189, 287; affective, 139, 140, 143, 159; bodily, 144, 150, 160, 163nn14, 16, 288; capitalist formations of, 142; chain, 142, 143, 151, 160–161; of child, 139, 144, 147; commodity, 139; embodied, 147; exchange, 185n5, Marxist concept of, 139–140; social, 141; surplus, 160
Van Gennep, 274

Wari'do, 70–71
weapons, 42
welfare, 6–7, 13, 65, 72–99, 117, 168, 172, 174, 205; mothers, 80
Whitbeck, Caroline, 30
Whitehead, Mary Beth, 29
whiteness, scholars of, 285
WIC, 80
Williamson, Judith, 158
Winnocott, D., 38–40; and transitional objects, 40
Women's Health Movement, 120n5, 280, 283
work. *See* labor
working class, 60, 66, 78, 80, 99n7. *See also* social class
Wozniak, Danielle, 6, 170, 178, 184, 186n10, 277, 278, 287

Yan, Hairong, 144
Yngvesson, Barbara, 9, 166n39, 174, 286
Yoxen, Edward, 192, 209n4